Religion in an Expanding Europe

With political controversies raging over issues such as the wearing of headscarves in schools and the mention of Christianity in the European Constitution, religious issues are of growing importance in European politics. In this volume, Byrnes and Katzenstein analyze the effect that enlargement to countries with different and stronger religious traditions may have on the EU as a whole, and in particular on its homogeneity and assumed secular nature. Looking through the lens of the transnational religious communities of Catholicism, Orthodoxy, and Islam, they argue that religious factors are stumbling blocks rather than stepping stones toward the further integration of Europe. All three religious traditions are advancing notions of European identity and European union that differ substantially from how the European integration process is generally understood by political leaders and scholars. This fascinating collection of papers makes an important addition to the fields of European politics, political sociology, and the sociology of religion.

TIMOTHY A. BYRNES is Professor of Political Science at Colgate University. He is the author of *Transnational Catholicism in Post-communist Europe* (2001) and *Catholic Bishops in American Politics* (1991). He is the co-editor of *Abortion Politics in American States* (1995) and *The Catholic Church and the Politics of Abortion: A View from the States* (1992).

PETER J. KATZENSTEIN is the Walter S. Carpenter, Jr. Professor of International Studies at Cornell University. He has written widely on issues of political economy and security in both Europe and Asia. He is the author of many books, including most recently *A World of Regions: Asia and Europe in the American Imperium* (2005) and *Beyond Japan: East Asian Regionalism* (co-edited with Takashi Shiraishi, forthcoming, 2006).

Religion in an Expanding Europe

Edited by

Timothy A. Byrnes and Peter J. Katzenstein

CAMBRIDGE
UNIVERSITY PRESS

CAMBRIDGE UNIVERSITY PRESS
Cambridge, New York, Melbourne, Madrid, Cape Town, Singapore, São Paulo

CAMBRIDGE UNIVERSITY PRESS
The Edinburgh Building, Cambridge CB2 2RU, UK

Published in the United States of America by Cambridge University Press,
New York

www.cambridge.org
Information on this title: www.cambridge.org/9780521676519

First published 2006

Printed in the United Kingdom at the University Press, Cambridge

A catalogue record for this book is available from the British Library

ISBN-13 978-0-521-85926-4 hardback
ISBN-10 0-521-85926-3 hardback
ISBN-13 978-0-521-67651-9 paperback
ISBN-10 0-521-67651-7 paperback

Contents

Contributors

PROFESSOR TIMOTHY A. BYRNES, Department of Political Science, Colgate University

PROFESSOR JOSÉ CASANOVA, New School for Social Research, New School University

REVEREND J. BRYAN HEHIR, Boston Archdiocese, Boston

PROFESSOR PETER J. KATZENSTEIN, Government Department, Cornell University

PROFESSOR DANIEL NEXON, Department of Government, Georgetown University

PROFESSOR VJEKOSLAV PERICA, Department of History, University of Utah

PROFESSOR DANIEL PHILPOTT, Department of Political Science, University of Notre Dame

PROFESSOR SABRINA P. RAMET, Department of Sociology and Political Science, Norwegian University of Science and Technology

DR. TIM SHAH, Senior Fellow, Religion and World Affairs, Pew Forum on Religion and Public Life

PROFESSOR BASSAM TIBI, Department of International Relations, University of Goettingen

PROFESSOR HAKAN YAVUZ, Department of Political Science, University of Utah

Preface

We developed the core ideas that inform this book in the fall semester of 2003 when we convened a seminar at Cornell University on "Fracturing an Integrating Europe from the Periphery? Religious Communities and Europeanization." These sessions were part of Cornell's Mellon-Sawyer Seminar, "Toward a Transnational and Transcultural Europe," which was sponsored by the Institute for European Studies at Cornell's Center for International Studies. We thank the Mellon Foundation, the Institute for European Studies, and the Carpenter Chair at Cornell University for the financial and logistical support of the seminar. And we thank the other members of the steering group of the seminar – Dominic Boyer, David Brown, Davydd Greenwood, and Sidney Tarrow – for their guidance and support.

A workshop hosted by Colgate University in April 2004 provided the venue for converting the conceptual and substantive discussions of our Mellon seminar into draft papers. We thank Colgate University's Center for Ethics and World Societies for the financial support that made this meeting possible. Substantial, subsequent revisions of these papers yielded a manuscript that received careful scrutiny by two anonymous readers of Cambridge University Press. We are grateful for their expert criticisms and suggestions that guided the final round of author revisions.

We would like to thank all of our authors for putting up with good humor what to them undoubtedly appeared like a never-ending cascade of email requests by their two editors imposing deadlines, suggesting changes, circulating and re-circulating drafts.

In preparing the final manuscript for submission, we relied on the unfailingly efficient help of Stephanie Hofmann.

Finally we thank each other. We have convinced each other that religion is of increasing importance in European and world politics and that students of international relations are far too reticent on this issue. We have learned from each other in other ways in the course of running this project. And, happily, our friendship has grown and deepened.

TIMOTHY A. BYRNES, *Hamilton, New York*
PETER J. KATZENSTEIN, *Ithaca, New York*

1 Multiple modernities as limits to secular Europeanization?

Peter J. Katzenstein

The casual reader of current news cannot help but notice the prominence of religious issues in contemporary European politics. In the 1990s hundreds of thousands of refugees from Croatia (Catholic), Serbia (Orthodox), and Bosnia (Muslim) were a painful reminder to all of Europe's religious heterogeneity. Declaration No. 11, appended to the 1997 Treaty of Amsterdam, innocuously proclaimed that the European Union (EU) respects and in no way prejudices national laws governing the status of Churches and religious associations as well as of philosophical and non-confessional organizations. Since then religious issues have become increasingly politicized (Soper and Fetzer, 2002).

In France a bitter debate has raged over the use of headscarves in schools. In Germany a similar political debate is occurring, at a less feverish pitch, with a more prominent role accorded to the Supreme Court. In Spain the Aznar government passed a law strengthening the position of the Catholic Church in public education, despite the public outrage of the opposition (Fuchs, 2003). Anti-Semitism is on the rise among Europe's Muslim population, especially since the beginning of the second Intifada in 2000. The public release of an EU-sponsored report on this subject became a matter of political controversy in the fall of 2003. In Kosovo that threat lingers. And the opening of negotiations between the EU and Turkey about eventual membership leaves religion on Europe's diplomatic agenda, and with it the issue of the compatibility between political Islam and secular Europe.

Europe, arguably the most secular part of the world, is increasingly forced to grapple with religious issues like these. Focusing exclusively on the Europeanization of secular politics – of who gets what, when, and how – misses two central aspects of European politics. First, as I shall argue in this chapter, European identity has remained largely untouched by legal and cultural processes of Europeanization, leaving the core of the emerging European polity hollow. Second, as Europe enlarges, transnational religious communities, defined here as entities spanning state borders, run up against the secular European polity. Because it has a strong influence in

1

many of the states that are joining, or seeking to join, the EU as fully-fledged members, religious politics in the West European core of united Europe is becoming more important. I view the variety of these political encounters and outcomes as manifestations of multiple modernities.

The core of secular Western Europe has preserved Christianity largely as glimmering embers that are no longer able to generate, on their own, much heat. European enlargement, however, is infusing renewed religious vitality into Europe's political and social life, thus chipping away at its exceptional secularism. This development is noteworthy for three reasons. First, religious vitality has the potential to revive political recognition of the Christian and specifically Catholic foundations of European integration. Second, renewed attention to religious differences could ignite political reactions that in the foreseeable future may well impede Europeanization. Third, the growing salience of religion is likely to demand new terms of coexistence with secularism. Legal and cultural Europeanization have left problematic and undefined the core of the European project. In the future religion may help fill that core by offering a focal point for political debate, engagement, and conflict.

A few decades back, the conventional European wisdom held that farmers were destined to disappear from the political stage. Yet half a century later, the Common Agricultural Policy remains a central and economically costly pillar of the European Union. The analogous view about religion is widespread in what many Europeans, in the West more than in the East, understand to be a secularizing or fully secular polity. This book is based on a different political intuition. European enlargement will feed rather than undermine the importance of religion in the EU. To a long shelf of books devoted to the enlargement of the core of a secular, capitalist, and democratic Europe, this volume adds an analysis of how transnational religious communities in the European periphery are reintroducing religion into the center of Europe. The book's analysis focuses on the role of Catholicism in contemporary European politics, with specific reference to Poland, the largest country that joined the EU on May 1, 2004; on the fusion of Orthodox Christianity with nationalism and the modern state in East and Southeast Europe, with specific reference to Serbia and the fateful position it occupies in the Balkans; and on the role of Islam and a large and rapidly growing Muslim diaspora, with specific reference to the possibility of Turkey's accession to the EU.

A long and tortuous debate on the preamble to the European draft constitution that José Casanova reviews in chapter 3 revealed just how difficult it is to strike a politically tenable balance between religion and secularization in contemporary European politics. The preamble defines Europe as a civilization whose people "have gradually developed the values underlying humanism: equality of persons, freedom, respect for reason." Religion appears obliquely only once, when the preamble speaks of the "cultural, religious, and humanistic inheritance of Europe" – a late addition to the final draft after the deletion of a specific reference to explicitly religious and secular symbols of identity, Christianity, Greco-Roman civilization, and the Enlightenment. Brokering a compromise between Ireland, Spain, Italy, Poland, and Christian Democrats from other countries on the one hand and France, Belgium, some of the Scandinavian countries, and socialists and liberals from other countries on the other, according to Leszek Jesień, a Polish expert, "put a certain fog on the issues" (Bernstein, 2003) that left the preamble (in the view of one British diplomat) "pompous and pretentious, but at first view not actively dangerous" (*Economist*, 2003).

The omission of an explicit reference to Christianity was harshly criticized in the summer of 2003 by both Pope John Paul II and the leader of the Greek Orthodox Church, Archbishop Christodoulos. The Pope addressed the future of Europe in "Ecclesia in Europa," a lengthy postscript to a 1999 Synod that he had hoped would be the beginning of a moral and civilizational renewal of Europe brought about by the Catholic Church. That renewal is, in the Pope's view, rooted in the recovery of a profoundly multicultural historical memory and in the imagination of Europe as a place open to entirely new possibilities. But the Pope at the helm of a traditionally pro-European Catholic Church, has sailed into rough waters. In the fall of 2004, the European Parliament opposed the nomination of Rocco Buttiglione, a conservative Italian politician, practicing Catholic, and friend and biographer of the Pope, as European Commissioner for Justice and Home Affairs. Buttiglione's conservative views on gay marriage, single mothers, and working women sparked outrage among secular parliamentarians. And so secular and religious views of European values came into conflict once more.

These illustrations point to what Grace Davie (2001: 467–68, 1994a) refers to as an odd irony abut the self-perceptions of Europeans:

At one and the same time, they perceive themselves as increasingly secular *and* draw the boundaries of their continent – known sometimes as "fortress Europe" – along Christian lines. Whether consciously or not, the effective barriers to entry coincide with a geographical definition of Christendom. Nations dominated by Western (Catholic) Christianity will, in my view, find it easier than their Orthodox equivalents to enter the European Union; Muslim states will find it harder still (if not impossible), despite the existence of significant Muslim communities within most, if not all, West European nations.

Why? Are the reasons to be found in the inherent characteristics of Catholicism, Orthodoxy and Islam, or in important historical processes,

such as the Renaissance, the Enlightenment, nineteenth-century industrialization, and prolonged periods of state-building, the growth of
nationalism, and democratization – all of which have differentiated
Southeastern from Western Europe? When Greece joined Europe in
1981, its Orthodoxy was trumped by the country's widely acknowledged
role as Europe's foundational civilization. Yet the legacy of 500 years of
Ottoman rule left Greece ill-prepared for functioning in the EU. Indeed,
if we imagine a Europe populated solely by states like Greece, it would
probably not be able to form a union (Katzenstein, 1997a). Greece's
falsification of its economic statistics before joining the European
Monetary Union illustrates the problem. Yet compared to the Serbian
Orthodox Church, as Vjekoslav Perica argues in chapter 7, Greece is
more skilled in its diplomacy and more open to European developments.
In Europe's historical evolution, religion is deeply entangled with other
factors. Compared to them, however, the salience of religion, what some
call its constitutive effects, lies in the intensity that perceived religious and
value conflicts generate in Europe, as they do elsewhere.

Multiple modernities in the era of Europeanization

At the beginning of the twenty-first century, the secular European project
of extending and securing peace among democratic welfare states is
helping to revitalize religion as a political force (Greeley, 2003). Inside
Europe, Grace Davie (2000) argues, a variety of mutating collective
memories provide a never-ending reconstruction of religious traditions:
in the Church and through churchgoers, in education, the media, and
law, in alternative formulations provided by new religions, and in the arts.
Less subtle and equally important, the number of Muslims living in
Europe has increased in less than a generation from about 1 million to
more than 15 million. Their social integration into European societies is a
complex political task. In addition, the southern and eastern enlargement
of the European Union has brought Catholicism and the Orthodox
Church into closer contact with the European project and incited lively
debate about the likely impact of the EU on "traditional Christian
values." How should we think about these political processes?

Multiple modernities disappoint those searching for one dominant
narrative, such as the growth of secularism or the inescapability of civilizational clashes. They are expressed in a variety of cultural programs that
reinvent themselves continuously in history. These programs adapt
themselves to (and also modify) large-scale historical processes such as
modernization, secularization, industrialization, and democratization.
Variable constellations of political context are brought together by

transnational contacts between global–local and international–regional sites of politics. In sum, multiple modernities and variable contexts shape and transfigure an enlarging Europe as it encounters transnational religious communities.

Shmuel Eisenstadt (1999a, 1999b, 2000a, 2000b, 2002; see also Berger and Huntington, 2002) has interrogated "multiple modernities" as a central topic in macro-history. This body of research examines long time periods and puts religion in a central place. Modern societies are not converging around common patterns. Rather, "the idea of multiple modernities presumes that the best way to understand the contemporary world . . . is to see it as a story of continual constitution and reconstitution of a multiplicity of cultural programs" (Eisenstadt, 2002: 2). This makes unavoidable the antinomies of modernity. Modernizing non-Western societies and modern, Western societies thus display different patterns of modernity. The cultural core of West European modernity offers a specific "bundle of moral-cognitive imperatives under the premises of the rationalization of the world" (Spohn, 2001: 501) and a secularizing reconstruction of religious traditions that radiates outward to other parts of Europe as well as North and South America through imposition, emulation, and incorporation.

Because Western modernity is adopted selectively and transformed in widely differing political and cultural contexts, it does not create a common global standard. Indeed, Western modernity is sufficiently broad to allow for tensions, even contradictions, between orthodox and heterodox orientations and identities, and unavoidable conflicts between geographic and socio-economic centers and peripheries. That difference is very evident across the Atlantic, as José Casanova argues in chapter 3, thus giving the current rift over the Iraq war a deeper significance than sharp political disagreements over the doctrine of preventive war and unilateral action outside of the UN framework. Difference also marks Germany and Japan, and not only as distinct models of capitalism. The difference created by Germany's exposure to Christianity as one of the world's great religions – in sharp contrast to Japan's tradition of religious syncretism – confirms the political plasticity and institutional plurality of modernity (Eisenstadt, 1986, 1996, 1998). Here Eisenstadt parts company with others, such as Ernst Haas (1997, 2000), who claim Japan as an example of secularization. Eisenstadt stresses instead Japan's syncretism. Considering Casanova's argument in chapter 3, this disagreement is instructive. Does the belief in secularism become compelling largely as a self-fulfilling prophecy – because of its foundational commitment to open-ended learning that by definition only it, not syncretism, can embody? Work on multiple modernities is rooted in Max Weber's writings on world religions. Secularist thought instead draws heavily on Weber's analysis of bureaucratic rationality. Writings in the secular tradition cling with determination to the idea that in the long term the self-reflexivity, open-endedness, and procedural thinness of secularism give it a decisive edge over all other forms of modernity. Multiple modernities make us look for and accept political antinomies that are perpetually recreated and that make even traditional fundamentalism modern.

Focusing on transnational communities also emphasizes a multiplicity of political balances that can be struck between secular and religious politics (Rudolph, 1997a, 2003). A transnational perspective undercuts the assumption of unitary, internally coherent religious or civilizational entities with an unquestioned identity. There are two general ways of articulating such a transnational perspective. One focuses on the connections between global and local factors in an increasingly deterritorialized world, the other on the links between national and regional factors in a world that continues to give the principle of territoriality its due (Katzenstein, 2005). A group of scholars who published under the name of the Group of Lisbon (1995: 15) insist that the two perspectives "refer to different processes and phenomena." Paul Hirst and Grahame Thompson (1996: 185 and also 8–13) concur, as they see a vast difference "between a strictly *global* and a highly *internationalized* economy." Globalization transcends space and compresses time and in so doing it has novel transformative effects on world politics. Internationalization refers to territorially based exchanges across borders and acknowledges basic continuities in the evolution of the international system. Globalization highlights the emergence of new actors and novel relations in the world system, internationalization the continued relevance of existing actors and the intensifications of existing ones. "Internationality," argues Jan Aart Scholte (2000: 49), "is embedded in territorial space; globality transcends that geography."

An analysis of various transnational religious communities in Europe benefits greatly from both perspectives. The growth of a European polity and transnational religious communities are both shaped by global and international processes. As this book illustrates, the transnational politics of Catholicism, with its elaborate and well-defined international structures, differs greatly from that of the Orthodox Church, firmly rooted in the nation-state, and the global–local connections that define Islam's institutional structure and outlook. Focusing on Catholicism and Poland, Orthodoxy and Serbia, and Islam and Turkey illustrates the complex interplay between globalization and internationalization.

The plausibility of focusing on multiple modernities is supported by central conclusions of a large number of sociologists of religion (for example, Esposito and Watson, 2000; Marty and Appleby, 1997; Race and Williamson, 1995; Beyer, 1994; Casanova, 1994; Johnston and Sampson, 1994; Robertson and Garrett, 1991) and a few political scientists who have written on the role of religion in world politics (for example, Thomas, 2000, 2005; Norris and Inglehart, 2005; Almond, Appleby and Sivan, 2003; Carlson and Owens, 2003; Hurd, 2004; Petito and Hatzopoulos, 2003; Byrnes, 2001; Dark, 2000; *Millennium*, 2000; Kurth, 1998; Haynes, 1998; *Orbis*, 1998; Rudolph and Piscatori, 1997; Janis, 1991; Berger, 1982). In the analysis of Europe and its international relations the rediscovery of religion is overdue. Specifically, scholars of Europe's emerging polity have so far neglected this topic in their voluminous writings. This oversight is true, specifically, for analyses grounded self-consciously in secular liberal and cultural realist perspectives. Instead of multiplicity these perspectives stress uniformity of outcomes: a progressive and cooperative secular politics for liberals, a divided and conflictual one for realists.

A secular liberalism is deeply ingrained in the self-understanding of most Europeans and in the interpretations of most scholars of European politics. Not long ago it was an article of faith, so to speak, among most scholars of religion and of Europe that secularization was the dominant trend in modernization. Francis Fukuyama (1989, 1992) went so far as to pronounce 'the end of history' after liberalism's final and decisive victory over the challenges posed by fascism in the first half of the twentieth century and communism in the second. Henceforth there would be no more ideological opposition to the rationalist secularism that Fukuyama had seen triumph in the Cold War.

As the collapse of communism and the disintegration of the Soviet Union occurred with the help of a devout Polish Pope and fervent Islamicist *mujahedeen*, Fukuyama's conclusion is less than fully convincing. It does not sit well at least with one of the pre-eminent sociologists of religion of this generation. In the words of Peter Berger (1997: 974, quoted in Stark, 1999: 16):

What I and most other sociologists of religion wrote in the 1960s about secularization was a mistake. Our underlying argument was that secularization and modernity go hand in hand. With more modernization comes more secularization. It wasn't a crazy theory. There was some evidence for it. But I think it's basically wrong. Most of the world today is certainly not secular. It's very religious.

And so, in its own way, is Europe. Berger (1999: 10) describes the European way with religion in the following terms: a "strong survival of religion, most of it generally Christian in nature, despite the widespread alienation from organized Churches. A shift in the institutional location of religion, then, rather than secularization, would be a more accurate description of the European situation."

José Casanova makes the same basic point in chapter 3 but with an interesting twist. The secularization of Europe is not a harbinger of broader developments in world politics. It is instead exceptional and distinctive of Europe, a self-fulfilling prophecy that takes something for granted that is not necessarily so. Large segments of the European population have accepted a teleological theory in which religions atrophy. In Casanova's view, the secularization of Western Europe is the result of the triumph of a specific knowledge regime rather than a deeper aspect of the process of modernization.

Cultural realism (A. Johnston, 1995; Nau, 2002; see also Niebuhr, 1940; D. Johnston, 2003) offers an alternative perspective that is more open to the influence of religion in world politics. In the aftermath of the Cold War and the collapse of the Soviet Union, Samuel Huntington's (1993, 1996) political intuition differed sharply from Fukuyama's. Huntington's "clash of civilizations" draws a pessimistic picture. The historical turn of 1989–91 removed one ideological conflict, but it revealed the existence of another. For Huntington, civilizations have become the relevant cultural context for states and non-state actors alike. Huntington insists that this is true in particular of "faultline" states that lie between civilizations, such as Serbia. Civilizational clashes are for Huntington the defining characteristic of a new era of international politics.

Because their building blocks are variable constellations of religion, culture, language, values, traditions, and memories, civilizations are not easily defined with any degree of precision. Today religion, specifically the rise of Islamicist political and religious fundamentalism in the Middle East, gives the civilizational argument much of its political prominence. Huntington's primary argument holds that underneath civilizational fluidity, a profound split exists between the "West" and the "rest." A secondary argument is less clearly identified with Huntington's main thesis. It holds that under the wide umbrella of civilization, identities are contested and can be reconstructed quite easily through a politics that by definition is forever in flux. For example, Huntington argues that Kemalist reformism can be explained within the context of Islam, as can significant reform efforts in Mexico and Russia (Huntington, 1993: 24, 42–44, 48).

Bassam Tibi deploys in chapter 8 both versions of the civilizational argument, although he stresses the first more than the second. In Tibi's view the radical nature of Islam in Germany is in part due to politics, specifically the monopolistic politics of representation that the German state imposes on its non-Christian immigrant communities (Fetzer and Soper, 2005: 98–129). And the radical nature of some Islamicist groups is due also to the radical doctrine and practices that are imported to Germany from Turkey through a variety of transnational ties. Islam is not simply a religion like contemporary Christianity, a matter of individual belief more or less firmly held. It is also a matter of intense practice and revered rituals, without which Islam would cease to exist. Political practice has created deep faultlines between the German state and important strands of Islamicist communities in Germany. Yet different German policies and different Islamic practices could alter, even erase, such faultlines.

Hakan Yavuz offers a different interpretation in chapter 9. He stresses the second argument much more heavily than the first. He emphasizes the political malleability and changeability of various Turkish identities within one Islamic civilization that, as it interacts with Europe, is creating competing versions of Islam. These versions find different ways of accommodating themselves to an expanding Europe. Yavuz's general point extends well beyond Turkey, as Islam's resurgence illustrates. "Islam" is a construct that now assigns to Iran a pivotal role in the Middle East. When the ideology of "Pan-Arabism" reigned supreme only a generation ago, as a non-Arab country, Iran was excluded from the Middle East. Since then anti-imperialism has given way to anti-Westernism. Twentieth-century Islam thus is not an unchanging and homogeneous actor or oppositional civilization (Trautner, 1999; Wedeen, 2003). Unsurprisingly, in contemporary Islam significant political differences exist between Saudi Arabian and Iranian visions of traditionalism and radicalism, just as within Saudi Arabia and Iran deep fissures also exist over the social and cultural purpose of Islam.

Secular liberalism and cultural realism have the virtue of simplicity. Both, however, suffer from limitations that invite us to move beyond them in our analysis of the interactions between Europeanization and transnational religious communities. Contra secular liberalism, there exists no teleology in history, secular or otherwise. And contra cultural realism, diversity and difference rather than unity and homogeneity are the markers of civilizational entities and the collective identities they foster. This is not to argue that concepts central to liberal and realist perspectives, such as efficiency and power, are irrelevant for the analysis of religion in world politics. They are most useful in combination with other concepts that better capture the ideas motivating religious politics.

By themselves liberal and realist perspectives do not yield a compelling answer to the mocking question that realists have traditionally posed to students of religion: "How many divisions has the Pope?" After the end of the Cold War and the collapse of the Soviet empire, students of international relations are likely to give a very different answer from the one proffered in the 1930s and 1940s and during the Cold War. Together with the Polish trade union movement, Pope John Paul II had a lot to do with the collapse and dismemberment of the Soviet Union at the end of the Cold War. And so did fervently Islamicist *mujahedeen* fighters in Afghanistan. Furthermore, efficiency as the master variable of a variety of liberal theories of international relations has great difficulties in engaging substantively the identities, motivations, and strategies of religious actors whose calculations typically cannot be reduced to simple instrumental reasoning (S. Thomas, 2000, 2005).

Grafted on to sociological approaches, liberal and realist analyses of religion in European and world politics yield more accurate analyses and deeper insights. As one manifestation of the sociological turn in international relations theory, constructivism insists that through interaction people construct the social and political world within the context of a material world they also inhabit. Agent, structure and language coexist and co-evolve without one enjoying ontological primacy over the other. In this view there is no reason to privilege actors, such as the unitary state, or levels of analysis, such as the international system, that have been central to most strands of realist and liberal international relations scholarship. This book's emphasis on the relations between state and non-state actors and their various transnational relations thus stretches beyond the core of realist and liberal analysis of international relations.

World politics reflects multiple historical experiences and social contexts rather than one outcome – be it secular cooperation or civilizational clash. Religious thought and practice, for example, reflect diverse experiences and contexts. That is one reason why Yasusuke Murakami (1996: 389) comes close to equating secular and religious thought.[1] The future, Murakami argues, will be marked not by homogenization but by diversity. The question of international understanding will not require a "communization" of cultures around standards set by modern science and the West. Instead it requires a growing "commensurability" of cultures based on the power of individual imagination and empathy as the basis for a rule- rather than a justice-based interpretive framework and approach to life. The difference between the revolutionary, transcendental reflections of historical religions (including contemporary science) in the West and the conservative, historiological, hermeneutic reflections in the East distinguishes between civilizations imbued with a sense of progress ending in the divine and the attainability of ultimate truth on the one hand and civilizations that remain in the world of the profane and sustain limitless reinterpretations on the other. "Thus religion [and science] and history form two different axes for reflexive action, and although one cannot say they are unconnected, they cross each other at right angles" (Murakami, 1996: 407). From a non-European vantage-point, the chasm between sacred and secular perspectives, between religion and science, is far from being decisive.

The disciplinary orientation of sociology and the analytical lenses of constructivism are particularly well suited to examine non-state actors such as religious communities. J. Bryan Hehir examines Catholicism in chapter 4, Sabrina Ramet the Orthodox Church in chapter 6, and Bassam Tibi Islam in chapter 8. Their analyses focus on how these religious communities relate to states. And Daniel Philpott and Tim Shah show in chapter 2 how states themselves are constituted in their varying relationships with religious communities. They inquire in particular into different patterns of the differentiation between state and Church that offer the political foundations for what Alfred Stepan (2001: 213–51) has called the "twin tolerations." Sociology and constructivism are open to inquiring into the transnational dimensions that are often central to religious politics and that connect global and international processes with national and local ones.

There are numerous avenues of inquiry into the processes by which religious communities and other non-state actors interact with states at the multiple levels that constitute the European Union and global culture. In their research practice, sociological schools of thought differ on specifics. For example, some display a bent for more (Almond, Appleby, and Sivan, 2003) or less (Esposito and Watson, 2000) theoretical self-consciousness and positivist commitment. But they all claim that social structures contain shared knowledge, material resources, and practices; that knowledgeable agents use these resources to construct through their practices variable and ever-changing norms and identities; and that through these practices they change themselves and the structures in which they are embedded. The intended outcome of the eclectic analytical perspective this book adopts is the "dehomogenization" of religious communities and the civilizational, regional, and political environments of which they are a part (Rudolph, 1997b). In short, the authors in this volume begin to translate into research practice the task of connecting concepts to data and thus help map an empirical terrain that students of European integration have left largely uncharted.

J. Bryan Hehir analyzes in chapter 4 the fundamentally international and pro-European outlook of contemporary Catholicism, and Sabrina Ramet describes in chapter 5 the role of Catholicism in Poland as a pivotal state involved in the process of European enlargement. Vatican II in the early 1960s constituted a decisive break with the traditionalist and often anti-democratic politics that had marked Catholicism in the preceding decades of clerical fascism and authoritarianism. Contemporary Catholicism demonstrates that the differentiation between religious and secular realms, as Daniel Philpott and Timothy Shah argue in chapter 2, is entirely compatible with a vibrant democratic politics. Christianity is part of a broader ensemble of European identities rather than a master key for encoding all rivals, illustrated, for example, by the importance of sacred music and church architecture in Europe's secular collective identity. It is in this context, Hehir argues, that the Pope's plans for Poland's Catholic mission in European enlargement should be seen. For the Pope is not merely content to participate in a set of transnational European processes for which the structure of the Catholic Church is well suited. He is also vitally interested in evangelizing Europe by exploiting the opportunity that the rechristianization of Central and Eastern Europe offers him. In the language of political economy, the combination of German (Church) money and Polish (Church) labor is to bring success to a new apostolic assignment of Europe's religious revival. Furthermore, the Pope is also intent on making Europe come to terms with its long history and likely future of religious diversity. The preamble to a European constitution that does not mention Christianity is for the Pope what the European anthem, Beethoven's Ode to Joy, stripped of its words, is to Beethoven – a political travesty. Catholicism is full of political possibilities. In recent decades it has been closely linked to liberation theology in Latin America, determined opposition against Soviet communism, and a wave of democratization that has spread all over the world (Philpott, 2004). It is thus easy to forget that for many decades the Catholic Church had often been an immovable force of reactionary politics. Today, however, human rights issues offer a perfect intersection where Catholic and secular politics embrace.

Historicizing the past is very important in Sabrina Ramet's discussion of a defensive Orthodox Church in chapter 6 and Vjekoslav Perica's discussion of the Serbian Orthodox Church in chapter 7. History has been harsh to the Orthodox Church. In recent decades the Orthodox Church has made its peace with fascist and communist governments. Now that the Cold War has ended and the opportunity for a democratic politics exists, it is highly defensive in the face of a demographically and ideologically expansive Islam and a degree of secularism in Eastern Europe comparable to that in the original six members of the EU (Laitin, 2002: 62–67; Norris and Inglehart, 2005: 111–32). The triumph of a nationalist-infused doctrine is occurring in a political space in which institutions – political parties, associational groups, social movements – are still relatively weak. The ambivalence between a Church-nation and a state-Church continues to bedevil the politics of the Orthodox Church in

Eastern Europe. It would be quite wrong to view Orthodoxy as a pro-gressive and liberal political force eager to promote inter-confessional dialogue, sexual tolerance, and European integration and enlargement. Indeed in chapter 7 Perica calls it a "warrior Church," which often provides political entrepreneurs who especially in times of crisis can be found at the forefront of anti-Westernism in the European periphery. Many radical monks and theologians in the Orthodox Church are educated in Greek seminaries and monasteries. Yet as the oldest carrier of the Byzantine tradition of Caesaropapism, or Church–state collabora-tion, Greek bishops know how to act as a moderating force and thus reinforce the general effects of Greece's EU membership.

Perica's discussion of Serbia in chapter 7 distinguishes between "Greek" and "Serbian" diplomatic styles and more or less openness in interaction with Europe. After living for decades under harsh communist rule, the Orthodox Church must surely take some comfort from the bonds that are building between it and its congregations. And after the disastrous failures of Serbia's foreign policy in the Balkans, Serbia's Orthodox Church has no better friend than the EU in its defense of the religious outposts of a rump Serbia. Even if religion in Central and Eastern Europe should prove to be a case of "belonging without believ-ing," a Church that is once again connected to its people and that must rely on a broader Europe as its main guarantor is unlikely to walk into the future with its head turned toward the past.

For Islam the problem of the past looms even larger as the possibility of European enlargement beckons. Bassam Tibi's analysis in chapter 8 alerts us to the problems an inherently transnational religious community faces if it does not recognize the distinction between a public and a private sphere. In Europe this has been traditionally a deeply contested issue, for example for transnational Catholicism in the late nineteenth century. That public–private distinction is now firmly enshrined in European law and political practice. A Europeanized Islam runs into the thicket of state Churches – for example in France, where the secular is coterminous with the public sphere, and also in Germany, where the state prefers to deal only with monopolistically organized religious communities. And Euro-Islam also runs up against the politics of a transnational diaspora that differs in its ethnic and social background, that is configured differ-ently in different European polities, and that acts as a funnel for money, books, and radical clerics entering European mosques, thus fanning flames of suspicion, especially after 9/11 and the March 2004 and July 2005 attacks in Madrid and London. In this European setting, neither the political choice between an outward-looking, open-link strategy, followed by the Jewish community in America, nor an inward-looking, ghetto strategy, traditionally adhered to by the American Catholic Church, is plausible. The global–local politics of Islam and a European polity emerging at the regional level must evolve new and different political strategies if accommodation is to be reached for the most rapidly growing portion of the European population.

The problem is posed with particular acuity in the case of Turkey's possible accession, as Hakan Yavuz argues in chapter 9. The political rejection of the elitist and often authoritarian secularist program of Kemalism by the Turkish population and the recent emergence of a democratic and reformist version of Islam, in the form of the AKP, offers the European Union a political opportunity for building a political bridge to Islam and a strategically important NATO ally. The opening of political space creates new coalitions in Turkey, between Islamic Europhiles and liberal-secularist Kemalists on the one hand, and Islamic Euro-skeptics and Kemalist nationalists on the other. In Europe a few things are also changing. The German CDU, a long-standing supporter of Turkish accession, altered its position in the winter of 2003–04. The EU's commitment for a definitive answer to Turkey's long-standing request for opening accession negotiations will probably not yield quick results. Millions of Turks now living in Europe will have an even harder time accepting Europe as part of their homeland.

This book's focus on the intersection of Europeanization and transnational religious communities in the era of enlargement entails three self-chosen limitations. Protestantism is not a major religious force in any of the new members or accession candidates of the EU, with the exception of the Czech Republic and Estonia. Consequently, this book does not give it the detailed analysis reserved for Catholicism, Orthodoxy, and Islam. We do not neglect Protestantism altogether, however. Daniel Philpott and Timothy Shah include in chapter 2 a brief analysis of Czechoslovakia before the Velvet Revolution as well as the stance of the Protestant Church toward Europe. And Daniel Nexon examines in chapter 10 the Protestant Reformation as the historical foundation for contemporary religious politics in Europe. A second limitation is that this book is not attempting to offer an encyclopedic survey of religious politics in all accession candidates and new EU members. Our intent is to focus instead on the configurations of Europeanization and transnationalism in three different religions, all of which are politically extremely salient for Europe's future. Finally, this book focuses on European enlargement from an institutional perspective, thus slighting the empirical analysis of religious practice at the micro-level. We take as given that Western Europe has become increasingly secular. Sociologists of religion have offered ample and detailed studies supporting the conventional view.

And that view is buttressed by cross-national survey research that points to Western Europe's widespread secularism as an outlier among the world's major regions (Norris and Inglehart, 2005). We know that sociologists of religion as well as anthropologists are collecting evidence on the intermingling of various religious practices and their engagement with deeply held secular views in an enlarged Europe. We are not contributing directly to that important field of scholarship here. Yet indirectly an analysis of the intersection between Europeanization and transnational religion speaks to the broader ramifications that a renewed, passionate, and at times violent engagement of secular and religious practices, for example in the Netherlands and Poland, are creating in Europe.

In sum, this book focuses analysis on Catholicism, Orthodoxy, and Islam in European enlargement. It singles out Poland, Serbia, and Turkey as the politically most prominent and problematic of the countries that have joined the EU, are trying to do so, and will probably try to do so in the future. It also sidesteps straightforward rationalist styles of analysis. Without neglecting power and efficiency, it emphasizes the multiple modernities that connect the secular with the sacred in novel ways on the one hand, and transnational contexts blending a variety of global, international, regional, and local processes on the other.

European enlargement and Europeanization

After 1989, throughout Central and Eastern Europe the notion was widespread that the time had finally come "to return" to Europe, an idea often held with fervent conviction. The collapse of the Soviet Union and communism had created not political choice but historical necessity. European enlargement and Europeanization are a result of that historical conjuncture.

Historically, attempts at political unification have failed in Western Europe. Since the demise of the Carolingian empire, German kings have continued to claim eligibility for the Roman imperial title and insisted on the right to be crowned by the Pope – an honor last bestowed on Emperor Charles V. Soon thereafter the Protestant Reformation and religious war eventually led to the Westphalian peace settlement. The decentralized state system that emerged became the main obstacle to Napoleon's and Hitler's bids for continental primacy. It also became the platform from which European governments began to export models of political organization, economic governance, and ideological hegemony beyond the European continent (Bull and Watson, 1984).

The collapse of the Habsburg and Ottoman empires at the end of World War One set the stage for one final unsuccessful German attempt at conquering the continent, World War Two, and a new bipolar international system. After 1945 the European integration movement was folded into the American camp. European integration had both international and domestic roots that blended secular and religious elements. The international source was balance-of-power politics, directed against both a possible revival of Germany in the midst of Europe and a Soviet Union that had pushed the borders of its sphere of influence in Central Europe as far west as the River Elbe. The domestic source was the revival of Christian Democracy as an important center of a democratic politics that was strongly committed to European integration.

International balance-of-power politics took a novel form after World War Two. The logic of "divide et impera" was operating on both sides of the Cold War divide: you keep down your Germans, while we keep down ours. The "German Question" that had bedeviled Europe for a century was finally ready to receive a "European Answer" (Calleo, 1978). The aim was to tame German power through European integration (Katzenstein, 1997a). The underlying political strategy was bold. Diplomacy moved away from the punitive policies that had been tried, and found wanting, after World War One. Instead it aimed to defang Germany by internationalizing its military and military-industrial complex. Building on the experience of European cartels in iron and steel during the interwar years, the European Coal and Steel Community (ECSC) of 1950 succeeded in doing just that. The second step was taken soon thereafter in 1952, with the creation of a European Defense Community (EDC) which guaranteed that a future German army would be put under a European command structure. The EDC's defeat in the French Assembly in 1954 looked like a total defeat of the strategy of balancing against German power through European integration. The establishment of the European Economic Community (EEC) in 1957 was a fall-back to achieve the same objective on an economic track. Over the next forty-five years the EEC has evolved in a complicated political process into an increasingly institutionalized European polity (Moravcsik, 1998; Stone Sweet, Sandholtz, and Fligstein, 2001). The original anti-German and anti-Soviet impulses have largely dissipated. Yet like the March of Dimes, the EU lives on.

It is difficult to imagine this history without the political contribution of Christian Democratic parties, as Dan Philpott and Tim Shah argue in chapter 2. Robert Schuman, Alcide de Gasperi, and Konrad Adenauer, the three "fathers" of the European integration movement, were all leaders of parties that had come to fill the spiritual void that fascism, communism, and the experience of the war had left. As Alan Milward (2000: 319) has argued:

far from renouncing the nation-state as the foundation of a better European order, they achieved prominence and success because they were among those who developed an accurate perception of the positive role it would play in the post-war order and who also recognized or stumbled upon the need for those limited surrenders of national sovereignty through which the nation-state and western Europe were jointly strengthened, not as separate and opposed entities, but within a process of mutual reinforcement.

In the words of Scott Thomas (2005: 167, 169) European integration "was an act of the political imagination of Christian Democracy," informed by a "different vision of faith, life, and politics."

The clerical roots of Christian Democracy were considerably stronger before Vatican II than after. Christian Democratic parties were, however, not simply instruments of the Catholic Church created to combat the rising tide of anti-clericalism in an era of mass politics. And they were not simply instruments of conservative political elites intent on appropriating Catholic social doctrine, which was supportive of some public welfare programs and intent on building mass parties to combat the rise of socialism. Instead, in their historical origins Christian Democratic parties were the contingent outcomes of decisions made by political actors who were pursuing interests often not related to confessional politics (Kalyvas, 1996: 2–6). They were carriers of the Catholic doctrine of subsidiarity as a pillar of the European integration movement (Holmes, 2000: 27–28, 50–56).

In the 1950s European integration was widely viewed, especially among Protestants and Social Democrats, as a Catholic conspiracy of conservatives, an ideologically tainted attempt to revive clerical politics as a hand-maiden of big business, orchestrated by the Vatican. True to that caricature, Christian Democracy has strongly supported European integration not only in the 1950s but throughout the second half of the twentieth century (Pridham, 1982). There are strong roots of this stance in the Church's historical skepticism of sovereign states and its enduring attachment to Europe's federal unity, dating back to the Middle Ages, as Philpott and Shah argue in chapter 2 (S. Thomas, 2005: 166–71). Although Social Democrats came to support the European project in growing numbers after the mid-1960s, a noticeable gap persists. Survey research reveals that since 1973, Catholics have been more supportive of European integration than Protestants; devout Catholics have been more supportive than conventional Catholics, who in turn are more supportive than nominal Catholics (Nelsen, Guth, and Fraser, 2001: 19; Nelsen and Guth, 2003a).

Fed by important international and domestic sources, the European integration movement has led to successive rounds of enlargement. The original six members (France, Germany, Italy, and the three Benelux countries) were joined in 1972 by Britain, Denmark, and Ireland. This enlargement bridged a gap that had opened in 1959 when Britain founded the European Free Trade Area (EFTA) as an alternative to the tighter customs union set up in 1957. Attempts to bridge that gap were stymied by French General de Gaulle, who remained deeply suspicious of and unalterably opposed to British entry and the dilution of French influence to which it would have led.

The second round of the EEC's enlargement occurred in Southern Europe in the 1980s, with the entry of Greece in 1981 and of Spain and Portugal in 1986. All three countries had troubled connections to an authoritarian past that was both anti-communist and pro-capitalist. In the case of Spain, the gradually evolving Franco regime, close security ties with the United States, and Franco's death in 1975 prepared the ground for a transition toward democracy; in Salazar's Portugal an eroding corporatism and military defeat in Africa set the stage for the 1974 revolution and a gradual transition to democracy; in Greece EEC associate membership since 1962 was interrupted by a military coup and the rule of a military junta (1967–74) before a return to democratic rule. Fear of Euro-communism and the prospect of instability along Europe's southern border made the EC seek in all three cases to stabilize both its borders and Southern European democracy through a strategy of enlargement. There was nothing inevitable about Europeanization, as a failed coup attempt in Spain illustrated in 1981. By and large, though, the things that Europe stood for were deeply appealing and to many appeared self-evident and inevitable: conformity with a liberal international order and multilateral security arrangements abroad, and democratic capitalist welfare states and modernizing civil societies at home. Conflicting political interests intervened, of course. Accession negotiations stretched over a decade and required tough bargaining over mundane issues such as agriculture and fishing; and they required also, in the case of Spain, a turn toward NATO membership that was difficult to bring about in domestic politics.

A third round of European enlargement came in the 1990s with the EU accession of Sweden, Finland, and Austria, three neutral members of EFTA. Norway and Switzerland preferred to remain outside of the EU, while unilaterally harmonizing their legislation with that of the EU. The other three members of EFTA, however, opted for shedding their neutral stance and calibrating their welfare states to the deregulation movement embodied in the EU's greatest achievement of the 1980s, the Single European Act of 1987. Because these three states had been deeply Europeanized for decades, the accession negotiations were uncomplicated and proceeded relatively quickly.

The fourth and largest round was the EU's enlargement toward the East, accomplished in 2004 with the joining of the Czech Republic, Estonia, Hungary, Latvia, Lithuania, Poland, Slovakia, and Slovenia. Cyprus and Malta joined at the same time, but Bulgaria, Romania, and Croatia, among others, are scheduled to join the EU at a later date. The accession negotiations were enormously complicated both by the entrenched interests of EU members and by the difficulties that post-socialist regimes had to overcome. Enlargement threatened established access to EU funds for agriculture and regional development, especially in Spain and France. With Germany unwilling to foot the bill for additional costs, negotiations were complex and contentious.

Equally important were the very different paths by which the accession countries extricated themselves from socialism, and the very different state and political capacities they could mobilize to meet the many and onerous requirements the EU imposed before full membership. In the end, the fourth round of enlargement poses the issue of the EU's constitution and methods of governance. Can methods of governance developed for a Europe of Six and gradually adapted to changing circumstances in successive decades be made to work in a Europe of Twenty-Five?

The question is of vital importance. For Europe's enlargement is likely to continue and extend deeper into Southeast Europe, and through special associate memberships perhaps also into Northern Africa and Central Asia. For example, European states have had an enormously conflicted and difficult relationship with their partners to the east in both the recent and distant past. At the end of 2004 the EU committed itself to begin accession negotiations with Turkey, as Hakan Yavuz discusses in chapter 9. Turkey has waited for decades, as Europe's authoritarian and religious "other" – and close NATO ally. In the political landscape transformed by the attacks of 9/11 and the Iraq war, the stakes could not be higher. The fate of Turkish accession will tell much about the mix of democratic and religious values that motivates European politics at the outset of the twenty-first century. The negotiation process will undoubtedly show the same kind of untidy learning-by-doing that has marked all of the prior stages of European enlargement: political creativity and leadership, crises that push issues to the top of the political agenda, and plain luck or misfortune.

Europeanization complements European enlargement. Various analytical perspectives – such as neo-functionalism, supranational governance, intergovernmentalism, and multilevel governance – all highlight the effects that Europe has on national-level politics and policy. Europeanization refers to the impact institutions and policy outcomes at the European level have on domestic polities, politics, and policies (Schimmelfennig and Sedelmeier, 2005: 5). It refers also, though less prominently, to the effect that various national polities and policies have on the EU and other European institutions. Broadly speaking, Europeanization is constructing, diffusing, and institutionalizing both formal and informal rules and procedures, policy paradigms and styles, shared beliefs, and ways of conducting political business.

Europeanization is not restricted to EU member states. It extends also to non-members such as Norway and Switzerland as well as to candidate countries in Eastern and Southeastern Europe. And Europeanization goes well beyond the issue of direct compliance with European rules to address also indirect effects that concern the organizational logic of national politics and policy-making on issues such as the functioning of political parties, local government, refugee policies, and citizenship (Vink, 2003). It is a process that to date has largely bypassed European mass publics.

Important to Europeanization are elites and states adopting European rules (Schimmelfennig and Sedelmeier, 2005: 7–8). Such rules concern issues of distribution, regulation, and redistribution, as well as of institutional design and jurisdictional conflict. The adoption of EU rules, for example, often focuses on their institutionalization at the domestic level. The directives and regulations that the EU has passed since its inception in 1957 are said to cover about 100,000 pages. By acceding to membership in the EU, new member states commit themselves to adopt, or "transpose," all of these rules into domestic law. This entails often far-reaching changes in the structure of domestic institutions and domestic political practices to meet EU standards. Formal adoption is one thing, practical implementation quite another. The behavioral dimension is shaped by the regulative and constitutive effects of rules that operate at the individual level through internalization and habituation and at the collective level through various sanctioning mechanisms. In addition to the formal and behavioral dimensions, there is also the discursive dimension of rule adoption in the process of Europeanization. Political discourse shows domestic actors merely paying lip-service, talking strategically, or being truly persuaded.

Rule adoption in its various guises is shaped by a variety of mechanisms. Johan Olsen (2002; see also Liebert, 2002), for example, highlights political mechanisms that are involved in various facets of Europeanization: diffusion for export of models of governance; purposeful decision-making for governance that occurs at the European level and that informs national politics; social learning broadly defined and competition for the changes that Europeanization induces in the various national polities that constitute Europe; and co-evolution and mutual adaptation in the creation of a distinct European polity.

The variety of mechanisms that are operating is explained by the intersection of an instrumental logic of consequences that is entailed in the incentives and disincentives of EU membership with a social logic of appropriateness (March and Olsen, 1989). European institutions thus have both constraining and constitutive effects. For other purposes Thomas Risse, Stephen Ropp, and Kathryn Sikkink (1999) have developed a multistage model that distinguishes between instrumental adaptation typifying early stages of Europeanization and persuasion and full institutionalization the late stages. Instrumental adaptation may take the form of manipulation through pressure and the strategic use of information, as typically conceptualized in rationalist accounts of politics. Persuasion operates through arguing and learning and institutionalization.

Europeanization can lead to socialization. This occurs when state elites interact in European institutions. European elites can adopt multiple roles in institutional settings where social and political pressures are absent, augmenting their national role conceptions with European ones (Trondal, 2001; Chayes and Chayes, 1995). Jeffrey Checkel (2003: 6–7) reviews in a recent paper the scholarship that has explored the socializing effects of numerous meetings over long periods in European institutions, particularly when those meetings promote deliberation and collective puzzling through complicated issues. Summarizing the existing research on elite socialization, he concludes that "the socializing effects of European institutions are uneven and often surprisingly weak, and in no sense can be construed as shaping a radically new, post-national identity" (Checkel, 2003: 13). This conclusion is even more true for mass publics.

Moving from the micro-level of elite socialization to the macro-level of domestic institutional change, Risse, Cowles, and Caporaso (2001: 1–2) conclude that Europeanization leads to distinct and identifiable changes in the institutional structures of member states. National adaptation to Europeanization is omnipresent. But this does not suggest either wholesale convergence or continued divergence in national institutions and policies. Instead, national adaptations retain distinctive national colors. Where national institutions fit well into emerging European ones, adaptation is minimal; where they do not fit well, pressure to adapt can be intense. Rather than favoring either the European or the national level, Europeanization meshes increasingly closely with both. An evolving European polity is experimenting with new methods of policy coordination that go beyond legal harmonization to include also codified practices such as target-setting, bench-marking, and peer review. Between perfect adaptation on the one hand, and hard-core resistance on the other, the messiness of Europeanization typically works itself out and creates "patched-up" institutional structures (Héritier, 2001: 54; Héritier, Knill, and Mingers, 1996; Ansell and Di Palma, 2004).

Legal and cultural Europeanization

European enlargement has spread from Western Europe to the south, north and east. It is accompanied by Europeanization. Enlargement and Europeanization are likely to continue, raising an important question: What constitutes the core of the Europe that is being enlarged and that is being made more European? I argue below that legal processes of Europeanization show that core to be problematic, and cultural processes reveal it to be undefined. Religious politics in Europe thus occurs on a terrain that remains relatively unoccupied.

Legal Europeanization

After World War Two Europe was rebuilt on the basis of two strong commitments: to political democracy, Christian and otherwise, and to harnessing Germany's destructive potential in a variety of European political arrangements. Whereas the religious motivation for the re-establishment of a democratic politics has waned over the last half-century, the commitment to taming German power and securing European peace has not. Various analytical perspectives on European integration alert us to the fact that the political process by which this objective has been sought has not changed over time. Legal Europeanization is a problematic process by which a secular Europe seeks to mold its constituent parts.

Legal Europeanization is illustrated clearly in the body of law, the *acquis communautaire*, that the European polity has created since 1957 (Iankova and Katzenstein, 2003). The *acquis* is the result of legislative decisions, legal rulings, and political practices. Although it is a legal concept that refers to a body of law, the *acquis* also represents the continuously changing institutional terms that result from a process of political integration through law. The European Union insists that any prospective member must, before accession, adopt the *acquis* – about 100,000 printed pages. This is a tall order, and a requirement that longstanding members of the EU themselves have difficulty meeting. Jonas Tallberg (1999: 125–26) reports that in about 10 percent of the cases member states did not comply with EU directives in the 1990s. Furthermore, various provisions of selective opt-ins and opt-outs have been fashioned to prevent Britain and Denmark from derailing the Europeanization of various policy sectors. Will the increasing heterogeneity of the EU member states that comes with enlargement lead to a further, substantial erosion of the legal and policy coherence of the EU?

The discrepancy between political reality and legal fiction is based on a system of institutional indulgence that acknowledges an unavoidable gap between law and compliance. In the process of European enlargement, a less philosophical and more political point deserves our attention. The decoupling of legal norms from political practice is central to Stephen Krasner's (1999) analysis of international legal sovereignty as a system of organized hypocrisy. International outcomes are created by rulers. Rulers violate or adhere to principles or rules because of calculations of material or ideational interests. They are not acting out taken-for-granted practices or following the scripts of overarching institutional structures. Norms and actions are decoupled. The logic of consequence trumps the logic of appropriateness.

Although it offers an important insight, Krasner's view is too one-sided. European enlargement contains elements of both political and institutional hypocrisy. This distinction describes the difference between voluntary and involuntary non-compliance. Social reality cannot be reduced only to the aggregations of individual rulers who create or break rules. Social reality is also the product of social interactions that create their own webs of meanings. Institutional rules and processes of rule-making are often at the heart of these webs. Once regularized, they become institutional orders that define the roles actors play and the social context in which actors define interests and adopt strategies (Olsen, 1997). Rulers neither precede these institutional orders nor do they stand outside of them. In the case at hand they are products of the institutions of the European welfare state and of a variety of European international institutions, most importantly the EU. Institutional hypocrisy is a systemic feature of legal Europeanization that occurs during enlargement. So is political hypocrisy, which results from the purposeful strategy of specific actors in specific countries or policy sectors.

Other scholars working on questions of legal compliance more generally have articulated a view similar to the one expressed here. Abram and Antonia Chayes (1995: 23–28), for example, see the principal source of non-compliance not in "willful disobedience" but in a lack of capacity or clarity of priority. Because sovereignty entails recognition by other states, enforcement of rules is less important than management through a variety of mechanisms including transparency enhancement, dispute settlement, capacity building, and persuasion. In an important book on European law, Lisa Conant (2002: 52) speaks of the ambiguities associated with the application of new rules across cases encouraging "contained compliance" as a distinctive trait of the EU. European law, Conant argues, "includes a myriad of limitations that obfuscates the responsibilities and opportunities states and individuals face under European law." Institutional and political hypocrisy capture the tensions between legal compliance or harmonization of law on the one hand, and policy compliance or policy implementation on the other.

It is therefore not unexpected that compliance with EU law poses problems for the Community and its member states. Lack of capacity, unclarity of priority, and obfuscation of responsibilities are characteristic of a European polity marked by the coincidence of both binding European rules and discretionary national applications. Institutional hypocrisy affects all member states of the EU, old and new, and points to the problematic core of legal Europeanization.

Cultural Europeanization

The vision of creating a European polity with a European public space is deeply appealing to many European intellectuals and readily invoked in the speeches of European politicians. Yet by all accounts political attempts to create a collective European culture have failed (Shore, 1996; Pantel, 1999). These attempts include, specifically, various policies focused on culture and education, such as initiatives aiming to correct national history books, adding a European dimension to national school curricula, setting up a European television channel, creating "European rooms" in national museums, and promoting a European lottery. A select few of these proposals have been adopted. Some were accepted without a binding resolution and never adopted by the member states. Still more were never acted on, as national governments have remained extremely reluctant to let the EU expand into the sacred domain of national secular culture (Theiler, 1999a: 2). Three decades of Europeanization thus have had minimal effects, a fact attested to by scattered evidence from opinion surveys. Public support for European integration is much weaker on questions of education, social, cultural, and media policy than, for example, on questions of economic and even foreign and security policy (Theiler, 1999a: 143–48, 1999b: 65; Dalton and Eichenberg, 1998: 263). A culturally largely undefined European collective identity leaves plenty of space for secular Europe's incorporation of the politics of religion.

European education policy has had a sorry history (Theiler, 1999a: 104–49). The Commission and the European Parliament have sought to introduce a European dimension into national school curricula, centering on the teaching of European material, Europeanized national histories, the display of European symbols in classrooms, a mandatory Europe day, and similar activities. The 1972 Janne Report developed the rationale for policy measures that would add a European dimension to education and thus help foster positive attitudes toward Europe. The intent of the measures the report proposed was to create a European identity and to enhance the perceived legitimacy of Community institutions and practices through the teaching of what one might call European civics. In 1973 the Commission reorganized itself and created a new Directorate for Education and Training, which was integrated with an equally new Directorate-General for Research, Science, and Education (DG XII) headed by the German Commissioner Ralf Dahrendorf, widely known for expanding the Community's role in education and culture (Theiler, 1999a: 107). Education research has confirmed that the material in national syllabi and textbooks mostly deals with European topics, covered in a national framework. The proportion of space allocated to the EU typically remains in the low single digits.

The political and legal obstacles to the Europeanization of national education materials proved to be simply too strong. During the 1970s, for example, European education ministers failed to attend a single joint meeting. And in the Community's educational policy, economic and vocational aspects of education crowded out all attempts to change the content of national school curricula. Policies facilitating international exchange, such as vocational training or the mutual recognition of diplomas, were adopted, in sharp contrast to total stalemate or failure in all attempts to increase a "European dimension" of national education. The picture changed little in the 1980s. In line with its single-market initiative, the EU adopted several measures that facilitated educational exchange and language training. But the EU refrained from inserting European content into national educational curricula, which member states continued to guard jealously.

One notable exception exists in university education. The Erasmus program has been an undeniable success of European educational policy. Adopted in 1987, its name evokes the European Enlightenment as constitutive of Europe's identity, without acknowledging the history of European imperialism, racism, and militarism (Shore, 1996: 483–86). In 1998 Erasmus sponsored about 200,000 student and 35,000 teacher exchanges. It also supported a large number of programs facilitating the mutual recognition of diplomas and cooperation in the training of language teachers. It is supplemented by the Jean Monnet program, through which the EU is supporting more than 400 university chairs and institutes dealing with European studies.

Yet this is the only notable success in the attempt to Europeanize education. The Treaty of Maastricht enlarged the EU's scope beyond the area of vocational training that had been part of its jurisdiction since 1957. It did not, however, compel national governments to relinquish their monopoly power over the content of educational policy. The Commission has been unable to enhance the European content in national curricula. In primary education in 1998 the EU sponsored some 10,000 teacher exchanges and 2,000 new school partnerships in an area (consisting of the EU, some EFTA countries, and parts of Central and Eastern Europe) with 300,000 schools, 4 million teachers, and 70 million primary and secondary school students (Theiler, 1999a: 137). Youth for Europe is by all accounts a very modest program aiming at short, one-week exchanges. And the Lingua program is much too small to be effective in advancing the promotion of the learning and teaching of languages.

Shifting the focus from education to culture reinforces the picture of minimal cultural Europeanization. Before the 1970s the EU had no mandate whatever in cultural policy. As the Commission began setting its sights beyond the economic dimension of European integration, the completion of a European customs union in 1968 changed its rhetoric. In the 1970s both Commission and Parliament pushed policies to strengthen a European consciousness. Tobias Theiler (1999a) has documented in great detail numerous political initiatives of the European Parliament and the Commission designed to give Europe a stronger symbolic profile and instill more of a European collective identity. Yet all these efforts failed to defeat political opposition and public indifference to the European project.

The "Declaration on European Identity" issued at the 1973 Copenhagen Summit was a forceful, first appearance of a new kind of identity rhetoric in European diplomacy. Although it was criticized as suffering from "conceptual confusion and phraseological gobbledygook" (Theiler, 1999a: 29), the rediscovery of a European cultural and civilizational identity and mission became the discursive underpinning for most subsequent policy initiatives. Soon after 1973 the European Parliament adopted proposals for the protection of Europe's cultural heritage and the free circulation of ideas and people. But it was the 1975 Tindeman Report with its blueprint for the future of the Community that contained proposals for creating a "citizen's Europe." The report suggested two different kinds of proposals: "vertical" ones seeking a greater symbolic representation of the Community in the everyday life of Europeans and "horizontal" ones facilitating the exchange of information. Despite the widespread interest that the report generated, national governments failed to act on its recommendations.

In the second half of the 1970s the Commission prepared a modest action program in the cultural sector, including the creation of European rooms in national museums and the creation of European Community cultural institutes. Although these initiatives did not succeed either, the Commission's activity did lead to small institutional innovations, such as the creation of a Community Youth Orchestra and a Community public relations campaign. By and large, though, throughout the 1970s comprehensive and far-reaching proposals by the Commission and Parliament were blocked by a number of national governments: always by France intent on excluding the EU from the issue of cultural policy, almost always by the United Kingdom and Denmark, and frequently, because of its federal structure, by Germany.

This political struggle continued throughout the 1980s, reflected in a series of proposals and draft treaties. The 1981 "Draft European Act," also known as the Genscher-Colombo proposal, paid much attention to cultural policy as did the "Draft Treaty of the European Union" drawn up by the European Parliament in 1984 under the leadership of Altiero Spinelli. The 1983 "Solemn Declaration on European Union" adopted at the Stuttgart Summit was much more reticent. And the Single European Act of 1987 excluded all cultural matters.

Against this track record of non-action, and with the political issue firmly settled in favor of national governments intent on preserving their exclusive political prerogatives on issues of culture, the Commission sought to make headway by pushing a few measures adopted at the regular meetings of the cultural ministers that had started in 1984, despite the continued lack of any institutional mandate by the Community (Shore, 1996: 479–80). The cumulative impact of the concrete measures adopted was modest at best. Some of the measures, such as the "European city program," had weak or non-existent links to either European integration or Community institutions or policies. Other measures facilitated transnational cultural exchanges, mostly focused in selected areas of "high culture" such as classical music or translations with inherently limited mass appeal.

Arguably the most important initiative of the decade was the Adonnino Report on a "People's Europe," delivered in two versions at the Brussels (March 1985) and Milan (June 1985) Summit meetings. It sought to strengthen the identity of the Community both internally and in relation to the outside world. In the specific area of cultural policy and communication it focused on audiovisual co-production, on the creation of a European academy of science, technology, and art, and on a Euro-lottery designed to appeal to a broader public. The reports also recommended border signs of a common design and the introduction of a European flag, the designation of Beethoven's Ode to Joy as the official Community anthem, and the issuing of postage stamps with European symbols and themes. With the exception of the adoption of a European anthem and "logo," and a number of public relations activities, by the early 1990s the European Commission had little to look back on after two decades of activity. The cumulative impact of the political initiatives that the European Commission and Parliament had undertaken in the face of stiff national opposition was reduced to an economic reinterpretation of its cultural objectives. Two decades of failure had taught the Commission that it could elicit minimal cooperation from national governments intent on protecting their cultural sovereignty only if it focused on the creation of a cultural space without borders in which cultural goods and services could circulate freely (Theiler, 1999a: 26–61).

The failed Europeanization of cultural policy was repeated in audio-visual policy (Theiler, 1999a: 62–103, 1999c, 2001; Collins, 1994; Schlesinger, 1994, 2001). Attempts to create a pan-European television station with non-national, European programming failed. Viewers simply did not like European programs. And national governments were unwilling to secure Community-wide distribution of the station's signals and offer adequate financial support. After these failures, EU policy shifted in the 1990s to a Europeanization of audiovisual production rather than consumption. In the hope of moving gradually to a partial denationalization of content, the European Parliament and the Commission sought to subsidize multinational co-productions. This policy also failed because of lack of support by member states. Instead EU policy was reduced to boosting domestic output and subsidizing circulation of audiovisual material throughout the Community. The EU's audiovisual policy encapsulates the failure of its cultural policy: it facilitated a horizontal exchange of information that is compatible with existing national and local identities. It conspicuously failed to have any noticeable effect on the vertical deepening of programming content that might help foster a European collective identity.

Cultural Europeanization has been a failure. It would be a mistake, however, to reduce Europe to any one of its many variegated aspects (Borneman and Fowler, 1997: 492). Some minor direct effects exist on religious matters: the EU and Europe's Churches, for example, collaborate in a program called "A Soul for Europe: Ethics and Spirituality." It funds projects with religious and ethical inspiration, thus neatly side-stepping the religious–humanist schism that so bedeviled the drafters of the preamble to the European constitution (Jansen, 2000: 105–06). Furthermore, the activity of new religious groups is of considerable concern to European institutions. In 1996, for example, the European

Parliament warned member states to be cautious in granting tax-exempt status to new religious organizations. And the European Court of Human Rights tolerates differential treatment of mainstream and peripheral Churches and denies Church status to certain religious groups. When states are found to violate the rights of religious groups, the court prefers to treat the issue not as freedom of religion but as freedom of speech (Enyedi, 2003: 224).

Europe's single-market initiative has had some indirect effects on issues of public morality. Paulette Kurzer (2001), for example, has examined "moral regulation" in contemporary European politics, touching on deeply institutionalized national values. Finnish and Swedish alcohol policy and Dutch drug policies, for example, have expressed very different approaches to substance abuse and public health. In recent years there has been an unmistakable trend toward less restrictive Nordic alcohol policies and less permissive Dutch drug policies. This diminution of cultural disparities operates indirectly through markets and not through any explicit set of EU cultural policies. Generally speaking, cultural Europeanization is distinguished by a lack of content rather than what Chris Reus-Smit (1999) has called the moral purpose of the state. The direct and indirect effects the EU has on religious and moral issues are small.

Existing survey data confirm the weakness of cultural Europeanization. No collective European identity exists. The data point instead to enormous variation across both countries and time. The lines between a European and an EU collective identity are blurred. After a decade of increasing Europeanization as measured by support for the EU in public opinion surveys in the 1980s, the 1990s have been a decade of "renationalization." The acceleration of the political integration of Europe in the 1990s has caused a substantial drop in public support for Europe. Between 2000 and 2003 growing transatlantic tensions, due to the unilateralist policies of the Bush administration and the US attack on Iraq unsanctioned by the United Nations, have re-energized European attitudes favoring integration. Research findings furthermore demonstrate that national identities differ in their openness to a European collective identity as a complement to existing collective identities, as in Italy, rather than a competitor with them, as in England (Breakwell, 1996: 18–26).

European identities are nested. In a 1991 opinion survey, on average, citizens in the twelve member states of the EU reported as strong an attachment to their local and regional communities as to national ones (Everts and Sinnott, 1995: 442). In 2002 the number of those identifying themselves only with their country, or first with their country and then with Europe, was more than five times larger than those who identified themselves only as European or with Europe first and then with their country (Eurobarometer, 2003: 36). Such nested attitudes tend to be stronger among the young, the better educated, and people having more positive attitudes toward Europe. Differences in epistemology, methods, and data notwithstanding, this conclusion is in basic agreement with broader sociological analyses that focus on complex processes of European identity construction through different governance mechanisms or in different issue areas, covering both internal and external interactions. Unity-in-diversity has thus become the core theme that the EU stresses (Pantel, 1999).

It would be a mistake to infer from this history of failure that Europe's secular identities are profoundly national. Europe, after all, is awash in a sea of American popular culture (Riding, 2004). On the basis of a cross-national analysis of language, religion, and popular cultures, David Laitin (2002) concludes that a pan-European cosmopolitan culture exists, complementary to persisting national cultures. Europe's cosmopolitanism has much to do with the United States. Americanization describes a process of selective appropriation by different social strata, which create their own subcultures and thus help constitute and perpetually reinterpret and re-enact national cultures. A popular joke, and French nightmare, defines a European as a person who watches American soap operas on a Japanese television set.

The openness of European nations to global culture is an important reminder of the minimal appeal and impact of Europeanization on mass publics in the domain of secular culture. The political salience and transnational effects of religion may prove to have greater political importance than the EU's secular culture in a Europe that is growing larger. Judging by the debates about Turkish accession and headscarves, on matters of culture it is Europe's religions rather than Europe's secular culture that are bound to provide the focal point for political debate.

Europe and religion

The rules for the relations between European states and the modern international state system were established at the end of the Thirty Years War in the seventeenth century (Philpott, 2000, 2001a). "Westphalia" has become shorthand for an interstate system that banished religion to the domestic and private realm, as Daniel Nexon argues in chapter 10. From a "melting pot" of freely co-mingling religions over which rulers had no jurisdictions emerged, after horrific violence, a "salad-bowl" of ruler-determined religious affiliations enshrined in the principle of *cuius regio eius religio* and in the doctrine and practice of state neutrality on religious matters (Madeley, 2003a, 2003b). Religious pluralism among states eventually became the rule, as did the principle of non-interference in domestic affairs. Because they are expressions of rationalist thought deeply antithetical to religion, the silence of realist and liberal theories of international relations on the role of religion in European and world politics is thus not surprising. Yet Nexon also shows in chapter 10 that the historical evolution from an international politics dominated by religion to a secular state system was anything but smooth. And a burgeoning literature on sovereignty demonstrates that the canonical view of sovereign states governed by the principle of non-intervention is bad history (Krasner, 1999, 2001).

Scott Thomas's (2005) analysis of religious movements and conflicts in world politics insists that the global resurgence of religion may have made the twentieth century the last modern century. Post-modernity recognizes explicitly the existence of multiple modernities. Religion is not an idiom of discontent. It is, rather, a set of ideas and practices that constitute the very content of a community's identity and the religious values, practices, and traditions that shape its political struggles. Religion is fundamentally a social tradition that encompasses and defines a community of believers rather than a body of beliefs, a social ethic, or a cultural system, as rationalist proponents of modernity argue.

The privatization and nationalization of religion that occurred in the seventeenth century in Latin Christendom was a decisive impetus for modern European and international society. But that process has remained far from complete in a world in which strong religions interact with weak states and in which religion is now experiencing a resurgence on a global scale. This resurgence is not primarily a "fundamentalist" or "anti-modernist" reaction to the ineluctable march of modernization and globalization. It is, rather, in its public form a normative critique of historical developments that have failed to bring about the Enlightenment's project of development and authenticity.

Thomas (2005: 49–50) grants Europe an exceptional status in the resurgence of religion in world politics. Secularization as an inherent feature of modernization, he argues, is applicable to European religion but not to the rest of the world. In pointing to European enlargement, this book argues otherwise and thus diminishes Europe's exceptionalism. Enlargement is bringing back into the center of the European Union what had been on its periphery: renewed attention to the dilemma of coping with the intersection between religious and secular politics.

The widening gap between an emerging European polity and the United States is underlining the multiple modernities between different parts of the West. After World War Two Reinhold Niebuhr and other

Christian "realists" and "liberals" made the case for an ecumenical Protestantism that helped shape US policy in the creation of the Bretton Woods system and the subsequent hegemony the US enjoyed over the capitalist part of a bipolar international system (Thomas, 2005: 159). The public theology of the time was internationalist, circumspect, tough, and self-critical, adhering to "due regard for the opinions of mankind," as Thomas Jefferson wrote in the Declaration of Independence (Thomas, 2005: 162) – a far cry from the religiously infused, unilateral actions of the United States as a military superpower at the outset of the twenty-first century.

In Europe in the late 1940s Christian Democracy and Catholicism laid the foundations of the European integration movement. Europe was not merely a site for state bargains and profitable economic transactions. It was also the focus of a political movement seeking to implement a particular, religiously infused vision. Arsène Heitz, who in 1955 designed what eventually became the European flag – twelve yellow stars on a blue background – has reported that he was inspired by a reference in the New Testament's Book of Revelation to "a woman clothed with the sun . . . and a crown of twelve stars on her head" (*Economist*, 2004). Christian Democracy legitimated the political entrepreneurs and much of the normative content of European integration – a far cry from the secularly infused, multilateral actions of the emerging European polity as a civilian superpower at the outset of the twenty-first century. The transatlantic divide in the 1940s and 1950s was tempered by religious commonalities and a shared anti-communism. Half a century later neo-conservative American Catholics are highly critical of European integration and thus at odds with pro-European Catholics and the Vatican. The transatlantic rift over Europe thus has important religious undercurrents that exacerbate an unprecedented wave of anti-Americanism spreading across Europe in the aftermath of the Iraq war.

The religious differences between Europe and the United States, as José Casanova argues in chapter 3, also point to the relevance of the idea of multiple modernity when applied to domestic developments in the United States and Europe. The sharp and ideologically charged divide between "retro" and "metro" America (Sperling et al., 2004) may become a possible future for an enlarged Europe, one that is less desirable than the comforting image of a Europe united around consensual, secular principles of democratic welfare states that seek to maintain their competitiveness and peace in international politics.

Conventional renderings of the historical origins of the modern European state system and religious politics are intellectually suspect. And so is the neglect of religious politics by scholars of Europe's contemporary international and transnational relations. Religion continues to lurk underneath the veneer of European secularization. Reinsertion of religious issues into European politics is beginning to occur, brought about by transnational religious communities which after many decades are "returning" to a Europe bent on enlargement. Problematic legal and undefined cultural Europeanization leave ample space at the core of the European polity that religious politics is beginning to occupy. Europe, it appears, is poised for a renewed encounter with its own multiple modernities.

Notes

I would like to thank all the participants in the Mellon-Sawyer seminar "Toward a Transnational and Transcultural Europe" where these ideas took their initial shape. The seminar was sponsored by the Cornell Institute for European Studies in the fall semester of 2003 and convened by the two editors of this volume on the topic of European enlargement and religion. All of the participants at a workshop at Colgate University in April 2004 gave me ample criticisms and suggestions, as did Tim Byrnes, friend, colleague, and co-editor, on that and all subsequent drafts. Robert Keohane, John Meyer, Vjekoslav Perica, Sabrina Ramet, Sidney Tarrow, Scott Thomas, and two anonymous readers for Cambridge University Press also offered insightful comments that helped me greatly in revising this chapter. At the Center for Advanced Study in the Behavioral Studies, Kathleen Much helped improve my prose. The remaining weaknesses are due to my stubbornness in not following the good advice I received.
1 This paragraph draws on Katzenstein (1997b).

2 Faith, freedom, and federation: the role of religious ideas and institutions in European political convergence

Daniel Philpott and Timothy Samuel Shah

The dramatic inauguration of democratic regimes in Eastern Europe after 1989 and their subsequent petitions to join the European Union (EU) are usually treated as separate events. But in fact they advanced a common political result: European unity. That the European Union promotes unity is plain. But democracy is an integrating force, too. The signers of the Helsinki Accords in 1975 asserted human rights as fundamental European values; at the end of the Cold War, heads of state spoke of a "common European home" of liberal democracies extending from the Atlantic to the Urals. Together European democratization and integration have curtailed the power, autonomy, and even sovereignty of the polity that has fragmented Europe for centuries: the nation state. Transnational unity is a historically notable end, for it has long been absent from Europe, achieved first in the Roman Empire, realized last in medieval Christendom, theorized in modern times in the philosophical visions of Rousseau, Kant, and Wilson, and attempted – without ultimate success – in the imperial ambitions of Napoleon and Hitler.

Europe's increasing transnational unity in its democratic and integrative dimensions greatly interests Europe's predominant religions: Roman Catholicism, Orthodoxy, and Islam.[1] Given their own aspirations to transnational unity and universality, this is entirely fitting. They have a stake in this momentous trend for an additional reason: Europe's elites increasingly cast democratization and integration as secularizing projects, as José Casanova argues in this volume. Notwithstanding this fact, we emphasize in this chapter that European faiths have made important contributions to shaping and realizing the supposedly "secular" political goals of European freedom and European federation. At the same time, they differ markedly in their stances toward them. The Catholic Church actively encouraged the democratic revolutions of 1989, albeit more vigorously in some settings than others, and has strongly favored European integration since its origins after World War Two. The Orthodox

Church, by contrast, lent negligible support to the revolutions of 1989 and remains ambivalent toward European integration. Activist Islam or "Islamism" in Turkey, though not involved in the democratic revolutions of 1989, has long fought for its own democratic rights within the secularist Kemalist republic but European integration it long opposed – until recently, when Islamist party leaders came to favor it partly as a means of democratizing the Turkish state.

Why have Europe's religious communities adopted different stances toward the continent's political convergence? The most promising explanation follows the lines of the "historical institutionalist" school of political science (Pierson and Skocpol, 2002) which stresses ideas and institutions. A religious body whose (1) theology of ecclesial and political authority and (2) institutional structure and relationship to the state together favor the circumscription of the sovereign state and the creation of continent-wide political institutions tends to support European convergence. Behind these ideas and institutions lies a long history of doctrinal debate and development and changing social and political contexts that together constitute a pathway to the present.

The impact of religious ideas and institutions on European convergence is difficult to disentangle from the concurrent influences of economic forces, political trends, secular ideas, and many other factors. However, the fact that numerous analysts cite the influence of religious communities on the formation of public opinion, elite opinion, oppositional activity, state policy, and international institutions in several episodes of European democratization and integration provides a warrant for further investigation.

A key to unlocking the complexity of religious communities' influence is the recognition that they are in fact complex conglomerates of agents, including upper hierarchies, lower hierarchies, a laity of official members, affiliated organizations (e.g. parties, civil society organizations, and labor unions), and the mass of people who publicly identify with a given religion. For example, building on the work of Timothy Byrnes, Bryan Hehir describes the dynamic and layered complexity of the Roman Catholic Church elsewhere in this volume. The recent controversy concerning the Catholic Church's role in the Holocaust underscores this complexity: it reflects not only a radical diversity of framing assumptions but also a smorgasbord of historical evidence created by diverse Catholic actors and even diversity within the lives of individual Catholics (for a sample of accounts, see Goldhagen, 2002; Rychlak, 2000; Cornwell, 2000). Different agents exercise different kinds of sway to achieve different sorts of ends with varying levels of vigor.

Ideas and institutions

What characterizes religious communities that promote European trans-national unity in its dual aspects of democratization and integration? What characterizes religious communities that oppose European unity? What accounts for these characteristics? Part of the answer lies in doctrines – religious conceptions of proper institutional form and views of temporal authority, especially that of the state. The differences are rich and have their roots in centuries of development. Comparatively favorable to convergence are the doctrines of the Catholic Church. We divide those most relevant to our inquiry into six propositions, which correspond to contrasting propositions and resulting stances in Orthodoxy and Islam, as Table 2.1 illustrates. Although these propositions have been subject to "internal pluralism" within religious communities (Appleby, 2000), consensus within single religious communities is wide and consistent enough to form a distinct contrast with other religious communities.

First, the Roman Catholic Church holds an ecclesiology that stresses visible unity centered upon a single hierarchy. Though the Church's structure today differs from its first-century form, its priestly hierarchy has always been capped by bishops, with the Bishop of Rome being *primus inter pares*, as Bryan Hehir and Timothy Byrnes elaborate in this volume. Second, since the Middle Ages, the Church has conceived Europe organically as a Christian civilization whose unity subsists in the Church itself (John Paul II, 2003; Southern, 1970: 15–23; Martin, 1978: 100). Third, the Church has long expressed skepticism toward what it views as the chief usurper of this unity – the sovereign state and particularly the sovereign-state system that emerged through the Peace of Westphalia in 1648. The contrast between this conception and the realist valorization of the state could hardly be greater, as Hehir notes in chapter 4. Catholicism is likewise reserved toward the nation or community that aspires to statehood (Weigel, 1999: 652). The Church continued to oppose the concept of sovereignty in the nineteenth century, rejecting international law as a "Protestant science" and censoring the works of Protestant international lawyer Hugo Grotius. Although in the twentieth century the Church came to allow the sovereign state as legitimate in principle, it still insisted upon its accountability to a larger moral order and promoted institutions to ensure this accountability (Philpott, 2001c: 85–88, 261–62). Fourth, the Catholic Church has long held some version of the "two swords" doctrine of Pope Gelasius: temporal and spiritual authority ought to reside in separate hands. Fifth, through a dialogue with the modern world, the Church came to graft into its doctrine of morally circumscribed state authority modern ideas of human rights

Table 2.1: *Religious communities' political ideas about the sovereign state and European unity*

Idea	Catholicism	Orthodoxy	Turkish Islam
Conception of religious unity	Visible unity, centered on hierarchy of bishops and pope	Visible unity, but decentralized, without Pope	Historically, strong conception, centered on Caliphate
Conception of Europe	United Christian civilization subsisting in Church itself	United Christian civilization, but not dominated by the West	Skeptical of Christian Europe; historically, only acceptable European unity is under Ottoman rule
View of sovereign state and nation	Skeptical, ought to be limited by universal authority	No enduring opposition; in twentieth century, autocephaly	Ottoman Empire outside of sovereign states system; opposition to Kemalism's embrace of nation-state
Relationship between temporal and spiritual authority	Ought to be separate	Close relationship, caesaro-papism	Ottoman Empire subordinated religious to political authority; Kemalists have continued tradition with hostility to Islam
View of human rights and democracy	Favorable after Vatican II in 1960s	No strong and uniform favor, only some voices	Historically, distrust of human rights and democracy, but recent embrace
View of role of Islam in Europe	After Vatican II, inclusive, stressing dialogue	Exclusion of Islam from United Europe	Historically, opposed to membership in Europe, but recent favor

and democracy. Its embrace of human rights began with Pope John XXIII's *Pacem in Terris* in 1963 and culminated in the 1965 document of the Second Vatican Council, *Dignitatis Humanae*, which endorsed religious freedom for the first time. Religious freedom, human rights, and democracy then became central themes in the teachings of John Paul II. Sixth, it was also in the Second Vatican Council that the Church adopted a more inclusive approach to Europe's Christian foundations, which called for dialogue and reconciliation with Protestants, Muslims, and Jews (Sutton, 1997: 23–25; Second Vatican Council, 1965; John Paul II, 1995).

Other major religious bodies in Europe have not necessarily espoused the mirror opposite of these six propositions but have been more ambiguous and sometimes skeptical. Eastern Orthodoxy has continued to teach an ecclesiology of visible unity since the schism of 1054 but in a more decentralized fashion than the Catholic Church. It also envisions a united Christian Europe but is wary of one dominated by the West, a concern dating back to the first millennium of Christianity (Ware, 1963: 18–72, 239–63). Never having struggled to defend its transnational unity against the Reformation or the rise of the sovereign state, Orthodoxy does not harbor Catholicism's skepticism toward the nation and the state. It has long embraced "Caesaro-papism," the originally Byzantine "symphonic" model of church–state cooperation, involving significant integration of spiritual and temporal authority. For over a century, its ecclesiastical structure has been divided along national lines in what is known as "autocephaly." Consistent with this national structure, the Orthodox Church in a historically Orthodox country such as Serbia, Russia, or Greece usually considers itself the unique guardian of its people's national identity and cultural autonomy, as Sabrina Ramet and Vjekoslav Perica note in their contributions to this volume (see also Perica, 2004). Unlike the Catholic Church, Orthodoxy has never decisively incorporated human rights and democracy into its central teachings and in some instances, according to Ramet, directly opposes religious freedom and other liberal-democratic principles. Though today Orthodoxy contains important voices favorable to these ideas, it lacks anything like a magisterium or encyclical tradition to give them unity and overriding authority. Finally, its notion of Christian Europe is comparatively more exclusive, particularly vis-à-vis Islam in general and Turkey in particular, in part because of Orthodoxy's historic experience of subjugation by the Ottoman Empire.

Islam in the Ottoman Empire placed a strong emphasis on visible religious unity, centered on the Sultan and Caliphate. With the Kemalist revolution and the abolition of Ottoman rule in 1924, Islam became subject to a radically secularist state. In relation to Europe, Ottoman Muslims had perceived European efforts to unify the continent as anti-Muslim and strategically threatening; the only European unity the Ottomans could accept was one wrought by Ottoman conquest. Until the eighteenth century, this remained a realistic prospect: the Ottoman Empire captured portions of Eastern, Central, and Southwestern Europe and was poised to expand further. Because the Kemalist revolution implied a radically more positive attitude to Christian Europe as a model of modernity and progress, traditionalist Muslims in Turkey came to distrust Europe even more profoundly (Yavuz, 2003: 249). In addition, Ottoman Islam was never part of the Westphalian state system: the polities negotiating the Peace of Westphalia, for example, conceived of themselves as the "Senate of Christian Europe" and did not consider Islam a member of "international society" (Naff, 1984). When European powers defeated the Ottoman Empire after World War One, they in effect imposed the Westphalian system on it and forcibly turned it into a collection of ethnically defined nation-states. Atatürk made a virtue of necessity and embraced the Western nation-state and Europeanization as essential to Turkey's progress (Yavuz, this volume). Traditional Islam was compelled to defer to and operate within Atatürk's authoritarian republicanism (Yavuz, 2000, 2003). Such deference actually continued – albeit in a radicalized way – the traditional Ottoman practice of subordinating religious to political authority, which the Ottomans arguably inherited from the Byzantine Empire (Quataert, 2000: 4). Recently, however, devout Muslims have struggled to secure greater freedom for themselves in Turkish civil society and politics. Both the Kemalist nationalists and Islamists have distrusted the Western tradition of human rights and democracy, though both have recently changed their attitudes. The groups continue to disagree, however, over how much public influence Islam should exert on Turkish politics and civil society (Yavuz, 2003: 249).

   Besides ideas, the institutional structure of religious communities and their institutional relationship to the state also influence their stance toward European unity. This is best described through a concept from the sociology of religion: differentiation (Martin, 1978: 69; Casanova, 1994: 11–66). Religious communities are differentiated when they are separated in their roles and jurisdictions from the state: one does not participate in the other's governance or perform the other's activities (Stepan, 2000, 2001). Most essential is independence from the state in governance. Does the state exercise influence over its selection of leadership? Its finances? Its doctrines? Its practice? Do religious leaders themselves perform temporal functions or hold state offices? Differentiation in governance often has important historical roots, arising from the religion's historical relationship to the state, its recent history of persecution or freedom, and its own response of resistance or accommodation. Another measure of differentiation is the strength of a religious body's transnational ties to co-religionists and external supporters, which can strengthen it with respect to the state. A differentiated religious body might also benefit from ties with civil society. Finally, a religious body might also differentiate itself from the state through identifying with the national identity of its inhabitants. If a religious body fuses itself with the nation and throws its allegiance behind a state as an expression of a shared religious nationalism, then it will be weakly differentiated (Perica, 2002, 2004). But a religious group sometimes identifies strongly and simultaneously with a particular nation *and* with a transnational religious community and, based on this dual affinity, sharply differentiates itself from the state – especially when the state is deemed hostile to both God and country (Martin, 1978: 100–08).

The more a religious body is differentiated from the state along these dimensions, the more likely it is to support European convergence. It can adopt such a commitment insofar as freedom from the state allows it to do so. Having identified its interests independently of the state, it is better able to articulate a vision of transnational unity. Ideas and institutions are related. A religious body's own ecclesiology determines its institutional structure, which in turn determines the prerogatives and distance it demands from the state. A religious body differentiated from the state is in turn more likely to espouse European unity in its democratic and integrative dimensions.

Together, ideas and the differentiation of institutions offer a powerful explanation of religious communities' divergent stances toward European unity. In the Catholic case, transnational unity, skepticism toward the sovereign state, and an embrace of human rights and democracy, combined with strong ecclesial resistance to state encroachment, generated a powerful opposition to communist regimes – especially in Poland and Lithuania – as well as strong support for European integration from its inception in 1950. The Orthodox Church, weaker in its institutional unity, less friendly to European unity, and less hostile to the nation and the state, possessed weak conceptual and institutional equipment with which to favor the revolutions of 1989 and was far more disposed to ally with the communist state. In addition, as the hierarchy of the Greek Orthodox Church illustrates, it has offered a mixed message toward European integration. Devout and politically assertive forms of Turkish Islam, also known as "Islamist," have opposed the Kemalist nation-state but remained weakly differentiated in their relationship to it, resulting in an ongoing and only partially successful struggle for a more autonomous space for Islam and hence for a more democratic politics. At the same time, Islamists traditionally opposed Turkish involvement in the "Christian club" of the European Union. Hakan Yavuz notes in this volume that, in pursuit of a "democratic Islamic identity," Islamists reversed this long-standing hostility in the late 1990s and now support Turkey's accession to the European Union precisely as a means of expanding an open democratic politics and hence the freedom of Muslims to shape public life. Islam in Turkey is thus a fascinating mixed case: in its basic ideas, it resists both the comprehensive claims of the secular state as well as either Christian- or secular-dominated European integration, but in its weak institutional differentiation as a historical legacy and contemporary fact, it embraces the EU in order to win by international means the political autonomy it cannot win by domestic means alone.

Religion and the democratic revolutions of 1989

Whatever differences in political form divided European states prior to the fall of the Berlin Wall – democratic socialism vs. free-market liberalism, firm alignment with the Western alliance vs. "third way" neutrality – no difference was sharper than the one created by what Winston Churchill termed the Iron Curtain. In the 1970s and 1980s, Spain, Portugal, and Greece had come to join and nearly complete the European community of liberal democracies outside the communist bloc. So when the revolutions of 1989 rocketed through Eastern Europe, and the Soviet Union suddenly collapsed in 1991, leaving the Baltic states and the Ukraine to emerge as democracies and Russia to begin its own troubled democratic development, Europe was more united in its basic political commitments than at any time since the Middle Ages (Nexon, this volume, chapter 10).

Among religious communities, the Catholic Church most vigorously promoted democracy in the revolutions of 1989. The Church in Poland, for example, advanced democracy in several ways. One was the direct protest of diverse voices in the Church – dissident statements, writings, and marches. During the early 1950s, as the communist regime was attempting to control the Church, Stefan Cardinal Wyszyński, who enjoyed enormous prestige and popularity, began to utter statements of defiance, a practice he would continue for several decades. Catholics at the grassroots also protested, supported by the Church's underground catechetical centers, summer camps, and educational programs (Rydel, 2001: 46–47; Broun, 1988: 333–34; Weigel, 1992: 111).

During the 1970s, Polish prelates adopted the language of human rights, following the lead of Vatican II. Then, too, a Catholic newspaper, *Tygodnik Powszechny* ("Universal Weekly") began to declaim against the regime. These and other instances led to a crescendo of dissent in the 1980s, when the Church cooperated with Solidarity in mounting mass demonstrations, speaking out against the martial law the regime imposed in 1981, and offering a place of sanctuary and organization for underground groups (Mojzes, 1992: 294–98; Jerschina, 1990: 94–95).

One of the most important modes of resistance was the Church's use of religious rituals and forms of piety through which it sustained its morale, guarded its independence, and defied the regime. As early as the 1950s, clergy spoke out against the regime through the mass and other religious meetings as well as summer camps, programs of religious instruction, and cultural activities, as Ramet details in chapter 5 of this volume (see also Rydel, 2001: 45–46). From 1957 to 1966, Cardinal Wyszyński led the Polish Church in a Great Novena campaign of prayer, pilgrimages, catechesis, and teaching deliberately designed to defy the regime. During the 1980s, open-air Catholic masses took on the flavor of public demonstrations. Particularly defiant were those celebrated by Father Jerzy Popiełuszko, a Solidarity priest who preached non-violent resistance. After the regime's security officers murdered him on October 19, 1984, hundreds of thousands attended his funeral, honoring him as a martyr priest (Weigel, 1992: 115–17, 149–50).

The Polish Church's most important asset of all was a richly transnational one: Karol Wojtyła, elevated from Archbishop of Krakow to become Pope John Paul II in October 1978, was the native son whom Poles would widely regard as "the fulcrum of the Revolution of 1989." In a decisive shift which Hehir analyzes in this volume, John Paul II departed from the earlier *Ostpolitik* of Pope Paul VI by refusing to engage with communism as a permanent political reality. Instead, he challenged it head-on by underscoring the inviolability of human rights, especially religious freedom, and emphasizing their transcendent foundation. Armed with these themes, he exercised skillful symbolic leadership. On his first papal visit to Poland in 1979, he drew hundreds of thousands, whom he galvanized through appeals to human rights – religious freedom above all – and his summons to the Polish Catholic Church to liberate Churches throughout the communist bloc. Later visits in 1983 and 1987 attracted similar crowds (Weigel, 1992: 129–37).

One of the greatest fruits of John Paul II's visits was the strengthening of the Solidarity trade union – the most important example of the Church's active cooperation with other civil society organizations against the regime. An organization of 10–12 million, Solidarity was the largest civil society organization in Polish history. It used religious symbols, was highly committed to religious freedom, turned to the Church for spiritual support – priests said mass for workers, for instance – and cooperated closely with the Church in leading resistance (though see Ramet, this volume, ch. 5). Though formally economic, it was importantly spiritual (Mojzes, 1992: 297–99).

Among religious communities in the 1989 revolutions, the Polish Church's democratizing activity was uniquely robust. The Church played a comparably significant political role in Lithuania. Here, too, protest enjoyed a mass base, involving rural and urban, rich and poor, educated and uneducated. It took the form of a series of popular petitions from 1968 to 1974, and, beginning in 1972, an underground newspaper, the *Chronicle of the Catholic Church in Lithuania*, inspired by Vatican II to promote the idea of human rights. A national opposition movement, Sajudis, used churches for political rallies. Ceremony was also a strong form of defiance in Lithuania, although less in the form of masses and more through national and religious songs (Vardys, 1978: 132–35, 144–45, 1981: 1).

In Czechoslovakia, the Church never galvanized a unified opposition movement of the sort that emerged in Poland or Lithuania, though in the early 1980s its opposition grew from sparse to palpable. The leading prelate, František Cardinal Tomášek, refrained from speaking out strongly against the regime through the late 1970s, adopting instead a strategy of accommodation to protect the Church. In the 1980s, a Catholic peasant, Augustin Navrátil, garnered 500,000 signatures on a petition demanding religious freedom, non-interference by the state in internal Church matters, and wider distribution of religious texts. During the 1980s Cardinal Tomášek then began to speak against the regime, emboldened by Navrátil and by the example and support of John Paul II. In a growing opposition movement, Catholics began to cooperate with non-Catholics, and Czechs with Slovaks, culminating in mass protests in 1988 and in 1989.

The Church in Hungary, save the steady but lonely voice of József Cardinal Mindszenty, opposed its communist rulers very little, at least until the 1989 revolutions. For decades an important symbol of opposition, Mindszenty was arrested and imprisoned in the earliest years of communism and then helped to bring about the short-lived revolution of 1956. He spent the next fifteen years protected within the walls of the US Embassy, where he remained a fairly isolated voice of opposition, hardly supported even by the Vatican. The period 1963 through 1989 was then a period of thaw, during which the regime allowed the Church to practice worship, education, and other activities and to exercise a joint role in the appointment of its own bishops, while the Church agreed not to oppose the state (Broun, 1988: 129–47; Ramet, 1998: 112–19).

The story of the Orthodox Church's stance toward communism was similar in both Bulgaria and Romania – by and large, one of subservience to the regime. Both churches, which had achieved autocephaly prior to the onset of the communist regime, suffered severe Stalinist purges during the late 1940s and early 1950s. Dissident priests, bishops, and nuns were killed; those who remained either supported the state or refrained from opposing it. In both countries, the Orthodox Church supported the regime by espousing propaganda on its behalf (Hale, 1971: 45, quoted in Ramet, 1998: 193). Once the Church's loyalty was established, the regime returned the favor. In Romania, for instance, the state celebrated the seventy-fifth anniversary of autocephaly, and after 1962, promoted the Church as representative of the Romanian nation. Only in the revolutions of 1989 did small dissident movements appear within Orthodoxy (Ramet, 1989: 20; Ramet, 1998: 191).

Due to a similar history of weak differentiation, Turkey also succeeded in subordinating religion to state – though in this case religion has increasingly sought to break out of its subordinate role. From the founding of the Turkish Republic under Kemal Atatürk, secular republicanism has come at the expense of robust democracy and autonomous civil society. Hakan Yavuz observes in this volume that for Atatürk, inspired by a positivist and Jacobin version of secularism, there could be no successful Westernization without state "reform" and repression of religion (see also Yavuz, 1999: 116–17). The tensions between Kemalist secularism and democracy became particularly acute after a military coup on September 12, 1980, which led to a revised constitution making the military the permanent guardian of the country's secular and republican values. Turkish politics has since been a story of unresolved struggle between the military guardians of Kemalist republicanism, who wish to preserve the secular republic against anti-modern religion, and Islamists, who wish to secure the freedom of religion to influence state and society (Insel, 2003).

However, a combination of weak differentiation and the persistence of secularist ideas and institutions has wrought important changes in Turkish Islam. In particular, the limited room for maneuver permitted by secularism has forced devout and traditionalist Muslims either to adapt to it or to accept having no public influence. Those who adapt *ipso facto* accept certain ideas: the state sets the parameters of religion's public existence; the only way to change the state is from the inside. So-called "Islamists" have adopted these ideas and organized a succession of political parties – the Welfare Party (RP), Virtue Party (FP), and today's governing Justice and Development Party (AKP) – reflecting them. Self-consciously inspired by European Christian Democracy, these parties adapt the Islamic faith to Turkish secular politics by emphasizing its ethical implications.

The gradualist "insider strategy" of the Islamists scored important successes in the early 1990s. In June 1996, the Islamist Welfare Party won enough votes to be the dominant partner in a coalition government, meaning that "for the first time since the formation of the Turkish Republic in 1923, Turkey's prime minister was a leader whose avowed political philosophy and personal identity was based on Islam" (Yavuz, 2003: 3). The generals struck back: unwilling to countenance a politically assertive Islamism, the military-bureaucratic establishment of the September 12 regime brought the government down in a "soft coup" in February 1997 and pressured the Constitutional Court to dissolve the Welfare Party in January 1998. The message to Islamists was clear: generals, not elections, would decide the appropriate parameters of secularist republicanism.

In November 2002, the latest Islamist political party, the Justice and Development Party (AKP), won an even larger share of the vote than the WP in 1996. The party leader, Tayyip Erdoğan, became prime minister. The party's rhetoric was striking for its incessant emphasis on democracy (Önis and Keyman, 2003: 99). But the question is whether the military remains the effective guardian of secularist republicanism, ready and able to intervene when it deems necessary. Until its role is officially and permanently transformed through constitutional change, democratic consolidation remains incomplete and precarious.

Explaining the democratic activity of religions

Behind the stark differences in these religious communities' democratic activity in the revolutions of 1989 was largely their respective political theologies. In the Catholic Church, long-standing themes of European unity, skepticism toward the secularizing tendencies of the sovereign state, and concern for the integrity of its visible unity evolved into support for liberal democracy in the context of the late twentieth century. Earlier in the century, these same themes had motivated the Vatican's censure of communism, which it spoke against repeatedly, as well as fascism, which Pope Pius XI condemned in several of its settings, including Nazi Germany in his encyclical of 1937, *Mit Brennender Sorge*.[2] After World War Two, fascism was defeated, but communism spread into Eastern Europe, where it brutally suppressed the Church. Accordingly, Pope

Pius XII was uncompromising in his opposition, as Hehir describes in this volume. His 1949 address in St. Peter's Square was typical:

It is only too well known what the totalitarian, anti-religious state ... demands of the church as the vice of its tolerance, a church that is silent when it should preach, a church that does not oppose the violation of conscience and does not protect the true freedom of the people and its well founded rights; a church that, with a dishonorable, slavish mentality, closes itself within the four walls of its temples. (Hehir, 1990)

By contrast, Western democracies had emerged as states in which the Church was protected through constitutional guarantees of religious freedom and where Catholic ideas could be expressed in politics through Christian Democratic parties. Such a rapprochement helped to set the stage for the Church's embrace of human rights in Vatican II.

In his teachings on the political order, John Paul II has interwoven these themes. Having participated influentially in Vatican II, he promoted its teachings on human rights throughout his pontificate and also commended democracy, most forcefully in his 1991 encyclical, *Centesimus Annus*. He supported European unity consistently and strongly, opposing the "logic of the blocs" before 1989 (Hehir, ch. 4), and all along viewing Europe as a common Christian civilization – even calling for an enlargement of the European Community to its eastern neighbors as early as 1988. Poland, he believed, plays a particularly important role in these developments. In 1980, he proclaimed Saints Cyril and Methodius, who brought Christianity to the Slavic people from the Byzantine Empire to the East during the tenth century, as co-patrons of Europe. Likewise, a Slavic and Christian Poland would strive to bring unity to Eastern and Western Europe through its struggle against communism. Such teachings could effect social change. It was a post-Vatican II Church that made possible the "Third Wave" of democratization from 1974 to 1990, roughly three-quarters of whose thirty states were Catholic. It was Pope John Paul II that made possible the Church's role in the 1989 episodes of the Third Wave (Sutton, 1997: 17, 22; Philpott, 2004).

The strength and breadth of these ideas in Catholic countries correspond to the varying degrees of Catholic democratic opposition found there. In Poland, these ideas were most empowered. In the 1970s, following Vatican II, the Polish hierarchy incorporated human rights, including religious freedom, into its statements against the regime. Pope John Paul then inspired Poles of all ranks with his call for the nation, through its very history of suffering, to be a carrier of freedoms to parts of Europe that did not yet enjoy them, thus uniting the continent. Catholic oppositional voices in Lithuania also embraced the Church's teachings on human rights vigorously and early after their proclamation. Czechoslovakia's embrace of human rights and democracy was weaker, as was its democratic activity. It wasn't until the 1980s that Catholic voices began to speak for human rights – Cardinal Tomášek, through his statements, Augustin Navrátil, through his petitions – though never with the numbers or the force of the Polish Church. In Hungary, Catholics who embraced the Church's teachings on human rights and European unity were fewer still (Mojzes, 1992: 294–95; Vardys, 1981: 1).

The Orthodox Church's heritage of ideas did not suit it well to oppose communism in Bulgaria and Romania. An ecclesiology that allowed far more division of its authority along national lines than that of the Catholic Church, a weaker stress on separation of authority and a relative openness to Caesaro-papism, and a lack of strong embrace of human rights and democracy all characterized the Church in Romania and Bulgaria, as it did elsewhere. Opposition to communism was feeble.

Again, ideas alone do not explain democratic activity. What gives ideas comparative efficacy across undemocratic regimes is the relative power that religious communities derive from their institutional relationship to the state – that is, the level of differentiation that they practice. In their relationship to religion, the most robust liberal democracies are characterized by what Alfred Stepan has called the "twin tolerations," by which the state respects the prerogatives of all religious bodies to practice and express their faith and to participate in democratic politics, while religious bodies consent to a thoroughgoing religious freedom and forgo legal or constitutional prerogatives that grant religious officials standing authority to formulate or approve public policy (Stepan, 2000, 2001: 213–53). Democratic differentiation is precisely what churches struggled for under the rule of communist regimes and precisely what these regimes sought to deny them – ruthlessly during their early years, steadily throughout their reign. Yet even under regimes determined to suppress religion thoroughly, more and less differentiation existed.

Where religious communities were more differentiated, they were more likely to challenge their regimes actively and effectively. What differentiation rendered for them is a sphere of autonomy – "moral extraterritoriality," as George Weigel has aptly called it – in which they could maintain an alternative discourse and wage oppositional activity (Weigel, 1992: 151). From their island of differentiation, religious bodies waged proto-democratic politics that ultimately resulted in the onset of democratic regimes (Stepan, 2001: 159–80).

In Poland, though the communist regime sought to denude the Church of its prerogatives over worship, expression, internal organization, education, and the running of hospitals, nursing homes, and orphanages, though it sought to delink the Church from the Polish nation, history, and culture, the Church here fought back with more success than churches elsewhere. Its leaders preserved a significant role in appointing their own bishops and church officials, and exercised autonomy in creating and running religious education programs and camps for children, publishing religious texts and periodicals, leading their people in national programs to instill piety, and traveling abroad and serving as chaplains in the armed forces. "The church – strong and independent – has far greater authority than the government with the population. To survive politically, the Polish Communist regime needs the support of the church," writes Janice Broun (1988: 168). Although Cardinal Stefan Wyszyński prided himself on not being subservient to Rome, especially during the Vatican's *Ostpolitik* of the 1960s and 1970s, the Polish Church's communication with Rome and its allegiance to its doctrinal authority remained strong. The strength and richness of this transnational tie only increased once John Paul II assumed the papacy. The Church was also strengthened in its independence from the state through its collaboration with Solidarity during the 1980s, and through its civic activity – for example, its priests ministering to prisoners and hospital patients, though they were housed in state institutions.

A particularly powerful source of differentiation was the Church's role as a symbol of Polish national identity. Against the efforts of the communist state to suppress this identity, the Church was viewed popularly as a carrier, a protector, and a standard bearer of the nation. All of this was the legacy of the Church's own long history of fighting to preserve its – and Poland's – autonomy against the harsh rule of both Russia and Prussia during its period of partition from 1795 to 1918. During the interwar period, it experienced a brief spell of favor from the Polish government, only to revert to a position of determined opposition during World War Two, when Poles mounted resistance to both Nazi and communist Russian invaders. A history of defiance bequeathed relatively strong institutional differentiation, which in turn enabled and permitted the Church to carry out strong democratic activity compared to religious communities elsewhere.

The Catholic Church in other states followed suit, the level of their democratic activity corresponding to their differentiation from the state. In Lithuania, strong democratic activity was the work of a Church that the Lithuanian people had viewed as a symbol of its nationhood since the nineteenth century. During communism, it became the "guardian of the nation's cultural heritage" (Girnius, 1989: 109). It was also a Church that managed to publish an underground newspaper and maintain an active organization despite harsh reprisals.

The Czechoslovakian Church, whose democratic activity was consistently weaker, had lost the support of the nation, especially in Bohemia, when the Catholic Habsburg Counter-Reformation state defeated and persecuted indigenous Protestantism in the seventeenth century. Subsequently the Habsburgs favored the Catholic Church, but exercised strong control over its internal leadership. Under communism, then, the Church retained few prerogatives in the face of persecution. It sought instead to negotiate agreements with the regime, but often to little avail: between 1973 and 1989, ten of thirteen dioceses remained without a residential bishop (Weigel, 1992: 173; Ramet, 1998: 112–19).

The Hungarian Church's affiliation with its national identity was stronger than the Czech Church's, but weaker than the Polish Church's. It had never dealt a major defeat to Protestant and nationalist aspirations, but it, too, had come under the strong control of the Habsburg state, even during the period of its disestablishment between 1867 and 1948. During World War Two, it did little to oppose its government's alliance with Nazi Germany. During communism, the Church practiced meaningful prerogatives in education, printing, and other areas, but only after making a deal with the communist government that it would mutually agree upon episcopal appointments and that its clergy would sign an oath of allegiance to the Hungarian constitution. It exercised very little true independence from the state, then, and undertook little democratic activity (Ramet, 1998: 104–12).

In the Orthodox countries of Bulgaria and Romania, the Church enjoyed little differentiation at all due to a history of division along national lines, a much less centralized and unified transnational ecclesiastical structure, and a history of close cooperation with, and often subsumption under, state authority. The Bulgarian Church gained autocephaly from the Patriarch of Constantinople in 1870, shortly before the Bulgarian state gained independence from the crumbling Ottoman Empire. Under King Boris III, who reigned from 1918 to 1943, the state established firm control over the Church, exercising strong governance, providing the Church with its finances, and taking over independent roles of the Orthodox Church in civil society. In the Romanian state, the government came to dominate the Orthodox Church soon after independence in 1878. Both states, then, were ripe for purge and takeover, when communist regimes came into power in the late 1940s. Both communist states exercised thorough control over their Orthodox Churches. Whatever prerogatives each Church practiced in education or publishing, they did so at the strict sufferance of the regime. Neither

Church exercised contact or communication with outside Orthodox Churches, except with Moscow, whose government controlled the governments of Bulgaria and Romania (Ramet, 1998: 181–201, 275–307).

Islam in Turkey illustrates the close interrelationship of ideas and institutions in explaining the democratizing impact of religion. Institutionally, of course, Islam has been intensively scrutinized and tightly controlled by the secularist Kemalist state, particularly since 1980. Islam in Turkey has enjoyed limited room for maneuver not only because of the radical secularism of the Kemalist revolution but also because of a long historical legacy of state-controlled religion going back to the Ottomans and even the Byzantines. "Like the Byzantines, the Ottomans practiced a kind of caesaro-papism, the system in which the state controlled the clergy" (Quataert, 2000: 4). This long-standing practice provides the Kemalist state with a certain legitimacy in keeping "religion within the limits of republicanism alone," to paraphrase Kant. Religions that oppose secularism and religious subordination, therefore, run the risk of being branded anti-national and unpatriotic. Consequently, Muslims who wish to exercise public influence and make state and society more open to religion must adopt certain ideas: above all, an Islamist ideology that emphasizes religious ethics and values over doctrines, and a political strategy that emphasizes gradual change from within the system. According to Yavuz's analysis in this volume, Kemalist "statism" fosters a weak, undifferentiated, and non-autonomous religious sphere cut off from transnational institutions and networks – one poorly equipped, in other words, to effect the dramatic political changes characteristic of the East and Central European revolutions of 1989.

Therefore, a religious body's level of differentiation from the state, together with its political theology, correlates closely with the vigor of its opposition to communist regimes in the revolutions of 1989 as well as to authoritarianism in Turkey after 1980 and thereby its contribution to the unity of Europe. But if religion matters, shouldn't more intensely religious countries be more effective opponents of anti-religious regimes? Shouldn't religious intensity matter at least as much as religious differentiation or religious ideas? As measured by belief and practice, religiosity would seem a powerful variable. Poland is by far the most religious of the countries that lived under communism; the Catholic Church there actually grew under communist rule. By contrast, the Czech Republic ranked as the least religious country in the world, and was indeed a weak democratizer. But the conclusion must be qualified. The Church in Czechoslovakia increased its democratizing activity even though popular levels of attendance and belief remained low. And to draw from a pre-1989 example, the case of Greece, a highly religious country, democratized with little participation by churches or religious believers. Democratic activity, then, depends far more on the ideas and autonomy of organized believers than on the level of religiosity in a country at large.

Religion and European integration

In contributing, more or less, to the democratic revolutions of 1989, religious communities thereby contributed, more or less, to a second major stage of European unity: the enlargement of the European Union. Only once they became democratic could formerly communist regimes accede to the EU. In 2004, many of them did.

Religious communities also contributed to European integration more directly, however. Again, more or less: the pattern here is similar to that of democratization. Due largely to Catholicism's historic theological and social ideas and legacy of institutional differentiation, the Catholic Church actively inspired, promoted, and shaped European integration in order to secure durable transnational ideals and interests. Other religious actors – particularly Eastern Orthodoxy and Islam, but also Protestant churches – favor religion–state differentiation more weakly in their theology, and, both historically and recently, have enjoyed less political independence and institutional capacity to transcend national contexts. They have consequently played a relatively weak and sporadic role in promoting and shaping European integration. Where they have publicly sought to do so, their support has been more ambiguous and less consistent over time and has had the aim of securing relatively shifting national religious and political goals.

Catholicism and European integration

Consider two recent statements. On March 3, 2004, the Vatican announced the final stage of the beatification of Robert Schuman, the French politician, devout Catholic, first president of the European Parliament, and founding father of European political unity (Zenit News Agency, 2004a). Less than three weeks later, on March 23, 2004, German Chancellor Gerhard Schröder praised Pope John Paul II for consolidating and extending the process of European integration, bridging Europe's East and West, and contributing decisively to the peaceful unification of the continent (Zenit News Agency, 2004b).

Catholic popes and Catholic politicians have indeed contributed decisively to European integration, from its postwar beginnings through its subsequent dramatic successes. Even before World War Two had ended, Pope Pius XII publicly advocated "a federated international system" as a check on future military aggression and insisted that "there is no time to lose" in establishing a "European union" to safeguard freedom and peace on the continent. He called all Catholics to support this effort. In 1953, clearly referring to the communist threat, Pius XII called on a "united Europe" to affirm its Christian foundations without which it would lack the "inner strength" to preserve its independence "in the face of more powerful adversaries" (Nelsen and Guth, 2003b: 18). Later popes continued to support European integration strongly. John Paul II has endorsed it in many statements, perhaps most strongly in his 1988 address to the European Parliament in Strasbourg, where, even before the Iron Curtain fell, he called for Eastern enlargement so that the whole continent might again "breathe with both lungs" (Sutton, 1997: 17).

Catholic politicians have supported European political integration at every crucial stage. Adrian Hastings observed that "almost everyone who has been really influential in the creating of the EU has been a socially minded Catholic from Schuman and Adenauer to [Jacques] Delors and [Jacques] Santer" (Hastings, 1997: 122). Hastings might have included in his list Jean Monnet (who was a nominal Catholic, though his sister was a prominent lay leader) and Catholic Italian Prime Minister Alcide de Gasperi among the founders, and Romano Prodi, the devoutly Catholic former Italian prime minister and current president of the European Commission, among the contemporaries (Gillingham, 2003: 16–33). The faith of these politicians was no mere window dressing on their integrationist efforts: most of them were steeped in Christian Democracy, a largely Catholic political movement. Christian Democracy stressed fidelity to Catholic social teaching, though it remained led by laity and independent of ecclesiastical control in the political sphere. Consequently, Christian Democrats could enthusiastically pursue European integration knowing that it enjoyed papal blessing, yet at the same time devise their own political strategy and institutions for realizing the general goal. In gradually constructing the edifice of European integration, beginning with the Hague conference in 1948, Christian Democratic politicians relied not on papal direction but rather on their own party institutions and pan-European networks and publications. They formed the most important nucleus of Europhiles since the postwar left was deeply divided over integration, while "the Protestants of Britain and the Nordic region were not interested in the supranational character of Continental proposals" (Nelsen and Guth, 2003b: 19). The Christian Democratic network was involved at later strategic points. Through the European People's Party (EPP), the pan-European network of like-minded and mostly Christian Democratic political parties,

it encouraged the formulation and passage of the Single European Act
in the mid-1980s – over the initial opposition of Protestant Britain
and Denmark as well as Orthodox Greece (Johansson, 2002; see also
Kalyvas, 1996).

All along, this pro-integrationist nexus of the Catholic hierarchy and
Catholic politicians generally supported an approach to the continent's
political integration that was faster, deeper, and broader than that
supported by any other distinct grouping. Those countries temporarily
delaying, selectively opting out of, or permanently holding out from such
rapid and robust integration were and are almost always majority-
Protestant countries, with much weaker or entirely non-existent traditions
of Christian Democracy – Iceland and Norway, which remain steadfastly
outside the EU, as well as Denmark, Sweden, and Britain, which have
repeatedly sought to slow, limit, or opt out of various aspects of integration,
most notably the single European currency.

The kind of European integration Catholic actors favor is one in which
Christianity plays a vigorous public role, yet respects the legitimate autonomy of the civil order – i.e. differentiation. To be sure, as Timothy Byrnes
points out in this volume, John Paul II hoped to re-evangelize Europe,
envisioning his native Poland as the leader of this effort, and to shape the
European Union's public policy, as evidenced by the Church's creation of
a Commission of the Bishops' Conferences of the European Community.
The Vatican itself, though, is interested less in imparting a religious
tincture to an otherwise secular institution than in ensuring that this
institution does not trespass on the legitimate autonomy and distinctive
"juridical personality" of the Church and other religious communities.
It envisions the EU embodying a pluralistic respect for Europe's religious
diversity, rather than imposing either a common secular ideology or a
confessionally derived church–state model. The Vatican therefore argued
(up until the issue was settled in June 2004, contrary to its position) that the
EU draft constitution ought to include a reference to Europe's "religious
heritage" and to the "particular" Christian contribution to that heritage in
much the same spirit that José Casanova conceives such a reference in this
volume: as an encouragement of the healthy public participation of religion, as a recognition of the historic role of Christianity in helping to
develop secular values like equality, freedom, and solidarity, and even as
a balm that might soften historical divides between religion and secularism.

Relevant to the Vatican's vision of legitimate religious and cultural
diversity is the controversial question of Turkish accession to the EU.
While Vatican officials, including former Cardinal Joseph Ratzinger, have
expressed hesitations about this possibility, more recently the Holy See
seems to have clarified its position: it does not oppose Turkish accession

in principle but only an excessively hasty accession process that might cause unnecessary conflict. Pope John Paul II himself in effect held that religious adherence alone is irrelevant to EU membership insofar as he unequivocally endorsed the accession of Bosnia-Herzegovina, whose population has a Muslim plurality of about 40 percent. Whether Ratzinger, now that he has become Pope Benedict XVI, will shift the position of the Holy See remains to be determined.

From popes to politicians, a wide array of Catholics have actively promoted European integration. They have promoted it, too, according to distinctive Catholic ends and emphases: the defense of Christian civilization against totalitarianism (during the Cold War); the restoration of Europe's original Christian unity; the recognition of Europe's Christian roots in the context of a respect for all of the continent's rich religious and cultural streams; the dependence of Europe's peace and security on authoritative supranational political structures; the recognition of the independence and distinct "juridical personality" of the Church and other religious communities; and a wide and religiously inclusive view of the limits of European Union expansion. The Catholicism of these actors was a crucial element in their support for European integration and in their conception of its depth, breadth, and form.

Orthodoxy and European integration

The Orthodox Church's relatively weaker compatibility with European integration is revealed by the contours of the 2004 enlargement of the European Union. Of the ten new entrants of that year, only Cyprus is at all (and only partially) Orthodox, while predominantly Orthodox Bulgaria, Romania, and Serbia were not admitted. All of the other new members are Catholic and Protestant, making the enlargement in effect a consolidation of Latin Christendom. The conclusion must surely be qualified: Bulgaria, Romania, and perhaps Serbia may well become members in the near future, while Orthodox Greece has been a member since 1981. Whatever these national governments eventually negotiate, though, the map of enlargement illustrates the comparative lack of support for integration among the several national Orthodox churches. Indeed, they range in their stances from qualified support to outright hostility, often expressed in distinctly civilizational terms, as illustrated by the case of Greece, by Vjekoslav Perica's treatment of Serbia (this volume, chapter 7), and by Sabrina Ramet's examination of a broader array of Orthodox churches (this volume, chapter 6).

No Orthodox country was part of the European Union until Greece joined in 1981, which means that the Orthodox Church became a relevant actor in the European integration process only at a relatively late stage. Of course, the main factor limiting the opportunity of Orthodox countries to join the European Union has been communism: with the exceptions of Greece and the Republic of Cyprus, all of Europe's Orthodox countries were under communist rule and inadmissible to the European Union until the early 1990s. Orthodoxy's relatively short period of engagement with European integration compels us to be wary of simplistic comparisons with other religious communities. Yet when the case of Greece is combined with the other locales where Orthodox churches have spoken out on integration since 1989, several themes emerge. Some Orthodox churches have come to support European integration, in part to support their governments' foreign policies, which seek to make their countries full members of a democratic and prosperous Europe, but also to prevent the EU from becoming a vehicle of Western secularism and a (second) Western betrayal of Christian Europe to the Islamic east. Many Orthodox Church leaders now guardedly support the European Union, but their support is predicated on the preservation of it as a Christian European project. Since the end of the Cold War, some Orthodox Church leaders have also voiced a far sharper hostility to the European Union, viewing it as an instrument of a rival Western civilization. Such was the perspective of Serbia during the 1990s and is now the perspective of leading clerics elsewhere in the Orthodox Church.

In the case of Greece, the public engagement of the Greek Orthodox Church and its leader, the Archbishop of Athens and All Greece, in European integration issues has been episodic, becoming significant only since 1998. Greece's original application for membership in 1975 under Prime Minister and later President Constantine Karamanlis and its early years of involvement in the EU following its entry in 1981 proceeded without significant Orthodox interventions. And pro-EU Greek politicians de-emphasized the cultural and religious particularities of Greece in making the case for accession. This was particularly true of the most fervent EU supporter, Karamanlis, who fought against both domestic and foreign opposition to Greek accession with the slogan, "We belong to the West" (Karamanlis, 1981; Pagoulatos, 2002: 3–4). Particularly because the European Community at the time of Greek accession was primarily a common economic market (though its states were also required to conform to common political standards), the dominant issue in the accession debate was not whether the EU would threaten Greece's sovereignty and Orthodox identity but whether its economy would benefit from market opening. On the latter grounds, there was "fervent domestic opposition" to the EU, but its main vehicles were the Panhellenic Socialist Movement (PASOK) and the Communist Party of Greece (KKE), with Orthodoxy playing no prominent part (Pagoulatos, 2002: 3).

Largely because the anti-integrationist socialists dominated Greek politics for much of the 1980s and early 1990s, Greek–EU relations became highly contentious and Greece came to be regarded as a notoriously "reluctant" and difficult member, the "black sheep" of the EU, comparable to Thatcherite Britain. Again, however, this had more to do with the country's entrenched clientelistic socialism and criticism of Northern European dominance in foreign policy and security matters than with any specifically Orthodox element, though it is probable that Orthodoxy played a secondary role in fueling the nationalistic spirit of PASOK's long-running confrontation with the EU.

A dramatic change began to occur, however, in the mid-1990s: Greeks as a whole began to move from skepticism to enthusiasm concerning the EU, while the Greek Orthodox Church, on the other hand, moved from indifference and silence to an unstable combination of guarded support and defensive hostility. A solid ideological consensus concerning the EU's essential contributions to Greece's political and economic stabilization and development had formed in the 1990s – a consensus that both reflected and fostered dramatically increased public support for the EU. This combination of elite and public support enabled Greece to join the EU's Economic and Monetary Union in January 2001 (Pagoulatos, 2002: 7–10).

At about the same time, the Orthodox Church became more publicly engaged on the subject of European integration spurred by at least four factors: the increasingly important question of the EU's religious and cultural identity, prompted by the draft Charter on Fundamental Rights as well as the later draft EU constitution; the related and increasingly discussed and controversial question of Turkey's accession to the EU; EU pressure on Greece to reform its church–state relations as a condition of deeper integration; and finally the activism of a highly articulate and outspoken churchman, Christodoulos Paraskevaides, in 1998.

As soon as he became Archbishop of Athens and All Greece, Christodoulos became a popular figure and soon used his political capital and impressive talents (including excellent English) to mount a sophisticated Orthodox campaign concerning the EU (Fokas, 2000: 12). Broadly, Christodoulos and other Orthodox Church leaders express support for European integration in general and the accession of Orthodox countries in particular, but their enthusiasm is conditioned on the preservation of the European Union as a Christian European project. If a single issue dominates the innumerable speeches Archbishop Christodoulos and other prominent Orthodox leaders have made concerning the EU, it is the EU's Christian identity, which encompasses both the recognition of Christianity in the EU constitution and the question of Turkish accession. In contrast to the Vatican, which has signaled that its most "weighty" concerns lie elsewhere, the Archbishop has vehemently insisted that the EU officially recognize Europe's Christian identity. In an address in 2003, appropriately entitled "Nostra Europa," he unmistakably referred to the question of Turkish accession to the EU. If "countries totally irrelevant to [Europe's] culture should also be included in the Union," then "Europe will have been murdered, and we shall have nothing else to do but to entomb its unburied body" (Christodoulos, 2003).

Finally, the Archbishop as well as Orthodox leaders from Russia sharply criticize EU pressure to institute greater church–state separation in member countries (Fokas, 2000; Perica, 2004; Stanley, 2000; Alfeyev, 2003). In part because of EU pressure, the Greek government in 2000 brought Greece in line with other members of the European Union by removing religious affiliation from state identity cards. In protest, Archbishop Christodoulos and other Orthodox Church leaders gathered hundreds of thousands of protesters carrying Greek flags and crucifixes (Stanley, 2000). He also attacked Greeks who advocate church–state separation as "people who are servile to all things foreign and undeserving of Greek identity, and therefore incarnating national decay" (Fokas, 2000: 12). Orthodox leaders outside Greece, such as Bishop Hilarion Alfeyev, head of the Representation of the Russian Orthodox Church to the European Union, have also attacked the EU as imposing "militant secularism" on Europe's believers (Alfeyev, 2003).

On some of these issues, the Greek government and the mass of ordinary Orthodox have different attitudes. In general, Greeks (about 98 percent of whom are assumed to be Orthodox) have become remarkably enthusiastic about the EU and deeper integration into its norms and structures. In fact, in 2002, Greek public opinion consistently ranked well above the EU average in its support. Pagoulatos notes that the "large majority of the Greek public considers EU membership to be beneficial for Greece, trusts the European Commission, supports the Euro (80%), supports a common foreign policy and a common defense and security policy" (Pagoulatos, 2002: 23). Furthermore, despite Archbishop Christodoulos's sometimes harsh criticism of the EU, the evidence suggests that the devoutly Orthodox support the EU at even higher levels than average Greeks (Nelsen and Guth, 2003a: 102). With respect to the EU's religious identity, the Greek government has not officially supported a reference to Christianity in the EU draft constitution, and, in a major shift, began to actively support Turkey's accession to the EU at the December 1999 European Council meeting in Helsinki (Pagoulatos, 2002: 17).

In his chapter in this volume, Vjekoslav Perica portrays a Serbian Orthodox Church whose stance is now quite close to the Greek Orthodox Church, but that was far more hostile to European integration from the 1980s up to Slobodan Milošević's electoral defeat and subsequent indictment on war crimes charges in 2000. Conservative, nationalist, Slavophile, eastward-looking, and steeped in a tradition of fallen martyrs, this was a Church that was highly hostile to Islam and that saw in the European Union a Catholic agenda dating back to its former imperialist rulers, the German Habsburgs. It found sharp confirmation of these suspicions in the EU's recognition, at Germany's behest, of Catholic Croatia's secession from Yugoslavia in 1992. After Milošević's demise, the Serbian Orthodox Church took a turn toward internationalism, ecumenism, and interfaith cooperation. It began to support the EU, but guardedly, largely out of a tactical alliance with Catholicism against both secularism and Islam. Similarly, Ramet shows in her chapter that although Orthodox churches elsewhere may support European integration, they do so for similar motives.

Islam and European integration

In contrast to Catholicism also stand Turkish Islamist movements, illustrated here by their most powerful organization, the Justice and Development Party (AKP). Though a single movement is admittedly a narrower phenomenon than the broad array of actors constituting the other religious traditions, both the party's relative autonomy from the Turkish state and the religiosity of its participants relative to other Turkish Muslims make it a valuable indicator of Islam's role in European integration. As with Orthodoxy, simplistic generalizations must be shunned: few Muslim-majority countries have had any significant engagement with the European Union.

Until recently, the party had fiercely opposed Turkey's accession to the European Union on the grounds of a deep-seated distrust of Europe as both Christian and the original fount of the repressive secularist republicanism of Kemal Atatürk (Yavuz, 2000, 2003, and chapter 9, this volume; Canefe and Bora, 2003: 141–42). One observer noted as recently as 1999 that "the Islamists would like to cut Turkey's ties to the West and improve relations with the Islamic world. This is most apparent in the position taken by the Refah and Fazilet (Virtue) Parties in recent years" (Yesilada, 1999: 145). Among the many surprises of the November 2002 Turkish national elections was that the successor of these Islamist parties, the Justice and Development Party or AKP (Adalet ve Kalkinma Partisi), which won the elections and took control of the National Assembly, vigorously supported Turkey's accession to the EU. Furthermore, the AKP made it clear that it would work to ensure Turkey's rapid fulfillment of the political (or Copenhagen) criteria for accession. Even allowing for a recent widespread shift in favor of European integration across the spectrum of Turkey's political parties and public opinion (Çarkoğlu, 2003; McClaren and Müftüler-Baç, 2003), the AKP stands out as unique in its devotion to the cause of European integration – comparing favorably, for example, even with the Kemalist Republican People's Party (Cumhuriyet Halk Partisi, or CHP). After the AKP's victory in the November 2002 elections, one observer noted that "the AKP, *much more than any political party of the previous era*, demonstrated a high degree of commitment to the goal of full EU membership" (Önis, 2003: 30, our emphasis). Though in this volume Hakan Yavuz and Bassam Tibi differ over whether the AKP's shift represents a genuine change in outlook or is merely tactical, the occurrence and scale of the change are indisputable.

The AKP's uniquely enthusiastic support for Turkey's participation in the European Union is even more surprising when put in the context of nationwide survey data. These data suggest, among other things, that Islamist attitudes generally correlate with lower levels of support for Turkey's accession to the European Union. In a multivariate analysis of data from a May–June 2002 survey, Çarkoğlu notes that religiosity exerts a strong and highly statistically significant independent negative effect on support for Turkish membership in the EU. However, while higher religiosity weakens support for EU membership, a majority of the most religiously observant people surveyed still supports the EU. In fact, the survey data show that no major identifiable subgroup (except the virtually tautologous one of Euro-skeptics) opposes full EU membership, and that overall Turkish support stands at about 64 percent. In other words, the data suggest that the AKP's staunchly pro-EU position separates it somewhat from its Islamist base – but not as dramatically as might be assumed (Çarkoğlu, 2003). Islamists in general, and the AKP leadership in particular, now believe that Muslim Turkey belongs in the European Union.

Explaining the posture of religions toward European integration

In their various postures toward European integration, the religious traditions we have examined have acted in accordance with their characteristic ideas, institutional relationship with the state, and historical experiences of Europe. For example, Catholicism's ecclesiology of visible transnational unity under a centralized hierarchy predisposes it to favor (or at least not be instinctively opposed to) federal and confederal political projects that transcend national boundaries (Weigel, 1999: 652). The historical experience of the Catholic Church led it to consider some form of political confederation necessary and appropriate for Europe: it believed the recent calamities of two world wars and ongoing calamity of totalitarianism made such a confederation urgently necessary, while its historical contributions to the continent's unification, civilization, and organization as a *Respublica Christiana* helped make it thinkable and realizable. The Church's long history of intense conflict with Europe's sovereign nation-states at least since Westphalia disposes it to deny that the modern nation-state is sacrosanct and to believe instead in the desirability of new political forms that revise and attenuate its "sovereign" powers. Its relatively strong hierarchical structure gives it both an interest in, and the possibility of, remaining independent from these sovereign states. All of these factors have yielded robust support for deep political integration in Europe – yet also one guided by Catholic social teaching and a pluralistic respect for other religions in the spirit of Vatican II.

Orthodox faith and practice and institutions are in some ways transnational, but Orthodox experience is inseparable from the most profound distrust of the Vatican and generally Western efforts to centralize power and authority over Christendom in Western capitals, whether Rome or Brussels. The Orthodox are also deeply committed to a view of their particular "autocephalous" national churches as carriers and preservers of particular national cultures; each national church is "an ark of the spirit of its people," according to Archbishop Christodoulos. The Orthodox Church enjoys closer affinity to particular nations and also, because of the legacy of Byzantine *symphonia*, particular states. The Orthodox Church is thus predictably anxious that an EU dominated by the West will be an agent either of Western Christian or militant-secularist suppression of Orthodox national cultures. The only way to prevent this, the Orthodox leaders we have examined believe, is by ensuring that the EU has more than a merely religious content but that it has some ecumenically Christian identity. Finally, for many Orthodox churchmen, only a European Union that keeps Islamic Turkey at arm's length can guarantee that the Islamic oppressions of the past remain in the past.

For Islamists in Turkey, exemplified by the Justice and Development Party, the European Union was profoundly threatening, particularly under the Welfare Party in its early days. As Yavuz describes, however, after the "soft coup" of 1997, Islamists came to hope that integration into

Europe would finally and irrevocably end the cycle of secularist repression of Islamic civil society and firmly entrench democratic norms and practices (this volume, chapter 9. At the same time, the military began to grow cool toward European integration for precisely the same reason: it feared that joining the EU would forever end its special status as the guardian of secularist republicanism. It was the weakness and non-autonomous character of Turkish Islam that prevented it from having the dramatic democratizing political effects other religious bodies delivered in the revolutions of 1989, and this weakness has caused it to reach outside Turkey in the hope that joining Christian Europe might enable Atatürk's republic to become fully democratic once and for all. According to Yavuz, "Given the long and deeply ingrained tradition of 'statism' in Turkey, it would have been very difficult to achieve the desired democratic transformation of the Turkish state and society relying on domestic factors alone" (this volume, chapter 9). Here, the relationship between differentiation and European integration, and for that matter, democratization, is strong, though it does not function quite as it does in the Catholic case. In Turkey, European integration is a strategy not of a religious community that is already differentiated and autonomous but of one that *seeks* to become differentiated and autonomous. Joining the European Union, for the AKP, is a way of cementing its freedom to participate openly in the Turkish state, and hence, a route to making the Turkish state more democratic. It thus contributes simultaneously to European transnational unity in both dimensions: integration and democratization.

Conclusion: religions and the uniting of Europe

What all of these cases powerfully illustrate is the immense transnational influence of religion on European politics, particularly the unification of the continent. Here, transnationalism means differentiation: the more a religious community entails an organization that extends across borders and enjoys independence from the state, the more likely it is to favor European political unity. In the case of both Catholicism and Turkish Islamism, religion is a force that deepens and extends common European values and institutions. The Catholic Church favors the eastward extension of the European Union and at least officially does not oppose the accession of Turkey. The Turkish Justice and Development Party favors uniting Turkey to the European Union, thus committing it to common norms of human rights and democracy. The Orthodox churches have a more divisive influence. To the degree that they favor European integration, they tend to do so as an alliance with Western Christianity against secularism and Islam. Among religions, then, the politics of unification is both unifying and divisive.

As for their future within the European Union, however, all of these European religions are more likely to be engaged in clashes with European secularism than with each other. The Catholic Church has already begun to object to secularizing trends in European Union law. Even if Turkey were to join the European Union under Islamist leadership, Islamist groups may well advocate laws that violate European norms – just as they attempted to outlaw adultery in autumn 2004. The Orthodox Church is likely to continue its vociferous condemnation of secularism in the European Union.

All of these trends pertain to what Charles Tilly has called "big structures, large processes, huge comparisons" (Tilly, 1984). "Long time horizons" might be added. Certainly, each religious tradition contains, and has contained over the course of centuries, competing voices on virtually every question regarding the political order. It is important to remember, too, that there are other sources of their positions on democracy and European integration besides political theology and institutional differentiation – their economic views, for instance. Still, the positions of these large religious communities are distinct and coherent enough to be compared. Ideas and institutions that have evolved over centuries strongly shape the stances of Europe's religious communities toward European unity.

The claim gains even more strength from comparison with another European religious community or more accurately set of communities – the Protestant churches. Though diverse in their theologies and institutions, ranging from the "magisterial Reformation" of Lutheranism and Anglicanism to the "low church" reformation of Baptists, Anabaptists, and Mennonites, Protestant churches are united historically in their "protest" against the Catholic Church of the sixteenth and seventeenth centuries and in their rejection of its aspirations to European unity. Ecclesiologically, Protestant churches either lack a notion of visible unity or hold a much weaker notion of it than either the Catholic or Orthodox Church, leaving them with a more circumscribed structure to sustain. At least the magisterial Reformation is a close historical ally of the sovereign state, whose armies could provide Protestants protection and whose powers usurped the remaining temporal powers of the Catholic Church, a desideratum of Protestant theology. The largest strands of the Reformation also embraced national and linguistic particularity, even forming national churches in Germany, Sweden, Denmark, England, and Scotland, as Nexon elaborates in this volume. Although in more radical forms of early modern Protestantism we find the origins of modern religious freedom as well as important roots of modern democracy, we also find in the magisterial Reformation a strong notion of church deference to state power, with relatively little institutional autonomy or exercise of accountability.

Contemporary Protestant stances toward European unity follow from these factors. In the democratic revolutions of 1989, the main Protestant country to leave communism behind was the German Democratic Republic (GDR), where the hierarchy of the Evangelische Church offered only weak opposition to the communist state, at least until the revolutions of 1989 were underway. The Evangelische Church was indeed a descendant of a historical state Church, long allied closely with state authority. Stronger opposition to the communist state came from the lower ranks of this Church, who were less tied to the institutional form and less theologically inclined. Similar patterns obtained in Protestant Latvia and Estonia (Monshipouri, 1996; Conway, 1994; Kellogg, 2001).

Protestant stances toward European integration are complex, including supporters and opponents. Generally, though, European Protestants are less enthusiastic about European integration than their Catholic contemporaries. Even leaders and groups that have supported integration have also expressed ambivalence and restrained enthusiasm. This includes George Carey, the former Anglican Archbishop of Canterbury, and the present Archbishop of the Finnish Lutheran Church, Jukka Paarma, as well as the most important network of Protestant churches, the Conference of European Churches (CEC) (Carey, 1999: 2; Paarma, 2002). Contrasting with this ambivalence is the unequivocal hostility of non-established evangelical churches as well as self-avowed "fundamentalists" such as Northern Ireland's Ian Paisley. Finally, surveys of public opinion data show Protestant masses to be systematically less enthusiastic about European political integration than their Catholic contemporaries (Nelsen, Guth, and Fraser, 2001; Nelsen and Guth, 2003a).

What the Protestant churches illustrate is that those religious communities most historically bound up in the creation of the sovereign state and most historically opposed to a united Christendom remained decidedly lukewarm toward European unity even in the late twentieth and early twenty-first centuries. This is precisely what a historical institutionalist explanation would expect. In contrast, those religious communities that most strongly envision and embody a European entity larger than the state have most vigorously supported the democratic revolutions of 1989 and the expansion of the European Union.

Notes
The research for this article was made possible by a grant for a collaborative project on "Religion and Global Politics" supported generously by the

64   European settings

Weatherhead Center for International Affairs at Harvard University and the Smith Richardson Foundation. We also thank Edgar Chen and Laurie Johnston for helpful research reports, Elizabeth Prodromou, George Weigel, David Lumsdaine, and Tony Messina for valuable comments and suggestions, and Colleen Gilg, Stephen Joyce, Jessica Lieberman, Kevin McCormick, Sarah Mehta, and Erin Urquhart for research assistance.

1 Protestantism is certainly also one of Europe's "predominant" religions, but space considerations prevent a full treatment of its relationship to European democratization and integration, but see our conclusion.

2 Again, complexity must be noted, for the Catholic Church's record against fascism is far from uniform. It signed a concordat with fascist regimes in both Nazi Germany and Mussolini's Italy during the 1920s and 1930s. A fascist Catholic priest ruled Slovakia in World War Two, the Catholic fascist *Ustasha* in Croatia allied with Hitler, and groups of fascist Catholics existed elsewhere in Europe.

3 Religion, European secular identities, and European integration

José Casanova

Since the signing of the Treaty of Rome in 1957 that established the EEC and initiated the ongoing process of European integration, Western European societies have undergone a rapid, drastic, and seemingly irreversible process of secularization. In this respect, one can talk of the emergence of a post-Christian Europe. At the same time, the process of European integration, the eastward expansion of the European Union, and the drafting of a European constitution have triggered fundamental questions concerning European identity and the role of Christianity in that identity. What constitutes "Europe"? How and where should one draw the external territorial and the internal cultural boundaries of Europe? The most controversial, yet rarely openly confronted and therefore most anxiety-producing, issues are the potential integration of Turkey and the potential integration of non-European immigrants, who in most European countries happen to be overwhelmingly Muslim. But the eastward expansion of the European Union, particularly the incorporation of an assertive Catholic Poland, and the debates over some kind of affirmation or recognition of the Christian heritage in the preamble of the new European constitution, have added unexpected "religious" irritants to the debates over Europeanization. It is the interrelation between these phenomena – the role of Catholic Poland, the incorporation of Turkey, the integration of Muslim immigrants, and references to the Christian heritage in the European constitution – and the European secular mindset that I would like to explore in this chapter.[1]

The progressive, though highly uneven, secularization of Europe is an undeniable social fact (Martin, 1978; Greeley, 2003). An increasing majority of the European population has ceased participating in traditional religious practices, at least on a regular basis, while still maintaining relatively high levels of private individual religious beliefs. In this respect, one should perhaps talk of the *unchurching* of the European population and of religious individualization, rather than of secularization. Grace Davie (1994b, 2000) has characterized this general European situation as "believing without belonging." At the same time, however, large numbers of Europeans even in the most secular countries still identify themselves as "Christian," pointing to an implicit, diffused, and submerged Christian cultural identity. In this sense, Danièle Hervieu-Léger (2003) is also correct when she offers the reverse characterization of the European situation as "belonging without believing." "Secular" and "Christian" cultural identities are intertwined in complex and rarely verbalized modes among most Europeans.

The most interesting issue sociologically is not the fact of progressive religious decline among the European population, but the fact that this decline is interpreted through the lenses of the secularization paradigm and is therefore accompanied by a "secularist" self-understanding that interprets the decline as "normal" and "progressive," that is, as a quasi-normative consequence of being a "modern" and "enlightened" European. It is this "secular" identity shared by European elites and ordinary people alike that paradoxically turns "religion" and the barely submerged Christian European identity into a thorny and perplexing issue when it comes to delimiting the external geographic boundaries and to defining the internal cultural identity of a European Union in the process of being constituted.

There is a certain irony in the whole debate, since the initial project of a European Union was fundamentally a Christian Democratic project, sanctioned by the Vatican, at a time of a general religious revival in post-World War Two Europe, in the geopolitical context of the Cold War when "the free world" and "Christian civilization" had become synonymous. But this is a forgotten history that secular Europeans, proud of having outgrown a religious past from which they feel liberated, would prefer not to remember. "Religious" issues serve as irritants to secular Europeans precisely because they serve to fuel the "glimmering embers" (Katzenstein, this volume) of Christianity, while at the same time confirming the widely shared secularist assumption that it is best to banish religion from the public sphere in order to tame the passionate conflicts and irrational attitudes which religion is assumed to bring into politics. Any public recognition of the Christian heritage or of the living religious traditions of contemporary Europeans, it is assumed, would make liberal political coexistence and pluralist toleration in a united Europe nearly impossible. Rather than recognizing the "really existing" religious and secular pluralisms and the multiple European modernities, the dominant discourses in Europe prefer to hold on to the idea of a single secular modernity, emerging out of the Enlightenment. Only secular neutrality is supposed to guarantee liberal tolerance and pluralist multicultural recognition in an expanded European Union. Thus, the secularist paradox, that in the name of freedom, individual autonomy, tolerance, and cultural pluralism, religious people – Christian, Jewish, and Muslim – are being asked to keep their religious beliefs, identities, and norms "private" so that they do not disturb the project of a modern, secular, enlightened Europe.

Catholic Poland in post-Christian Europe: secular normalization or great apostolic assignment?

The fact that Catholic Poland is "rejoining Europe" at a time when Western Europe is forsaking its Christian civilizational identity has produced a perplexing situation for Catholic Poles and secular Europeans alike. Even though as a Roman Catholic country Poland has generally followed Western European religious developments, it has also manifested long-term historical patterns of divergence from Western developments (Casanova, 2003b; Kloczowski, 2000). It suffices to state here the most significant patterns.

Prince Mieszko's decision to adopt Latin Christianity as the official cult of the Piast court in 966 was to determine the civilizational identity of Poland as an integral part and borderland of Western European civilization, particularly after the Prince of Kievan Rus, Volodymyr, adopted Byzantine Christianity two decades later. Medieval Poland followed general Western European religio-political developments.

In the early modern era, however, the Polish–Lithuanian Commonwealth followed a noticeably divergent development as a decentralized and religiously pluralistic "aristocratic *res publica*" at a time when Western European monarchies were consolidating their centralized absolutist rule and subjecting the national churches to state control. At a time of generalized religious warfare and state repression of dissenting religious minorities in the rest of Europe, the Commonwealth offered a striking example of peaceful coexistence of various Christian churches (Catholic, Lutheran, and Orthodox), of toleration of dissenting Christian sects (Calvinists, Anabaptists, Brethren, Anti-Trinitarians, and Armenian Monophysites), and of religious freedom for non-Christian minorities (Jews, Karaites, and Muslim Tatars). In fact, early modern Poland became a haven for dissenting faiths fleeing generalized religious warfare in Europe. It was at this time that Poland emerged as the largest center of Jewish settlement in the world and remained so until the Holocaust.

The nationalization of Polish Catholicism took place in the nineteenth century not as a process of state formation from above, but as a process of resistance from below to foreign state power. Church and nation became identified at a time when the Catholic Church became the only institution able somewhat to cut across the partition of Prussian, Russian, and

Austrian Poland. During the nineteenth century, Catholicism, romantic nationalism, and Slavic messianism fused into a new Polish civil religion. Nineteenth-century Poland avoided the typical Western European patterns of conflicts between the Catholic Church and the secular liberal state, between the Church and a secular humanist intelligentsia becoming increasingly anti-clerical, and between the Church and a socialist workers' movement turning first anti-clerical and then militantly atheist. In fact, the first generations of Polish workers were neither dechristianized nor denationalized, at least not to the extent that was common elsewhere. On the contrary, often there was a fusion of class, religious, and national identities, a pattern that re-emerged with the Solidarity movement in 1980.

Throughout the communist era Polish Catholicism underwent an extraordinary revival at the very same time when Western European societies were undergoing a drastic process of secularization. But, it is important to view Polish Catholicism not as a vestigial residue of a traditional society, as theories of modernization and secularization tend to imply, but as the result of modern processes of religious revitalization. Indeed, with the establishment of a Polish independent state after World War One, the unity of Church and nation began to dissolve, and in the interwar era, despite the nostalgia with which, according to Ramet (chapter 5), the Church hierarchy may view this period, Catholic Poland began to approximate more general European religious–secular developments. The unity of Church and nation began to dissolve. There appeared the standard cleavages between classes, parties, and ideologies. Anti-clericalism, though mild by Latin standards, also began to emerge. It appeared in the quarrels between the non-confessional Polish state and the Church. It appeared among large sectors of the intelligentsia, which had finally incorporated the Enlightenment as well as the positivist and Marxist critiques of religion. It appeared within the socialist left and within the peasants' movement led by Wincenty Witos. It was the Nazi occupation and the clumsy attempts of the communist regime to impose the Soviet model of forced secularization from above that created the conditions for the revitalization of Polish Catholicism and the persistence of Polish "exceptionalism."

The reintegration of Catholic Poland into secular Europe can be viewed therefore as "a difficult challenge" and/or as "a great apostolic assignment." Anticipating the threat of secularization, the integralist sectors of Polish Catholicism have adopted a negative attitude toward European integration. Exhorted by the Polish Pope, the leadership of the Polish Church, by contrast, has embraced European integration as a great apostolic assignment.[2]

Looking at Polish attitudes (Stadtmüller, 2000) toward European integration one can distinguish four different types of "europhobes," i.e. those who are against integration because of what "Europe" represents. First, there are those on the communist left who are not against European integration *per se*, but only against integration into capitalist Europe, and who would therefore be ready for integration after a European social revolution. Second, there are those who on nationalist grounds are against any type of multinational integration because it limits national sovereignty and is dangerous for national identity and Polish national values. Third, there are those who are still afraid of German expansionism and view the EU as a front for such expansionism, and may therefore be regarded as a particular variant of the nationalist "europhobes". Finally, there are the Catholic "europhobes", those who are against European integration because today's Europe has lost its Christian identity and therefore its secular, materialist, hedonist values represent a threat to Poland's Catholic identity and values. This is the view held by integralist sectors of Polish Catholicism, such as Radio Maryja, father Tadeusz Rydzyk or Bishop Stanisław Stefanek. What Catholic "europhobes" fear is the threat of secularization inherent in cultural Europeanization.

The anxieties of the "europhobes" would seem to be fully justified since the basic premise of the secularization paradigm, namely, that the more modern a society the more secular it becomes, seems to be a widespread and taken-for-granted assumption in Poland also. Since modernization, in the sense of catching up with European levels of political, economic, social, and cultural development, is one of the goals of European integration, most observers tend to anticipate that such a modernization will lead to secularization also in Poland, putting an end to Polish religious "exceptionalism."[3] Poland becoming at last a "normal" and "unexceptional" European country is after all one of the aims of the "Euroenthusiasts." But the European "norm" of secularization warrants some more critical scrutiny, as I will try to show in the final section of this chapter.

The Polish episcopate, nevertheless, has accepted enthusiastically the papal apostolic assignment and has repeatedly stressed that one of its goals once Poland rejoins Europe is "to restore Europe for Christianity." While it may sound preposterous to Western European ears, such a message has found resonance in the tradition of Polish messianism. Barring a radical change in the European secular *Zeitgeist*, however, such an evangelistic effort has little chance of success. Given the loss of demand for religion in Western Europe, the supply of surplus Polish pastoral resources for a European-wide evangelizing effort is unlikely to prove effective. The, at best lukewarm, if not outright hostile, European response to John Paul II's renewed calls for a European Christian revival, points to the difficulty of the assignment.

One could propose, perhaps, a less ambitious, though no less arduous, apostolic assignment with equally remarkable effects. Let Poland prove the secularization thesis wrong. Let *Polonia semper fidelis* keep faith with its Catholic identity and tradition while succeeding in its integration into Europe, thus becoming a "normal" European country. Such an outcome, if feasible, could suggest that the decline of religion in Europe might be not a teleological process necessarily linked with modernization but a historical choice which Europeans have made. A modern religious Poland could perhaps force secular Europeans to rethink their secularist assumptions and realize that it is not so much Poland which is out of sync with modern trends, but rather secular Europe which is out of sync with the rest of the world. The delineation of such a provocative, though unlikely, scenario here is only meant to break the spell which secularism holds over the European mind and over the social sciences.

Granted, even this more modest apostolic assignment of keeping faith with the Polish Catholic tradition may prove too lofty a task. To maintain a tradition under modern conditions demands a constant renewal of this tradition and creative responses to the changing challenges, and not just a traditionalist defense of the faith against the threats of liberalism, hedonism, and relativism. Religious trends in post-communist Poland are not encouraging. The Polish Church has squandered much of its authority with its protectionist defense of its institutional power, with its heavy-handed interventions in parliamentary proceedings, in electoral processes, and in public debates, with its clerical resistance to giving greater autonomy to the laity, and with its mistrust of modern individual freedoms, of freedom of conscience as well as of intellectual, artistic, and moral freedoms, particularly, as pointed out by Ramet in chapter 5, with its fundamentalist resistance to modern transformations in gender relations and sexual morality.

Obviously, only the future will tell whether Polish Catholicism has been up to the opportunity and the challenge presented by European integration. Western European observers are accustomed to discount manifestations of Polish religious effervescence and Polish messianism as annoying and hopelessly anachronistic, if not reactionary, expression of the Polish romantically heroic, yet desperate, penchant to resist the march of history. It happened during the nineteenth-century Polish uprisings and it happened during the Solidarity movement. Polish and Western European developments appeared seriously out of sync. Yet, in both cases the Poles confounded the prevailing *Zeitgeist*. The surprising, some would say miraculous, elevation of Cardinal Wojtyła to the papacy

as John Paul II, his triumphal visit to Poland in 1979, the rise of Solidarity
a year later, and the collapse of the Soviet system in 1989, bringing to an
end the Cold War and the division of Eastern and Western Europe, altered
radically the march of history and global geopolitical configurations.[4] The
repeatedly demonstrated power of renewal of Polish Catholicism, which
should not be confused with a residual and recessive tradition, has confounded skeptics and critics before. It could happen again.

Could a democratic Muslim Turkey ever join the European Christian club or which is the torn country?

While the threat of a Polish Christian crusade awakens little fear among
secular Europeans confident of their ability to assimilate Catholic Poland
on their own terms, the prospect of Turkey joining the European Union
generates much greater anxieties among Europeans, Christian and post-
Christian alike, but of a kind which cannot be easily verbalized, at least
not publicly. Turkey has been patiently knocking on the door of the
European club since 1959, only to be told politely to keep waiting,
while watching latecomer after latecomer being invited first in successive
waves of accession.

The formation of the European Coal and Steel Community (ECSC) in
1951 by the six founding members (Benelux, France, Italy and West
Germany) and its expansion into the European Economic Community
(EEC) or "common market" in 1957 were predicated upon two historic
reconciliations: the reconciliation between France and Germany, two
countries which had been at war or preparing for war from 1870 to
1945, and the reconciliation between Protestants and Catholics within
Christian Democracy. Indeed ruling or prominent Christian Democrats
in all six countries played the leading role in the initial process of
European integration. The Cold War, the Marshall Plan, NATO, and
the newly established Washington–Rome Axis formed the geopolitical
context for both reconciliations. Greece in June 1959 and Turkey in July
1959, hostile enemies yet members of NATO, were the first two countries
to apply for association to the EEC. That same July, the other Western
European countries formed EFTA as an alternative economic association. Only Franco's Spain was left out of all initial Western European
associations and alliances.

Granted, the EEC always made clear that candidates for admission
would have to meet stringent economic and political conditions. Ireland,
the United Kingdom, and Denmark formally applied for admission in
1961 but only joined in 1973. Spain and Portugal were unambiguously
rebuffed as long as they had authoritarian regimes, but were given clear

conditions and definite timetables once their democracies seemed on the road to consolidation. Both joined in 1986. Greece, meanwhile, had already gained admission in 1981 and with it *de facto* veto power over Turkey's admission. But even after Greece and Turkey entered a quasi-détente and Greece expressed its readiness to sponsor Turkey's admission in exchange for the admission of the entire island of Cyprus, Turkey still did not receive an unambiguous answer, being told once again to go back to the end of the waiting line. The fall of the Berlin Wall once again rearranged the priorities and the direction of European integration eastward. In 2004 ten new members, eight ex-communist countries plus Malta and Cyprus, joined the European Union. Practically all the territories of medieval Christendom, that is, of Catholic and Protestant Europe, are now reunited in the new Europe. Only Catholic Croatia and "neutral" Switzerland and Norway are left out, while "Orthodox" Greece as well as Greek Cyprus are the only religious "other." "Orthodox" Romania and Bulgaria are supposed to be next in line, but without a clear timetable. Even less clear is if and when the negotiations for Turkey's admission will begin in earnest.

The first open, if not yet formal, discussions of Turkey's candidacy during the 2002 Copenhagen Summit touched a raw nerve among all kinds of European "publics." The widespread debate revealed how much "Islam," with all its distorted representations as "the other" of Western civilization, was the real issue rather than the extent to which Turkey was ready to meet the same stringent economic and political conditions as all other new members. About Turkey's eagerness to join and willingness to meet the conditions, there could be no doubt now that the new AKP government had reiterated unambiguously the position of all the previous Turkish "secularist" administrations. Turkey's "publics," secularist and Muslim alike, have spoken in unison. The new government is certainly the most representative democratic government of all of Turkey's modern history. A wide consensus has seemingly been reached among the Turkish population, showing that Turkey is no longer a "torn country" on the issue of joining Europe and thus "the West." Two of the three requirements stated by Samuel Huntington (1996: 139) for a torn country to redefine successfully its civilizational identity had clearly been met: "First, the political and economic elite of the country has to be generally supportive of and enthusiastic about this move. Second, the public has to be at least willing to acquiesce in the redefinition of identity." It was the third requirement that apparently was missing: "the dominant elements in the host civilization, in most cases the West, have to be willing to embrace the convert."

The dream of Kemal, "Father of the Turks," of begetting a modern Western secular republican Turkish nation-state modeled after French republican *laïcité* has proven not easily attainable, at least not on Kemalist secularist terms. But the possibility of a democratic Turkey, truly representative of its ordinary Muslim population, joining the European Union, is today for the first time real. The "six arrows" of Kemalism (republicanism, nationalism, secularism, statism, populism, and reformism) could not lead toward a workable representative democracy. Ultimately, the project of constructing such a nation-state from above was bound to fail because it was too secular for the Islamists, too Sunni for the Alevis, and too Turkish for the Kurds. A Turkish state in which the collective identities and interests of those groups that constitute the overwhelming majority of the population cannot find public representation cannot possibly be a truly representative democracy, even if it is founded on modern secular republican principles. But Muslim Democracy is as possible and viable today in Turkey as Christian Democracy was half a century ago in Western Europe. The Justice and Development Party (AKP) of Tayyip Erdoğan defines itself as a "Muslim Democratic" rather than as an "Islamist" party. Yet it has been repeatedly accused of being "fundamentalist" and of undermining the sacred secularist principles of the Kemalist constitution which bans "religious" as well as "ethnic" parties, religion and ethnicity being forms of identity which are not allowed public representation in secular Turkey.[5]

One wonders whether democracy does not become an impossible "game" when potential majorities are not allowed to win elections, and when secular civilian politicians ask the military to come to the rescue of democracy by banning these potential majorities, which threaten their secular identity and their power. Practically every continental European country has had religious parties at one time or another. Many of them, particularly the Catholic ones, had dubious democratic credentials until the negative learning experience of fascism turned them into Christian Democratic parties. Unless people are allowed to play the game fairly, it may be difficult for them to appreciate the rules and to acquire a democratic habitus. One wonders, who are the real "fundamentalists" here?: "Muslims" who want to gain public recognition of their identity and demand the right to mobilize in order to advance their ideal and material interests, while respecting the democratic rules of the game, or "secularists" who view the Muslim veil worn by a duly elected parliamentary representative as a threat to Turkish democracy and as a blasphemous affront against the sacred secularist principles of the Kemalist state? Could the European Union accept the public representation of Islam within its boundaries? Can "secular" Europe admit "Muslim" democratic Turkey? Officially, Europe's refusal to accept Turkey so far is mainly based on Turkey's deficient human rights record. But there are not too subtle indications that an outwardly secular Europe is still too Christian when it comes to the possibility of imagining a Muslim country as part of the European community. One wonders whether Turkey represents a threat to Western civilization or rather an unwelcome reminder of the barely submerged yet inexpressible and anxiety-ridden "white" European Christian identity.

The widespread public debate in Europe over Turkey's admission showed that Europe was actually the torn country, deeply divided over its cultural identity, unable to answer the question of whether European unity, and therefore its external and internal boundaries, should be defined by the common heritage of Christianity and Western civilization or by its modern secular values of liberalism, universal human rights, political democracy, and tolerant and inclusive multiculturalism. Publicly, of course, European liberal secular elites could not share the Pope's definition of European civilization as essentially Christian. But they also could not verbalize the unspoken "cultural" requirements that make the integration of Turkey into Europe such a difficult issue. The specter of millions of Turkish citizens already in Europe, but not of Europe, many of them second-generation immigrants caught between an old country they have left behind and their European host societies unable or unwilling to fully assimilate them, only makes the problem the more visible. "Guest workers" can be successfully incorporated economically. They may even gain voting rights, at least on the local level, and prove to be model or at least ordinary citizens. But can they pass the unwritten rules of cultural European membership or are they to remain "strangers"? Can the European Union open new conditions for the kind of multiculturalism that its constituent national societies find so difficult to accept?

Can the European Union welcome and integrate the immigrant "other"? Can Islam and other non-Western immigrant religions become "public" European religions?

Throughout the modern era Western European societies have been immigrant sending countries, indeed the primary immigrant sending region in the world. During the colonial phase, European colonists and colonizers, indentured servants and penal laborers, missionaries, entrepreneurs, and colonial administrators settled in all the corners of the globe. During the age of industrialization, from the 1800s to the 1920s, it is estimated that around 85 million Europeans emigrated to the New World and to the southern hemisphere, 60 percent of them to the United

States alone (Hirschman et al., 1999). In the last decades, however, the migration flows have reversed and many Western European societies have become instead centers of global immigration. A comparison with the United States, the paradigmatic immigrant society (despite the fact that from the late 1920s to the late 1960s it also became a society relatively closed to immigration), reveals some characteristic differences in the contemporary Western European experience of immigration.

Although the proportion of foreign immigrants in many European countries (United Kingdom, France, Holland, West Germany before reunification), at approximately 10 percent, is similar to the proportion of foreign-born in the United States today, most of these countries still have difficulty viewing themselves as permanent immigrant societies or viewing the native second generation as nationals, irrespective of their legal status. But it is in the different ways in which they try to accommodate and regulate immigrant religions, particularly Islam, that European societies distinguish themselves not only from the United States but also from one another. European societies have markedly different institutional and legal structures regarding religious associations, very diverse policies of state recognition, of state regulation and of state aid to religious groups, as well as diverse norms concerning when and where one may publicly express religious beliefs and practices.

In their dealing with immigrant religions European countries, like the United States, tend to replicate their particular model of separation of Church and state and the patterns of regulation of their own religious minorities. France's étatist secularist model and the political culture of laïcité require the strict privatization of religion, eliminating religion from any public forum, while at the same time pressuring religious groups to organize themselves into a single centralized church-like institutional structure that can be regulated by and serve as interlocutor to the state, following the traditional model of the concordat with the Catholic Church. Great Britain, by contrast, while maintaining the established Church of England, allows greater freedom of religious associations which deal directly with local authorities and school boards to press for changes in religious education, diet, etc., with little direct appeal to the central government. Germany, following the multiestablishment model, has tried to organize a quasi-official Islamic institution, at times in conjunction with parallel strivings on the part of the Turkish state to regulate its diaspora. But the internal divisions among immigrants from Turkey and the public expression and mobilization of competing identities (secular and Muslim, Alevi and Kurd) in the German democratic context have undermined any project of institutionalization from above. Holland, following its traditional pattern of pillarization, seemed, until very recently at least, bent on establishing a state-regulated but self-organized separate Muslim pillar. Lately, however, even liberal tolerant Holland is expressing second thoughts and seems ready to pass more restrictive legislation setting clear limits to the kinds of un-European, un-modern norms and habits it is ready to tolerate.

If one looks at the European Union as a whole, however, there are two fundamental differences with the situation in the United States. In the first place, in Europe immigration and Islam are almost synonymous. The overwhelming majority of immigrants in most European countries, the UK being the main exception, are Muslims and the overwhelming majority of Western European Muslims are immigrants. This identification appears even more pronounced in those cases when the majority of Muslim immigrants tend to come predominantly from a single region of origin, e.g. Turkey in the case of Germany, the Ma'ghreb in the case of France. This entails a superimposition of different dimensions of "otherness" that exacerbates issues of boundaries, accommodation, and incorporation. The immigrant, the religious, the racial, and the socio-economic disprivileged "other" all tend to coincide.

In the United States, by contrast, Muslims constitute at most 10 percent of all new immigrants, a figure which is actually likely to decrease given the strict restrictions to Arab and Muslim immigration imposed after September 11, 2001. Since the US Census Bureau, the Immigration and Naturalization Service, and other government agencies are not allowed to gather information on religion, there are no reliable estimates on the number of Muslims in the United States (Leonard, 2003). Available estimates range widely between 2.8 million and 8 million. Moreover, it is estimated that between 30 and 42 percent of all Muslims in the United States are African-American converts to Islam, making more difficult the characterization of Islam as a foreign, un-American religion. Furthermore, the Muslim immigrant communities in the United States are extremely diverse in terms of geographic region of origin from all over the Muslim world, in terms of discursive Islamic traditions, and in terms of socio-economic characteristics. As a result, the dynamics of interaction with other Muslim immigrants, with African-American Muslims, with non-Muslim immigrants from the same regions of origin, and with their immediate American hosts, depending upon socio-economic characteristics and residential patterns, are much more complex and diverse than anything one finds in Europe.

The second main difference has to do with the role of religion and religious group identities in public life and in the organization of civil society. Internal differences notwithstanding, Western European societies are deeply secular societies, shaped by the hegemonic knowledge regime of secularism. As liberal democratic societies they tolerate and respect individual religious freedom. But due to the pressure toward the privatization of religion, which among European societies has become a taken-for-granted characteristic of the self-definition of a modern secular society, those societies have a much greater difficulty in recognizing some legitimate role for religion in public life and in the organization and mobilization of collective group identities. Muslim organized collective identities and their public representations become a source of anxiety not only because of their religious otherness as a non-Christian and non-European religion, but more importantly because of their religiousness itself as the "other" of European secularity. In this context, the temptation to identify Islam with fundamentalism becomes the more pronounced. Islam, by definition, becomes the "other" of Western secular modernity, an identification that becomes superimposed upon the older image of Islam as the "other" of European Christianity. Therefore, the problems posed by the incorporation of Muslim immigrants become consciously or unconsciously associated with seemingly related and vexatious issues concerning the role of religion in the public sphere, which European societies assumed they had already solved according to the liberal secular norm of privatization of religion.

By contrast, Americans are demonstrably more religious than Europeans and therefore there is a certain pressure for immigrants to conform to American religious norms. It is generally the case that immigrants in America tend to be more religious than they were in their home countries. But even more significantly, today as in the past, religion and public religious denominational identities play an important role in the process of incorporation of the new immigrants. The thesis of Will Herberg (1983: 27f.) concerning the old European immigrant, that "not only was he expected to retain his old religion, as he was not expected to retain his old language or nationality, but such was the shape of America that it was largely in and through religion that he, or rather his children and grandchildren, found an identifiable place in American life," is still operative with the new immigrants. The thesis implies that collective religious identities have been one of the primary ways, race being the other one, of structuring internal societal pluralism in American history. Religion and race and their complex entanglements have served to structure the American experience of immigrant incorporation, indeed are the keys to "American exceptionalism."

Today, once again, American religious pluralism is expanding and incorporating all the world religions in the same way as it previously incorporated the religions of the old immigrants. A complex process of mutual accommodation is taking place. Like Catholicism and Judaism before, other world religions – Islam, Hinduism, Buddhism – are being "Americanized" and in the process they are transforming American religion, while the religious diasporas in America are simultaneously serving as catalysts for the transformation of the old religions in their civilizational homes, in the same way as American Catholicism had an impact upon the transformation of world Catholicism and American Judaism has transformed world Judaism.

This process of institutionalization of expanding religious pluralism is facilitated by the dual clause of the First Amendment which guarantees the "no establishment" of religion at the state level, and therefore the strict separation of church and state and the genuine neutrality of the secular state, as well as the "free exercise" of religion in civil society, that includes strict restrictions to state intervention and to the administrative regulation of the religious field. It is this combination of a rigidly secular state and the constitutionally protected free exercise of religion in society that distinguishes the American institutional context from the European one. In Europe one finds on the one extreme the case of France, where a secularist state not only restricts and regulates the exercise of religion in society but actually imposes upon society its republican ideology of *laïcité*, and on the other the case of England, where an established state church is compatible with a wide toleration of religious minorities and a relatively unregulated free exercise of religion in society.

As liberal democratic systems, all European societies respect the private exercise of religion, including Islam, as an individual human right. It is the public and collective free exercise of Islam as an immigrant religion that most European societies find difficult to tolerate precisely on the grounds that Islam is perceived as an essentially "un-European" religion. The stated rationales for considering Islam "un-European" vary significantly across Europe and among social and political groups. For the anti-immigrant, xenophobic, nationalist right, represented by Le Pen's discourse in France and by Jörg Haider in Austria, the message is straightforward. Islam is unwelcome and un-assimilable simply because it is a "foreign" immigrant religion. Such a nativist and usually racist attitude can be differentiated clearly from the conservative "Catholic" position, paradigmatically expressed by the Cardinal of Bologna when he declared that Italy should welcome immigrants of all races and regions of the world, but should particularly select Catholic immigrants in order to preserve the Catholic identity of the country.

Liberal secular Europeans tend to look askance at such blatant expressions of racist bigotry and religious intolerance. But when it comes to Islam, secular Europeans tend to reveal the limits and prejudices of modern secularist toleration. One is not likely to hear among liberal politicians and secular intellectuals explicitly xenophobic or anti-religious statements. The politically correct formulation tends to run along such lines as "We welcome each and all immigrants irrespective of race or religion as long as they are willing to respect and accept our modern liberal secular European norms." The explicit articulation of those norms may vary from country to country. The controversies over the Muslim veil in so many European societies and the overwhelming support among the French citizenry, including apparently among a majority of French Muslims, for the recently passed restrictive legislation prohibiting the wearing of Muslim veils and other ostensibly religious symbols in public schools, as "a threat to national cohesion," may be an extreme example of illiberal secularism. But in fact one sees similar trends of restrictive legislation directed at immigrant Muslims in liberal Holland, precisely in the name of protecting its liberal tolerant traditions from the threat of illiberal, fundamentalist, patriarchal customs reproduced and transmitted to the younger generation by Muslim immigrants.

Revealingly enough, Prime Minister Jean-Pierre Raffarin, in his address to the French legislature defending the banning of ostensibly religious symbols in public schools, made reference in the same breath to France as "the old land of Christianity" and to the inviolable principle of *laïcité*, exhorting Islam to adapt itself to the principle of secularism as all other religions of France have done before. "For the most recently arrived, I'm speaking here of Islam, secularism is a chance, the chance to be a religion of France" (Sciolino, 2004). The Islamic veil and other religious signs are justifiably banned from public schools, he added, because "they are taking on a political meaning," while according to the secularist principle of privatization of religion, "religion cannot be a political project." Time will tell whether the restrictive legislation will have the intended effect of stopping the spread of "radical Islam" or whether it is likely to bring forth the opposite result of radicalizing further an already alienated and maladjusted immigrant community.

The positive rationale one hears among liberals in support of such illiberal restriction of the free exercise of religion is usually put in terms of the desirable enforced emancipation of young girls, if necessary against their expressed will, from gender discrimination and from patriarchal control. This was the discourse on which the assassinated Dutch politician Pim Fortuyn built his electorally successful anti-immigrant platform in liberal Holland, a campaign which is now bearing fruit in new restrictive legislation. While conservative religious people are expected to tolerate behavior they may consider morally abhorrent such as homosexuality, liberal secular Europeans are openly stating that European societies ought not to tolerate religious behavior or cultural customs that are morally abhorrent insofar as they are contrary to modern liberal secular European norms. What makes the intolerant tyranny of the secular liberal majority justifiable in principle is not just the democratic principle of majority rule, but rather the secularist teleological assumption built into theories of modernization that one set of norms is reactionary, fundamentalist, and anti-modern, while the other set is progressive, liberal, and modern.

Anti-immigrant xenophobic nativism, secularist anti-religious prejudices, liberal-feminist critiques of Muslim patriarchal fundamentalism, and the fear of Islamist terrorist networks, are being fused indiscriminately throughout Europe into a uniform anti-Muslim discourse which practically precludes the kind of mutual accommodation between immigrant groups and host societies necessary for successful immigrant incorporation. The parallels with Protestant-republican anti-Catholic nativism in mid-nineteenth-century America are indeed striking. Today's totalizing discourse on Islam as an essentially anti-modern, fundamentalist, illiberal and undemocratic religion and culture echoes the nineteenth-century discourse on Catholicism (Casanova, 2001b).

Does one need references to God or to its Christian heritage in the new European constitution or does Europe need a new secular "civil religion" based on Enlightenment principles?

Strictly speaking, modern constitutions do not need transcendent references nor is there much empirical evidence for the functionalist argument that the normative integration of modern differentiated societies requires some kind of "civil religion." In principle there are three possible ways of addressing the quarrels provoked by the wording of the preamble to the new European constitution. The first option would be to avoid any controversy by relinquishing altogether the very project of drafting a self-defining preamble explaining to the world the political rationale and identity of the European Union. But such an option would have been self-defeating insofar as the main rationale and purpose of drafting a new European constitution appears to be an extra-constitutional one, namely to contribute to European social integration, to enhance a common European identity, and to remedy the deficit in democratic legitimacy.[6]

A second alternative would be the mere enumeration of the basic common values that constitute the European "overlapping consensus," either as self-evident truths or as a social fact, without entering into the more controversial attempt to establish the normative foundation or to trace the genealogy of those European values. This was the option chosen by the signatories of the Declaration of American Independence when they proclaimed *We Hold These Truths As Self-Evident.* But the strong rhetorical effect of this memorable phrase was predicated on the taken-for-granted belief in a Creator God who had endowed humans with inalienable rights, a belief shared by republican deists, establishmentarian Protestants and radical-pietist sectarians alike. In our post-Christian and post-modern context it is not that simple to conjure such self-evident "truths" that require no discursive grounding. The 2000 Solemn Proclamation of the Charter of Fundamental Rights of the European Union attempts to produce a similar effect with its opening paragraph: "Conscious of its spiritual and moral heritage, the Union is founded on the indivisible, universal values of human dignity, freedom, equality, and solidarity." But the proclamation of those values as a basic social fact, as the common normative framework shared by most Europeans, could hardly have the desired effect of grounding a common European political identity. It simply reiterates the already existing declarations of most national European constitutions, of the 1950 European Convention on Human Rights, and most importantly of the 1948 Universal Declaration of Human Rights of the United Nations. Without addressing explicitly the thorny question of Europe's "spiritual and moral heritage" and its disputed role in the genesis of those supposedly "universal values," it is unlikely that such a proclamation can have the desired effect of inscribing those values as uniquely, particularly or simply poignantly "European."

The final and more responsible option would be to face the difficult and polemical task of defining through open and public debate the political identity of the new European Union: Who are we? Where do we come from? What constitutes our spiritual and moral heritage and the boundaries of our collective identities? How flexible internally and how open externally should those boundaries be? This would be under any circumstance an enormously complex task that would entail addressing and coming to terms with the many problematic and contradictory aspects of the European heritage in its intra-national, inter-European and global-colonial dimensions. But such a complex task is made the more difficult by secularist prejudices that preclude not only a critical yet honest and reflexive assessment of the Judeo-Christian heritage, but even any public official reference to such a heritage, on the grounds that any reference to religion could be divisive and counterproductive, or exclusionist, or simply violates secular postulates.

The purpose of this argument is not to imply that the new European constitution ought to make some reference to either some transcendent reality or to the Christian heritage, but simply to point out that the quarrels provoked by the possible incorporation of some religious

reference into the constitutional text would seem to indicate that
secularist assumptions turn religion into a problem, and thus preclude
the possibility of dealing with religious issues in a pragmatic sensible
manner. In the first place, I fully agree with Bronisław Geremek (2003)
that any genealogical reconstruction of the idea or social imaginary of
Europe that makes reference to Greco-Roman antiquity and the
Enlightenment while erasing any memory of the role of medieval
Christendom in the very constitution of Europe as a civilization evinces
either historical ignorance or repressive amnesia.

Secondly, the inability to openly recognize Christianity as one of the
constitutive components of European cultural and political identity
means that a great historical opportunity may be missed to add yet a
third important historical reconciliation to the already achieved reconciliation between Protestants and Catholics and between warring
European nation-states, by putting an end to the old battles over
Enlightenment, religion, and secularism. The perceived threat to secular
identities and the biased overreaction to exclude any public reference to
Christianity belies the self-serving secularist claims that only secular
neutrality can guarantee individual freedoms and cultural pluralism.
What the imposed silence signifies is not only the attempt to erase
Christianity or any other religion from the public collective memory,
but also the exclusion from the public sphere of a central component of
the personal identity of many Europeans. To guarantee equal access to
the European public sphere and undistorted communication, the
European Union would need to become not only post-Christian but
also post-secular.[7]

Finally, the privileging of European secular identities and secularist
self-understandings in the genealogical affirmation of the common
European values of human dignity, equality, freedom, and solidarity
may not only impede the possibility of gaining a full understanding of
the genesis of those values and their complex process of societal institutionalization and individual internalization, but also preclude a critical
and reflexive self-understanding of those secular identities. David Martin
(2003) and Danièle Hervieu-Léger (2003) have poignantly shown that
the religious and the secular are inextricably linked throughout modern
European history, that the different versions of the European
Enlightenment are inextricably linked with different versions of
Christianity, and that cultural matrixes rooted in particular religious
traditions and related institutional arrangements still serve to shape and
encode, mostly unconsciously, diverse European secular practices. The
conscious and reflexive recognition of such a Christian encoding does not
mean that one needs to accept the claims of the Pope or of any other

ecclesiastical authority to be the sole guardians or legitimate administrators of the European Christian heritage. It only means to accept the right of every European, native and immigrant, to participate in the ongoing task of definition, interpretation, renovation, appropriation, transmission, or rejection of that heritage. Ironically, as the case of French laic étatism shows, the more secularist self-understandings attempt to repress this religious heritage from the collective conscience, the more it reproduces itself subconsciously and compulsively in public secular codes.

The four issues analyzed in this chapter – the integration of Catholic Poland in post-Christian Europe, the integration of Turkey into the European Union, the incorporation of non-European immigrants as full members of their European host societies and of the European Union, and the task of writing a new European constitution that both reflects the values of the European people and at the same time allows them to become a self-constituent European demos – are all problematic issues in themselves. But the chapter has tried to show that unreflexive secular identities and secularist self-understandings turn those problematic issues into even more perplexing and seemingly intractable "religious" problems.

The secularization of Europe

As stated at the beginning of the chapter, the general secularization of Europe is an undeniable social fact. It is true that the rates of religiosity vary significantly across Europe. East Germany is by far the least religious country of Europe by any measure, followed at a long distance by the Czech Republic and the Scandinavian countries. At the other extreme, Ireland and Poland are by far the most religious countries of Europe with rates comparable to those of the United States. In general, with the significant exception of France and the Czech Republic, Catholic countries tend to be more religious than Protestant or mixed countries (West Germany, the Netherlands), although Switzerland (a mixed and traditionally pillarized country comparable to Holland) stands at the high end of the European religious scale, with rates similar to those of Catholic Austria and Spain. In general, Romania being the most notable exception, former communist countries in East and Central Europe have rates of religiosity lower than the European average, but many of them, most notably Russia, have experienced remarkable religious growth since 1989 (Greeley, 1994).

European social scientists tend to view these European facts through the analytical lenses of the inherited theory of secularization (Wilson,

1966). According to the orthodox model of secularization, most force-fully restated by Steve Bruce (1992, 1996), secularization is intrinsically and structurally linked to general processes of modernization. Social differentiation and other components of modernization, like societaliza-tion and rationalization, lead to a decline in the societal significance of religious institutions, which in turn leads eventually to the decline of religious beliefs and practices. As a general rule the theory postulates that the more modern a society the less religious will be its population.

Leaving aside the exceptional cases of oversecularization (East Germany, Czech Republic) or undersecularization (Ireland, Poland), for which one could offer ad hoc historicist explanations, in general the traditional theory of secularization would seem to hold well against the European evidence. The core European countries – Great Britain, France, Holland, Germany – the ones which have led the processes of European modernization, fit well the model of secularization. Yet, even though the drastic secularization of post-World War Two Western Europe may be an incontrovertible fact, the standard explanations of the phenomenon in terms of general processes of modernization, by reference to either increasing institutional differentiation, increasing rationality, or increasing individualism, are not persuasive since similar processes of modernization in the United States and in the cultural areas of other world religions are not accompanied by the same secularizing results.

We need to entertain seriously the proposition that secularization became a self-fulfilling prophecy in Europe, once large sectors of the population of Western European societies, including the Christian churches, accepted the basic premises of the theory of secularization: that secularization is a teleological process of modern social change; that the more modern a society the more secular it becomes; that "secul-arity" is "a *sign of the times.*" If such a proposition is correct, then the secularization of Western European societies can be explained better in terms of the triumph of the knowledge regime of secularism, than in terms of structural processes of socio-economic development such as urbaniza-tion, education, rationalization, etc. The internal variations within Europe, moreover, can be explained better in terms of historical patterns of church–state and church–nation relations, than in terms of levels of modernization.

It is time to abandon the Euro-centric view that modern Western European developments, including the secularization of Western Christianity, are general universal processes. The more one adopts a global perspective, the more it becomes obvious that the drastic secularization of Western European societies is a rather exceptional phenomenon, with few parallels elsewhere other than in European settler societies such as New Zealand, Quebec, or Uruguay. The collapse of the plausibility structures of European Christianity is so extraordinary that we need a better explanation than simply referring to general processes of modernization. Holding on to the traditional theory of secularization, by contrast, reassures modern secular Europeans that this collapse was natural, teleological, and normal.

What makes the European situation so unique and exceptional when compared with the rest of the world is precisely the triumph of secularism as a teleological theory of religious development. The ideological critique of religion developed by the Enlightenment and carried out by a series of social movements throughout Europe from the eighteenth to the twentieth centuries has informed European theories of secularization in such a way that those theories came to function not only as descriptive theories of social processes, but also and more significantly as critical-genealogical theories of religion and as normative-teleological theories of religious development that presupposed religious decline as the telos of history.

Three dimensions of the Enlightenment critique were particularly relevant: the cognitive critique of religion as a primitive, pre-rational world view to be superseded by the advancement of science and rational thought; the political critique of ecclesiastical religion as a conspiracy of rulers and priests to keep the people ignorant and oppressed, a condition to be superseded by the advancement of popular sovereignty and democratic freedoms; and the humanist critique of the very idea of God as human self-alienation and as a self-denying other-worldly projection of human aspirations and desires, a critique which postulated the death of God as the premise of human emancipation. Although the prominence and pertinence of each of these three critiques may have changed from place to place, each of them in various degrees came to inform modern European social movements, the political parties associated with them, and European theories of secularization (Casanova, 1994).

In this respect, theories of secularization in Europe have functioned as self-fulfilling prophecies to the extent to which a majority of the population in Europe came to accept the premises of those theories as a depiction of the normal state of affairs and as a projection of future developments. The premise that the more modern and progressive a society becomes the more religion tends to decline, has assumed in Europe the character of a taken-for-granted belief widely shared not only by sociologists of religion but by a majority of the population. The postulate of progressive religious decline has become part of the European definition of the modern situation with real consequences for church religiosity. It is the assumed normality of this state of affairs that points to the exceptional character of the European situation, a situation which tends to self-reproduce itself and to appear increasingly irreversible, in the absence of either a general religious revival or a radical change in the European *Zeitgeist*.

It is instructive here to look at the contentious and protracted debate between European and American sociologists of religion concerning the validity of the theory of secularization. The disagreements are not so much factual as terminological and theoretical. The first and most basic disagreement is terminological. Europeans tend to use the term secularization in a double sense, switching constantly back and forth between two related meanings. There is, firstly, secularization in the broader sense of secularization of societal structures or diminution in the social significance of religion. There is, secondly, secularization in the narrower sense of decline of religious beliefs and practices among individuals. The broad meaning of social secularization is related to the long-term historical processes of social differentiation and emancipation of the secular spheres (state, capitalist economy, science, etc.) from religious institutions and norms and the concomitant relegation of religion to its own greatly reduced and delimited sphere.

In the European context, secularization is a concept overloaded with multiple historically sedimented meanings which simply points to the ubiquitous and undeniable long-term historical shrinkage of the size, power, and functions of ecclesiastical institutions vis-à-vis other secular institutions. The second, narrower, meaning of the term, the decline of religious beliefs and practices among individuals, is secondary, posterior, and mainly derivative from the primary meaning. Europeans, however, see the two meanings of the term as intrinsically related because they view the two realities, the decline in the societal significance of religious institutions and the decline of religious beliefs and practices, as structurally related. Supposedly, one leads necessarily to the other.

Americans tend to view things differently and practically restrict the use of the term secularization to its secondary and narrower meaning, to the progressive decline of religious beliefs and practices among individuals. It is not so much that they question the secularization of society, but simply that they take it for granted as an unremarkable fact, as a *fait accompli*. The United States, they assume, has always been, at least constitutionally since independence, a secular society, as secular if not more so than any European society. Yet they see no evidence that this unquestionable fact of *desacralization* of society has led to a progressive decline in religious beliefs and practices among Americans. If anything the historical evidence, as historians and sociologists of American religion have amply documented (Butler, 1990; Finke and Stark, 1992; Greeley, 1989), points in the opposite direction of progressive growth in religious beliefs and practices and progressive *churching* of the American population since independence. Consequently many American sociologists of religion tend to discard the theory of secularization, or at least its postulate of the progressive decline of religious beliefs and practices as a European myth (Stark, 1999; Stark and Bainbridge, 1985).

Indeed, despite some lingering disagreements concerning the factual evidence of the extent of religious vitality on both sides of the Atlantic, there is a relative consensus that religion, in its institutional as well as in its individual manifestations, is doing generally much better in America than throughout most of Europe. Even after discounting the tendency of Americans to inflate their rates of church attendance (Hadaway, Marler, and Chaves, 1993) and to exaggerate the depth and seriousness of their religious beliefs, the fact remains that Americans are generally more religious than most Europeans with the possible exception of the Irish and the Poles. Moreover, the very tendency of the Americans to exaggerate their religiousness, in contrast to the opposite tendency of Europeans to discount and undercount their own persistent religiosity, tendencies which are evident among ordinary people as well as scholars, are themselves part of the very different and consequential definitions of the situation in both places. Americans think that they are supposed to be religious, while Europeans think that they are supposed to be irreligious.

European visitors have always been struck by the vitality of American "salvational" religion. In comparison with Europe, at least since the early nineteenth century, the United States appeared simultaneously as the land of "perfect disestablishment" and as "the land of religiosity par excellence" (Marx, 1975: 217). Yet until very recently Europeans rarely felt compelled to put into question the thesis of the general decline of religion in view of the American counter-evidence. Progressive religious decline was so much taken for granted that what required an explanation was the American "deviation" from the European "norm." The standard explanations have been either the expedient appeal to "American exceptionalism," which conveniently does not require one to question the European rule, or the casuistic strategy to rule out the American evidence as irrelevant, because American religion is supposed to have become so "secular," so "commercialized," or so "privatized" that it should no longer count as authentic religion (Weber, 1946; Luckmann 1967; Wilson, 1979).

It is in reaction to the European failure to confront seriously the evidence of American religious vitality that a new American paradigm has emerged offering an alternative explanation of the American religious dynamics, which challenges the basic premises of the European theory of secularization (Warner, 1993). In and of itself, the explanation of religious vitality in terms of the beneficial effects of the dual clause of the First Amendment to the US Constitution, "no establishment" and "free exercise" of religion, is not novel. Tocqueville (1990), and Marx (1975) following him, had already maintained this basic insight. The combination of high secularization in the broad primary sense of social differentiation ("perfect disestablishment") and low secularization in the narrower secondary sense of religious decline ("land of religiosity par excellence") already put into question the alleged structural relationship between the two dimensions of secularization in the orthodox model. Tocqueville (1990: 309), moreover, had already used the American evidence to question two basic premises of modern theories of secularization which, as he pointed out, had their origins in the Enlightenment critique of religion under the *ancien régime*: that the advancement of rationalism (i.e. education and scientific knowledge) and individualism (i.e. liberal democracy and individual freedoms) would necessarily lead to the decline of religion.

What is new in the American paradigm is the move to turn the European "orthodox" model of secularization on its head and to use the American evidence to postulate an equally general structural relationship between disestablishment or state deregulation, open free competitive and pluralistic religious markets, and high levels of individual religiosity (Finke, 1997; Stark and Iannaccone, 1994). With this reversal what was until now the American exception attains normative status, while the previous European rule is now demoted to being a deviation from the American norm. But it is this very move to turn what is a highly illuminating account of the exceptionally pluralistic and competitive American religious market into a general "supply-side" theory of religious economies that is problematic. As Bruce (2000) has convincingly shown, internal comparative evidence within Europe simply does not support the basic tenets of the American theory. Monopolistic situations in Poland and Ireland are linked to persistently high levels of religiosity, while increasing liberalization and state deregulation elsewhere are often accompanied by persistent rates of religious decline. Thus, the impasse; the orthodox model works relatively well for Europe but not for America, the American paradigm works for the US but not for Europe. Neither can offer a plausible account of the internal deviations within Europe. Most importantly, neither works very well for other world religions and other parts of the world.

Bruce (2000: 40) is correct when he implies that the general "secularization of demand" throughout much of Europe imposes almost insurmountable constraints to "supply-siders." These constraints work both upon the many new and unsuccessful religious entrepreneurs in Europe attempting to supply "supernatural compensators" for which there is apparently little religious need, and upon supply-side theories of religion which assume that there is a universal constant demand for supernatural compensators and one only needs to liberalize religious markets in order to generate supply, competitive pluralism, and religious growth (Stark and Bainbridge, 1985). The notion of a constant demand for supernatural compensators is a-historical, a-sociological, and flies in the face of European facts.

The truly puzzling question in Europe, and the explanatory key in accounting for the exceptional character of European secularization, is why churches and ecclesiastical institutions, once they ceded to the secular nation-state their traditional historical function as community cults, that is, as collective representations of the imagined national communities (Anderson, 1991) and carriers of the collective memory (Hervieu-Léger, 2000), also lost in the process their ability to function as religions of individual salvation. The issue of greater or lesser monopoly is relevant but not the most crucial one. We could rephrase the question and ask why individuals in Europe, once they lose faith in their national churches, do not bother to look for, or actually look disdainfully upon, alternative salvation religions. Such a kind of brand loyalty is hard to imagine in other commodities' markets. Why does religion today in Europe remain "implicit," instead of taking more explicit institutional forms? It is this peculiar situation that explains the absence of a truly competitive religious market in Europe. The culprit is not so much the monopolistic laziness of the churches protected by state regulation, but the lack of demand for alternative salvation religions among the unchurched, even in the face of new, enterprising yet generally unsuccessful religious suppliers.

From the point of view of this chapter the interesting issue is not the fact of progressive religious decline among the European population, but the fact that this decline is accompanied by a "secularist" self-understanding that interprets the decline as "normal" and "progressive," and therefore as a quasi-normative consequence of being a "modern" and "enlightened" European. It is this "secular" identity shared by European elites and ordinary people alike that paradoxically turns "religion" and the barely suppressed Christian European identity into a thorny and perplexing issue when it comes to delimiting the external geographic boundaries and to defining the internal cultural identity of a European Union in the process of being constituted.

Moreover, as Katzenstein makes evident in chapter 1, the conception of a single universal secular modernity has serious repercussions for conceptions of the emerging global order, for contested definitions of the West and its multiple modernities, and for the failure to recognize the plurality of modern interrelated civilizational dynamics. It is not accidental that the discourse of global secular cosmopolitanism is a paradigmatically European discourse, while the discourses which emerge from America are either evangelical imperial callings to eradicate evil and make the world safe for democracy or realist warnings of a global civilizational clash between the West and the rest. The model of cosmopolitan Europeanization is that of expansion of its territorial borders through integration of the external periphery into an internally homogeneous space. As the successive enlargements and the aspirations of Turkey, and most recently of Ukraine, to join the European Union demonstrate, the model has tremendous appeal for neighboring countries which would rather be within this privileged space that guarantees democracy, economic prosperity, and security, than outside its borders. But such a model of cosmopolitan Europeanization must sooner, rather than later, face its internal and external limits. The inability to Europeanize its immigrants is the most obvious manifestation of the internal limits of cultural Europeanization. Externally, the European Union cannot continue expanding unless one imagines the process of cosmopolitan globalization as the enlargement of a single European nation-state until it encompasses the entire globe. Once territorial enlargement comes to an end and Europe closes its borders to further immigration in order to protect its cosmopolitan, universal values what remains is exclusionist "fortress Europe."

Notes

This chapter is a much expanded version of an article first written for *Transit. Europäische Revue* (Casanova, 2004) within a series of issues dedicated to explore the interrelations between religion and European integration, as a result of the mandate given by the President of the European Commission, Romano Prodi, to the Vienna Institut für die Wissenschaften vom Menschen in spring 2002 to form a working group to reflect upon the role and relevance of "values" in the formation and expansion of the European Union.

1 This chapter does not aim to offer either a comprehensive analysis of the four issues or a systematic explanation of European secularization. Its sole purpose is to show how the secularist self-understanding built into modern European identities affects the handling of "religious" issues, turning them into paradoxes.

2 Sabrina P. Ramet's contribution in this volume offers a detailed analysis of the tensions between "europhobes" and "europhiles" within Polish Catholicism in the broader context of an extended analysis of the role of the Catholic Church in political conflicts and "culture wars" in communist and post-communist Poland. I have covered some of the same issues from a different perspective in other writings (Casanova, 1994: ch. 4, 2003b). This section is only meant to point out some of the paradoxes of the integration of a still militantly Catholic Poland in a post-Christian secular Europe.

3 This expectation is aptly captured in the heading of chapter 1 of George Sanford's (1999) *Poland. The Conquest of History*, which reads: "From God's Playground to Normality."

4 In chapter 11, Timothy A. Byrnes makes evident the importance of viewing the Catholic Church as a transnational religious regime, even in order to understand the dynamics of national churches. This is obvious in the complex dynamics between the Roman center headed by the Polish Pope and the Polish Catholic Church. But it is equally important to keep in mind that all the transnational characteristics of the Catholic Church that we take for granted today – papal supremacy, control of the ordination of bishops worldwide, ecumenical councils, transnational religious cadres, transnational religious movements, transnational religious centers, transnational pilgrimages – are relatively recent (post-Vatican I) modern revivals of medieval developments, which had either disappeared or been much weakened throughout the modern era with the emergence of the Westphalian system of states and the control of the Catholic churches by Catholic monarchs (Casanova, 1997). Religious regimes are always embedded in worldly regimes. Contemporary processes of globalization offer opportunity structures for the Catholic Church to reconstitute itself as a transnational religious regime with global reach. Whether Orthodoxy will respond to the transnational challenges and opportunities of Europeanization and globalization is, of course, an open question. But one should also keep in mind that although autocephaly may be a very old ecclesiastical tradition within Orthodoxy, the division of Orthodox Christianity into autocephalus "national," "patriarchal" churches is a "modern" development that accompanies the expansion of the system of nation-states into Orthodox territories, beginning with the establishment of the Moscow Patriarchate in the sixteenth century, a move that parallels the establishment of Protestant and Catholic national churches.

5 It should be clear that my analysis here is fully in agreement with M. Hakan Yavuz in chapter 9, rather than with Bassam Tibi in chapter 8. Tibi's argument would only be plausible if indeed one was to assume that the AKP's project of joining the European Union, their new discourse of human rights, democracy, civil society, and rule of law, is only a diversionary tactical move by "pseudo-democrat" Islamists to reach their real strategic goal of imposing an Islamist *sharia* state by instrumentally using legal Europeanization, that is, the adaptation of Turkey's constitutional and legal system to European standards, in order to dismantle the secularist Security Council that is controlled by the military as guardians of the Kemalist order and is the only thing that stands in the way of their conquest of the state. I find such an argument totally implausible. Even if one was to concede that, indeed, all their public statements and their decisive moves toward democratic and legal reforms notwithstanding, this is the true hidden agenda of the Islamists which they adopted after the experience of the 1997 military coup, it should be evident that such a tactic of legal Europeanization could never lead to the strategic goal of establishing an Islamist state. Parallels with the fascist democratic road to power in the 1930s, the communist strategies of the 1940s, or the Algerian FIS in the 1990s are simply misplaced. The AKP are using their electoral victory to

advance legal and cultural Europeanization in order to meet the conditions to join the European Union. The notion that once they are accepted, they will reveal their true intentions and impose an authoritarian Islamic state seems to me preposterous. Yavuz offers a much more plausible argument, buttressed by convincing sociological empirical evidence of the transformation of the AKP from an Islamist to a Muslim Democratic party, that is akin to earlier transformations of the dubiously democratic Catholic parties of the 1930s into the Christian Democratic parties of the late 1940s and 1950s, the very ones which sponsored the project of the EEC. For a comparative analysis of Catholic and Muslim *aggiornamentos* see Casanova (2001b).

6 This point was forcefully made by Dieter Grimm at his keynote address, "Integration by Constitution – Juridical and Symbolic Perspectives of the European Constitution," at the conference "Toward the Union of Europe – Cultural and Legal Ramifications," at New School University, New York, March 5, 2004.

7 Even in his new post-secular openness to the religious "other" and in his call for the secular side to remain "sensitive to the force of articulation inherent in religious languages," Jürgen Habermas (2003: 109) still implies that religious believers must naturally continue to suffer disabilities in the secular public sphere: "To date, only citizens committed to religious beliefs are required to split up their identities, as it were, into their public and private elements. They are the ones who have to translate their religious beliefs into a secular language before their arguments have any chance of gaining majority support." Only by holding to a teleological philosophy of history can Habermas insist that "post-secular society continues the work, for religion itself, that religion did for myth" and that this work of "translation," or rational linguistification of the sacred, is the equivalent of "non-destructive secularization" and enlightenment.

4   The old Church and the new Europe: charting the changes

J. Bryan Hehir

This chapter combines old and new themes in the study of religion and politics. The entire volume testifies to the rising interest in the academy and in government bureaucracies about the role of religion in world politics. Religious ideas, institutions, and communities have either stepped into or been pushed and pulled toward the center of world politics and the foreign policy of states. Many would argue they have always had an influence in these arenas, but have been ignored. But that is surely no longer the case. The analytical attention now centered on the role of religion reverses a long-term pattern which was rooted on the confluence of the end of the religious wars in Europe and the rise of the modern tradition of international politics. These two events of the seventeenth century yielded a conviction among scholars and statesmen that drawing firm boundaries between the role of religion and the realities of interstate politics was both prudent and necessary (Philpott, 2002). This conviction, forged in the brutal experience of religious conflict, became a premise of the study and the practice of modern diplomacy. In the last twenty years that premise has been challenged and found wanting.

The Church and world politics

This volume testifies to the broadly based conviction of scholars that the failure to analyze systematically the role of religion in world politics will yield both inadequate intelligence and bad policy on some of the world's most conflicted problems. This development, while likely not a majority opinion among scholars of international relations, can claim enough support to be designated a "new theme" in the field. The older characteristic is the fact that, even when religion was accorded a marginal status in world politics, the Catholic Church was routinely given some systematic attention. The reason for this exception was not due to the intrinsic significance of this faith community but to its size, structure, and standing in the world of diplomacy. To some degree these are "external" characteristics of this religious community, distinguishable from its internal content of faith, but they each make Catholicism an object of analytical and practical interest to scholars and practitioners of diplomacy. With roughly 1 billion adherents, with an institutional presence at every level of the international system, and with recognized diplomatic standing in the international community, the Catholic Church has often been studied simply as an "actor" in world politics (Madelin, 2001: 886).

The new attention now paid to religion in world affairs has also influenced the way in which Catholicism is now understood. In the past the Church was most often the subject of analysis in diplomatic histories. The stress fell upon a narrative treatment rather than analytical attention. A standard theme of postwar European politics was the role of Christian Democracy – as a party and through the leadership it produced – in the recovery from World War Two. In a variety of settings account was taken of the Church's role, of the personality or the policy of different popes, and of the way in which major actors (e.g. Bismarck, Napoleon) in the game of nations sought to confront, cajole, or cooperate with papal power. The scope of the narrative runs from the Roman Empire to the collapse of the communist bloc (Rhodes, 1983). As history, the narrative makes for interesting (sometimes dramatic) reading; what is missing, however, is the analytical lens which modern scholarship brings to bear upon states, international organizations, or transnational actors. The tools of contemporary social science and international relations theory are seldom brought to bear upon the evolution of the Church's role in world politics. Even though the Vatican and the Holy See is understood as a state, it has not often been analyzed as one. That has now begun to change. The new attention to the role of religion includes a series of studies engaging the standard "level of analysis" method to understand Catholicism in its systemic, national, and local dimensions.

The dividing line between the older diplomatic studies and today's work may lie with Ivan Vallier's chapter in the Keohane and Nye (1971) volume on transnational actors (TNA). The impact of the volume itself, challenging the dominance of state-centric studies, provided a unique platform for Vallier's effort to draw an analogy between the Church and other TNAs (Vallier, 1971: 129–52). His work, intrinsically important in itself, also opened the way for other scholars to assess the role of Catholicism in the modern world.

Vallier wrote in the shadow of the Cold War and he also understood the Church in terms of the powerful pontificate of Pius XII (1939–58). This perspective yielded a strong stress on a pyramidical conception of Catholicism in which the dominant dynamic moved from the papacy down through the rest of the life of the Church. Such an understanding did capture the Church of Pius XII, but it failed to incorporate the changed dynamic initiated by the Second Vatican Council (1962–65). While affirming the unique role of the papacy, the teaching of the Council also stressed the necessity of a collegial understanding of leadership in the Church among all the bishops, and it highlighted the significance of local churches (at the national and regional level) as sources of ideas and initiatives for the wider Catholic community (Rahner, 1979). Vallier successfully depicted the Church as a counterweight to global communism, but his analysis failed to capture the post-conciliar complexity of Catholicism as it confronted not only communist regimes but authoritarian states with impeccable anti-communist credentials but terrible human rights records (Chile, Brazil, South Korea, and the Philippines). Nonetheless Vallier opened a new path which others followed.

In 1973 Samuel Huntington invoked the concept of the Church as a transnational actor in his effort to refine the use of the phrase. Huntington approached the Church not as a theologian or sociologist of religion but as a secular political scientist and analyst of world politics. Describing what he termed a "transnational revolution" in world politics, he identified a widely diverse list of organizations which fit the following description:

These twelve organizations appear to have little in common. They are public and private, national and international, profit-making and charitable, religious and secular, civil and military, and, depending on one's perspective, benign and nefarious. Yet they do share three characteristics: *First*, each is a relatively large, hierarchically organized, centrally directed bureaucracy. *Second*, each performs a set of relatively limited, specialized, and in some sense, technical functions: gathering intelligence, investing money, transmitting messages, promoting sales, producing copper, delivering bombs, saving souls. *Third*, each organization performs its functions across one or more international boundaries and, insofar as is possible, in relative disregard of those boundaries. They are, in short, *transnational organizations*, and the activities in which they engage are *transnational operations*. (Huntington, 1973: 333)

Huntington returned to the role of the Catholic Church in his study on the "Third Wave" of democratization. His concern in this study was to highlight the changed normative status of democracy and human rights in Catholic teaching, and the comparative advantage Catholicism had in advancing its support of these values particularly in traditionally Catholic cultures like the Philippines and Latin America (Huntington, 1991). Like Vallier, Huntington was only marginally interested in the internal dynamics of the Church; both of them focused on its functional capabilities in a world increasingly open to non-state actors with international capabilities. Neither addressed in any depth or detail the impact of

Vatican II on Catholic theology and policy within states or in the wider global system. But both authors helped to move the analysis of Catholicism closer to the work of social scientists and policy analysts.

The next stage of this process is ably represented in Timothy Byrnes's work *Transnational Catholicism in Postcommunist Europe* (2001). The book represents a new generation of scholars who bring to their work a complex understanding of the internal structure and dynamics of the Catholic Church, and join this to prevailing arguments in political science and international relations. I do not seek to engage Byrnes's position as a whole, but simply to affirm two of his basic points and dissent from a third. I am in agreement with his effort to establish the relationship of religion and politics as a legitimized arena of study among analysts of international relations, and even more strongly in agreement with the way he joins the internal analysis of Catholicism with his study of the external relations of the Church with political actors. Byrnes has it just right, in my view, when he recognizes, on the one hand, that the policy choices of the Church can be analyzed in the standard categories of political science, but, on the other hand, the analysis will be thin rather than thick if the normative positions of Catholic teaching and the internal complexity of Catholic institutions are not given equal attention. In affirming both of these positions Byrnes advances the argument beyond Vallier and Huntington.

My difference with Byrnes is the way in which he categorizes the levels of institutional presence of the Church in world politics. He distinguishes international, national, and personal roles of decision-making and influence in the Catholic polity. My difference lies only with the last category. I would hold for systemic, national, and local analysis, with recognition that personal actors – in this case uniquely the papacy – shape and direct all three levels of religious presence and policy. The local provides – I believe – a more structural insight into the Church's life. Undoubtedly the personal determination and dynamism of John Paul II attracted the attention of any analyst, but by including the level of the local church (within a nation) as an essential category of analysis, there is ample room to assess the influence of any pope, and it allows space for the recognition that most holders of this office have had less direct public influence than the Polish Pope.

Distinguishing systemic, national, and local levels of analysis facilitates joining the understanding of Catholic policy and influence with standard assessments of foreign policy and politics. The crucial category in doing so is the idea of analogy, the comparison of two entities which are somewhat alike yet totally different in other dimensions. The *systemic level* of Catholic presence and influence should focus on the office of the papacy, the actions of the Holy See carried out through the Secretariat of State and the diplomatic corps, the bilateral relationships of the Holy See with individual states, and, quite importantly, the normative positions taken in both policy statements and moral teaching about international affairs. The analytical tools of both international relations theory and foreign policy studies are applicable at this level. At the systemic level the Catholic Church fits the description of both a transnational actor and a state. Playing this proposition out is obviously beyond the scope of this chapter, but illustrative examples will indicate its potential. Using the dominant systemic theories of international relations one can identify analogous relationships of Catholic theory and policy with both realism and liberalism, but it is not helpful to reduce the Church's role to either theory completely (O'Brien and Shannon, 1992: 1002).

Roman Catholicism's centuries-long engagement with world politics reflects some realist premises but also qualifies them. It takes sovereignty seriously, grants the state substantial but limited moral standing, and acknowledges (in its adherence to Just War theory) the persistent possibility of conflict and the necessity at times of using coercive force (within defined moral limits) to protect basic human values. Realist analysis can also be used to explain aspects of the Holy See's choices in world politics. There are, however, clear and distinct differences which highlight the limits of realist categories to explain Catholic theory and practice. In moral terms Catholic positions on the sovereign state grant it less legitimacy than any version of realism (classical, modern or neo) simply assumes in its treatment of the state. Similarly, while the legitimization of the use of force is part of Catholic moral doctrine, the limits imposed by the contemporary understanding of Just War theory are much more stringent than modern states are willing to accept. Finally, the role accorded international institutions in modern Catholic thinking and practice is far more expansive than realist analysis would acknowledge.

The same exercise of defining shared and conflicting positions can be carried out by comparing Catholicism and liberal theories of world politics. Shared perspectives can be identified in the emphasis they give to values and norms as both motivating and restraining forces in international relations. There is a similarity of values about the importance of the transnational fabric of world politics, particularly as it functions to restrain and limit the power of the state. But there are basic philosophical differences in the premises of the Catholic and liberal positions which can lead to divergence in policies and positions. These differences involve the contrast between organic and individualistic conceptions of the person and society; flowing from this broad distinction lie differences about theory and policy. The understanding of human rights, for example, while similar, is not always identical. Catholic teaching, evidenced in John XXIII's encyclical *Pacem in Terris* (1963) or John Paul II's *Address to the United Nations* (1979), stresses the equality and interdependence of political-civil and socio-economic rights. Some versions of liberal theory would give clear philosophical and policy priority to civil and political rights. At the policy level, Catholic positions on the role of the market in domestic and international politics, and particularly the understanding of free trade, would differ from standard liberal analysis in the limits imposed on the market and on the rules for trade in the international arena. These policy differences would be matters of degree, but could still amount to significant differences in concrete cases.

In spite of these divergences with both major theories of international relations, it is both possible and productive to use the conceptual framework of each theory to analyze the role, the position, and the influence of Catholicism in world politics. The Church may not be a state, pure and simple, but a standard analysis of state policy will yield insight into the positions taken by the Holy See. The latter may always state its positions in normative terms, but it is often possible to identify specific interests which direct policy and to determine the strategies and tactics of the Church in its relations with state and international organizations.

At the *national level*, analysis of Roman Catholicism has similarities with the field of comparative government. How might this provide insight into the role of the Church in Europe? There is no question that Vallier was accurate in identifying the powerful role of Rome in shaping similarity of belief and practice across national and cultural lines. But there remains, at the margin, significant space in which churches within nations shape distinctive styles of analysis and make choices or policy questions which are not simply a carbon copy of a grand systemic plan. The national context or "character" within which churches function, their relationships with their state and its place in the international system, all contribute to how a given "national church" sees issues and makes decisions. Two policy examples illustrate the potential of comparative analysis within the Catholic system.

The first was the political and ecclesiastical debate in the 1980s about the morality of nuclear deterrence. While the main focus of this question was about US policy, the consequences of that policy for Europe turned an intensive national debate into a transatlantic one. Both the French and German episcopates, while drawing on the same normative theory as the US bishops, were far less convinced that a stringent critique of deterrence policy and a declaratory policy of "No First Use" were positive steps. The point of the lance in this transatlantic debate were these issues of strategic policy, but the wider horizon of the discussion included differences about

how the bishops of each country saw their role in addressing their societies, how they defined their relationships toward state policy and practice,
and how they related to public opinion in the Catholic community. To be
sure the differences among the Americans, the French and the Germans
lay at the margin; there was much shared space in their analysis. But for
the student of comparative politics there was rich material to be explored
in a supposedly monolithic religious institution.

A second example is the moral evaluation of globalization, a shift from
political-strategic to political-economic issues. The contrast in this case
lies not only among local or national churches, but in the assessment of
globalization found in the southern hemisphere (particularly Latin
America), and the evaluation by the Holy See. The Pope, in multiple
statements and through his representatives in many official forums, has
expressed a clear critique of globalization both because of its potential
impact on the poor, and because of the all too frequent reduction of the
process to purely economic categories when its consequences clearly
extend to social and cultural questions. This critique is made, however,
from the standpoint of a basic acceptance of the fact (and the potential
benefits) of globalization with the caveat that it must be given moral
direction by public and political decisions at many levels. Catholic voices
from Latin America, Africa, and Asia are clearly supportive of the papal
critique of globalization, but they often bring a more skeptical and critical
eye to the question of whether this powerful process is being given moral
direction. The differences, a matter of degree to be sure, are examples of
the standard bureaucratic adage that "where you sit determines where
you stand." The Holy See approaches the question systemically; it must
assess the multiple forces behind globalization, the different consequences it has for different parts of the globe, and the overall direction
of an admittedly complex empirical phenomenon. The voices of the
southern hemisphere are neither unaware of these factors nor lacking in
an understanding of the process. But they experience a vulnerability to
powerful forces which, however beneficial they may be systemically and
in the long term, can be powerfully chaotic and even destructive in the
short term to their interests.

Comparative analysis in ecclesiastical terms can assume a basic commonality of religious and moral doctrine, but it must account for some
differentiation of conclusions which is often rooted in the complexity of
institutional relations within the Church and difference of either experience or assessment of empirical data in deciding a policy.

At the *local level*, i.e. the concrete pastoral level within a national
setting, the appropriate tools of analysis will principally be those of
domestic politics, law, and culture. My difference with Byrnes in stressing

this level of analysis is because of the importance it has assumed in post-Vatican II Catholicism and the potential it offers to highlight the uniqueness of this transnational actor because of the simultaneous interplay of systemic and local perspectives about policy choices. The issues which arise at the local level of the church involve church–state questions, the impact of cultural diversity on Catholic belief and practice, the socio-economic conditions in which local churches exist and seek to live out the broader themes of Catholic social vision. These broad complex questions, however, do not exhaust the potential of local analysis. Both Vatican II and Paul VI supported the notion that the local level of church life could be a source of innovation theologically, liturgically, and socially. In many ways the local churches of Western Europe produced influential theological and pastoral resources in the 1940s and 1950s. The most powerful contemporary example of this potential has been the influence of the Theology of Liberation. This religiously based vision arose in the context of the Church in Latin America; its emergence illustrated a complex interplay between religiously inspired reflection and the concrete conditions of socio-economic life in that continent. The theological perspective which emerged owed something to the wider social tradition of Catholicism and to the spirit and substance of Vatican II, but it cannot be explained solely from these two perspectives. While not confined to the Latin American setting, there is a concrete connection between the themes articulated in the various versions of the Theology of Liberation and the pastoral and political experience of the Church in that region. Other parts of the Church have drawn on this theology but it takes an act of translation and adaptation to do so. The central point to be made here, however, is the local origins of the theological vision, then the way in which it has been drawn into critical dialogue (with some substantial conflict involved) with John Paul II and the papal magisterium. The dialogue, to be sure, has been a critique of some aspects of this theological vision, but it has also been a testimony to the positive influence of the themes it has pressed at the local, regional, and systemic levels of the Church.

Contrary to Vallier's emphasis, this review of the systemic, national, and local levels of the Church's life leads to a more dialectical, pluralistic, and dynamic understanding of how transnational Catholicism functions. There is a clear comparative advantage which the papal office provides in the Church's engagement with world politics. Internally, of course, the papal office holds a uniquely authoritative role for Catholics; the concern here, however, is external, the ability of a religious voice to engage the international system. The office is not limited to words and witness; as exemplified by John Paul II, there is the capacity to enter a situation and by word and action catalyze a process of change which extends far beyond the time of a pastoral visit (Ash, 1989). Both these capacities are further expanded by the ability of the Pope to make key appointments within a national or local church; these often are joined to explicit or implicit directions which take shape in local or national ecclesial policy.

This process of vertical integration within the Church does not exhaust the potential for international influence and coordinated action. Since Vatican II and in the context of growing global interdependence, at the transnational level of national churches there has been increasing collaboration around policy issues that may affect a group of countries but not engage the whole Church. Prime examples of this strategy of collaboration include human rights issues, the debt of developing countries, and specific bilateral questions where a church in the southern hemisphere calls on a northern ecclesial community to influence its government's policy. Finally, there are interesting examples of clear divergence of local church perspectives and priorities from those of the Holy See. The clearest public case was the role of the Philippine bishops in the crucial days of the deposition of Ferdinand Marcos. The Church in the Philippines over a number of years had become the dominant critical voice calling for reform. When the crucial weekend arrived after Marcos had won re-election in a corrupted process, the bishops denounced the election as illegitimate. Later evidence demonstrated that the Holy See, while supportive of Marcos's departure, wanted the bishops to pursue a less visible role in the national drama. The bishops were convinced that failure to speak and lead could result in a violent clash in the country. They were vindicated when their leadership both deposed Marcos and did it in collaboration with non-violent "people power." The leader of the Philippine episcopate, Cardinal Sin, later visited Rome and emerged from an audience with John Paul II with the report that he and the Pope agreed that the Philippines were like Poland – both cases were victories (Claver, 1986)!

Catholicism and Europe: past and future

There is not a region of the world that has the depth and breadth of relationships with the Roman Catholic Church which Europe has had. To move into this history is to find constant contact from the systemic to the national and local levels of Catholicism. It is commonplace today to note the dramatic decline of religious affiliation generally and of Catholicism particularly in Western Europe. But even recognizing this fact does not negate the continued importance of the tradition of European Catholicism for the life of the larger Church. That importance is rooted in the region's historical role, its theological contributions, and its political role in world affairs. Historically, Europe's relationship to the Church is documented from the New Testament until this new century. The history is rich and deep, it is a history of collaboration and conflict. The historical narrative has been the source of much of the teaching of the Church in theology, canon law, liturgical life, and the political and social traditions of Catholicism. Europe was a mission land, then it became the source of missionaries for Asia, Africa, and North and South America. It was a united continent, then a divided one, and now faces again a united future, one sure to be different from either of the two earlier periods. The process of Europeanization, therefore, with its many new and original dimensions, will undoubtedly be seen by the Church as another chapter in a long and complex story.

Part of that history is the theological contribution of Europe to the universal Church. Here again, the narrative began with classical Greece and Rome, found unique expansion in the medieval era, was dramatically changed by both the Reformation and the Enlightenment, and produced systemic results in Catholic thought and life in the twentieth century. Those results were the influence which European theology had at the Second Vatican Council. The Council's product, sixteen documents touching every major area of Catholic life, was primarily the work of theologians from Western Europe. They had prepared for Vatican II without knowing it by the enormously creative research carried out in the interwar years and just after World War Two. The Council provided the opportunity for this research to find expression in authoritative teaching which opened a new era in Catholic history – one that is still in process. Both the historical and the theological narratives are well beyond treatment in this chapter, and neither has the immediate significance for this volume that the political and diplomatic dimensions of Europeanization hold for the Church. It is that dimension of Catholic and European life which engages the systemic, national, and local relationship cited above. To address this example of transnational Catholicism, I will briefly examine the past and present status of the Vatican's role in Europe through three recent papacies: Pius XII (1939–58), Paul VI (1963–78) and John Paul II (1978–2005). Having looked through this vertical lens, I will sketch the transnational agenda of the Church in Europe.

The first era is the diplomacy of Pius XII; it was characterized most clearly by the Vatican's very close relationship with the Christian Democratic movement in Western Europe. Here one sees Vallier's conception of transnational Catholicism at work; Pius XII shaped Catholic life from the top, particularly in the critical arena of Western Europe

(Falconi, 1967: 234–303). As World War Two drew to a close, the Pope had a definite vision of what was at stake for the Catholic Church in Europe, and he was determined that his vision would be endorsed and implemented in the public and pastoral life of the Church. The Pope's view, in simple terms, was that communist regimes were by their nature illegitimate, and, therefore, what the Church should do, essentially, was to work toward isolating them, by having nothing whatever to do with them. He set a policy in place of frontal opposition and no collaboration between the Church and communist states. Second, he sought to extend this policy of isolation from the Vatican into the life of local churches in Europe. When the possibility arose of the Communist Party actually being elected in Italy, for example, the Vatican declared that voting communist would be cause for excommunication. The Pope's notion was that there simply was no shared space whatever between Catholicism and communism, and based on that notion, he pursued a firm policy of confrontation.

The policy had two consequences. The first was that the Vatican, and the Catholic Church more broadly, became closely associated with Christian Democratic parties in Western Europe. The EU is built on the EC and the EC was powerfully influenced by Christian Democracy, a political movement but one directly rooted in Catholic social thought and close collaboration with the Holy See's role in postwar Europe. As many analysts have put it over the years, the European Community acquired a distinctly Roman flavor from its very early days, embodied in the lives and careers of men like Monnet, Schuman, de Gasperi, and Adenauer. These people were all strong-minded political leaders in their own right. It is too simple to think of them passively taking orders from clerical leaders. But they, like Jacques Delors later, drew from a social vision shaped by the Catholic tradition.

The second effect of Pius XII's policy of strict anti-communism was the creation of the widespread perception that Catholicism was *de facto* aligned with the West and Western policy in Europe. This perception was much less accurate in relation to the papacies of Pius XII's successors; it may have been a bit overstated even in the 1940s and 1950s. But there is no doubt that Pope Pius's rejection not only of communism itself, but also of the very prospect of dealing with communism or with communist states, complemented much of allied policy during the Cold War era.

The second era, or model of Vatican diplomacy, is associated with Pope Paul VI and runs through the period from 1963 to 1978. Paul VI had been a leading official in Pius XII's Secretariat of State; even in this major diplomatic post, he harbored doubts concerning Pius's policy of

104   Catholicism

refusing to interact with communist states. When he suggested that the policy of no conversation and total isolation had been exhausted and was proving counterproductive, he was "rewarded" with leadership of an Italian diocese, and thereby removed from office in the Vatican foreign affairs bureaucracy. It was recognized clearly throughout that bureaucracy at the time that the then Monsignor Montini had been removed because Pope Pius XII simply would brook no opposition to his approach to relations between Catholicism and communism (Hebblethwaite, 1993: 242–60).

As occasionally happens throughout Church history, however, a man banished through the "reward" of a diocese can sometimes return to the Vatican, not to his old role as functionary, but as Pope. In just such a circumstance, Montini followed Pius XII's successor, Pope John XXIII, to the Chair of Peter in 1963. Now as Pope Paul VI, Montini had a second opportunity to reshape Vatican policy toward communism and Europe, and he set out to do so (Stehle, 1981). The key collaborator in this rethinking of policy was Paul VI's Secretary of State, Cardinal Agostino Casaroli. Casaroli was a fascinating personality who served in the Vatican's Secretariat of State for a full half century, from 1939–89; he was at the very center of Vatican foreign policy for that whole period. He was known for a time as the Vatican's Kissinger, and though he may not have appreciated the analogy, he certainly had a similarly profound effect on policy, particularly in terms of what came to be known as the Vatican's version of *Ostpolitik*.

Much like its secular counterpart, Vatican *Ostpolitik* was predicated on the pragmatic conclusion that the effort at total isolation and delegitimation of communism was simply not working; the institutions of the local churches in the communist bloc were eroding and it was increasingly difficult to maintain secure contact with bishops or make appointments to key positions; the Vatican had to accept the responsibility of "saving what could be saved" within these very difficult circumstances. What this meant in practice was Paul VI's decision to open up dialogue, through Casaroli and his office, on a series of tactical issues with the communist regimes of Eastern and Central Europe.

It was assumed that there was little agreement in principle between Catholicism and communism but concrete, specific tactical objectives bearing on the Church's life and freedom could be addressed diplomatically. This change in the Holy See's policy toward the Soviet bloc was part of a broader change initiated by Paul VI. Without eroding Catholic interest in and commitment to Europe, the Pope reshaped the Vatican's role by focusing intently on the churches and countries in the southern hemisphere. By word and deed, in his statements and his travels, he stressed the responsibility of East and West to the poverty, conflicts, and struggles of the South.

Karol Wojtyła of Poland brought a very different understanding of Europe to the papacy as Pope John Paul II. His overall approach from the very beginning in 1978 was not so much a critique of *Ostpolitik*, but rather a conviction that it did not go far enough (Weigel, 1999: 226–34). In response to this conviction he also executed a far-reaching change in the architecture of Vatican policy. First of all, of course, John Paul II acted to bring Europe back into the center of the Church's concerns. He did not in any way reject Paul VI's broader understanding of the role of the Catholic Church in world affairs, but he linked that broader concern to a renewed emphasis on the role that he and his Church could play in shaping the future of Europe, particularly the part of Europe that had lived for decades under communist rule (G. H. Williams, 1984). Second, the Polish Pope simply never accepted his predecessor's premise or assumption that the Vatican and the Catholic Church had to deal with communism as a permanent aspect of the European political landscape. More explicitly, John Paul II never shared the widely held assumption that the division of the European continent into competing political blocs was a fact of political life that had to be accepted. In fact, he viewed Yalta as a fundamental moral failure in international relations, and he came to the papacy with a vision that the overturning of Yalta, in other words the fundamental redrawing of European political structure, was possible and even necessary.

Talk of overturning Yalta, or of overcoming communism, was usually regarded as not only unlikely but too risky to advocate at the time. Surely, it did not conform with the assumptions or prescriptions of the dominant realist paradigms in the academy or diplomacy. Moreover, Pope John Paul II put a distinctive twist on such "unrealistic" hopes by combining a firm conviction that the structure of European politics could be radically altered through non-violent means. This was a bet, of course, a kind of high-stakes wager on the future, but it was these basic assumptions from which the Vatican operated throughout the 1980s and 1990s (O'Brien and Shannon, 1992: 454–61). Karol Wojtyła brought with him to Rome an unparalleled knowledge of East and Central Europe, and a very distinctive conception of Europe and its politics that involved three basic elements.

First of all, John Paul II set out to do what he could do as Pope, and to encourage others to do what they could do, to break what he called in his 1987 encyclical *Sollicitudo Rei Socialis* "the logic of the blocs" (O'Brien and Shannon, 1992: 406–07). He wanted to move beyond the definition of Europe implied by the role of the two superpowers, and he also wanted to question the very notion of world politics being driven by competition between those two powers. Second, and in a related sense, the Pope wanted to create space for Europe that would not be controlled by this superpower competition and that would allow Europeans to move beyond the cramped notions created by Yalta and the Cold War. For John Paul II the notion that Europe existed in two halves was fundamentally mistaken. In what might be called Gaullist terms, the Pope conceived of a single European entity, stretching from "the Atlantic to the Urals," and he encouraged his fellow Europeans to explore their common history and shared identity. Finally, for Pope John Paul II it was crucial for Europeans to reground that identity in some sense of Christian values, or in a reaffirmation of Europe's Christian history. This theme took on greater and greater prominence over the course of Wojtyła's papacy, but from the very beginning John Paul II articulated the idea of creating political space for Europe outside of the logic of the blocs while also recentering Europe in a Christian vision.

This identification of three distinct eras of recent papal history and three very different models of Vatican diplomacy in regard to Europe brings us up to the present period while setting the appropriate historical context in which the present can be best understood. At this point, then, I want to turn from this matter of how the systemic related to the regional, and move on to a closer examination of the region itself, particularly in terms of the challenge presented to the Catholic Church by what is called in this volume the processes of Europeanization. This challenge has three characteristics. There is a challenge of structure; there is a challenge of scope; and there is a challenge of substance. The challenge of structure involves the creation of new political institutions in Europe. There is now a more complex web of governing institutions as the continent evolves from a Europe of states to a system of European states interwoven with a multiplicity of transnational and international bodies and institutions. This new complexity requires all interested parties to rethink and reorient their approaches to European political structures, and the Vatican is certainly no exception to this rule.

The Vatican, of course, is very familiar with Europe, and has long experience dealing with European political institutions, but it now has to take action to formulate new church structures that can engage the new political structures of the European Union. This need has been recognized quite clearly within the Catholic Church, and these new structures are indeed being constructed. There are still nuncios, or papal representatives in each European country, there are still individual conferences of bishops within each nation. But there is now an organization called the Commission of the Bishops' Conferences of the European Community (COMECE), with a secretariat in Brussels that coordinates the relationships both among the various episcopal conferences across the continent, and between those conferences and the governing institutions of the European Union. The COMECE has existed for a number of years, but its role will be particularly important in the coming years as the parallel ecclesiastical structure best capable of responding to the challenges posed by the integration of European politics and society. In fact, there is now a formal committee of European bishops charged explicitly with dealing directly with the European Union.

By the challenge of scope posed to European Catholicism I mean the question of reconciling the very different religious realities that exist in Eastern and Western Europe, a pervasive theme of this volume. There is obviously a very striking difference between East and West; John Paul II had to face this divergence as he articulated and advanced his vision of a unified and Christian future for Europe and its people. In its simplest terms, the challenge facing the Church in this regard is the challenge of preserving the faithfulness of the East as it integrates with the more secularized West. In fact, John Paul II's preferred vision of the future ran in exactly the opposite direction. Rather than countenancing the secularization of the East through integration with the West, he envisioned the re-evangelization of the West through integration with the East.

I agree with Byrnes's perspective in this volume that John Paul II's intent in Europeanization was tied to evangelization, but I do not agree that it was his only interest. The Holy See historically has always had an interest in the secular status of Europe, its ability to continue on the path of peace and political integration. Those goals have intrinsic merit and are actually supported by the teaching and practice of Vatican diplomacy.

However, it is clearly the case that the Pope sees the cultural and religious state of Europe as alarming on the one hand, and a source of personal sadness on the other. In *Ecclesia in Europa* (2003), the papal reflection on the European Synod, he offered the following very sober assessment of the religious situation in Western Europe:

I would like to mention in a particular way the loss of Europe's Christian memory and heritage, accompanied by a kind of practical agnosticism and religious indifference whereby many Europeans give the impression of living without spiritual roots and somewhat like heirs who have squandered a patrimony entrusted to them by history. At the root of this loss of hope is an attempt to promote a vision of the person apart from God and apart from Christ. European culture gives the impression of silent apostasy on the part of people who have all they need and who live as if God does not exist. This is the context for those attempts, including the most recent ones, to present European culture with no reference to the contribution of the Christian religion. (John Paul II, 2003)

The Holy See has both a pastoral interest in reversing the trend of "silent apostasy" and a political-moral commitment to the continued development of the process described in these pages as Europeanization.

On the question of the substantive challenge posed to Catholicism by the processes of Europeanization, we need to turn to a Catholic social vision that developed over the course of the twentieth century. That social vision encompasses a view of society, of the state, and of the common good, all of which hold direct relevance for this particular moment in European history. There are three main sources of this vision. The first is the documents of the Second Vatican Council, and the legacy that those documents have left to the Church. Particularly important for these chapters are two texts of the Council, *Gaudium et Spes* ("The Pastoral Constitution on the Church in the Modern World") and *Dignitatis Humanae* ("The Declaration on Religious Liberty"). These two documents taken together had a double effect on Catholicism's conception of its own role in the world. I have described that effect as making the Church less political and more social. "The Declaration on Religious Liberty," in particular, encouraged a distancing of the Church from the state, a distancing in the sense of eschewing the previous model of tight intimate collaboration between the Catholic Church and individual states. The previous model assumed that the closer the Church could get to the state, the better off the Church would be, and that model was embodied in a multiplicity of concordats.

These concordats, formal arrangements, or treaties between states and the Catholic Church still exist, of course, but they no longer serve as the governing model of how the Church should relate to the state. The idea now, following the Council and "The Declaration on Religious Liberty," is to recognize the state's appropriate secularity, to engage it selectively, but not to tie the Church's fate and fortune to formal engagement with the state (Murray, 1966). It is a less specifically political model in that sense; it envisions and leads to a more social form of engagement between Church and society. When the Church creates space between itself and the state, it provides itself with more freedom and greater opportunities for participating more fully in the life of civil society. The legacy of the Second Vatican Council, in this regard, is a movement to set the Church free from close ties with the state expressly for the purpose of rendering the Church more able to engage the state, in either positive or negative terms, from a position within civil society. This dynamic has taken root quite clearly in Europe since the end of the Council, but it has been an important development in places like Latin America as well.

The second source of this substantive contribution are the personal teachings of Pope John Paul II himself, teachings derived from and building on a rich tradition of Catholic social thought that has been constructed by a number of popes over the last century. This tradition is embodied in a series of documents, usually in the form of papal encyclicals that have sought to address socio-economic issues, as well as a range of other social questions, from the point of view of social philosophy. Generally dated from Pope Leo XIII's *Rerum Novarum* in 1891, Catholic social teaching through the 1930s grew out of the Church's efforts to respond to the social and moral consequences of the industrial revolution. Beginning with Pope Pius XII in the 1940s, however, the focus of that body of teaching expanded to include a greater emphasis on the implications of the emerging international system. Finally, in the 1970s, a part of this teaching tradition began to respond to the consequences of what might be called post-industrial society, particularly in settings like the United States and Western Europe (O'Brien and Shannon, 1992; Hehir, 1983).

John Paul II's contribution to this body of Catholic teaching, and his substantive response to the challenges of Europeanization, are best understood in the context of this historical development. Most prominently, his encyclical *Centesimus Annus*, marking the centennial anniversary of Leo XIII's seminal *Rerum Novarum*, was written, in part, to lay out the Polish Pope's views on exactly why communism collapsed in Europe. There was great interest in that analysis, of course, because of the widespread understanding that the Pope and his support of Solidarity had played an important part in bringing that collapse about in the first place. But *Centesimus Annus* went well beyond the question of communism to address issues like the proper relations between state and culture, and the moral implications of the market economy, matters of great significance throughout the world, but certainly matters of particular importance on a European continent already in 1991 struggling with the daunting prospect of reintegrating after four decades of sharp and pervasive division.

The third, and perhaps the most direct, source of Catholic response to the substantive challenges of Europeanization is *Ecclesia in Europa*, John Paul II's "post-synodal apostolic exhortation" referenced above. As I have already noted, this document struck a very somber tone in terms of the general religious situation in Europe, particularly in the West. However, it also went into great detail in terms of the public role that the Pope thought that the transnational Catholic Church *should* play in contemporary European society. In this important document, the Pope was clearly articulating his hope that the Church could recover a meaningful public role from the ravages of European secularism; he was laying out his vision, in fact, of a re-evangelization of a newly unified Europe; and perhaps most relevantly for our purposes in this volume, he was seeking public institutional recognition of the place of the Catholic Church in the public life of an expanding European Union. In *Ecclesia in Europa*, for example, he renewed his impassioned call for inclusion in the new European constitution of a prominent reference to the religious foundations of European civilization, and particularly to the Christian foundations of authentic European history.

From these sources the Catholic response to Europeanization must address four issues: (1) relations with secular states; (2) the challenge of religious pluralism; (3) managing a market economy; and (4) responsibilities in a changing world order. I pick these four (which I have used in other essays to analyze American Catholism) because they are exactly the kinds of structural questions with which the processes of Europeanization must be engaged at both the level of individual states, as well as at the level of a uniting Europe.

In terms of Catholic response to the secular state in Europe today, it is interesting to note that in *Ecclesia in Europa*, a document in which the Pope re-emphasized his conviction that the Church ought to play a prominent public role in Europe, he nevertheless made a point of reminding his readers that "in her relations with public authorities, the church is not calling for a return to the confessional state" (John Paul II, 2003). Why would he do that? Because for centuries in Europe, the position of the Catholic Church was that the confessional state, union between Church and state, should be the norm, particularly in settings characterized by large Catholic populations (Murray, 1964). The Vatican Council's teaching on religious freedom eroded that argument; "The Declaration on Religious Liberty" asserted the right of religious liberty for each person and every religious tradition. John Paul II, building on the Council, clearly wanted a public role for religion in society and for the Church in Europe, but he did not seek the privileges of an ancient time; today they are inappropriate.

This perspective and policy fits the model of a social rather than political approach to the Church's public role. To be sure, John Paul II had plenty to say to state authorities of all kinds, but he was determined to have his say as a participant in a wider civil society. More than any of his papal predecessors, John Paul II was very clear in his desire to maintain a distance between institutional representation of the state and institutional representation of the Church. This is an important reason why, for example, he so strongly opposed priests and nuns holding public office. He believed that such roles confuse the proper relationship between political and religious authority. If a priest or nun is elected to an office, or even takes a formal position in state administration, that creates an inappropriate starting point for the Church's interaction with the state.

In similar terms, the post-Vatican II Catholic Church now accepts religious pluralism as the normal context in which it carries out its pastoral mission. John Paul II was a strong supporter of religious freedom throughout his life, and he was very comfortable articulating this commitment to pluralism in Europe and throughout the world. The challenge of religious pluralism in modern Europe (Peter Katzenstein's theme of multiple modernities) means that the Church must address multiple audiences and it must rely on persuasion to make its public policy case. At times John Paul II moved directly from Catholic moral positions to proposals for civil law, but we should not dismiss the importance of a Catholic Pope calling clearly and articulately for respect within European society for a broad range of religious traditions. The traditional Catholic approach to establishing the moral grounding for public policy within pluralist circumstances is to advance philosophical arguments in a process of testing existing law and policy against a wider moral vision. Such an approach might prove very useful within the context of a European unity emerging out of complex political and cultural diversity.

Moreover, on a range of issues involving social justice and war and peace, Pope John Paul II might well have found substantial overlap between his own views and mainstream European opinion. Catholic teaching, in short, might serve as a kind of moral backdrop for political views held more widely. This was arguably the case during the lead-up to the war in Iraq when the Pope made the White House very uncomfortable through his continual assertion, corresponding to many European political leaders, that the war was neither necessary nor advisable. In contrast, of course, a range of bioethical issues have arisen on the public agenda about which the Catholic argument is decidedly not congruent with mainstream European opinion. Given the human and moral significance of these policy debates, the Church will always feel obligated to address them, but it will face a cultural and social context which will not be easily shaped by the content of Catholic bioethical positions.

Third, in terms of the market economy, it is true that John Paul II was more positive than any of his predecessors in his assessment of the market as a mechanism for organizing the economy. But his essential argument was that the market has both assets and limits, and therefore it is necessary that there be a broader social policy that complements the moral limits of the market (O'Brien and Shannon, 1992: 464, 469). The moral limits of the market were evident for John Paul II in a number of ways. In the first place, he emphasized the simple but important observation that the market is irrelevant to the lives of persons who do not have the resources necessary for meaningful participation in it. Second, since the market does not know how to evaluate different kinds of goods, some highly valued human goods (e.g. health care) ought not to be submitted totally to the dynamics of the market. Because of the moral limits of the market, John Paul II argued in favor of a social policy which accepts the market but also protects basic rights and fundamental social goods. There is in this view substantial affinity with social policy in modern Europe. But some aspects of the European social welfare state drew criticism from John Paul II, a point to be developed below.

Finally, in terms of the Catholic Church's substantive response to current circumstances in an expanding Europe, Pope John Paul II articulated a very clear belief that the OECD countries, the rich countries of world capitalism, have deep, powerful, and expansive obligations toward the countries of the South and elsewhere. This is particularly true in the crucial questions of international political economy, but the Pope spoke in similar terms about matters of humanitarian aid, and about the issue of military intervention by major powers. In this reaffirmation of the global view articulated by Pope Paul VI in the 1960s and 1970s, Pope John Paul II made clear both the broadly transnational nature of world Catholicism, and the degree to which that Church will bring its broader global concerns with it as it resumes what he considers to be its rightful place in the public life of European society.

Transatlantic Catholicism: contrast and comparison

In secular political analysis discussion of the new Europe sooner or later includes some assessment of the impact of Europeanization on the Atlantic alliance, NATO, the OECD, or other ties which bind Europe and the United States. In these discussions, the primacy of influence of the United States is virtually taken for granted. But in Catholic relationships the primacy of Europe is assumed. Neither European churches nor the Holy See are in doubt about the political, military, and economic power of the United States, and there is a clear-eyed recognition that this puts the Church in the United States in a crucial position. But the logic of ecclesial relations do not simply follow the patterns of secular power. Particularly in relations between the systemic and the national levels there is an acquired skill which European Church leaders possess, almost an innate sense of how to relate to Rome which Americans neither have by instinct nor necessarily acquire even with diligent effort. The reciprocal relationship from the side of the Holy See also manifests a kind of familiarity and confidence about shared vision and ease of communications not always present in US–Vatican ecclesial relationships.

Precisely because so many of the political-diplomatic issues, from human rights, to humanitarian intervention to globalization, have a

The old Church and the new Europe

13

transatlantic context, it is useful to close this chapter with a synthetic comparison of the US and European similarities and differences. In terms of secular characteristics there is much shared between them. Much of Europe is, like the United States, an example of an advanced industrial democracy. Europeans are middle powers in the international hierarchy but possessed of a status and role which assure them a place in major international debates. There is a European presence assured on the Security Council, a European heading the IMF, a substantial European role among international civil servants and a European press read around the world. None of this as yet translates into a "pole" of European power which rivals the US role, but it has provided a unique status for Europe in world affairs.

Within the Catholic Church the very disparity of power between the United States and Europe is an important characteristic in the way the Holy See interacts with them. There is a discernible if never articulated premise in Catholic polity that the Holy See should protect the status and self-determination of small and middle-sized churches against the influence of large and powerful churches (e.g. the United States, Brazil). The abiding realism of the Vatican means that it understands the inevitably different scope of influence of some local churches, but it also means that at key moments the Holy See will intervene if that influence is simply sweeping other churches into a given posture or position on crucial issues. Popular interpretations of Catholic organizational life often assume a unique influence for the Church in the United States; the opposite is, in my view, closer to the reality. The Holy See does not want to translate secular power into special privilege within the universal Church. This basic organizational premise is then complemented by the fact that both geographical proximity and historical ties provide the European churches with access to the Holy See and a style of engagement which makes communication a simple matter.

It should be noted that another example of this balancing role played by the Holy See can apply directly to some European churches (e.g. the German) that exercise significant influence in the southern hemisphere. They too can, at times, experience the restraining role of Rome.

A counterpoint to the restraining role of Rome is its coordinating function. At times it will call upon the transatlantic churches to reinforce the position of the Holy See either on transnational issues (like Third World debt forgiveness) or in high-profile international conferences (like UN Conferences on Women or Population). In these instances the normal pattern is for the Holy See to set the policy and to represent it in intergovernmental forums or conferences, while the local churches within key nations address their governments directly.

Shifting the analytical focus to the transnational relations among the European and US churches highlights differences in spite of their common character as advanced industrial societies. At the political level, while all the major actors are democracies, the pattern of church–state relations differs in structure and style. Some of the European churches maintain concordats with the Holy See; others have the cultural character of being "Catholic countries"; both of these factors can shape how Church and state interact, even though the relationship observes all the expected distinctions of a secular democratic state. The US case is governed by rather strict construction of the First Amendment which, of course, grants neither any special status nor special access to the decision-making of the executive, legislatures, or courts.

Moving from church–state to church–societal relationships, a distinguishing characteristic of the US Church is the extensive range of Catholic social institutions – educational, social, and health care institutions. While all of these exist – some of uniquely historical significance – in Europe, it is the number and size of these sectors which sets off the US Church from its European counterparts. Over 200 colleges and universities, several hundred primary and secondary schools, a network of social services second only to federal and state governments, and the largest non-profit health care system in the country: these elements of the Catholic social system are not only a unique manifestation of the Church's ministry but a major social influence in a secular, democratic, capitalist nation. The differences between Europe and the United States is not confined to size and numbers. These institutions are part of what distinguishes the manifestation of the social welfare state in Europe and the United States. Both have the welfare state; in many ways the European expectations of the state correspond more closely to Catholic social teaching than in the US (e.g. on universal access to health insurance). But, as noted above, John Paul II in *Centesimus Annus* went out of his way to criticize aspects of the modern welfare state. While the critique did not identify specific examples, it seemed to be aimed at the all-encompassing role of the welfare state found in some European societies (O'Brien and Shannon, 1992: 476). In specifically Catholic terms, the lack of subsidiary or pluralism in the provision of social services gave the state too intrusive a role in civil society. The US model, with both room for and reliance upon non-profit institutions, corresponds to the logic of subsidiary even if its outcome in key areas like health or housing falls short of the substantive expectations of the social teaching.

It seems unlikely that there will be any major expansion of the Catholic social system in Europe; neither need nor tradition calls for such a development. In the United States, while all three sectors are under financial pressures, and while each manifests some church–state conflicts about how they are to function, the likely (and desired) future will maintain these institutions as a major form of Catholic witness in society.

At the local level of Church life within Europe and within the United States substantial differences exist in style of pastoral ministry and formal participation in ministerial roles. Throughout the twentieth century US participation in liturgical life (i.e. mass and the sacraments) was generally far higher than in Europe. Although US numbers have declined since the 1960s, there is still, on a national basis, significantly higher rates of participation than Western European countries have.

The broader point of comparison is the public role of religion in the transatlantic relationship. While both sides of the Atlantic have in place secular democratic institutions, US public debate about general themes of society and culture as well as about specific issues, ranging from bioethics through non-profit institutions to international affairs, is thoroughly pervaded by appeals to religious convictions, values, and conclusions. If anything, the tendency to invoke religious positions in these debates has intensified in the last twenty years. To repeat an earlier theme, Catholicism, by teaching and tradition, expects to play a public role in society, and the Church was urged to do so by John Paul II. So the image of an engaged US Church and a silent European Catholic voice would be totally mistaken. But the style of extensive public engagement by the Catholic bishops of the United States on issues like abortion, war and peace, and social policy creates a different manifestation of ministry than is evident in most European countries.

The reasons for this difference lie in both secular and ecclesial soil. The secular setting of the United States is shaped by the seeming paradox of a carefully structural constitutional order of "separation" of religion and government along with the pervasive religiosity of popular culture. The constitutional lines are clearly drawn and enforced by multiple decision of the courts; but within this formidable structure of restraint there is much open space for appeals to religious themes concerning American public life. The European structures have their own clear divisions (e.g. France) and they seem to create in civil society greater reticence about intensifying public debate through invocation of religious language and values.

Having drawn this distinction, two qualifications need to be added. The tremendous impact of the sexual abuse crisis on the Church in the United States may well, in the immediate future, seriously erode the capacity of Church leadership to play an effective role in public policy until the consequences of the crisis have been thoroughly addressed. On the other hand, as a key theme of this volume asserts, recent debates in Europe, sparked principally by trends in Muslim immigration, have necessitated public discussion of the role of religion in law and culture. Europe may manifest a greater public role for religious voices at a time when the US Church will face new obstacles to playing an effective public role.

Conclusion

Europeanization as understood in this volume is a fact with long-term consequences for the countries of the continent and their role in the world. Catholicism has lived with Europe through centuries of deep, powerful, secular and religious change and conflict. The new questions of the new Europe will require the Church once again to adapt but also to reaffirm its role in the personal and public life of the continent. The question is not whether it will do so but how.

Note
I acknowledge with thanks Timothy Byrnes's collaboration in this chapter.

5 Thy will be done: the Catholic Church and politics in Poland since 1989

Sabrina P. Ramet

Poland and its Church have long fascinated observers. The Church's role in the legendary resistance of the Poles to tsarist rule and later to communist rule, the devotion of Polish bishops and priests to the interests of the Polish people in times of hardship, and the enormous popularity of the Church throughout the communist era and its considerable political clout in the post-communist era make this Church worthy of study. The Catholic Church in Poland has, moreover, been able to make its voice heard and to make a difference in the continent-wide debate, in a way that, let us say, the Catholic Church in Slovenia or Croatia or Slovakia or Austria or Romania has not.

Traditionally, in Catholic teaching, what happens on earth should reflect, as much as possible, God's will; political power, accordingly, can be viewed as a sword, whose wielder can either contribute to realizing the promise that "thy will be done on earth as it is in heaven," or set up obstacles to that project. This is also an important reason why, as Daniel Philpott and Timothy Shah note in their contribution to this volume, the Catholic Church has been wary of state sovereignty; but the problem is not the institutional form of the state as such, so much as its secular character, and, insofar as the EU is conceptualized as a *secular* union, its threat to Church interests is greater, not less, than the threat already posed by the secular state. In traditional Catholic teaching, thus, there is no such thing as neutrality in politics: there is apathy, of course, just as there are uninvolvement and abnegation and disengagement and disestablishmentarianism, which is nothing less than the effort to keep the bishops at a maximum distance from the swords they so yearn to wield. But neutrality in issues that involve God's will or God's plan is an absurdity – at least as understood in traditional Catholic teaching. Not all Catholics will agree with this formulation, but I dare say that all conservative Catholics will, and it is the conservative wing of the Catholic Church which reigns supreme in the Vatican and in the Catholic Church in Poland (hereafter, Church in Poland) alike.[1]

In conditions in which a force hostile to Catholicism maintains a political monopoly, the Church is thrown on the defensive and looks in the first place to protect its own interests. Although there were differences in the Church's strategy in Nazi Germany, fascist Italy, communist Poland, and socialist Yugoslavia, the objective was, in all of these cases, the same: survival and self-defense. Church leaders criticized violations of human rights in all of these cases as well, and the figures of Pope Pius XII (1876–1958; pope 1939–58), Stefan Cardinal Wyszyński (1901–81), and Alojzije Cardinal Stepinac (1898–1960) still provide inspiration to many, even if Pius and Stepinac have found detractors, as well as advocates. Wyszyński and Stepinac were both imprisoned by the communists as a result of their refusal to collaborate, while the Nazis considered kidnapping Pius at one time. And in all of these cases, the Church was prepared to come to a modus vivendi, whether that found expression in the form of a concordat or, in the Polish case, in the form of the April 1950 agreement, or, in the Yugoslav case, in the form of a protocol between Belgrade and the Vatican signed in 1966, six years after Stepinac's death.

Where the Polish case is concerned, the Church in Poland was clearly on the defensive during the years of communist rule. During these years, the Church could not hope to realize the kingdom of God on earth. But the years 1988–89 marked a transition in which the opportunity was opened for Church leaders to lay hold of the swords of power and take up the ecclesiastical agenda. While it is conceivable that other prelates might have reacted differently, Pope John Paul II (1920–2005, pope 1978–2005), Józef Cardinal Glemp (b. 1928) of Warsaw, and Bishop Tadeusz Pieronek, executive secretary of the Episcopal Council of Poland until 1998, were not disposed to let this opportunity pass; indeed, they would have considered such neglect unconscionable. It would have been no less than a sign of – neutrality! As a result, led by the late Pope John Paul II, Józef Cardinal Glemp, and Tadeusz Pieronek, the Church in Poland has fought energetically, since 1989, to make the system itself conform to its own programmatic preferences. Those programmatic preferences are, of course, the preferences not just of the Church in Poland but of the Catholic Church as such.

The chapter which follows is divided into five parts: in the first part, I shall provide a brief sketch of the experiences and activities of the Church in Poland during the years 1945–89; an understanding of these years is critical if what has come later is to be brought into focus, because it was in those earlier years that Polish prelates drew certain lessons and developed a strategy for effecting change in Poland. Part two looks at the years since 1989, examining both the Church's charitable and social engagement and the various controversies in which it has been involved. In part three,

I shall focus on the battle over abortion, outlining the changes in legislation since 1989 and the effects of such changes, and summarizing the arguments and rhetoric on both sides of the controversy. In the fourth part, I shall look at the debates surrounding Polish accession to the European Union (EU) and explain why John Paul II, Glemp, and Pieronek, in spite of their concerns about the draft EU constitution, chose to give EU accession their strong backing. In this context, it will be clear in what sense the Church views the integration of Poland into the EU as "a great apostolic assignment" – as José Casanova puts it in his chapter. I shall also note the role of the ultra-conservative Radio Maryja in the controversy over EU accession. And finally, in the conclusion, I shall show how an important sector of the Catholic Church has become mired in the past, thus finding itself uncomfortable with some of the contemporary trends in Europe and the world, and suggest ways in which the Church can move beyond the present impasse to regain its balance and contribute to the moral dialogue in the years to come. Throughout this chapter, it will be my assumption that tendencies toward globalization, secularization, pluralization, and growth in tolerance are largely irreversible, and that the Church, which has shown a remarkable capacity to adapt to historical change over the past centuries, has the capacity to adapt to these tendencies, provided that it does not allow itself to make a fetish of some completely unnecessary trappings of the faith, which are dear to the more atavistic conservatives but which depend, among other things, on a studied de-emphasis of the Gospels.

Church and state, 1945–1989

The present mindset of the Church in Poland is very much a product of its experiences in the communist era, which can be seen as consisting of four phases: repression, 1945–56; retrenchment, 1956–70; stabilization, 1970–80; and system decay, 1980–89. In the phase of repression, the communist regime voided the concordat of 1925, banned Catholic publications from public libraries, and seized the facilities of the Caritas charitable organization and much of the Church's holdings in land and livestock. Pope Pius XII pronounced an anathema on communist authorities (in 1949) and urged Catholics to withhold obedience and loyalty to the new authorities. Then, at the end of 1952, three Silesian bishops disappeared and the following year, Archbishop Wyszyński and Bishop Czesław Kaczmarek were arrested and locked up. The Catholic weekly *Niedziela* was banned in 1953. Then, in 1954, the communists forced the theological faculties in Warsaw and Kracow to close, establishing the Academy of Catholic Theology (in Warsaw), which they controlled, to take the place of the suppressed faculties of theology. The Catholic University of Lublin (KUL) was forced to shut down its faculties of law and economics and to fire some professors, and when KUL refused to pay taxes, the communists confiscated some of KUL's land, erecting a hotel there (Szostek, 2004). Wyszyński and Kaczmarek were released only in October 1956, when local disturbances and a change of regime ushered in a new phase not only for the Church, but for all of Poland.

The release of Wyszyński and Kaczmarek was only the most visible signal of the new phase, which coincided with the general secretaryship of Władysław Gomułka (1905–82) and which saw a truce between Church and regime. In the years 1956–70, the Church's publishing activity revived, Catholic Intelligentsia Clubs were launched, and the faculties of law, economics, political science, and education in Lublin were returned to Church control at the Catholic University of Lublin (KUL). But the regime was undertaking only a tactical adjustment, not a change of strategy. One sign of this is that, soon after the release of Wyszyński from prison, the regime made renewed efforts to curtail religious instruction, which was still being offered in the state schools at the time. In fact, during the 1959–60 school year, religious instruction was still available in 21,500 schools (out of a total of 28,000); but the authorities now moved decisively, and in the following year religion was still being taught in only 6,500 schools (Staron, 1969: 586).

The third phase, 1970–80, coincided with the years that Edward Gierek served as first secretary of the Polish United Workers' Party (PUWP). Gierek continued the dual strategy of Gomułka, endeavoring simultaneously to win the support of the hierarchy and to undermine the Church's ties with the people. Already in July 1971, the Gierek regime transferred to the ownership of the Church in Poland property which had been confiscated from the German Catholic Church at the end of World War Two. Altogether, about 7,000 church facilities were involved. Gierek also ended the policy of obstructing the construction and renovation of church buildings. But the regime also pressed "for an increase in the 'socialist content' in elementary school curricula and, in particular, for recasting curricula on Polish history to minimize the Church's role" (Ramet, 1998: 45).

Everything changed in the course of 1980–81, when communist power crumbled, the independent trade union Solidarity emerged, and Marshal Wojciech Jaruzelski restored order on the basis of de facto military rule. During the years 1980–89 (the fourth phase), the Church abandoned its defensive posture and became heavily involved in promoting recognition of its own past role in Poles' struggle for independence during the years 1795–1918, in defending the rights of imprisoned Solidarity activists, playing host to a human rights seminar (in December 1987), and in organizing a private agricultural fund. The Church also began supporting an independent culture, by sponsoring poetry readings, film festivals, art exhibitions, and theatrical production. But many observers were struck by the way in which the Church seemed to be acting alone, rather than in concert with the now-underground Solidarity trade union; rather than engaging in a tactical alliance with the devout activists of Solidarity against the communist authorities, the Church preferred to position itself as a third force, independent of both regime and Solidarity. The regime fought back by handing Archbishop Glemp, who had succeeded the late Wyszyński as primate of Poland in 1981, a list of sixty-nine "extremist priests" who should be reined in, if not muzzled altogether. Then, on October 19, 1984, members of the state security apparatus kidnapped and murdered Rev. Jerzy Popiełuszko, a highly popular young priest who had been saying "masses for Poland" and speaking in defense of Solidarity's principles.

The communist regime was more than aware that the Church possessed both institutional and popular strength. Its institutional resources, as of 1988, included 98 bishops, 23,432 priests, 23,711 nuns, and 9,038 seminarians, operating 10,719 churches, 1,835 chapels, 2,506 convents, 447 monasteries, 12 high schools, and the Catholic University of Lublin, as well as 35 mass periodicals (Chrypinski, 1989: 138; Turowicz, 1987: A682–83; *Słowo Powszechne*, 1985, 68–78). But it was its popular strength which lent the Church its real power. Invigorated by the informed attention of "the Polish pope," buttressed by the hugely popular cult of the Virgin Mary and cults of the saints, and legitimated in the eyes of the Polish people by its confrontational engagement with the regime over the previous four and a half decades, the Church was trusted by fully 87 percent of Poles, according to an October 1989 poll – well ahead of ratings for the army (70 percent), the government (68 percent), or even Solidarity (66 percent), and far ahead of the PUWP (11 percent) (OBOP Center, 1989: 74; PAP, 1989: 78–79). It was the sheer strength of the Church which compelled communist authorities to tread lightly, at least after 1956, where sacerdotal interests were at stake.

A new era, since 1989

As Tim Byrnes points out in his chapter, the collapse of communism presented the Church with new opportunities, and, indeed, the authoritarian system crumbled, new pluralist institutions were put in place, and the Church moved quickly to operationalize its agenda. Those who remember Pope John XXIII may be tempted to speculate how history might have been different if he, Angelo Roncalli, had been occupying St. Peter's throne since 1978, rather than Karol Wojtyła. Certainly, it is hard to imagine that the Italian Roncalli would have displayed so steady an interest in Poland. Moreover, judging from what he actually did, one might speculate that he would have given a higher priority to continued *aggiornamento* (bringing the Church up to date and in tune with the world) rather than undertaking measures which put the Church in confrontation with secular forms of globalization. One might also speculate that Roncalli would have given a higher priority to ecumenism and charitable work than to the various issues related to sexuality which have absorbed so much of the attention of the Wojtyła papacy. The only utility of such speculation, however, is to remind us that much in history depends on specific personalities, and that the direction which the Church has taken under Wojtyła's leadership is not a direction which it would necessarily have taken regardless of who was pope. Moreover, it was Wojtyła who, acting on the last wishes of Wyszyński, named Glemp primate of Poland, and it was Wojtyła who, acting entirely on his own initiative, strengthened Glemp's position by raising him to the College of Cardinals. And yet, Pope John Paul II was Polish, Glemp never enjoyed the kind of freedom which his predecessor had enjoyed until 1978. Stefan Cardinal Wyszyński would repeatedly tell Pope Paul VI (Giovanni Montini) that he (the Pope) was not familiar with conditions in Poland and should let those who knew Poland make decisions affecting her ecclesiastical interests; Glemp was hardly in a position to treat Karol Wojtyła in the same way.

The Church's priorities

Be that as it may, the Church's first priority as communism crumbled in Poland, becoming the subject of discussions between the episcopate and sympathetic figures in the Sejm and in the opposition as early as the winter of 1988/89, was abortion, which the Church wanted to see banned. Later, in May 1989, after the elections in which Solidarity won 99 of the 100 seats in the newly created Senate, Glemp and Solidarity leader and future Polish president Lech Wałęsa met so that the bishop could impress upon Wałęsa the seriousness with which he regarded abortion. Pressure on both the legislature and the medical establishment built quickly, and as early as September 1990, the Senate passed a restrictive bill on abortion and forwarded it to the lower house, the Sejm, for approval. In the meantime, the Polish episcopate had issued a communiqué calling for the return of religious instruction to the schools and began to air a proposal to declare Catholicism the state religion of Poland. The latter proposal was eventually dropped, apparently because the Pope quashed it, but as early as August 1990, a special subcommittee of the Joint Commission of the Government and the Episcopate peremptorily announced the restoration of religious instruction in the public schools. Ombudsman Ewa Letowska challenged the constitutionality of this decree, but on January 30, 1991, the Constitutional Court of Poland ruled that the decree did not violate Church–state separation or any other existing statute. The following year the number of religion classes was increased from one period per week to two per week, though a new subject, ethics, was introduced as an alternative to religion class. Although representatives of non-Catholic denominations initially expressed concern that their children would face peer pressure, if not pressure from teachers, to submit to Catholic religious instruction, the religion classes soon became popular, with Catholics and non-Catholics alike valuing them as a unique occasion on which to discuss metaphysical questions in an open way (Kosela, 2004b; Biedron, 2004). At the same time, Church leaders did their best to keep sex education out of the schools. In December 1992, under pressure from the Church, the Sejm voted 198 to 172, with 12 abstentions, to institute a new law mandating that radio and television broadcasts respect "Christian values"; the nature of such "Christian values" would be ascertained by an eight-member council, on which the Church was well represented (Law on Radio and Television Broadcasting, 1993; Ramet, 1998: 299–300). Then, in January 1993, both houses of the Polish legislature, voting separately, approved a law criminalizing abortion (details in the next section), which was signed into law by President Wałęsa on February 15.

Throughout the period 1989–93, the Church sought to negotiate a concordat. A joint governmental–ecclesiastical commission, meeting in Warsaw, produced a draft and forwarded it to the Holy See for approval. But the Holy See rejected the draft and, after a long delay, produced a new draft which was said to be in conflict with sixteen existing laws, two codices, and a number of decrees; among these laws were the law on liberty of conscience and faith, the law governing Church–state relations, and the law concerning marriage (Polskie Radio First Program, 1995: 50–51; Korboński, 1995: 15). In spite of this, Prime Minister Hanna Suchocka, who had less than two months left in office before parliamentary elections would sweep her out of power, signed the Vatican's draft text on July 28, 1993, forwarding it to the Parliament for its approval. The concordat was not approved, in fact, until 1997, but then it was approved without revisions; the problem of its incompatibility with existing laws largely disappeared with the enactment of Poland's new constitution in 1997, though it was necessary to change the law on marriage, so that a church wedding would be recognized by the state (Mazurkiewicz, 2004). But there were many Poles – some 53 percent in fact, according to a 1999 poll – who felt that the Church's political influence had grown too large (PAP, 1999). As is very well known, the Pope continued throughout his papacy to speak out on issues of social justice (his *Sollicitudo Rei Socialis* of 1988 standing as a prominent example), addressing the theme of poverty, and excoriating both communism and capitalism for their excesses. The reason that the Church in Poland gave priority to issues of abortion, divorce, and the protection of Christian values on the airwaves is that these issues were readily susceptible to legislation, whereas the problems of global injustice and poverty can scarcely be solved by the passage of a few laws in Warsaw.

The role of Aleksander Kwaśniewski

The concordat was, itself, not finalized until a bitter dispute concerning the constitution had been resolved and not before Wałęsa had been voted out of office. In fact, prominent Church leaders did their best, during the 1995 presidential elections, to persuade Poles to vote for either Hanna Gronkiewicz-Waltz, president of the National Bank of Poland and a firm defender of the Church's interests, or incumbent Lech Wałęsa, denouncing the candidate of the post-communist Democratic Left Alliance (SLD) Aleksander Kwaśniewski as "anti-religious," "anti-God," and "neo-pagan." In spite of the Church's efforts, Kwaśniewski won 51.72 percent of the vote in the second round and assumed the presidential office (see Ramet, 1998: 303–04; Eberts, 1998: 829). But Kwaśniewski was not prepared to go into battle against the Church, and, inspired more by pragmatism than by conviction, steered the unaltered concordat to approval in the legislature. It was also during Kwaśniewski's first term as president that, on April 2, 1997, the new Polish constitution was finally approved, after nearly eight years of discussion and negotiation. Initially, the Polish episcopate had wanted to see an invocation of the Godhead in the preamble, an explicit guarantee in the constitution protecting human life from conception, a definition of marriage as a relationship between persons of opposite sex, and an emphasis on the Christian history and culture of Poles. The final compromise satisfied the Church's demand for an invocation (the preamble begins with the words, "In the name of God ...") and in the preamble, a clause was inserted referring to the Christian heritage of the Polish nation. At the same time, Article 25 of the constitution defines the Polish state as neutral in matters of religion, while, ambiguously, referring to Church–state "cooperation for the good of mankind and for the common good" (quoted in Eberts, 1998: 834).

The educational and charitable engagement of the Church

A survey conducted among 1,241 Poles in 2001 found that only 38 percent said that God was "very important in their lives" (Koseła, 2004a: 125, 130). Only 45.2 percent of Poles attended Sunday mass regularly (in 2002), while a mere 17.3 percent said they took communion regularly (Zdaniewicz and Zaręba, 2004: 292–94). Some 61 percent of Poles are pro-choice (Nowicka, 2004), and "only" 83% of Poles reported (in 1998) that religious belief was an important constituent element of their identity.[2] Yet, in spite of these discordant results, fully 95 percent of Poles declare themselves Catholics. What accounts for the absence of any overt signs of secularization among Poles?

I believe that at least four factors must be mentioned in this connection. The first in terms of chronology, but the weakest of the four at this point in time, is the feeling that "the Church is on our side," inherited from the era of the partitions, when local clergymen joined Poles in rebelling against Russian occupation in 1830 and 1863, and from the Church's solidarity with the Polish people during World War Two. Much more vivid is the second factor, viz., the Church's firm defense of human and civil rights during the communist era when, for many years, the Church was the only institution protecting Poles from communist repression.

In the present, post-communist context, two other factors must be mentioned, viz., the Church's educational and charitable commitment. Where education is concerned, it is worth noting that the Church operates not only the Catholic University of Lublin (KUL, founded in 1918 and reactivated in 1944) and the Cardinal Stefan Wyszyński University in Warsaw (founded in 1995, transforming the state-run Academy of Catholic Theology into a fully-fledged university), but some 277 primary and secondary schools as of 2002 – up from ten in the communist era, and from 186 in 1997 (Mazurkiewicz, 2004; see also Mazurkiewicz, 2001: 359–80).

But factor number four – the sheer scope of the charitable and social engagement of the Church in Poland – must also, to my mind, be taken into account, if one is to make sense of the Polish people's deep love of their Church. The Caritas charity and the Polish branch of the Catholic Youth Organization (known in Poland by the initials KSM) – both of them revived after May 1989 – are well known; the latter organization has some 20,000 active members and organizes charity drives. But there are other organizations, such as: the Christian Voluntary Center, which works with hospitals, hospices, and orphanages; Novo Millennio, a charitable organization set up by Fr. Mieczysław Puzewicz after the floods of 2000, in order to help affected villagers; and soup kitchens for the poor, such as the "Mensa" soup kitchen operated by the Church in Lublin. To this one may add therapy organized by the Church for children of pathological families (such as families affected by alcoholism), assistance to women trafficked into forced prostitution (with the Sisters of Our Sorrowful Heart, in Silesia, being especially active in this regard), and therapy for homosexuals who have entered into heterosexual marriages, to help them make their marriages work (Puzewicz, 2004; Cisło, 2004; Kadżiołka, 2004; Bień, 2004).

We may add to the equation the engagement of the Church press on behalf of working Poles. While the Church press is intended to serve as the organ of the Church, *Niedziela* (with a circulation of 250,000) criticized a draft government budget at one point, warning that the factory closures called for by the government would throw large numbers of people out of work (Buglewicz, 2004).

In the late 1980s, the number of priestly vocations declined, leading some observers to speculate that the Church in Poland might be faced with a shortage of priests at some point in the future. But the numbers of vocations rose again in the 1990s, hitting a fifty-year high point in 2003 (Pawlina, 2003: 44; Mazurkiewicz, 2004). The continued strength of vocations is, in turn, not merely a factor for the strength of the Church but also a symptom of the continued vitality and credibility of the Church.

Homosexuality and homophobia

For the Polish left, however, the Church's strongly expressed views about various aspects of sexuality remain troubling. Indeed, the sexual concerns registered by Pope John Paul II, Cardinal Glemp, and others go far beyond the exclusion of abortion and sex education, and have extended to fighting a host of perceived "evils" including contraception, prenatal medical testing (such as amniocentesis), artificial insemination,[3] divorce, homosexuality, and pornography, not to mention the Church's continued resistance to certain notions advocated by some would-be reformers in the US, Germany, Austria, and elsewhere – the ordination of women, an end to priestly celibacy, and a more general celebration by the Church of human sexuality.

When 24-year-old Karolina Bregula, having lived in Sweden for three years, decided to launch a billboard campaign in Warsaw in May 2003, showing gay and lesbian couples holding hands and showing affection, Catholic groups protested to city officials, and the posters were variously taken down or painted over. But even so, Robert Biedroń, leader of the Campaign Against Homophobia, counted the campaign as a success.

"For the first time," he said, "homosexuals were shown as ordinary people, not as paedophiles from a railway station or freaks from a gay parade" (as quoted in *The Scotsman*, 2003). By summer 2003, moreover, Senator Maria Szyszkowska (SLD), a professor of philosophy at the University of Warsaw whose ethical development had been influenced by the writings of Immanuel Kant, was preparing legislation to expand gay rights. Among the problems which the legislation is intended to overcome are the fact that a life partner lacking a marriage certificate cannot obtain information about the condition of a hospitalized partner or be consulted in connection with proposed surgical procedures, the lack of inheritance rights when one's life partner dies, the inability to obtain a special visa when one's partner has professional opportunities or obligations in certain countries requiring such visas (e.g. Japan), and a more nebulous but no less real awareness that one's life partner is not recognized as such. Senator Szyszkowska's bill is designed to eradicate these forms of inequality and would grant same-sex couples all the rights and prerogatives enjoyed by heterosexual couples, except the right of adoption, which she left out reluctantly in the conviction that Polish society is not yet ready to accept such a provision. Immediately after the publication of the draft bill (*Magazyn Trybuny*, 2003: 6–7), she received a death threat, and the Catholic Church sent letters to people's homes saying that it was not in accord with the social teachings of the Church to accept homosexual relationships (Szyszkowska, 2004). The Congregation for the Doctrine of the Faith also issued an instruction, claiming that love between two persons of the same sex was contrary to Natural Law and informing Catholic politicians that they had a moral duty to oppose any legislation supportive of homosexuality. Among Poles, however, one out of every five respondents in a May 2002 opinion poll felt that there was no need to have recourse to religion in order to explain morality or make moral choices (by contrast more than a third of respondents felt that *only* religion could serve as a foundation for moral dictates) (Zaręba, 2004: 88).

Homosexuality has become highly politicized, with the right-wing League of Polish Families promising to establish Maoist-style "re-education" camps for gays and lesbians and with the introduction, in the Parliament, of a draft law which would have prohibited homosexuals from teaching in schools; the bill was, however, struck down by the Parliament in early 2004 (Biedroń, 2004). The League's youth organization has also used violence to prevent Polish gay people from marching for tolerance and its members have pelted marchers with bottles and stones, even throwing acid at them – all this in the name of Christian love! Yet the Catholic media and the Catholic bishops, who seem never to tire of calling

128   Catholicism

homosexuality "unnatural" and "sinful," have been eerily silent when it comes to anti-gay violence, and after one such attack in Kracow (in May 2004), the archbishop of that city described the marchers as having staged a "demonstration of sin," while saying nothing about their attackers (Ivanovs, 2004).

But the ranks of those supporting the bill for gay partnerships includes Rev. Florian Lempa, a Catholic professor of canon law at the University of Białystok, and Rev. Ernest Ivanovs, pastor of Warsaw's small Reformed Free Church, who has made gays, lesbians, and transgendered people feel welcome in his congregation (Ivanovs, 2004). Nor are those offering a vision of a more tolerant Poland likely to give up. "I am optimistic about the eventual outcome of this struggle," Senator Szyszkowska told me in 2004, "although it is going to be an uphill struggle. There have been some doors closed to me because of this. For example, I used to have my own radio program; now that's over. But I will never give up" (Szyszkowska, 2004).

Sexuality and the elections

By 2001, it was hard to portray President Kwaśniewski as being particularly "left-wing" on matters of interest to the Church. He had backed the Church's position on the concordat, on the *Invocatio Dei*, and even on abortion, had made no effort to repeal or revise the guidelines protecting "Christian values" in the public media or to resecularize the schools, and, at least for the time being, his party had postponed any action to grant legal equality to same-sex couples. But, for all that, the Church viewed Kwaśniewski as, at best, a pragmatic politician, if not as a "bolshevik" (Kadziołka, 2004), and certainly not as an ideological ally. Hence, when the 2000 presidential campaign got underway, Cardinal Glemp gave his blessing to the Catholic Election Action (WAK), as an alternative to the SLD, while Wałęsa made a long-shot effort to regain the presidency, using homosexuality as a campaign issue. At a campaign rally in July 2000, for example, Wałęsa mused, "I believe those people need medical treatment. Imagine if all people were like that – we wouldn't have any descendants!" (as quoted in Agence France Presse, 2000). With Catholic lawmakers pressing presidential candidates to declare their views concerning homosexuality, Marian Krzakowski, the candidate of Solidarity Election Action (AWS), spoke out against homosexual marriage and adoptions. Candidates from the center and left were more circumspect; Andrzej Potocki, a spokesman for the Liberty Union Party, for example, told PAP that "people of different sexual orientations enjoy the same rights guaranteed under the constitution" (as quoted in Agence France

Presse, 2000). The focus on homosexuality during the campaign drove some observers to distraction. Marek Sawicki, for example, the deputy vice-president of the Polish Peasant Party, referring to economic challenges, muttered in exasperation, "There are so many questions to be resolved . . . and now here we are [pre]occupied with homosexuality" (quoted in Agence France Presse, 2000). An opinion poll conducted during the 2000 presidential elections showed that some 55 percent of Poles had a negative view of homosexuality with 62 percent declaring that they were opposed to same-sex marriage (even though 88 percent of Poles admitted that they did not know anyone who was gay or lesbian); but in spite of the SLD's lack of hostility toward same-sex unions, Kwaśniewski easily won re-election, while the SLD went on to win the largest bloc of parliamentary seats in September 2001 – once again in spite of ecclesiastical exhortations to voters not to cast their ballots for the former communists (*Polish News Bulletin*, 2001a, 2001b). Perhaps not irrelevant is the fact that, even in 2003, some 31 percent of Poles told pollsters that they had positive memories about communist Poland, with roughly the same number – 33 percent – saying that they had negative memories (PAP, 2003). Presumably the remaining 36 percent either had mixed memories or did not want to admit to remembering anything before 1989!

Controversy over Auschwitz

There is a further controversy from the post-communist period which deserves at least some mention, viz., the controversy which flared during 1998–99 concerning the planting of Christian crosses near the entrance to the Auschwitz concentration camp where more than 1 million persons, perhaps as many as 2.5–3 million persons, mostly Jews, were liquidated by the Nazis during World War Two.[4] Controversy surrounding Auschwitz actually began in 1984 when Carmelite nuns took possession of a nearby building and converted it into a convent. Jewish organizations expressed outrage and eventually, in 1987, an agreement was reached requiring the nuns to vacate the premises – which they did, albeit only in 1993. Where the crosses are concerned, a large 26-foot (8-meter) high wooden cross had been erected already in 1988, in spite of Jewish protests, to commemorate a mass celebrated by the Pope at a nearby site in 1979 "to commemorate the spot where 152 Polish prisoners had been shot by the Nazis in 1941" (BBC News, 1998). Given the strength of Jewish opposition, and in particular Jewish insistence that Jews could not pray in the presence of a cross, a consensus was eventually reached in the first half of 1998 that, out of respect for Jewish sufferings and sensitivities, there should be no religious or political symbols placed at Auschwitz, and, thus, that the cross should be removed. In response, a Catholic group calling itself the Cross Defense Committee began putting up smaller crosses (ranging from 3 feet, or 1 meter, to 13 feet, or 4 meters, in height) in July 1998. By August 10, the committee, egged on by the right-wing Catholic radio station Radio Maryja, which had already run afoul of the episcopate, had planted more than ninety crosses at Auschwitz; eventually, committee members and sympathizers planted some 300 crosses at the former concentration camp, thereby devaluing the site as one associated especially with Jewish suffering (Turek, 1998). The key figure in this drama was Kazimierz Switon, then 67 years old, a distributor of anti-Semitic pamphlets who took up residence in a "tiny caravan" parked at the edge of Auschwitz and who, decked out "in gumboots and a grubby felt hat," used the sudden media attention he was receiving to denounce Jews, liberals, freemasons, and other supposed "enemies of Poland" (*The Independent*, 1998).[5] While Poland's chief rabbi, Pinchas Menachem Joskowicz, joined the Israeli government and the Yad Vashem Holocaust Museum in Israel, among others, in protesting the presence of the crosses, Cardinal Glemp protested the Israeli protest as an endeavor to "impose foreign will" (quoted in Turek, 1998: 1). By June 1999, however, all the smaller crosses had been removed and only the tallest cross remained. The Poles were rewarded for their understanding of Jewish concerns a year later, when the European Parliament issued a report praising Poland as the least xenophobic country in Central Europe, specifically highlighting Polish understanding of Jewish concerns as regards Auschwitz (*Polish News Bulletin*, 2000; also Zubrzycki, 2004: 176–204), although sociological data from the late 1990s showed that, among post-communist countries in Central and Eastern Europe, Poland recorded the *highest* score for anti-Semitism (Ambrosewicz-Jacobs, 2000: 576).

The fight over abortion

While one can find churchmen who differ with the Vatican over contraception, artificial insemination, and sex education, one would be hard pressed to find any churchman advocating on behalf of abortion. That said, there are at least three complications with abortion in the case of Poland: first, the ban on abortion, instituted at the behest of the Catholic Church and on the basis of Catholic values, applies to all residents of Poland, whether Catholics or not; second, according to a poll taken in 2003, some 61 percent of Poles believe that the law on abortion is overly strict and should be liberalized, with only 20 percent wanting to make the law even more restrictive and 19 percent having "no opinion" (Agence France Presse, 2003d); and third, the law has had consequences which no one welcomes – indeed, it could be said not to have achieved its purpose at all!

Opening salvoes and effects

Abortion was illegal in Poland until 1956, but with the legislation passed that year, social reasons (including financial reasons) were sufficient to obtain an abortion, with the result that abortion was, *de facto*, available on demand. This situation lasted for nearly forty years, during which time an average of 180,000 to 300,000 abortions were performed each year (Nowicka, 1997: 1). What the Church wanted was a bill which would make abortion illegal, with no allowable exceptions – not even to save the woman's life or in the case of rape. Only a small minority of parliament-arians were prepared to go that far, but a bill drafted in 1992 by members of the Christian National Union would have permitted abortion only in cases where pregnancy endangered the woman's life. Two members of the Parliament – Zbigniew Bujak of the Labor Union and Barbara Labuda of the Democratic Union – took the initiative to set up a Social Committee for a Referendum, to press for a national referendum on the future status of abortion. Bujak and Labuda gathered more than 1,300,000 signatures in support of a referendum. The Church's position, then as now, was that morality could not be the subject of a referendum. As a result of the Church's pressure, there was no referendum.

In the meantime, in May 1990, the Ministry of Health had decided that contraceptives would no longer be covered by national health insurance – a decision which put contraceptives effectively out of reach of many Polish women. At the same time, the ministry issued new guidelines for abortion, already restricting its availability, even in advance of new legis-lation (Ramet, 1998: 297). Opinion polls conducted around that time found that some 80 percent of Poles felt that abortion should continue to be legal and available, within unspecified constraints. But the Parliament continued to work on the bill, in spite of public hostility, settling on a draft bill which excluded prenatal tests. The exclusion was later dropped, and the bill passed by the Sejm on 7 January 1993 and ratified by the Senate on 30 January, was signed into law by President Wałęsa on 15 February. The new law outlawed abortions except in the following instances:

- when a panel of doctors certifies that the pregnancy endangers the mother's life or seriously threatens her health;
- when a prosecutor certifies that the pregnancy is the result of rape or incest;

- when the fetus is determined by prenatal tests to be seriously, irreparably damaged;
- and during the course of emergency action if needed to save the mother's life.

Since the Church had not wanted any exceptions to the prohibition, this law was not fully satisfying as far as either the Holy See or the Polish episcopate was concerned.

But the application of the law proved to be tougher and more restrictive than might have been anticipated. Specifically, according to Wanda Nowicka, many women who were entitled by law to access to an abortion were denied such access in practice (Nowicka, 1997: 2). Shana Penn cites two examples. The first concerns Barbara, a 28-year-old woman, who already had a four-year-old son afflicted with hypochondroplasia, a rare disease causing underdevelopment of the limbs, disfigurement, and chronic pain. Although she was using contraceptives, Barbara became pregnant once more, but was denied a prenatal test and was even advised, by the hospital administrator, that even if tests detected deformity, she would not be granted an abortion, because "nobody wants to have any problems." In fact, under the law, she would have been entitled both to a prenatal test and, under the circumstances, to an abortion. Barbara eventually gave birth to a daughter, suffering from the same affliction as her son, but receives no state support for her two disabled children. Penn's other case concerns Alicja, a 31-year-old mother of two, who had severe eyesight deficiency resulting from retinal damage. When she became pregnant again, she saw an ophthalmologist, who advised her that continuing with the pregnancy would be likely to cause further damage to her eyesight. Allegedly, however, "[t]he gynecologist at the public hospital, to whom Alicja was referred, opposed the diagnosis and destroyed the medical report, thus blocking her ability to seek medical treatment elsewhere." Alicja, whose finances were marginal, could not afford any alternative recourse and went through with the pregnancy, with the result that her eyesight was further damaged to the extent that she became unable to work or even to care for her newborn (Penn, 2001).

But for many Polish women, the criminalization of abortion merely drives them to seek abortions abroad (if they are more well-to-do) or illegally (if they do not have the funds to travel). Indeed, there have been an estimated 80,000 to 200,000 illegal abortions per year since the passage of the 1993 law on abortion, and that estimate does not even count the number of abortions performed abroad (Nowicka and Tajak, 2000: 3). Where the illegal abortions are concerned, facilities are generally not as well equipped as public hospitals are, with the result that illegal abortions are less safe than legal abortions. There have also been cases of women leaving their newborn babies at the hospitals where they are delivered (as 738 mothers did in 1995), leaving them at the doorstep of the local church, selling them to foreigners, or dumping their newborn babies in the trash (as 162 women did in 1994) (Ramet, 1998: 298). As of 1992–93, most Poles favored making abortion available in cases of financial hardship. Since the number of abortions conducted abroad for Polish women and illegally at home is roughly the same as the number of abortions conducted legally before, and given the additional problems which have ensued, as itemized above, it can reasonably be argued that passage of the law has not yielded the results for which its advocates had hoped.

Indeed, these trends have continued with, for example, just 159 legal abortions in 2002 (*Sprawodanie*, 2003). Moreover, according to official government statistics, there were on average fifty cases of infanticide in Poland annually during the years 1990–2003 and an average of sixty-one cases of child abandonment (involving newborn babies) annually during the same period (*Statystyka – Dzieciobójstwo i porzucenie*). Another problem is that there have been cases of women with health problems who have been denied abortion, in spite of the risk to their health posed by childbirth, and who have died shortly after giving birth (Nowicka, 2004).

Radio Maryja

In 1991, Father Tadeusz Rydzyk of the Redemptorist Order – a kind of latter-day Fr. Coughlin – established Radio Maryja in Torun, broadcasting a combination of religious programs, prayers, news (chiefly about the Catholic Church), and calm religious music. Pope John Paul II welcomed the new station when it began broadcasting in 1991, and by 1993, Radio Maryja was broadcasting nationwide. By 2002, the station claimed a radio audience of about 10 percent of adult Poles (BBC News, 2002). But Rydzyk's radio station soon proved to be considerably to the right of the Vatican, broadcasting programs characterized by xenophobia and authoritarian attitudes, and blaming privatization, the market economy, Jews, and liberals for Poland's problems (*Polish Business News*, 1998). In 1997, Polish ecclesiastical leaders reprimanded Rydzyk for repeatedly ignoring a summons to appear before the court in connection with a slander allegation. Archbishop Henryk Muszyński of Gniezno also had the occasion to reprimand Rydzyk after a broadcast in which Fr. Waldemar Chrostowski, director of the Catholic–Judaic Dialogue Institute, was maligned, while Archbishop Józef Życiński of Lublin has compared Rydzyk to French racist Le Pen and Austrian racist Jörg Haider (Życiński, 2004). Bishop Pieronek, who, as long as he was secretary of the episcopal conference, represented the center of gravity in the Church in Poland at least as much as Cardinal Glemp, accused Rydzyk of fostering "a kind of psychosis" about "some hidden external enemy wanting to destroy Catholicism in Poland" (quoted in *Polish Business News*, 1998). But Rydzyk's Radio Maryja has also played a part in the abortion drama, by demanding that legislators and other politicians who wanted to liberalize Poland's strict abortion law should have their heads shaved, reviving a practice adopted in the early 1940s against Polish women who were suspected of prostituting themselves to Nazi occupation troops. Radio Maryja also claimed that those advocating liberalization of the regulations concerning abortion were trying to build "a pagan cult of power" (Turska, 1996: 3). And Radio Maryja also helped to organize transportation for persons wishing to join a March for Life on the eve of an important vote in the Sejm on abortion. After the march, in which about 40,000 persons allegedly took part, organizers of the march "encouraged protesters to visit parliamentary deputies in their homes and offices and convince them to vote against [a proposed] amendment" to the law (Turska, 1996: 3).

In 2001, Radio Maryja, which had formed links with the right-wing League of Polish Families, which in turn had thirty-six seats in Parliament after the 2001 parliamentary elections, succeeded in obtaining "social broadcaster" status – which exempted the station from having to pay for its broadcasting license. This followed a vote in the Sejm, which ruled that the National Radio and Television Broadcasting Council had unfairly discriminated against the station. But in autumn 2002, Cardinal Glemp, increasingly exasperated at Radio Maryja's broadcasting excesses, issued a decree banning the station from operating in Warsaw and restricting the station from raising funds. Among other things, Radio Maryja had usurped some of the prerogatives of the episcopacy itself, thereby setting itself up as an independent (or, if one prefers, potentially schismatic) movement and engaging itself in quasi-educational activity. As Glemp pointed out in his decree, "No ecclesiastic organization, even those well-known, popular and charismatic [movements], can organize religious offices, meetings, or other forms of religious education without the approval of the bishop of the diocese" (as quoted in Agence France Presse, 2002). And for that matter, Radio Maryja was competing with the Polish Episcopate's own official radio station – Radio Józef.

In communist times, every diocese having the means to do so set up its own diocesan radio station; as of the mid-1990s, there were some thirty diocesan radio stations across Poland, but only one truly national Catholic radio station – Radio Maryja. However, in 1998, the episcopal conference decided to promote the merger of these diocesan stations, in order to form an official national Catholic radio station – in effect, an

alternative to Radio Maryja. Some twenty-two diocesan stations responded positively to this appeal, forming Radio Plus, headquartered in
Lublin and directed, since 2000, by Fr. Jarosław Jęczeń. Eight archbishops – among them, Archbishop Józef Michalik of Przemyśl (who
was elected to a five-year term as chairman of the Conference of the
Polish Episcopate in April 2004) and Archbishop Henryk Gulbinowicz
of Wrocław – feared that Radio Plus would be too open to alternative
ways of thinking and therefore preferred to continue to manage their
broadcasting on the diocesan level (Jęczeń, 2004).

Radio Maryja has remained controversial, however, and, on October 1,
2002, a decree signed by Cardinal Glemp, banning the station from
broadcasting in Warsaw, came into effect, although, in practice, its
broadcasts continued to be received in Warsaw. The decree also
restricted the fundraising activities of the station. Shortly after that, an
investigation into the station's financial affairs was reopened.

Revising the abortion law

In response to the law passed in 1993, various women's organizations
were created – among them, the Women's Rights Center (founded in
Warsaw in 1994), which offers legal advice and assistance to women, and
training for police, prosecutors, and judges dealing with domestic abuse;
a women's counseling center set up by the feminist organization eFKa
(in Krakow); the League of Polish Women; and various feminist groups.
In 1995, the National Women's Information Center was set up with
headquarters in Warsaw; directed by Barbara Limanowska, the center
seeks to foster a discussion of reproductive and sexual rights.

In fact, in the wake of the September 1993 elections, which strengthened parties on the left, the Polish Parliament voted in June 1994 to
amend the bill, in order to make some allowance for financial difficulties.
President Wałęsa vetoed the measure, however, and the lower house
failed to override the presidential veto. Subsequently, after the election
of Kwaśniewski, the Parliament reopened the question, and in late
August 1996, the Sejm approved changes to the law to allow abortion
during the first twelve weeks of pregnancy where financial hardship was
present, to restore a partial subsidization of contraceptives, and to introduce sex education in the schools. Although the Church continued to
oppose the use of contraceptives, some 48.1 percent of Poles reported (in
an opinion poll conducted in May 2002) that they thought that the use of
contraceptives should be allowed; among young people 18–24 years of
age, the proportion favoring the accessibility of contraceptives was as high
as 67.7 percent (Zaręba, 2004: 98). But the hierarchy deplored these

measures taken by the Sejm and organized a protest by 50,000 faithful to put pressure on the Senate. On October 4, the Senate overturned the Sejm's vote, rejecting the amendments by a vote of 52 to 40. But under Polish law, the Sejm enjoys the authority to override a vote in the Senate, and did just that three weeks later. President Kwaśniewski signed the bill into law on November 20, 1996.

The Polish primate compared the measure to World War Two, in an ill-conceived reference which prompted a protest from the World Jewish Federation. But the following year, the Constitutional Tribunal reviewed the amendments and struck down the provision for the termination of pregnancy on social or financial grounds. In 1999, in the Sejm, where the center-left dominated, amendments to the health law were passed which would have allowed prenatal testing in cases where family members had genetic problems, where there was reasonable suspicion that the fetus might have genetic flaws which could be treatable before birth, and when there was reasonable suspicion that the fetus might be damaged. The Senate, however, controlled by parties more conservative in political coloration, rejected the amendments in mid-June 1999. Then, in July 2001, the Federation for Women and Family Planning (the FWFP) staged a mock tribunal, to inform public opinion about the impact of the law and about violations of women's reproductive rights guaranteed by the albeit restrictive legislation. By this point, with growing polarization between liberals and conservatives in Poland and with the FWFP undertaking legal action against hospitals it accused of having refused abortions to women who were legally entitled to them, the SLD let it be known that it wanted to try once more to liberalize the law, specifically to restore the provisions struck down in 1997. A poll conducted by *Rzeczpospolita* in January 2003 among a representative sample of 1,025 Polish adults found that 63.6 percent thought that a referendum concerning the law on abortion should be conducted in Poland (*Poland.pl*, 2002). That same month, Polish women's organizations renewed pressure on the government to ease up on restrictions on abortion, and the following month, in an interesting development, religious leaders, women's rights groups, and 150 politically prominent figures from forty-six countries signed a letter sent to President Kwaśniewski calling on him to liberalize the law on abortion. Encouraged by these developments, women deputies of the SLD drew up a proposal to liberalize the law. But in June of that year, President Kwaśniewski met with the papal nuncio to Poland, Archbishop Józef Kowalczyk, and assured him that he was opposed to the proposal drawn up by the women deputies.

But Kwaśniewski's party has remained committed to easing the restrictions on abortion. Thus, in March 2004, the SLD announced its intention to pass a new bill which would not only ease such restrictions but also introduce universal sex education, assure access to birth control, and legalize in-vitro fertilization (*HLI-EUROPA News*, 2004a). The following month, Izabela Jaruga-Nowacka, by now serving as deputy prime minister, proposed further to make post-coital contraceptive medication available to victims of rape (*HLI-EUROPA News*, 2004b).

The Church and the EU

The collapse of communism opened up not only the possibility of repluralization but also the prospect of Polish entry into what had hitherto been West European organizations, and in the first place the EU. Poland submitted an official application for admission to the EU on April 8, 1994, and Polish support for membership in the EU, already higher than 75 percent at the time, rose to an estimated 80 percent by May 1996 (Grabowska, 2002: 15–16). But for the Church in Poland, which had not fully absorbed the full impact and spirit of the Second Vatican Council, the notion of integration into European structures – into "Europe," as the shorthand has it – seemed as much threatening as beckoning. As Bishop Pieronek put it in a 1998 lecture:

Europe not only falls short on Christian ideas, but there are tendencies to sever the link with the transcendental dimension altogether. In today's Europe there is a tendency to gain independence from all powers existing outside the human world, in particular, to become free from dependence on God and live "as if God did not exist", in individual as well as social life.

John Paul II is aware of these attitudes and realises what dangers they may pose to Christianity, the Church and man himself. In spite of this, or perhaps because of this, he calls for a new evangelisation. In this way Europe of the future could be identified with Europe of the past, which appeared on the stage of history thanks to Christianity. (Pieronek, 1998)

The danger, in a word, posed by European integration was secularization, which, in the minds of Polish bishops, included the displacement of spiritual values by material values and by ever greater absorption with sexuality. The Church's task, then, must be to restrain the libido and uphold divine law.

In communist times, questions of ecclesiastical survival, the independence of trade union activity, and human rights dominated the Church's agenda. But with the satisfactory resolution of these challenges and the development of a normative structure within the EU, the Church has inevitably, and for completely obvious reasons, paid attention to that normative structure. What the Church would like ideally, as Tim Byrnes notes in the conclusion to this book, is to play a decisive role in defining what will be understood as European values. But in July 2002, the

European Parliament called for the legalization of abortion across both current and prospective EU member states, emphasizing, at the same time, the importance it attached to seeing sex education in the public schools and to easy access to contraceptives. This was a shot across the bow, as far as the Holy See and Catholic prelates were concerned, signaling to the Church that it would have to fight if it wanted to see the normative structure of the EU conform to Catholic moral teaching. The EU's additional encouragement of the legalization of same-sex partnerships in member states and prospective members further dismayed the Church, inducing deep consternation among Catholic prelates and provoking expressions of concern lest EU integration completely undermine the Church's ability to defend its Catholic mores.

But in spite of these expressions of concern, support for EU membership grew among the bishops and clergy. Bishop Pieronek's warning notwithstanding, he and Archbishops Muszyński and Tadeusz Gocłowski of Gdańsk came to be called the "pro-Europe vanguard" of the Church as early as 1995 (*Poland Outlook*, n.d.). In recognition of his outspoken support for integration, Pieronek was later awarded the Polish European Award from the Polish Robert Schuman Foundation (*News from Poland*, 1998). Then, in 1997, Archbishop Muszyński led an episcopal delegation to Brussels for discussions with EU officials; Muszyński returned even more determined to support the cause of EU integration. Józef Cardinal Glemp also became an early supporter of EU membership, though he warned, in 1998, lest the EU suffocate Poland's Christian identity and culture. Glemp has been a cautious supporter and, on another occasion, warned that accession to the EU might bring "abortion, euthanasia, pornography, gay movements and anti-family policy" to Poland. Indeed, as of October 2001 the proportion of Poles who still favored membership had slipped to about 60 percent (Grabowska, 2002: 19, 21), while, as of late 2002, an estimated 59 percent of Catholic priests supported EU membership, with only 20 percent opposed (Agence France Presse, 2003a).[6] But the cause of EU integration has also had its foes. Leading the pack have been Radio Maryja's Fr. Rydzyk, who went so far as to urge Poles to boycott EU products, and Andrzej Lepper, the controversial leader of the Self-Defense Party, which gained notoriety for depositing manure outside ministry buildings. Not too surprisingly, right-wing Catholics used anti-pornography campaigns in an effort to mobilize anti-EU sentiment. But even Archbishop Życiński of Lublin, generally regarded as a moderate, warned in February 1998, "The suggestion to let Europe into Poland is a denial of the word of Christ, who commanded us to preach the Gospel to the ends of the earth" (quoted in Jackowska, 2003: 167).

In spite of these somewhat amorphous concerns about the EU fostering secularism, homosexuality, and pornography, it was only in March 2002 that the Polish episcopate issued the first official document dealing with Poland's bid to join the EU. In forwarding the document to the president, the prime minister, the Vatican, and the European Convention, Archbishop Muszyński underlined that "the Church regards the EU as a community of the spirit" and that "according to the Church, Europe is above all an entity of the spirit and of certain values" (*Warsaw Voice*, 2002). The following month European minister Danuta Huebner met with representatives of Poland's Catholic media, to pass along assurances that the EU had no influence on the moral decisions of its member states and, in fact, has never interfered in questions of abortion or euthanasia specifically. Then in May, Church concerns came into focus when Cardinal Glemp and President Kwaśniewski issued a joint statement promising that Polish representatives to the European Convention would endeavor to ensure that the eventual EU constitution would include a reference to Europe's Christian tradition. A spokesperson for the episcopate offered that the *Invocatio Dei* as featured in the Polish constitution could serve as a model for the EU constitution.

In June 2002, the *Polish News Bulletin* reported that some deputies of the SLD and its coalition partner, the Labour Union, continued to prioritize the liberalization of the law on abortion and the restoration of sex education in the schools but that Prime Minister Leszek Miller and his cabinet colleagues wanted to avoid "an open war" with the Church until Poland had been admitted into the EU. Accordingly, the *Bulletin* reported, the SLD came up with the idea of appointing the more ideologically committed members of these parties to the civil rights team, "where they can freely investigate and explore what have been described as 'radical initiatives' ... the intention is to keep the party's anti-clerical and feminist wings busy until the EU referendum scheduled for next summer" (*Polish News Bulletin*, 2002). In spite of the implicit medium-term threat to the Church's vital interests, the Church did not react at the time. But in the course of that summer, the European Parliament issued a non-binding appeal to member states to liberalize their legislation in the sphere of reproductive rights; the Church in Poland responded by offering this as evidence that "Europeanization" could undermine "Polish values" (Penn, 2003). The controversy escalated in December, when Marek Dyduch, secretary general of the SLD, reportedly told a newspaper that his party would take up the question of liberalizing the law on abortion after the referendum on EU entry, scheduled for June 2003, was behind them. The publication of Dyduch's statement provoked an immediate reaction, with Archbishop Muszyński demanding that a clause be added to the EU constitution guaranteeing that there would be no EU pressure on Poland to change its legislation in that sphere, and Cardinal Glemp demanding that the EU guarantee Poland's right to adopt its own regulations on abortion independently. Foreign Minister Włodzimierz Cimoszewicz protested that there was no reason to think that the EU even *could* impose such legislation on Poland, while Prime Minister Miller declared that the government had no plans to reopen the abortion question. In fact, Cimoszewicz added, the Polish government had no intention of seeking the addition of any special clause either to the EU constitution or to Poland's accession treaty. But Glemp and Muszyński, acting in harmony with the Holy See, insisted that a recognition of Poland's "separateness" be included in *both* the accession treaty *and* the EU constitution itself. In fact, Ireland had obtained something along these lines in the accession treaty it had signed at the time it joined the EU, and, among the other nine countries scheduled to join the EU in 2004, Malta had already negotiated a clause safeguarding its proscription of abortion. So, whether it was unnecessary or not, at least two other countries had thought it worthwhile to obtain explicit guarantees on the subject of abortion.

Former French President Valery Giscard d'Estaing chaired the thirteen-member committee assigned to draft the constitution for the EU. They released the first sixteen articles of the draft constitution, including the preamble, to the public on February 6, 2003; the draft they produced began with a preamble which acknowledged the humanistic values developed in ancient Greece and Rome, the principles of the Enlightenment, and the rights articulated and defended in the course of the French Revolution. The only recognition of Christianity was the acknowledgment "that the 'values' of Europe's 'religious' heritage 'are always present' along with those of its cultural and humanist heritage" (*European Report*, 2003). The virtual invisibility of God and Christianity in the preamble, especially in the light of the explicit mention of ancient Greece and Rome, dismayed Christians across Europe, and there were public calls from Ireland, Italy, Spain, and Poland, and later also from Lithuania and Latvia, to add an explicit allusion to the continent's Christian heritage. In an official statement released later in the year, Pope John Paul II argued that "Christian roots are a foundation of freedom because they make Europe a melting pot of different cultures and experiences ... [and inspired demands for] the universal right to justice and peace" ("Pope argues," 2003). In the Pope's mind, it was, accordingly, unthinkable that mention of God and Christianity might be omitted from the EU constitution.

The Vatican continued to hammer at this theme. In February 2003, for instance, an official spokesperson at the Vatican described the proposed text as "totally unsatisfactory" (Agence France Presse, 2003b), while, in June of the same year, Roberto Cardinal Tucci, director of Radio Vatican, described God's absence as "an offense to reason, to good sense, and to a good part of Europe's citizens" (Dixon, 2003: 26). Elmar Brok, a European deputy from Germany, added his voice to the chorus, declaring that "Europe as a whole is based on a Christian heritage" (as quoted in *Christian Science Monitor*, 2003a: 7). Others felt that the draft constitution was not secular enough and demanded that there be "a guarantee of the separation of Church and state" in all member states (*Christian Science Monitor*, 2003a: 7). And still others claimed that a reference to the continent's Christian heritage would be discriminatory because it would suggest that only the contribution of Christianity but not the contribution of Judaism and Islam to European history and civilization is worth mentioning. Thus, for example, Richard Prasquier, a member of the executive committee of France's Representative Council of Jewish Institutions, warned that "mentioning only Christian values would fail to recognize the Jewish contribution to European culture" (*Christian Science Monitor*, 2003a: 7). Then there was Les Semaines Sociales de France, a French Christian policy group, which threw its support behind an amendment which would insert a mention of God together with an advisory that God and religion should not be misused for political profit.

Back in Poland, the government caved in to Church pressure and sent a note to EU councils in Brussels in January 2003 asking for an assurance that "no EU treaties or annexes to those treaties would hamper the Polish government in regulating moral issues or those concerning the protection of human life" (*The Guardian*, 2003a: 17). Michal Tober, a government spokesperson, said that the note would serve to prevent opponents of EU accession (such as Radio Maryja) from misleading people about the consequences of joining the EU. A few months later, immediately after Archbishop Józef Życiński criticized the draft constitution and traced the French revolutionary ideals of freedom, equality, and fraternity to Christian virtues (*Gazeta Wyborcza*, 2003), President Kwaśniewski called for the addition of a reference to Christianity in the European constitution. But while fringe groups marched in Warsaw carrying banners that read "The Poles will not build the Europe of Sodom and Gomorrah" (*Manchester Guardian Weekly*, 2003: 33), Archbishop Życiński emphasized that the disagreements over the preamble should not discourage Poles from voting for Polish accession. Cardinal Glemp himself declared, on the eve of the Polish referendum on accession, "I am not a Euro-enthusiast. I'm a Euro-fatalist. Europe is Poland's destiny" (as quoted in *The Guardian*, 2003b: 17). In the event, more than 59 percent of Poles took part in the referendum on 7–8 June 2003, with 78 percent voting in favor of accession (*The Guardian*, 2003c). Subsequently, Poland joined the EU on May 1, 2004.

But the controversy over the absence of any mention of either God or Christianity in the preamble continued, and in October 2003, Poland's bishops added another buchette to the fire by noting their "great concern" that the preamble omitted "any reference to conscience as a basic criterion of moral evaluation" (Associated Press Worldstream, 2003). Europe's leaders had set December 12 as the date on which they would sit down, under the chairmanship of Italian Prime Minister Silvio Berlusconi, to hammer out details still in dispute in the draft constitution, and Berlusconi promised the Pope that he would ask his fellow prime ministers to agree to add a reference to Christianity to the constitution. But Turkish Prime Minister Recep Tayyip Erdoğan declared his unmitigated opposition to any such idea. According to Erdoğan, "Freedom of conscience and a ban on all discrimination are the founding principles of modern Europe. If the concept of religion is included in the constitution, it would contradict those principles and centuries of progress on the continent" (as quoted in Agence France Presse, 2003c).

But the December 12 summit ended in fiasco – not because of any differences of opinion about the alleged benefits or damage entailed in including mentions of God and/or Christianity in the preamble, but because Germany and France wanted to revise a voting system which had been agreed in Nice in 2000, under which Poland and Spain, in spite of their smaller populations, were to receive almost as many votes as Germany and France. The latter two countries also wanted to introduce a system of "double majority voting" under which decisions would have to be supported by half of all member states having at least 60 percent of the population of the EU. When Poland and Spain refused to give up what the French and Germans characterized as an overgenerous allotment of votes, the summit collapsed. But by late March 2004, Spain had a new prime minister, who was prepared to give up the system established in Nice, and, with their Spanish partner talking compromise, the Poles too softened their line. Meanwhile, by April 2004, about ten of the projected twenty-five member states of the EU were supporting the inclusion of a reference to Christian values in the eventual EU constitution.

By June 2004, the EU constitution had been finalized. The preamble still reflected the original formulation (although the Greeks and the Romans had disappeared from the text, together with the French Revolution). God and Christianity had not been added to the text, but the embracing reference to religious traditions remained – a formulation which implied the inclusion not only of Christianity but also of Judaism,

Islam, and perhaps of other traditions as well. Poland's bishops were divided about whether the constitution should be accepted.

After Glemp

In March 2004, Cardinal Glemp retired as chair of the Conference of the Polish Episcopate, though retaining his title as 'Primate'; as already mentioned, the more clearly conservative Archbishop Michalik was elected to take over the duties of chair. Michalik is more sympathetic to the political message of Radio Maryja, including its EU-phobia, than either John Paul II or Primate Glemp, according to one informant, who sees Michalik as more of a maverick (Szostkiewicz, 2004). What this will mean for the polarization of Polish society remains to be seen. But, as of 2002, one could divide Poland's twenty-one bishops into four groups: there were only two "Euro-enthusiasts" (having no fear of the EU and seeing more opportunity than danger in EU membership), alongside six "Euro-skeptics" (fearing that Polish membership in the EU would, on the whole, prove to be negative for Catholicism in Poland), four "Euro-realists," and nine "Euro-neutrals" (who did not get engaged in the issue) (Leszczyńska, 2004: 270–71). Michalik, quite obviously, is a skeptic.

What needs to be stressed is that it is religion itself, or rather the Catholic Church, which constitutes the vector along which Poland is polarized. This is also reflected in the press, with, for example, *Nasz Dziennik*, a daily newspaper owned by Fr. Rydzyk, staking out a position on the far right, the Church's daily *Niedziela* and the secular weekly *Polityka* occupying a more moderate but still conservative niche, and *Gazeta Wyborcza*, a daily newspaper (circulation of 1.3 million) edited by Adam Michnik, striving for a centrist position and often publishing views from both left and right, side by side. There are also center-left and progressive publications such as *Nie*, edited by Jerzy Urban, *Trybuna*, a left-wing newspaper published in 70,000 copies, and *Bez dogmatu*, a weekly magazine founded and edited, 1993–2002, by Barbara Stanosz. *Bez dogmatu* has maintained a dignified posture, and has opened its pages to contributions by the aforementioned Robert Biedroń, among others (Stanosz, 2004; Biedroń, 2004). There are also several hard-left publications – *Lewa noga*, *Walka Trwa*, and *Nowa lewica* – and a sophisticated center-left weekly magazine called *Przegląd*; these hard-left publications have minimal influence, however, on either policy debates or public opinion. *Nie*, an irreverent weekly edited by Jerzy Urban, is a widely respected and influential periodical (with a circulation of 300,000), and then there is the anti-clerical weekly, *Fakty i mity*, owned and edited by ex-priest Roman Kotliński who, in 2002, launched the Reason Anticlerical Party and who has joined in gay rights events in order to declare his support for gay and lesbian marriage (Kotliński, 2004).

Yet, even though the foregoing account takes note of the presence of at least six distinct opinion groups in Poland, Poles themselves speak of "left" and "right," and tend to aggregate much – though not all, to be sure – into one or the other camp, friend or foe. For the Church, what is at stake is morality itself, and the Church sees itself as the protector of Natural Law, headed by the vicar of Christ (as the Pope is called). For the Church's critics, on the other hand, some of the Church's positions – most especially its opposition to the declaration of legal equality of women and men (see *HLI-EUROPA News*, 2004c) and its hostility to same-sex unions – are morally indefensible and, instead of focusing on the *primary principles* of Natural Law, which, according to St. Thomas Aquinas, are immutable, the Church is concentrating at least some of its efforts on defending certain *secondary principles*, which, in line with Aquinas's predictions (Aquinas, 2002: 120–28), are already in the process of change. And hence, too, as Jerzy Urban told me in June 2004, there are real concerns, among some, about "the very idea that Catholic teaching should be reflected and anchored in state structures and state law" (Urban, 2004).

Conclusion

In a brilliant survey of the politics of the Roman Catholic Church in Poland published in *Europe-Asia Studies* some years ago, Mirella Eberts notes that what the Church hoped to see realized in post-communist Poland was a state which would be "democratic in form, but Christian in content." The problem with this ideal, however, she argues, is that it is in the nature of pluralist democracy "that the content cannot be firmly predetermined in advance" (Eberts, 1998: 836, quoting from Gowin, 1995: 73). The result, Gowin suggests, has been that "antagonism toward democracy and a tendency to pit it against the natural law principle grew in Church circles" (Gowin, 1995: 73, as quoted in Eberts, 1998: 836). Eberts even suggests that "many, if not the majority, of the Church hierarchy hold an inter-war vision of a democratic Poland" (Eberts, 1998: 837), though, as already noted, it is not necessary to refer to historical examples to understand what the Church wants. At the same time, Tim Byrnes is surely correct in thinking that the Church in Poland sees the fight over abortion as a battleground on which its vision of what Poland should be and will, in part, be determined. Thus, when in 2000 the Vatican issued a controversial document, which seemed to backpedal on the ecumenically inspired recognition of Protestant organizations as "Churches," which had been extended at the Second Vatican Council, by asserting that Protestant denominations are not, in fact, Churches at all, but "ecclesial communities," Roman Catholic leaders in Poland gave their strong endorsement (Luxmoore, 2000: 1). The document – *Dominus Iesus, on the Unicity and Salvific Universality of Jesus Christ and the Church* – was aimed at those Catholic theologians who "have argued that all religions may be equally valid ways of salvation" (as quoted in Luxmoore, 2000: 1). The episcopal conference of Poland's 92,000-member Lutheran Church released a statement declaring, "This claim to exclusiveness on questions as fundamental as salvation evokes our deepest concern," while Orthodox Archbishop Jeremiasz, head of Poland's 570,000-member Orthodox Church, expressed his personal hope that *Dominus Iesus* would soon be "quietly forgotten," adding that "We have to learn to live in a Christian way without doing injustices to each other" (both as quoted in Luxmoore, 2000: 2). Archbishop Życiński replied to these critics, however, by suggesting that they subscribed to a

post-modernist mentality in which there is no center or single reference system, and where all interpretations are equally good. The Holy Father has reminded us through Cardinal Ratzinger that we are the Church of Jesus Christ, not a collection of private chapels. It is not that people can go to church and choose [what to believe] – there are certain fundamental truths which a Christian should know. (as quoted in Luxmoore, 2000: 1; insertion by Luxmoore)

This exclusivist mentality was reflected in the establishment by then-Prime Minister Cimoszewicz of an Inter-Ministerial Team for New Religious Movements in August 1997, which, in a report issued in June 2000, called on governmental agencies to train personnel in how to deal with the "religious sects." Complaints were registered by high-ranking figures in the Adventist Church, the Church of Evangelical Christians, and the Church of Christian Assemblies that their bodies and allegedly "all non-Catholic groups" were being "treated as sectarian and dangerous" by Catholic bishops and government officials (Luxmoore, 2001a: 1–2). But in early 2001, Krzysztof Wiktor, secretary of the aforementioned Inter-Ministerial Team, announced that his agency would shortly be replaced by a new Inter-Ministerial Team for Psycho-Manipulative Groups and would dedicate itself to combating "therapeutic, health and crypto-political groups which have nothing in common with religious associations" (Luxmoore, 2001a: 1). The very existence of this agency constitutes a demonstration of the fact that the Polish state has, at least to some extent, endeavored to accommodate the programmatic desiderata of the Catholic Church, ignoring the protests by members of minority religions that the agencies of the state consider it quite normal to engage themselves in the religious sphere. The Catholic Church also set up a network of anti-cult centers, operated by the Dominican Order (Kościanska, 2001).

In view of the firm opposition of the Church globally, and hence also in Poland, to gay and lesbian equality and its disinclination to see sex education in the schools, we may conclude that the Church remains a bastion of conservatism, at least where sex is concerned. Still, it is worth reminding ourselves that the Church in Poland is not homogeneous, and that there are liberal (i.e. cosmopolitan) tendencies in its ranks, such as Fr. Adam Boniecki, editor-in-chief of *Tygodnik Powszechny*. The late Fr. Józef Tischner, whose liberality and tolerance were legendary, urged, at one point, that "the Church should do a very heroic thing and start accepting the state, even if it is not exactly as the Church would like it to be" (as quoted in Eberts, 1998: 837). Indeed, there may be other roles for the Church to play, besides that of judge. The roles of prophet (where the Church may warn about the dangers of environmental destruction,[7] world overpopulation, and widespread poverty), of teacher (especially in popularizing Natural Law and tolerance in an age where moral relativism and even nihilism have indeed become widespread, with stubborn pockets of intolerance enduring both within the Church and outside it), and of moral guide (for example, in reminding its flock that the story of the Good Samaritan was not intended to apply only to persons from Samaria) are not only worthy roles for the Church, but, I would argue, are precisely where the Church can make an important contribution in the years to come.

Notes

This chapter reflects, in part, interviews conducted in Warsaw and Lublin June 20–July 7, 2004. I am grateful to the Department of Sociology and Political Science of the Norwegian University of Science and Technology (NTNU) for making my trip to Poland possible, to Prof. Krzysztof Koseła and Fr. Piotr Mazurkiewicz for translating some of the Polish materials cited herein, and to Prof. György Péteri for translating the Hungarian material cited in this chapter. I also wish to thank Professor Ola Listhaug for his support of this project, Beata Eggan, Professors Maryjane Osa and Andrzej Korboński, and Luba Fajfer for practical assistance, and Professor Krzysztof Koseła in Warsaw and Archbishop Józef Życiński in Lublin for taking it upon themselves to put me in touch with appropriate persons. This chapter was first presented at a regular meeting of the Program of East European Cultures and Societies at the Norwegian University of Science and Technology, Trondheim. I am grateful to Professor György Péteri and other participants in that event for their helpful comments. I am also grateful to the participants in the conference held at Colgate University about the same time for making some suggestions. I also wish to thank the editors of this volume,

Tim Byrnes and Peter Katzenstein, as well as the anonymous reviewers, for helpful feedback on both of my chapters for this volume.

1 Against this view, some critics may wish to assert that the "real" question is not whether the Church can stand aside when questions such as abortion come up, but whether the Church's engagement is "legitimate." While the latter question is not entirely irrelevant to this chapter and will, in fact, be taken up toward the end, to make assessments of the legitimacy of the Church's engagement in the political sphere the center of focus would shift the emphasis from a discussion of the Church's political engagement with the EU to public opinion as such.

2 The poll was conducted among 1,107 Poles and reported in Koseła (2003: 60).

3 The Church fears that heterogenic insemination, in which sperm are selected for certain desired traits, reduces human life to a commodity.

4 Raul Hilberg writes that 1 million Jews were killed at Auschwitz; Aharon Weiss writes that between 1.2 million and 2.5 million died there; and Yehuda Bauer writes that there were between 1.5 million and 3.5 million victims at Auschwitz. These estimates are reported by Karsai (2001: 116). I am indebted to Prof. György Péteri for hunting down this information for me. Higher estimates are also available. For example, William Carr, in the fourth edition of his *History of Germany*, writes that "The camp commandant at Auschwitz calculated in 1945 that two-and-a-half million Jews had been gassed there and a further half-million had died of hunger and illness, a total of three million Jews murdered coldly and scientifically." In addition, according to Guenter Lewy, some 20,000 Gypsies were also killed at Auschwitz. See Carr (1991: 334); and Lewy (2000: 166).

5 Switon was later given a six-month suspended sentence for slandering Jews and Germans and for calling Polish parliamentarians "national traitors."

6 The poll was conducted on October 11 and November 5, 2002 among 600 priests.

7 Indeed, the Roman Catholic Church, like the Evangelical Church of Germany and the Norwegian Church, and no doubt other religious bodies as well, has begun to alert people to the dangers of environmental deterioration and to the importance of environmental protection.

6 The way we were – and should be again? European Orthodox Churches and the "idyllic past"

Sabrina P. Ramet

Mainline Churches are, by nature, conservative. This is not so much because they are loath to change a successful formula, as because they are loath to change any formula, come what may. It is the essence of the great monotheistic religions (Christianity, Islam, Judaism) to experience difficulty in distinguishing between those formulae developed thousands of years ago which have lost whatever utility (if any) they may have had and such moral truths as are truly universal and everlasting. While most, if not all, religions embrace a range of opinion, from conservative to liberal (if not from ultra-conservative to left-liberal), the Orthodox Church is distinguished from other large religious organizations by the greater dominance of conservatives in its power structure and by the largely conservative orientation of even its "liberals." Orthodoxy, thus, is a religion which – to quote Shakespeare – "looks on tempests and is never shaken" – not even when it should be. Whatever changes may impact the world, the Orthodox Church refuses, for the most part, to accommodate itself to change, standing fixed in time, its bishops' gaze riveted on an "idyllic past" which serves as their beacon. For Orthodoxy, time stands still. Why is this? It would be nice to offer a simple, one-line answer. But I believe that the answer must be traced to several factors, among them: the fact that the Orthodox world did not experience either the Renaissance or the Enlightenment, thereby proceeding along an alternative intellectual trajectory in which Slavophilia, for example, derived its energy in part from the rejection of values which had gained currency in the West precisely as a result of these two epochs; the fact that urbanization came late to these areas and the lower educational attainment, until recently, of the population in the eastern stretches of Europe, so that the Church in the East has retained an authority which it has not enjoyed in the West for at least three-quarters of a century; the long communist rule in the areas to be discussed in this chapter, running through more than four decades when Western Europe was building (or in Britain, Switzerland, and Scandinavia, continuing) democratic institutions; and the fact that this long period of communist rule was experienced by all those Churches in communist countries, including the Orthodox Churches, as a period of siege, requiring cunning, a strong defensive posture, and a determination to survive. I am not persuaded, on the other hand, that it makes sense to talk about Orthodox Churches having been in a state of crisis throughout the two millennia of their existence; indeed, such a view of Orthodox history would require an enormous leap of faith.

None of the foregoing should be taken to suggest that Orthodox clergy do not bear any responsibility for their actions. At various points in time, Orthodox bishops faced crucial choices – such as the choice faced by Metropolitan Sergii in Soviet Russia in 1927, whether to accept the Soviet regime or to adopt a posture of defiance. But an elaborate rehearsal of such choices would be beyond the scope of this chapter and exceed its length limitations.

No institution – and that means also no Church – can be understood outside its historical context. In the case of the Orthodox Churches to be discussed here, that means that the four centuries of Ottoman rule, five centuries of tsarist rule (in Russia and Georgia), and more than four decades of communist rule (indeed, more than eight decades in the case of Russia and Georgia) inevitably shaped patterns of accommodation with state authorities, strategies of survival, and perhaps also tendencies to see denials of Church claims about morality in terms of profound ideological threat. In communist conditions, moreover, the possibility for dissent, even against established Churches, was limited – and, besides, there was less motivation for such dissent than there was in the West. Thus, in the Churches under communist rule, protests on behalf of gays and lesbians, women priests, and ecclesiastical democratization were absent, there was tangibly less interest in ecumenism – the Russian Orthodox and Bulgarian Orthodox Churches joined the World Council of Churches, for example, on orders from their respective governments in order to defend communist interests – and free-thinking clergy such as Romania's Fr. Gheorghe Calciu tended to concentrate their energies on resisting state penetration of their Churches rather than on trying to reform their Churches. The Churches in most of the communist world were persecuted, controlled, placed under surveillance, and obstructed in their publishing activity, and nationalism entered into the ecclesiastical discourse of the Russian, Bulgarian, Georgian, Romanian, and Serbian Orthodox Churches, the Roman Catholic Church in Poland, the Eastern-rite Catholic Church in Ukraine, and other ecclesiastical bodies. These differences were systematic and fundamental, and left those Orthodox Churches which lived under communism less disposed toward liberalization and habituated them to thinking in terms of threat and survival. It also habituated them to thinking back to the relatively more idyllic past which they had enjoyed before the communists had come to power.

In the present context, the historic transnationalism of the Orthodox Church, expressed through and manifested in the Church councils and conclaves, the contacts between the patriarchs, and the unity of doctrine, confronts a new and rising transnationalism – that of the EU. The draft constitution of the EU (presented to the public in 2003) expressed the confidence that the values of the Enlightenment are truly universal and that the institutions and legislation which enforce those values as standards have something approaching a transcendent validity. But from the Orthodox standpoint, the pressure emanating from the EU on Orthodox countries to compromise on questions considered matters of doctrine for the Orthodox Church, so that the laws of those countries might come into conformity with the allegedly universal standards of the EU, has turned the natural order on its head. From the Orthodox viewpoint, it is the EU, if anything, which should be adjusting its standards to those of the Orthodox Church!

In the pages which follow, I shall discuss the role of the notion of an idyllic past in the (European) Orthodox Church, examining that body's deeply ingrained homophobia, its inward-looking sacralization of the nation, its hostility toward liberalism and cosmopolitanism, and its consequent hostility toward both ecumenism and European unity. In this discussion, I shall draw upon the recent history of the Russian, Georgian, Romanian, and Serbian Orthodox Churches, with some reference also to the Bulgarian Orthodox Church. It should be kept in mind that although one may characterize a given Church with broad brush strokes, there is always some diversity within a given organization.

The "idyllic past" and the prospect of repristination

Romantic ruminations about a lost but retrievable "idyllic past" are associated with a rigid repudiation of the rotten present, seen as decadent, unholy, and impure. In Russia, for example, neo-Slavophiles associated with the Russian Orthodox Church point to declining birth rates, increasing rates of reported alcoholism, homosexuality, and Western influences and conclude, in fear, that the Russian nation is itself in decline. Their hopes, when they do not sink into despair, focus on repurification, revival, and regeneration, returning Russians to the more pristine state supposedly characteristic of Russia eons ago. In the same spirit, a report on the state of Serbian young people, commissioned by the Holy Synod of the Serbian Orthodox Church and published in 1996, traced the rising incidence of "drug addiction, alcoholism, criminality, superstition, pornography, sexual deviance, AIDS, the collapse of the family, the decline in the birth-rate, the crisis of national identity and the other evils and trials that have recently descended on the Serbs" to religious change – specifically to New Age religions. Against this impure world, the Orthodox Church preserves its purity, maintains its claim to embody the Heavenly Kingdom on earth, and fights against all those who would champion anything the Orthodox Church considers "impure."

But where is this "idyllic past" to be found? It is to be found, in the first place, in the mythology of Christianity itself. The story of Adam and Eve places them in the Garden of Eden, an idyll which they lost, according to myth, because of their sins; but, paradoxically, through the murder of the living God incarnate, a limited redemption was achieved – limited because it did not enable people to return to the Garden of Eden – at least not immediately – and because the collective absolution which it allegedly ensured did nothing to assure the individual salvation of one or another person, who still had to earn it on his or her own merits. This mythic Garden of Eden is, however, not the only "idyllic past" operative on the Orthodox mind. There is also the historic "idyllic past" in which two themes are blended. For the Russians and the Georgians, the mythic past is a blend of pre-schism Christianity, i.e. before the separation of Christianity into Eastern and Western Churches, and of pre-communist piety. For the Bulgarians, Romanians, and Serbs, the idyllic past is a compound of, likewise, pre-schism Christianity, and of pre-Ottoman self-government, recalled, especially in the cases of the Serbs and the Bulgarians, as a time of glory. The Serbs recall the rule of Tsar Dušan the Mighty in the fourteenth century as an age of power, while the Bulgarians recall how their medieval empire attacked and pillaged Constantinople.

But how does one get back to this "idyllic past," if that is even possible? For the Orthodox Church, the path lies through undeviating adherence to changeless strictures. But, in the case of the Serbs, at least, it is, allegedly, precisely because of their undefiled beliefs, their Orthodox religion, that the international community failed to understand the Serb nationalist point of view in the 1990s. For the Serbian Orthodox Church, as for its sister Churches, the transnational standards being promoted in the name of "Europeanization" represent "vice, vanity, and hypocrisy." Yet it is interesting to find the Orthodox condemning secular societies for "necrophilia," given the Orthodox cult of the dead. For the Orthodox Church, relics – such as the bones of fourteenth-century Tsar Lazar that were exhumed and paraded around Serbia on the 600th anniversary of the 1389 Battle of Kosovo or "the honorable foot of the holy and glorious Apostle Andrew the First-called" (Alexy II, n.d.), which "visited"

152   Orthodoxy

Moscow, Kiev, Minsk, and other cities more recently – are the objects of reverence and are thought to have healing powers which may properly be described as magical. Reverence for relics is not itself piety, but, for the Orthodox, it is considered a potent signifier of true piety. To show reverence for relics is to show that one is a pious person, a person trying to live morally in emulation of the person whose relics they are.

Liberals, cosmopolitans, and democrats

It is not only in Serbia that one finds sections of the Church allied with the extreme right. This phenomenon, which may also be found in Catholic countries,[1] is present in contemporary Bulgaria, where Fr. Georgi Gelemenov figures as the leading figure in the local skinhead movement, openly expressing his admiration for Nazism, in Romania, where fifteen Orthodox priests from Bihor county were reported (in 2001) to have joined the revived Iron Guard, with meetings of the fascistic Guard taking place in several Orthodox monasteries (*Evenimentul zilei*, 2001), and in Russia where there have been similar phenomena.

We may identify the liberal project with six core principles – the rule of law, individual rights, tolerance, the harm principle, equality, and the neutrality of the state in matters of religion (except insofar as one or another religious association poses a serious threat to individual rights, or egregiously violates the harm principle). That said, it is clear that liberalism cannot be reduced to mere "secular rationalism." Yet what is striking is that, at least in the cases being considered here, the Orthodox Church – like the Roman Catholic Church in Poland – is antagonistic toward or seeks seriously to qualify each of the six principles. The problems which the Orthodox Church has with most of these should be obvious by this point. But perhaps it may be helpful to say something about the rule of law and about the harm principle. Rule of law entails, among other things, the subordination of the Churches to the secular government. The Orthodox Churches, by characterizing the legalization of homosexuality as grievous sin, for example, set their own authority over that of the civil government. To the extent that a religious organization, whether the Muslim Brotherhood or the Judaic community or the Roman Catholic Church or the Orthodox Church, seeks to make the civil government the agent for the instrumentalization of its own specific moral agenda, dictating its doctrines in areas where there is controversy, that organization may be said to be displaying theocratic tendencies, which is to say, the aspiration to realize the Kingdom of God, as interpreted by the religious elite of the specific religious organization, on earth. It is the impossibility of creating harmony on the basis of a theocratic principle in a multiconfessional society which impelled Locke and Rawls alike, among others, to urge religious toleration and non-confessionality as the guiding principles of government. As for the harm principle, this principle holds that there is no right to harm any other person except in defense of life, limb, or property, and even then one may not inflict any greater harm than is necessary to make such defense effective. When it comes to respect for the harm principle, adherents of the Georgian Orthodox Church (to be discussed at some length in the next section) and the Serbian Orthodox Church are perhaps the most obvious offenders in the set being considered here.

The fact that each of the five Orthodox Churches being discussed here has sought, and to some extent or other achieved, privileged status for itself within the religious market, prioritizing the introduction of Orthodox religious instruction into the public schools, illustrates all too clearly that the episcopal establishment within the Orthodox Church is not yet prepared to live by the rules of liberal democracy and points to one of a number of reasons as to why that Church resists "Europeanization." The denunciation of J. K. Rowling's *Harry Potter* books by the Bulgarian and Russian Orthodox Churches in 2002 came as a bolt from the blue, though the nature of their objections fits the already established pattern of their thinking. Rowling's flights of fantasy, the Holy Synod of the Bulgarian Orthodox Church warned, diminished their readers' immunity to black magic and therefore constituted a kind of "spiritual AIDS" which left their readers "open to evil"; Fr. Stefan Stefanov, the parish priest at St. Nikolai Church in Russe, who first spoke out against *Harry Potter*, explained to Reuters that Rowling's books "make children believe that witchcraft is something innocent, existing only in literature, which is not the case" (RFE/RL, 2002). Shortly thereafter, the Russian Orthodox Church demanded that the *Harry Potter* novels be banned, arguing that they "promoted occultism and witchcraft" (*Ogam*, 2003).

To Western eyes, Harry Potter is a magical character for children and a commercial success. To Orthodox eyes, however, Harry Potter represents cosmopolitanism in its worst manifestation, the legitimation of witchcraft and black magic, Western cultural infiltration and ideological subversion, and a challenge to the Orthodox monopoly on how to understand magic and the supernatural. The repugnance which the Orthodox feel for Harry Potter is not unrelated to the more general Orthodox distrust of liberalism, cosmopolitanism, and even democracy. It is true, of course, that Orthodox Churches throughout the post-communist world have welcomed the fall of communism and that, in Serbia, Patriarch Pavle repeatedly called for Milošević to step down. But what the Orthodox Churches welcome in the new political reality are the chance to retrieve their former properties confiscated by the communists, the opportunity to build church facilities without having to overcome cumbersome and obstructive bureaucratic obstacles, the possibility to proselytize and distribute religious propaganda to the limit of their financial resources, the possibility for people to once more take an active part in the Church without negative repercussions for their careers, and the prospect of being able to dictate their moral agenda to the state, especially in the sexual sphere. The Orthodox Churches do *not* welcome the fact that neo-Protestant groups and various other religious groups which they call "sects" have also enjoyed new freedom, and, in at least some cases, look back with nostalgia to the days of monarchy. Even local advocates of democratization may sometimes look over their shoulders. Take, for example, the Belgrade magazine *Slovenski glasnik*, launched in early 1997 by an editorial board inspired by liberal-democratic ideals. In an editorial declaration of intent published in the first issue, the editors declared that, in their view, there was "no question of the value of maxims such as democracy, individual liberties, human rights and the rights of minorities"; in the next breath, however, they noted that "it was 'in recent years, the greatest world power' that [had] insisted most on these 'maxims', and that, under the excuse that it was defending democracy, was in fact carrying out 'global unification' and 'threatening the sovereignty of individual Slav countries' " (Čolović, 2002: 247).

A decadent world: Orthodox fear of contact with the impure

To the extent that one may identify the formula "live and let live" as axiomatic for liberal democracy, it is immediately apparent that this formula is problematic for the European Orthodox Churches discussed here. Universalism – the notion that all people enjoy equal rights and equal duties – and cosmopolitanism – the conviction that one owes one's loyalty to humankind more generally in the first place and to one's own nation only insofar as national loyalty does not harm the wider human community – "have acquired bad connotations among the Orthodox," being associated with "the destruction of patriotism" and the extirpation of "the last vestiges of the nations that still bear the name of Orthodoxy" (Moss, 1998). It is not that the Orthodox wish to deny the common humanity all people share; the fear of universalism and cosmopolitanism reflects, rather, the fear that what characterizes traditional Orthodox culture will be eroded by exposure to Western cultural artifacts and

Western thinking. Moreover, to the extent that the Orthodox way is the way of the pure and the just, anything which threatens that way comes to be seen as impure and dangerous. Insofar as the EU is championing a relaxation of strictures against homosexuality, it champions that which is impure – at least as far as the Orthodox Church sees it. Indeed, Fr. Aleksandr Men, one of the most liberal churchmen to come out of Russian Orthodoxy, warned in an interview given on September 5, 1990, just four days before he was murdered, about conservative currents within the Russian Orthodox Church.

Anti-ecumenism

Ecumenism is the ecclesiastical counterpart to EU integration and is a reliable measure of a Church's willingness to accept diversity of viewpoints. A Church which can accept engagement in the World Council of Churches only on its own terms, therefore, can be expected to insist that EU integration likewise be accepted only on its own terms. The Orthodox Church embraces both those interested in participating in the ecumenical movement (who probably constitute the majority among churchmen) and those opposed.[2] It is possible to recount a history of ecumenism in the Orthodox Church. In 1573, for example, a delegation of divines from the Lutheran Church in Tübingen initiated contact with the Ecumenical Patriarch, but the Patriarchate terminated the contact in 1581. Later, Patriarch Cyril Lucaris displayed an interest in Calvinism, but the Orthodox communion repudiated the Patriarch's ideas on this subject. In the eighteenth century, "non-juring" Anglicans took up correspondence with the Russian Orthodox Church and the Eastern patriarchs, but there were no results and contacts withered. Ecumenism is, however, above all a twentieth- (and twenty-first-) century phenomenon, and there has been a livelier ecumenical interest also in Orthodox circles since Patriarch Joachim III's 1902 encyclical calling for an Orthodox consensus on relations with Catholics, Old Catholics, and Protestants. The Pan-Orthodox conferences held during the interwar period and then again, after an interruption, beginning in the 1960s, the International Theological Dialogue between the Orthodox and Catholic Churches, and the Orthodox involvement in the World Council of Churches have all proven to be fruitful forums for ecumenical contacts. But that is only one side of the story.

The other side of the story is that much of Orthodoxy has been permeated by suspicion about ecumenism; why, after all, spend time with the adherents of schismatic or heretical Churches unless the point is to convert them to the true Church? In this spirit, a 1998 statement issued by the Moscow Patriarchate characterized the "ecumenists" as being motivated by their wish "to testify about Orthodoxy before the rest of the world" (Moscow Patriarchate, 1998). While such a motivation will scarcely provoke shock or outrage, what was not mentioned was any indication of interest in hearing the representatives of other Churches testify about their own faiths. In fact, even among Orthodox "liberals," if one may use this term here, the stress is on those features of other faiths which provoke Orthodox disapproval, such as Protestantism's alleged "relativism" (manifested in the so-called "branch theory" which holds that the various denominations may be seen as branches of a single Christian Church) and the alleged "resistance of Protestant Christians to the idea that there is one True Church," which Orthodox identify with their own Church, and the Catholic institution of the papacy, described by one Orthodox cleric as "a destructive innovation" (Gregory, n.d.: 1). Hence, even when Orthodox writers appear to concede that "there is a greater agreement between Rome and Orthodoxy ... than exists with Protestantism," this concession is immediately undermined by the declaration, to which probably all Orthodox clerics would subscribe, that "the main obstacle to ecumenism in the Roman camp is the papacy" (Gregory, n.d.: 1). Ecumenism, thus, has been problematic for both wings within the Orthodox communion because, insofar as the Orthodox Church claims to be the one and only true and divinely sanctioned Church, and views the Catholic Church as a corruption of the divinely established Church and all other Christian organizations as sects having no claim to divinity, it is ill-prepared for the kind of give-and-take which is expected in such ecumenical bodies as the World Council of Churches.

The World Council of Churches (WCC) was established in 1948 by Protestant Churches; over time various Orthodox Churches joined, though the Catholic Church has kept its distance down to today. The WCC slid into deep crisis in the course of 1997–98, when the Georgian and Bulgarian Orthodox Churches decided to terminate their association with that body. But the roots of the crisis go back further in time, and reflect growing differences between the more liberal Protestant groups which have dominated the 342-Church member organization (as of 2001) and the more conservative evangelicals and Orthodox, who have been upset about the Council's debates concerning the ordination of women, gender-inclusive language in biblical translations, same-sex unions, the ordination of homosexuals, and abortion. Already at the WCC's 1991 assembly at Canberra, Australia, Orthodox clerics threatened to abandon the organization unless there was a return to more biblically rooted ethics. By March 1992, five Orthodox Churches of North America had discontinued their membership in the National

Council of Churches in America, though four eastern Churches in North America remained members. Then, in early 1997, Archimandrite Lazar Abashidze of the Georgian Orthodox Church (which had joined the WCC in 1962) published a forty-page booklet condemning ecumenism. This proved to be only the first salvo in an intra-ecclesiastical battle in Georgia. The St. Shio-Mghvime Monastery, a center of anti-ecumenical sentiment, pressed the Patriarch to abandon his ecumenical activity and issued an open letter on 14/27 April 1997, demanding the withdrawal of the Georgian Church from the WCC, the severing of communion with any and all Orthodox Churches which remained affiliated with the WCC, and the promulgation of a formal anathema against ecumenism (Ecumenism in Georgia, n.d.). Within weeks, the Lavra of St. David Garedze, the Betania Monastery, the Monastery of Zarzma, and the monastics and parish clergy of the Shemokmedi diocese echoed the call for disassociation from the ecumenical movement. In the event that the Church would not withdraw from the WCC, at least some of these units threatened schism; indeed, Archimandrite Georgi, Father Superior of the St. Shio-Mghvime Monastery, announced that his monastery no longer considered itself in communion with Patriarch Ilia II because of his endorsement of the "ecumenical heresy" (RFE/RL, 1997: 1). The Georgian hierarchs caved in to the pressure, and, at a hastily convened synod on May 20, announced that they would be pulling their Church out of both the WCC and the Conference of European Churches. On the same occasion, however, the hierarchs announced the suspension of the rebellious clergymen from their positions and a ban on protesting laymen from receiving holy communion.

A year later, the Bulgarian Orthodox Church, under pressure from the ultra-conservative Old Calendarist Church, followed in the footsteps of its Georgian sister Church, sending shockwaves through the WCC. The decision was taken in April 1998, and on July 22, the Holy Synod of the Bulgarian Orthodox Church confirmed the decision. In addition to the aforementioned concerns, Orthodox hierarchs were, by this point, up in arms over their lack of weight in the organization (constituting just twenty member-Churches after the withdrawal of the Georgian and Bulgarian Churches) and were beginning to agitate for an abandonment of the principle of decisions by majority vote, which they dismissed as an "Anglo-Saxon" conceit (*Christian Century*, 1998a, 2000b; Zolotov and Brown, 1998: 2). Archbishop Anastasios of Tirana (Albania), offered the observation that "the New Testament was not written by majority vote. It is the work of the Holy Spirit" (quoted in Doogue, 2001: 2–3). As the polarization deepened, the Serbian Orthodox Church considered following the Georgian and Bulgarian Churches out of the WCC, eventually

deciding to remain in the organization, and the Greek and Polish
Orthodox Churches also opened a discussion of the question, but eventually rejected the anti-ecumenists as "fanatics . . . motivated by particular
interests" who "are not representative of Orthodoxy" (Archbishop
Jeremiasz of Wrocław-Szczecin of the Polish Orthodox Church, as
quoted in *Christian Century*, 1998a). The Russian Orthodox Church,
riven into more and less ecumenically inclined factions, was also affected
by the growing controversy and threw the WCC into virtual panic when it
announced that it too was considering withdrawing from the organization; in mid-December 1998, on the occasion of the WCC Eighth
Assembly, held in Harare, Zimbabwe, just hours after the WCC had
appointed a special commission to address Orthodox concerns, the
Russian Orthodox delegation announced that it was suspending its involvement in the WCC Central Committee until the commission had completed its deliberations. The strength of anti-WCC sentiment prevailing
in Russia was displayed on the occasion of a visit by Konrad Raiser,
General Secretary of the Council, to the Moscow Theological Academy
and Seminary the previous winter when, at the end of his talk, Raiser was
shouted down as a "heretic" and "accused of never having read the Bible
and of heading an organization that promotes homosexuality" (*Christian
Century*, 1998b: 2).

   As the special commission, composed of thirty representatives from
Orthodox Churches and thirty representatives from non-Orthodox
Churches, began its work, Vladimir Shmaliy of the Russian Orthodox
Church issued a warning that "any move to develop a homosexual
agenda would severely jeopardize Orthodox participation in the WCC,"
and endeavored, without success, to bar the commission from even
discussing sexuality (quoted in World Council of Churches, 1999).
After three-and-a-half years, the commission finished its work,
presenting its report to the WCC Central Committee, which approved
the report in early September 2002. Instead of settling the dispute, however, the report only inflamed it. The report brought about three changes
in the operations of the World Council. First, the Council abandoned the
principle of majority vote, replacing it with a consensus process – in effect
adopting a veto system; this decision provided a guarantee that the WCC
would henceforth be unable to take any courageous decisions. Second,
alongside "member Churches," the Council has now introduced a new
category of "associated Churches," which will cooperate only in an
advisory capacity and which will not be committed by any decisions
taken by the WCC. Third, the Council agreed to abandon "joint services
of worship," since the Orthodox Church rejected the notion that a service
lacking a celebration of the Eucharist could be characterized as

"worship"; instead, the WCC will henceforth hold "confessional" and "inter-confessional" *prayers* (*EKD Bulletin*, 2002). Inevitably, some delegates viewed this decision as a capitulation to the Orthodox Churches; for example, Margot Käßmann, the Lutheran Bishop of Hanover, criticized the report and its acceptance in sharp tones and, in protest, resigned as the German delegate in the Central Committee after nearly twenty years of work in the Council. Orthodoxy, by contrast, has been pleased with the result; Archbishop Christodoulos of the Greek Orthodox Church, for example, told a Symposium on Orthodox Theology and Ecumenical Dialogue at Thessaloniki in July 2003 that the chances that the Greek Church would leave the WCC were fading. Moreover, in the wake of these concessions, the WCC sent an appeal to the Bulgarian and Georgian Churches to resume membership in the body.

This outcome notwithstanding, the Russian Orthodox Church had been displaying a clearly defined anti-ecumenical hubris in the years that the commission was at work: already in 2000, Metropolitan Filaret of Minsk and Slutzk demanded that the World Council of Churches change its name, since most of the member organizations could not qualify, in his view, as "Churches" (he may have had in mind that the organization should call itself "the World Council of Sects") (*Christian Century*, 2000a). Then, the following year, the Moscow Patriarchate rejected the *Charta Oecumenica*, drawn up on the basis of cooperation of more than 120 Protestant, Anglican, and Orthodox Churches, as well as the Catholic Church, because of its affirmation that all the Christian Churches were "branches" of a single Church. And finally, in April 2001, Metropolitan Kirill of Smolensk and Kaliningrad, who heads the Moscow Patriarchate's department for external relations, called on Western Churches to "reform" their calendars and to celebrate Easter according to the Orthodox calendar (which is to say, according to the obsolete Julian calendar, rather than the standard Gregorian calendar in use in Russia itself as well as elsewhere in the world) (Zolotov, 2001).[3]

Turning the other cheek

The Orthodox attitude toward ecumenism – viewing it, at most, as an opportunity to promote Orthodox faith among non-Orthodox Christians, and at worst, as a risk of exposure to impure and heretical notions – is also reflected in its attitude toward other Christian organizations. As one Orthodox clergyman put it in 1999, "Orthodoxy is maximalist – everything matters" (Moses, 1999). Because of this, it is the *other side* – the non-Orthodox – which is expected by Orthodox clergy to turn the other cheek. While the Orthodox Church has considered itself completely authorized to establish dioceses and parishes in Protestant Berlin, in Catholic Paris, in Protestant and Catholic America, and even in Shinto-Buddhist Japan, it has resented and resisted efforts by non-Orthodox ecclesiastical organizations to establish organizational structures in traditionally Orthodox areas. The repudiation of the principle of reciprocity is grounded in the Orthodox conviction that only the Orthodox faith counts as worthy in the eyes of God. Nor do appeals to reason carry much truck, since Orthodox prelates prefer to refer the moral questions of the day to the Scriptures, rather than consider arguments outside that framework. Hence, for example, when, in February 2002, Pope John Paul II announced his decision to upgrade four "apostolic administrations" in Russia to the rank of dioceses – a decision having no significance in terms of proselytization but reflecting, at the most, an expectation that the 1.3 million Catholics living in Russia (many of them of German, Polish, or Baltic descent) could expect to continue to practice their faith unmolested – the Holy Synod of the Russian Orthodox Church chose to interpret this to mean that "the Roman Catholic Church is ... seeking to have as its congregation the Russian people, which culturally, spiritually and historically is the congregation of the Russian Orthodox Church" (*Monitor*, 2002).[4] Russian Orthodox Church leaders joined prominent MPs in calling for anti-Catholic demonstrations across Russia to defend Russia's spiritual values, while Bishop Jerzy Mazur, an ethnically Polish prelate heading the Catholic diocese of Siberia, was stripped of his visa in April 2002 and declared *persona non grata*, in reprisal for the Pope's decision. Already in 1992, Metropolitan Ioann of St. Petersburg and Ladoga had sent an open letter to the mayor of St. Petersburg, objecting to the "throngs of upstart preachers falsely calling themselves Christians [who] have poured into our country, Holy Rus'," and warning that they brought only "religious refuse" and "moral degeneration."[5] To combat their fellow Christians, Russian Orthodox bishops initiated a patriotic education program with the Ministry of Defense in 1997, with the goal of reviving "the Orthodox traditions of the Russian army and navy," have pressed for the introduction of a class on "The Foundations of Orthodox Culture" in state schools, and have insisted that Orthodoxy be accorded a special place under Russian law. Interestingly enough, opinion poll data suggest that ordinary Russians are significantly more tolerant of non-Orthodox religions than are the Orthodox prelates (Filatov, 1995).

Religious intolerance is also rife in Serbia, where Serbian Orthodox Bishop Filaret has earned a particular reputation for religious chauvinism and, among political parties, apparently only the Social Democratic Union has spoken out against the widespread anti-evangelical violence, issuing a statement in April 2001 accusing members of the Socialist Party of Serbia of spreading religious intolerance. The religious intolerance of the Serbian Church has its counterpart in national intolerance, manifested not only in the Church's well-known endorsement of the program of Serbian expansionism being promoted on the battlefield during 1991–95, but also in that Church's broad support for the radical Serbian Democratic Party (SDS) in the Serbian Republic (*Republika Srpska*) in Bosnia-Herzegovina.

The same pattern of intolerance may be found in Romania where, in 1994, the Orthodox Church declared itself the "National Church" of Romania – a move lacking legal status but provocative in its effect. In fact, the Romanian Orthodox Church has fought to obtain establishment as the state religion and to block the return of property seized from the Greek-rite Catholic Church after World War Two to that Church, and succeeded in obtaining the introduction of religious education in state elementary and high schools (compulsory in the elementary schools, optional in the secondary schools) (Stan and Turcescu, 2000: 1477–79, 1482–85). Archbishop Anania of the Romanian Orthodox Church even suggested, in 1998, that all members of the Holy Synod be granted seats *ipso facto* as senators (Stan and Turcescu, 2000: 1476–77). There have been fist-fights between Greek-rite Catholics and adherents of the Romanian Orthodox Church over property disputes, because of the failure of the state to produce definitive rulings and because of the Bucharest Patriarchate's stubborn rejection of Catholic pleas for restitution (for details, see Ramet, 2003).

According to John Anderson, the Bulgarian Orthodox Church has been less insistent on obtaining special legal status than the Greek and Russian Orthodox Churches (Anderson, 2003: 96). This is probably due, in the first place, to the internal dispute which briefly divided that Church into two rival bodies, each swearing allegiance to its own patriarch (for details, see Ramet, 1998: 283–85). Organized immediately after the change of leadership at the end of 1989, the Committee for the Defense of National Interests and its weekly newspaper, *Zora*, have fought notions of multiculturalism and cosmopolitanism tooth and nail, and "have also been active in an effort to suppress or sharply limit the activities of evangelical Christian sects that have gained a foothold in the country since 1989" (Bell, 1999: 247). By the mid-1990s, religious intolerance was starting to move into the mainstream, as Bulgaria witnessed the outbreak "of an often virulent and generally misinformed wave of media attacks on 'non-traditional' religions ... an assault often joined by politicians of a nationalist persuasion" (Anderson, 2003: 99).

But it is in the post-Soviet Republic of Georgia that some of the most noxious forms of religious intolerance have been seen. Under the constitution, the Georgian Orthodox Church's "special role" in history is recognized, though the constitution is silent about what this should mean in practice. The Georgian Orthodox Church has, in fact, lobbied the Parliament and the government for the passage of laws which would enshrine the Church as the official Church of Georgia and restrict the activities of "non-traditional" religions. The Georgian Church scored a victory of sorts when, in February 2001, the Supreme Court of Georgia ruled that, in the absence of a law on religion, it was not possible for the Jehovah's Witnesses to be registered; the Court did not extend this conclusion to other religious bodies such as, for example, the Georgian Orthodox Church itself. The Georgian Orthodox Church has also managed to exert influence on the educational curriculum in the republic (Tchkuaseli, 2001).

Organized violence against the clergy and members of non-Orthodox Christian denominations can be traced back to the Georgian Orthodox Church's active lobbying during 1998–99 for a government ban on such groups altogether. The first mob assault on non-Orthodox believers took place on October 17, 1999 in Tbilisi. Between then and July 2003, non-Orthodox Christians were targeted in more than 100 violent attacks, involving principally Jehovah's Witnesses, Pentecostalists, Baptists, and adherents of the Assembly of God (Corley, 2003). In spite of this, the government did not make any credible efforts to investigate or prosecute the offenders. Most of the initial attacks were organized by Vasili Mkalavishvili, a defrocked Orthodox priest, whose followers attacked Jehovah's Witnesses at worship on April 30, 2001 with sticks spiked with nails (*Georgian Mobs*, 2001). Mkalavishvili's group has also been held responsible for the distribution of hate-mongering leaflets.

Mkalavishvili and his supporters have enjoyed wide-ranging impunity. Even when they were put on trial, in 2000, after an attack which had left at least sixteen Jehovah's Witnesses injured, some of them seriously, the court brought only charges of the destruction of property against the defrocked priest's band, while prosecuting two of the victims on charges of hooliganism. During the trial itself, Mkalavishvili's followers assaulted a number of persons attending the trial, including human rights activists, Jehovah's Witnesses, and even one journalist, beating up Giga Bokeria and Kote Vardzelashvili, representatives of Liberty Institute, a Georgian human rights organization. Ultimately, the court cleared Mkalavishvili's people of all charges, but convicted the two accused Jehovah's Witnesses of hooliganism.

During 2000–01, anti-Orthodox violence escalated and, at this writing, shows no signs of subsiding; indeed, Mkalavishvili no longer has the monopoly on such violence. Orthodox clergy in good standing have taken part in some attacks,[6] with one Orthodox priest on horseback leading a charge – Cossack-style – against a Jehovah's Witnesses prayer meeting in Sachkhere in March 2001. Other groups have also been affected. In February 2002, for example, an Orthodox mob looted the premises of the Baptist church in Kaspi (35 km. northwest of Tbilisi), burning hundreds of Bibles and other religious books. To be sure, Archbishop Garmelia, chief of the Orthodox Church's Department of External Affairs, has condemned the physical attacks on non-traditional denominations, but he has also characterized the Witnesses as "totalitarian" – terminology which suggests that legal prosecution should be, in his view, the only suitable course of action. In fact, the Georgian Orthodox Church has recently pressed for legislation to divide religious organizations into three groups: the Georgian Orthodox Church would, under this scheme, be the single member of the privileged first category; Catholicism, Judaism, Islam, and the Armenian Apostolic Church would enjoy broad toleration within the category of "other traditional faiths"; and all other faiths would enjoy strict regulation at best, if not outright proscription.

Orthodoxy's war with the EU

The same fear of spiritual pollution which inspires conservative Orthodox concerns about participation in the World Council of Churches also underlies the engagement of the Orthodox hierarchy from across the Orthodox world in a battle against the liberalism enshrined in the European Union's new constitution and the insistence on the incorporation of an explicit acknowledgment of God's presence into this secular-political document.

The Presidium of the Convention on the Future of Europe, chaired by Valery Giscard d'Estaing, began work drafting the constitution in March 2002, being tasked to complete its work by April 2003; almost immediately after the convention began its work, tensions started to escalate between the Orthodox Churches and the EU. Aware of the EU's insistence on certain minimal standards in legislation, the Russian Church issued a statement on October 7 of that year, holding that the EU's "eastward expansion should not be about the imposition of Western culture and lifestyle on the rest of Europe" and urging that the "[c]ultural and spiritual diversity of European regions can be preserved through the division of powers between Union, national, and regional authorities." In particular, the statement stressed the Moscow Patriarchate's demand that each member state be able to legislate, with full autonomy, in education, family life, and ethics (*Eurasian News*, 2002: 1–2).

The Patriarchate tipped its hand by equating gay marriage with pornography, prostitution, and drug abuse as all equally "unacceptable" to Orthodox Christianity (*Eurasian News*, 2002: 2) – an equation which reveals as clearly as anything the Orthodox Church's complete opposition to the liberal project, to feminism (which condemns pornography and prostitution, but not gay marriage), and even to Christian traditions of tolerance embedded in the New Testament.

In February 2002, the first sixteen articles of the draft constitution were published, and soon after, major European Churches sent responses to the drafters. In a letter addressed to Giscard d'Estaing, Metropolitan Kirill of Smolensk and Kaliningrad objected to the constitutional Charter's guarantee that religion was the "private affair of an individual" and expressed his "real anxiety" concerning "[t]he danger of absolute dictatorship of an ideology guided only by the earthly well-being of people, their material prosperity and free self-realization in activities of this world without any system of moral values" (*Russian Orthodox Church News*, 2003: 2). In fact, in the next breath, Metropolitan Kirill conceded that liberalism *did* offer a program of moral values, that these values include "human dignity, freedom, supremacy of law, tolerance, justice and solidarity," and that such values, established in the constitutional Charter, "are not alien to Christian morals." But he also insisted that, unless they were associated with an explicit recognition of the primacy of Christian values in Europe, these values could be, as they had been in the past – according to the Metropolitan – "exploited to establish tyranny, to manipulate human consciousness, to justify various vices, etc." (*Russian Orthodox Church News*, 2003: 3). In view of this, Metropolitan Kirill urged that the constitutional Charter also contain a reference to the Christian heritage of the European lands, a provision for consultations between the European institutions and the Churches of the EU so that ecclesiastical viewpoints could be taken into account as future policy decisions are taken, and a provision guaranteeing the right of the governments of the member states to regulate their own religious spheres with an eye to preserving their cultural and religious identities (i.e. the right of governments to restrict the activity of religious organizations of whose activity they did not approve) (*Russian Orthodox Church News*, 2003: 3–4). These demands reflected a broad Orthodox consensus that the secular state is "unacceptable" and that only a state or union in which the religious principle is connected with the political principle, i.e. in which there is no clear separation of Church and state, may be considered legitimate.

On 18–19 March 2003, an inter-Orthodox conference was held in Heraklion, Crete, to review the constitutional Charter and to formulate recommendations for its revision. Chaired by His Holiness Bartholomew, Patriarch of Constantinople, the conference drew attention to the Church's interest in seeing governments develop "criteria of classifying the destructive or criminal organisations which pretend to be religious in the same category with recognised Churches" (*Novosti*, 2003: 1). By the close of the conference, the participants had reached an agreement on six points, recommending to the EU that the constitutional Charter incorporate Christian values, recognize the principles of "Christian, Biblical, Greek and Roman ancient heritage," protect not only the individual rights of people but also their collective rights, ensure "the right of all the traditional European Churches and religions" (presumably to advance their social agendas through government legislation), include provisions for the regulation of relations between Church and state, and "set clearly specified criteria that would stipulate a clear attitude toward sects and proselytism" (*Novosti*, 2003: 1–2). But churchmen did not remain calm, and tempers flared. In June 2003, for example, Archbishop Christodoulos blasted the EU for its omission of a reference to God or the Christian heritage in the draft constitution and complained that those who had drafted the Charter were "*expelling* Christianity from the constitution of the European Union."[7] Along similar lines, the Russian Orthodox Church issued a statement, about the same time, complaining that a reference, in the Charter, to the influence of Enlightenment philosophy in shaping European civilization was "evidence of the ideological bias of the draft" and insisting that "those ideas ... are not universal or generally accepted" (Interfax, 2003). Metropolitan Kirill had offered a fuller statement of the Orthodox view of the liberal tradition in an article for *Ecumenical Review*, published in 2001. In that context, the Metropolitan asserted that, in his view, "the liberal concept, quite alien as it is to the notion of sins includes the idea of the emancipation of human beings as they are, which actually means the release of the potential of sin in the human person. Free people, this asserts, have the right to discard everything that bind[s] them and prevent[s] them from asserting their sinful ego[s] ... [T]he liberal idea stands diametrically opposed to Christianity" (Kirill, 2001: 3). If one took this declaration of war at face value, it would appear that at least some highly placed Orthodox clergymen want nothing to do with individual rights and duties, with tolerance, with the principle that it is wrong to harm other people except to the extent and degree necessary to protect oneself or another, with the notion of human equality, or even, perhaps, with the rule of law (see Ramet, 2001a: 46–67). One might also conclude, if one wanted to give the Metropolitan credit for having read Kant, that he objected to the German philosopher's insistence that people act only in accord with principles which could serve as universal law (Kant, 1991) – a notion which does not have any obvious point of conflict with Christian ethics. But, in fact, at least some of the Orthodox polemical rhetoric against liberalism takes aim not at the ideas associated with the classics of liberalism (Locke, Kant, Mill, Rawls) or even at liberalism as it is understood by its practitioners in the West today, but at an amalgam of select features associated with the liberal project (tolerance of homosexuality, neutrality of the state in matters of religion), pathological symptoms of social decay (pornography, drug abuse), and an assortment of groups of whom it disapproves (Jehovah's Witnesses, prostitutes, and advocates of globalization). In other words, one of the reasons for the ferocity of Orthodox attacks on what some of its spokespersons identify with the liberal tradition is precisely the fact that what they are attacking is a bastardized version of liberalism; it is a picture containing features which *at least some* liberals themselves identify as problems (drug abuse, pornography) and which are, at any rate, not part of the liberal legacy, while leaving out some of the most essential elements in the liberal tradition (individual rights and duties, tolerance, respect for the harm principle). It is true, of course, that there is no common ground between the liberal plea for tolerance in the religious sphere and the Orthodox aspiration to see the theocratic principle anchored in the political systems of the states in which Orthodoxy is dominant, but there is nothing to be gained from the pretense that liberalism is somehow a philosophy of pornography and drug abuse, or from ignoring its essential affirmation of universalist ethics.

Fear of the "other": the battle about sexuality

In 1994, the American Psychological Association issued a statement on homosexuality, summarizing global scientific research into the subject. According to this statement:

[t]he research on homosexuality is very clear. Homosexuality is neither mental illness nor moral depravity. It is simply the way a minority of our population expresses human love and sexuality. Study after study documents the mental health of gay men and lesbians. Studies of judgment, stability, reliability, and social and vocational adaptiveness all show that gay men and lesbians function every bit as well as heterosexuals. (*American Psychological*, 1994)

The Orthodox Church has held to an entirely different view of homosexuality, however, emphasizing (in a 1984 statement of its position) that homosexuality should be interpreted in terms of "moral failure" and claiming that it "interferes with the normal development of societal patterns and as such it proves detrimental to all." But this consequenti-alist appeal is not where the Church wishes to place its emphasis. Rather, the Church "condemns unreservedly all expressions of personal sexual experience" which do not serve the "unalterable function ascribed to sex by God's ordinance – the procreation of the human kind" (*The Word*, 1984). It follows, for the Church, that "any and all uses of the human sex organs for purposes other than those ordained by creation, run contrary to the nature of things as decreed by God." And finally: "No one has the right to do whatever he wishes with his body" (*The Word*, 1984). For the Orthodox Church, homosexuality is a perversion and a mental disorder, and homosexuals should be referred to psychiatric care. That summary remains valid for the dominant voices in the Russian, Bulgarian, Georgian, Greek, Romanian, and Serbian Orthodox Churches, where Christian love is made conditional on unquestioning conformity to the rules of the Church.

For the Orthodox Church, ecumenism, so-called "Europeanization" (i.e. the establishment of EU standards in legislation), and tolerance of homosexuality are organically interrelated. Taken together, they embody the threat of "post-modernism," even the battlefront on which "purity" must be defended.

The embattled Romanian Orthodox Church

Homosexuality has become especially controversial in Romania, where the practice became illegal in 1936, during an era of growing fascicization of Romanian society. Three decades later – in 1968 – the communist dictator Nicolae Ceaușescu revamped the anti-gay legislation under Article 200, dropping the qualification about public scandal and raising the penalty to one to five years in prison. In 1993, four years after Ceaușescu's fall from power, Romania was admitted to the Council of Europe on condition that it change eleven of its laws, to conform with European standards. The only change required by the Council to pro-voke controversy was the requirement that Romania decriminalize homo-sexuality. Immediately there were protests and expressions of fear for the future of Romanian culture. At the forefront of the campaign to defy the Council of Europe and retain the anti-gay legislation was the Romanian Orthodox Church, which had been promoting religious, ethnic, and sexual intolerance for decades (see Ramet, 1998: ch. 7). Already in the 1930s, hundreds of Orthodox priests had joined the fascistic Legion of the Archangel Michael (later called the Iron Guard). According to *Monitorul*, a daily newspaper, a document uncovered by historian Dobrincu proves that the current Patriarch Teoctist was among those joining the Iron Guard at that time; allegedly, as a young man, Teoctist even took part in the burning of a Jewish synagogue in Iași (*Monitorul*, 2001: 6).[8]

Be that as it may, the prospective decriminalization of homosexuality became the driving inspiration for the Romanian Orthodox Church's political engagement in the first decade after communism – not corruption, not human rights, not organized crime, not the widespread poverty in Romania, certainly not democratization, but the Church's fear, as Archbishop Ana put it in 1998, that the Council's demand that homosexuality be decriminalized constituted a direct threat to the moral purity of the Orthodox way (*Evenimentul zilei*, 1998, as cited in Stan and Turcescu, 2000: 1480). In choosing to fight on this issue, the Church could count on sympathy among a large number of Romanians. A 1995 poll found, for example, that 53 percent of respondents felt that gays and lesbians "should not be accepted" in society (Barscy, 1999: 3). Another poll, taken in 2000, found that 86 percent of respondents did not want to live next door to a gay or lesbian (BBC News, 2001: 2). Orthodox student organizations and other student groups rallied to the Church, and in 1994, more than 100 theology students began to stage anti-gay demonstrations in front of the Parliament building and to collect signatures on a petition demanding that there be no liberalization for lesbians and gays or, at a minimum, that lesbians and gays be prevented from operating bars or publishing magazines. Under pressure from both sides and fearing that they would lose their seats in Parliament if they conceded too much, the legislators tried to have it both ways by eliminating the general ban on same-sex relations while restoring the clause concerning public scandal, thereby allowing the jailing and harassment of gays and lesbians to continue.

The Council of Europe was not favorably impressed by the revised legislation and noted that the pressure on gays and lesbians in Romania had not eased. Indeed, it remained impossible even to stage a gay theater performance. In 1998, then-President Emil Constantinescu met with Scott Long of the International Gay and Lesbian Human Rights Committee in Public Scandals and Jeri Laber of Human Rights Watch and promised to pardon all those incarcerated under Article 200 and to give priority to the repeal of the discriminatory Article. By this point, the Romanian government had been advised that it would be accepted into the European Union – but only if it abolished the legal discrimination against lesbians and gays. Accordingly, a year later, the Chamber of Deputies voted 180 to 14, with 40 abstentions, to repeal the controversial Article, and the measure went forward to the Senate. The Romanian Orthodox Church summoned the Holy Synod, as the assembly of its hierarchs is called, to an emergency meeting in September 2000, on the eve of the Senate's vote, and once more reiterated its view that homosexuality is a sin and that it should therefore remain illegal in Romania. Interestingly enough, while the Church emphasized that gays and lesbians should be denied any public forum in which to defend their position, Archbishop Nifon insisted on the Church's right to condemn sin.

On September 13, 2000, Patriarch Teoctist sent a letter to the Romanian Parliament, in the name of the Holy Synod, asking the Senators "not to pass laws in contradiction with the Christian morals [as interpreted by the Orthodox Church], with the natural law, as well as with the dignity and vocation of the family," and insisting that the stress by the European Parliament that the repeal of Article 200 was a condition for Romania's entry into European structures should not be taken seriously. "We are sure," the letter argued, "that in spite of all appearances, the European structures will receive us, in their bosom, with our specific features, with our Christian traditional identity. We also think that a dialogue and a richness of spiritual values [are] desired, not a unity artificially imposed" ("Church against Homosexuality," 2000). In spite of the Church's continued opposition, Article 200 was finally repealed and in November 2001, Bucharest saw the opening of the country's first gay nightclub.

The Russian Orthodox Church and homosexuality

Like their Romanian counterparts, the bishops of the Russian Orthodox Church have felt that there can be no room for same-sex relations. Thus, on August 15, 2000, the Russian Orthodox Church issued a formal statement condemning homosexuality, alongside transsexual operations, artificial insemination, drug addiction, euthanasia, and abortion. Where homosexuality is concerned, the statement declared that "people advocating homosexual practices should not be allowed to carry out teaching or educational work with children or young people or take positions of authority in the army or in penitentiary institutions" (quoted in ReligiousTolerance.org, 2001).

Where homosexuality is concerned, the Russian Orthodox Church has been drawn into battle not on the home front so much as at the World Council of Churches (WCC). There, in the course of its 1999 meeting at Harare, Zimbabwe, the WCC authorized a study of sexual diversity, as a first step toward accepting the legitimacy of same-sex relations. The Russian Church petitioned the WCC to drop all discussion and, when it failed in that petition, threatened to resign its membership in the ecumenical body.

Gay Pride and Orthodox morality in Serbia

In June 2001, Serbia's nearly invisible gay community bravely set out for what they hoped would be the country's first Gay Pride march. The march never took place. As the small group of gay Serbs assembled at Belgrade's central square, two groups of skinheads – with Fr. Žarko Gavrilović, a retired Serbian Orthodox priest, at the head of one of them – attacked the gays, beating them up. The mob, which swelled to more than 1,000 persons, carried posters which read "Orthodox for a Morally Clean Serbia" and "No to Immoral Homosexuality and Depraved Orgies," and chanted "Serbia is for Serbians, not for homosexuals!" (Simo, 2001: 1–2). Boško Buha, Belgrade police chief, whose police watched while the skinheads injured dozens of people, explained that Serbia is "not mature enough to accept such demonstrations of perversity" (quoted in Simo, 2001: 1–2).

Later that year, the Serbian Orthodox Church organized its own event. With the right-wing St. Justin the Philosopher Association of Students, the journal *Dveri srpske*, and the Church Choir of the Shrine of St. Alexander Nevsky as sponsors, the "first assembly of Orthodox-national Serbian youth at the University of Belgrade since 1944" took place on the premises of the Philosophy Faculty on December 6, 2001. Serbian Orthodox clergy took part in the meeting, which was attended by students and other locals. Bora Kuzmanović, a professor at the University of Belgrade, told those present that "retraditionalization" was the answer to the "crisis of values" which he believed was gripping Serbian society, while Branimir M. Nešić, a student at the Philosophy Faculty, condemned liberal student organizations for espousing "sick views" such as "the legalization of gay and lesbian marriages, the legaliza-tion of softer drugs, [and] looking for collective forgiveness from all manner of Albanians, Croats, Americans, English ..." (both quoted in Milosavljević, 2001).

The Serbian Church's view of homosexuality does not differ from that of its Romanian and Russian sister Churches. What it adds is an intense nationalism, in which homosexuality comes to be seen not merely as a betrayal of Christ and as a grievous sin against nature, but also as a betrayal of the Serbian nation.

Conclusion: Orthodoxy and intolerance

It has not been my purpose in this chapter to suggest that the Orthodox Church has a monopoly on intolerance, or that intolerance is the only salient feature of that ecclesiastical body. But this is not the place to develop a history of religious intolerance among all Christian and non-Christian religions. In limiting the discussion to the Orthodox Church, insofar as the story of Orthodox–EU "dialogue" has been largely conflictual, it seems to make sense to focus on the sources of their discord.

As already noted, the Orthodox Church is both national and transnational. Its "national" aspect is dictated not only by the tradition of autocephaly but also by the framework of states, each with its own legal system and its own traditions. But as European integration proceeds, taking the form, *inter alia*, of legal standardization, and as sovereignty sheds its Westphalian meaning and becomes more subordinate to international norms, autocephaly will become ever less necessary and transnational coordination within the Church ever more a matter of necessity. Autocephaly is, to be sure, a tradition in the Orthodox Church, but it is not a matter of doctrine; and hence, if Orthodox prelates were to conclude that some reassessment of administrative and juridical organization is in their own best interests, then it is not to be ruled out that the principle of autocephaly might be revised or amended. Already, the creation of the World Council of Churches and the promotion of EU integration have confronted the Orthodox world with the need for coordination, to find a common response. Thus, there have been intra-Orthodox conclaves at which matters of common concern have been discussed. And because of the recent EU advocacy of decriminalization of homosexuality – an issue which is scarcely the point of principal emphasis for the EU, but which has assumed vast importance for the Orthodox Church – Orthodox prelates have felt under pressure and have responded defensively.

The homosexual is, for the contemporary Orthodox Church, what the Jew was in bygone days. Thus, Church hierarchs have signaled, from time to time, their rejection of anti-Semitism,[9] while continuing to rail against gays, lesbians, and transsexuals, warning that the "evil [of sexual diversity] threatens to take over the world and what is abnormal is increasingly being taken as normal" (Patriarch Teoctist, as quoted in Agence France Presse, 2001). Conservatives in the Orthodox Church, even while swearing their fidelity to the Bible, do not, apparently, see that Christ's admonition not to cast the first stone unless one is oneself free of sin applies in the case of homosexuals, do not believe that the story of the Good Samaritan could possibly be recast as the story of the Good Homosexual, do not accept that Christ's exhortation to love one's neighbor as oneself could apply also to gays and lesbians; the Orthodox Church has, it appears, "improved" upon the very Gospels to which it swears its undeviating loyalty. But the Church's very revisionism serves as a warning against trying to locate the source of ecclesiastical intolerance in the Gospels. The source of Orthodox intolerance is not to be found in the New Testament.

In fighting the decriminalization of homosexuality in Romania, the Orthodox Church called, as noted above, for "a dialogue" and claimed to value "a richness of spiritual values." But it is a "dialogue" in which the homosexual must read from a prepared script (confession of sins, penitence, humble request for absolution); and "richness" refers not to diversity, which has never been part of the Orthodox tradition, but to the richness of the Orthodox faith itself. What the Orthodox Church has wanted in Russia, in Georgia, in Romania, and in Serbia is to impose moral uniformity, sexual conformity, and, to the extent possible, cultural homogeneity. Cultural heterogeneity enters on the coat-tails of neo-Protestant and New Age religions, which threaten to induce cultural shifts, as well as changes in the attitudinal patterns of locals, and change, apparently, is to be abhorred, unless it is change in the direction of repristination – a political version of what Carl Jung once called "the return to the womb." Repristination is sometimes offered quite explicitly, for example in the January 2002 Christmas message by Serbian Patriarch Pavle, who promised Serbs that, to the extent that they "return to the path taken by Saint Sava" they could once more "be as pure as children" (*Glas javnosti*, 2002).

It is striking, in this connection, that the aspiration to return to the "idyllic past" in which men ruled their women by force, in which homosexuality was completely taboo, and in which believers felt that they were "as pure as children," could involve the rehabilitation of outright rogues. In Russia, for example, there has been a campaign underway to canonize Ivan the Terrible, the crazed sixteenth-century tsar who allegedly enjoyed torturing prisoners and who killed his own son, the heir to the throne, as well as Grigorii Rasputin, the lecherous monk who insinuated himself into the tsarist family and preached that the best way to conquer sexual temptation was to give in to it. Although Russian Patriarch Alexy II has repeatedly spoken out against these particular candidates, the pressure has grown so strong that, by early 2003, the Moscow Patriarchate was reported to be reconsidering its position. Meanwhile, Aleksandr Dvorkin, the Russian Orthodox Church's leading expert on sects, noted that there were already claims being registered that Stalin, the man responsible for the killing of more people than anyone else in history, even Hitler, was secretly a monk and predicted that there would soon be demands to canonize the sanguinary despot (Zolotov, 2003).

One finds the same syndrome in Romania, where there have been continuing efforts to promote the canonization of anti-Semitic Iron Guard leader Corneliu Zelea Codreanu and wartime Axis collaborator

Marshal Ion Antonescu, who is thought to have been responsible for the extermination of about 200,000 Jews. In 1993, for example, a political party calling itself the New Christian Romania held its founding congress in Bucharest and demanded that Codreanu be raised to the communion of saints – a demand seconded by the Cluj-based Sarmisegetuza Association in 1998. In 2001, a symposium organized by the Greater Romania Party saw the demand that Antonescu be canonized by the Romanian Orthodox Church, and on June 2 that same year, a statue to the wartime leader was unveiled in the yard of the Christian Orthodox church in Bucharest.

Or again, there is the case of Serbia, where, in May 2003, the Holy Synod of Bishops of the Serbian Orthodox Church *unanimously* declared the canonization of Bishop Nikolaj Velimirović, who died in 1956. Velimirović is notorious for his endorsement of the chauvinistic Chetnik movement which massacred Muslim civilians during World War Two and aspired to create an ethnically homogeneous Greater Serbian state, and for his anti-Semitism and praise of Hitler (in 1935) (Saponja-Hadžić, 2003). In celebration of the canonization, the reliquary with the new saint's relics was removed from the Lelić Monastery and taken to St. Sava's Church in Belgrade, allowing Serb believers to pay homage to "Saint Nikolaj."

Bishop Velimirović was a well-educated man, who earned a Ph.D. at the University of Bern, Switzerland, continuing with postgraduate studies at Oxford University, before returning to Serbia in 1909 to be tonsured. But far from developing a love of the West during his years in Switzerland and England, Velimirović, who would end his days as Dean of St. Tikhon Seminary in South Canaan, Pennsylvania, reviled the West, among other things because people in the West were allegedly guilty of excessive bathing. "Are you with Europe or with your people?" he asked on one occasion. Nor did the bishop have any use for democracy or tolerance or pacifism or the Jews, lumping all of these together. "All modern European principles have been made by the Jews," the bishop claimed, "who nailed Christ to the cross: democracy, strikes, socialism, atheism, religious tolerance, pacifism and universal revolution. These are the inventions of the Jews, or their father the Devil . . . The most important thing is that Christian Europe has become a servant of the Jews, has rejected the Father of light and recognized the Devil as its father in thought and deed" (*Vreme*, 2003: 43). Given the availability of such men of virtue as Boris Godunov, the Russian tsar who, when famine struck his country, distributed food and money from the royal treasury, and Dragoljub Jovanović, the Serbian progressive who headed the left wing of the Agrarian Union and did his best to fight against hegemony of all kinds, I find myself driven to the conclusion that the canonization of rogues is attractive to some people precisely because they are rogues; in other words, those pressing for the canonization of Velimirović, Rasputin, Ivan the Terrible, and potentially Iosif Vissarionovich Stalin know precisely what they are about, viz., to establish firm group boundaries and establish the Church as the champion of the national group, by glorifying figures who have perpetrated great harm, especially when that harm was perpetrated on group "outsiders."

The Orthodox Churches of Russia, Georgia, Romania, and Serbia yearn for a lost "idyllic past," and while they may not imagine that they can retrieve it entirely, they do believe that through religious instruction in the schools and what they themselves call "retraditionalization," they can *approach* this "idyllic past." The European Orthodox Churches discussed here are suspicious of the foreign world and believe that it is good to be nationalist – for *some* Orthodox, even to be good in a chauvinistic sense (as demonstrated in the canonization of Bishop Velimirović). Leading Orthodox figures can be found blasting liberalism, cosmopolitanism, and democracy, and blaming society's troubles variously on Jews, homosexuals, the World Council of Churches, the European Union, and globalization.

Can the Orthodox Church change? At the outset of this chapter, I expressed some skepticism as to the prospects of an Orthodox "Reformation" or even of an Orthodox *aggiornamento*. The decentralized structure of the Orthodox Church makes sweeping reform across the entire Orthodox world more difficult to accomplish than was the case with the Catholic Church, and even in the latter case, the Second Vatican Council, like the First Vatican Council, provoked a small secession on the part of those unwilling to accept the new scheme.[10] But the challenges of the twenty-first century – which will include global warming, the continued extinction of species, food shortages, massive environmental damage, and perhaps the bankruptcy of the United States– will drastically reshape the environment in which we live and, I cannot help but think, force the religious associations, among them the Orthodox Church, to address new problems which are, at this writing, barely on the horizon.[11] Moreover, it may be helpful to recall that, in 1864, the Catholic pontiff, Pius IX (1792–1878; reigned 1846–78) issued his ill-famed *Syllabus of Errors*, anathematizing 80 "errors" – among them advocacy of religious freedom, the notion that non-Catholics could also go to heaven after death, the denial of the Catholic Church's perfection, the rejection of force to promote Catholicism, the claim that secular government may limit or regulate the activities of the (Catholic) Church, secular education as such, and the very principle of Church–state separation. Yet, a century later, at its historic Second Vatican Council, the Catholic Church embraced *all* of these "errors" and began to promote ecumenical contacts with an energy it had never before displayed. Thus, while it is difficult to detect liberals in positions of power within the Orthodox Churches discussed herein, what history teaches us, among other things, is never to exclude the possibility of change.

Notes

I have benefited in this draft from the comments offered at the conference held at Colgate University in early April 2004.

1 Such as Poland, where Fr. Tadeusz Rydzyk operates a radical radio station known as Radio Maryja, spewing out intolerant messages, including anti-Semitism.

2 In the Russian context, the ecumenists tend to be the same persons who favor introducing more contemporary Russian language into liturgical services, while anti-ecumenists tend to be the same persons who want to retain Old Church Slavonic without any compromise or attenuation.

3 Kirill was not proposing that Western Churches adopt the obsolete Julian calendar, only that they celebrate Easter on the same day as the Orthodox Churches.

4 The figure of 1.3 million Catholics in Russia is taken from *National Catholic Reporter*, March 1, 2002.

5 Ramet (1998: 269–70).

6 Orthodox clergy were said to have taken part in two attacks on Jehovah's Witnesses and Pentecostals in July 2002 alone. See *Christian Century*, 2002.

7 Since one cannot "expel" something which was not there in the first place, the archbishop was either operating under the mistaken impression that a reference to God had been included in an early draft of the constitution or speaking in an inflammatory manner.

8 Whether or not the particular document is authentic remains in doubt, but Stan and Turcescu report that the information about Teoctist's earlier membership in the Iron Guard has been confirmed from (other) materials found in the Romanian state archives. See Stan and Turcescu (2000: 4).

9 In February 2002, the Holy Synod of the Serbian Orthodox Church condemned the anti-Semitic comments made by retired priest, Fr. Žarko Gavrilović. The Associated Press reports did not mention anything about Gavrilović's anti-gay statements and activities. See Associated Press Worldstream (2002).

10 The First Vatican Council's declaration of the doctrine of papal infallibility provoked the secession of the Old Catholic Church, whose members refused to accept the new doctrine. The Second Vatican Council provoked the secession by "integralists" such as Archbishop Marcel Léfebvre, who refused to accept the mass in the vernacular and other reforms.

11 Environmental concerns were addressed by the Ecumenical Patriarch, Bartholomew I, as early as 1997, when he described the "wanton destruction of nature" as a sin, and warned against the extinction of species, changes to the global climate, deforestation, and pollution. He returned to these themes in July 2003. See "Orthodox leader blesses green agenda", in *Christian Science Monitor* (2003b).

7　The politics of ambivalence: Europeanization and the Serbian Orthodox Church

Vjekoslav Perica

Religion and Serbia's ambivalent attitude toward the West

The post-1989 Europe's East saw the recovery and growing influence of national Orthodox Churches. In the countries of Eastern Christian tradition religion is a public affair. Eastern Churches are some kind of branches of government often under special laws. Also by tradition, Caesar is always first and the Patriarch (head of the Church) is the ruler's benevolent mentor. The Eastern Orthodox Church remains reserved toward political activism generally much more than Western churches, except in extraordinary circumstances, most notably when a secular authority does not exist or cannot function. The Church then becomes a provisional government of sorts until restoration of secular authority. This practice was in fact strengthened during five centuries of Ottoman rule by the so-called *millet* system. The Ottomans destroyed Serb nobility and statehood but tolerated and recognized the Church as both spiritual and political representative of the community. This was because Muslim Ottomans knew only one type of community, namely religious community (in this case Christian or "Roman" i.e. *Rum millet*). This historical experience reinforced the Church's roles as a guardian of national identity and a form of *de facto* statehood. Thus Orthodox churches entered the modern age of nations as "ready-made nation-states" albeit different from the Western model. By the same token, the Western liberal principle of separation between Church and state in Eastern Orthodoxy has two powerful traditions against it, namely the Byzantine tradition ("caesaro-papism") and the experience of Ottoman rule. Conservatism in politics in Europe's predominantly Orthodox societies emphasizes the critical link between Orthodoxy and nationhood. By contrast, liberalism insists on separation between Church and state and grants religion a lesser role. As Europe unites, this controversy deepens and divides societies of the East. National Orthodox Churches are important allies of various Euro-skeptical and nationalist-conservative blocs.

This chapter will explore the case of the Serbian Orthodox Church (SOC). Founded in 1219 as a self-governing ecclesiastical and state institution that acquired a supreme Church authority called the Patriarchate in 1346, the SOC has been traditionally one of the most militant European Orthodox Churches. Under foreign rule its patriarchs became political leaders and the Church encouraged uprisings and wars of liberation. Full national independence under Serb kings and patriarchs became the highest political ideal, cultural value, and marker of nation-hood. Drawing from my research on the Church's international policies since 1989,[1] I will examine the prospects for Europeanization in a particularly instructive case.[2] With an image of bellicose empire-breaker and nemesis of multinational states, Serbia (currently under the official name "Serbia and Montenegro" – henceforth "Serbia") will be a test for the success of the hitherto most delicate stage of the EU project. According to this volume's design and structure, I will try to avoid overlapping with Sabrina Ramet's comparative analysis of several Eastern Orthodox Churches. Ramet examines their attitudes on political issues and clerical policies in the "public square" concerning the EU's "liberal project." I will focus instead on what I see as a militant or "warrior church" in the European Orthodox world. I examine the Serbian Orthodox Church's remarkable activist role in international and inter-religious affairs and specifically its ambivalent attitude toward the EU.

At least since the 1980s, Europeanization of Serbia has met with a vibrant resistance. Nevertheless, Serbia–West interaction is rather complex. In many respects it is analogous to the famous nineteenth-century Russian Slavophile–Westerner controversy.[3] It is an ambivalent love–hate relationship that entails both conservative West-haters and liberal pro-Westerners. The Serbian Church, however, rarely manifested pro-Westernism and remained one of the fountainheads of the new wave of Serbian anti-Westernism. Yet, Church leaders try to deal with the EU via some sort of "neo-Byzantine" diplomacy combining collaboration and compromise with conflict and defiance. The SOC's foreign policy priorities have been Balkan affairs, especially territorial arrangements such as consolidation of the Serbian nation-state and inclusion of the local Serb communities in Bosnia-Herzegovina, Kosovo, and Macedonia. Regarding domestic political issues, the SOC pursues an anti-liberal agenda as analyzed by Sabrina Ramet in her chapter. I would, however, underscore the problem of separation between Church and state. Here Western liberalism, which insists on the separation, and Eastern tradition-alism, which emphasizes the "symphony" principle, remain at loggerheads.

What makes Serbia so unique and, in the light of Europeanization, problematic? In the eyes of the West, Serbia and Montenegro are notorious Balkan warrior nations. Their Churches' liturgies commemorate martyrdom myths and warrior spirit (although Christians, Serbs, and Montenegrins sometimes say that vengeance is sacred). The Kosovo myth – representing both the martyrdom cult and warrior spirit – is preserved in the Serbian Church's liturgy and folk tradition and is mentioned in the relevant literature beyond Balkan boundaries (Eliade, 2005; Emmert, 1990). Serbs and Montenegrins fascinated Europe by their resistance to Turkish subjugation but worried the West when they also resisted Western hegemony especially in the wake of World War One. In modern European international politics, Serbia is considered Russia's faithful ally and Russian leaders' outpost in the West. Serbia, however, is in Europe. In contrast to Russia and Turkey, described recently by Samuel P. Huntington as "torn countries," Serbia is wholly European. Thus, during the Balkan wars of the 1990s, a Serb leader, addressing a nationalistic rally, sent a message to Europe that Serbia is, in his words, one of the oldest European "political nations" (Perica, 2002: 162).

The Church's ethnic label and the title of the Serbian patriarch emphasize the ideal of national–ecclesiastical unity. Religion, culture, and national identity entail ideals of independence and sovereignty in both Church and state affairs. Eastern Orthodoxy is therefore considered more nationalistic than, for example, the internationally structured, universal Roman Catholicism, and Serbian Orthodoxy is perhaps the most nationalistic in the Orthodox world. Some recent Catholic–Orthodox rivalries even compelled Catholicism to "nationalize" and "ethnicize." For example, Croatian Catholicism and Serbian Orthodoxy added much fuel to the fire of ethnic conflict and civil wars in former Yugoslavia. Through this interaction, the Catholic Church in Croatia adopted a semi-official label "The Church of the Croats" so as to "get even" with its Serbian religious-nationalistic rival (Perica, 2002, 2006).

Imperial and other supranational structures dominating over the Church–national community of Orthodox Serbs are viewed as alien and "unnatural." This is so even in the case of Christian empires, not to mention non-Christian ones. To be sure, Orthodox theology insists that the Church is one Christ's Church and Christianity must be understood as a whole; yet, in practice, Orthodox Christianity cherishes above all the principle of *autocephaly* or self-governance in ecclesiastical affairs and each Eastern Orthodox Church desires a Patriarchate – a supreme religious authority of its own. By extension, autocephaly means also national, i.e. political, sovereignty. In the West, sovereignty typically comes from either the ruler or the people as an aggregate of individuals. In the East, sovereignty can derive from the ethnic community, the ruler, or the

Church represented by its Patriarch. The patriarch is also traditionally called *etnarch* after the Greek term that means the one who leads a people or nation.

Being national-autocephalous, Orthodox churches are by no means isolated sectarian communities. In addition to the theological concept of "wholeness" of Christianity, including its monotheism, Orthodox Churches actively interact with states and other Churches. Historical experience sometimes turned these Churches into peculiar "reserve governments" standing by ready to assume functions of political leadership in times of crisis of the kingdom or nation-state. These "reserve governments" had departments for foreign affairs and conducted active policies concerning relations with states, Churches, and other international factors. Many times in history Orthodox patriarchs represented the nation in international affairs. The Ottoman *millet* system, under which Eastern Orthodox Churches lived for centuries, strengthened the political-representative role of the Church in that only religious communities were recognized and tolerated by the imperial authorities.

According to historians of Serbia Michael B. Petrovich and Charles Jelavich, the SOC developed a religion of "public identity" and became a "quasi political organization" (Petrovich, 1976; Jelavich, 1954). The SOC is a national institution and element of the nation-state structure. The only international association that might be acceptable as a partner for "fraternal" cooperation among equals is some kind of a successor of the Byzantine Empire, for example, the idea of the Eastern Orthodox Christian Commonwealth that sporadically appeared before and after the fall of Constantinople. In the modern era, Russian imperialist "messianism" aspired to unite all the Orthodox under the tsars. A Russo-Serbo-Montenegrin brotherhood in arms grew strong particularly from the first Serbian uprising against Ottoman rule in 1804, through the Balkan crisis of the 1860s–70s, down to the outbreak of World War One. World War Two and communism revived Russophilia and pan-Slavic sentiments but the 1948 Tito–Stalin split and subsequently Tito's Yugoslav national communism ended it. Nonetheless, historian Ivo Banac discovered that an overwhelming majority of rebellious Orthodox communists who sided with Stalin against Tito were of Orthodox Serb and Montenegrin background (Banac, 1988).

The Western perception of Serbia fit in the "Other Europe" pattern, due, among other things, to the Orthodox faith (Wolff, 2001). However, Orthodox Europeans took pride in being in the first line of defense of Europe against Islam and in this role received Western encouragement. This "antemurale myth" thus became one archetypal myth of nationhood in Southeastern Europe (Hosking and Schöpflin, 1997; Kolstø, 2005).

Serbian Church historian Dimitrije Bogdanović compares the significance of the 1389 Kosovo battle between Serbs and Ottomans with landmark battles between European Christians and Muslim invaders such as the Battle of Poitiers (732) and the Battle of Kulikovo (1380) and even draws an analogy between Kosovo and the ancient Battle of Thermopylae to stress the Euro-Asian conflict (Bogdanović, 1985: 286). In a similar vein, bishop and poet Petar II Petrović-Njegoš of Montenegro created a modern supplement to the Kosovo cycle of legend and folk poetry entitled *Gorski vijenac* (the correct translation would be "The Mountain Range") in which he depicts the Christian–Muslim "ceaseless struggle" until complete annihilation of one of the warring parties. During the recent war in Bosnia, Serbia's view of this war as a Christian defense against the resurgent Islamic threat received significant support notably in Britain and France (Klimon, 1994). Help also came from the East from Russian diplomacy, the Orthodox Church, and even volunteer fighters on the Serbian side.

However, behind the grand myth of the Balkan warrior churches, lies their real character of survivors by all means possible. The history of the SOC records both collaboration and resistance. Within the multireligious and multinational Ottoman Empire, the SOC collaborated out of necessity and sometimes for its own material benefit as a "political" representative of Serbs while only occasionally plotting against the regime and assisting rebellions. Likewise, the SOC did not suffer so terribly under the Habsburg "yoke" as the contemporary political mythology would have the people believe. In the Serbian modern national state, the Church found its ideal order. It therefore legitimized every regime and policy even in cases of the worst corruption, genocidal crimes, and aggressive wars. Lay theologian Marko P. Đurić (the few outspoken inside critics of the SOC are all lay theologians) sees the Church–state symbiosis as the major problem. In his words, this "holy political matrimony with the nation-state" compelled the Church to tolerate state policies that Christianity would otherwise condemn. Đurić calls for a new ecclesiology of an "actively peacemaking Church" (*mirotvorna crkva*).[4]

The Serbian Church and international aspects of the Balkan crisis, 1989–1999

In the late 1980s and through the 1990s, the European unification in the West coincided with the disintegration of the Yugoslav federation. The western, predominantly Catholic Yugoslav republics of Croatia and Slovenia cheered the rise of the EU and publicly showed pride in their Western heritage. Concurrently, anxiety mixed with spite spread across

Serbia. The multiethnic federation split into Western and Eastern "blocs" with the wavering Bosnian Muslims caught in the crossfire. In the discourse of Serbian nationalism of the 1980s, the EU was portrayed as a revived Habsburg Catholic Empire backed by the reunited Germany and the Vatican. The momentarily dormant Serbian anti-Germanism erupted on the occasion of the 50th anniversary of the beginning of World War Two that in the SOC was commemorated as a "martyrdom of the Serbs." Anti-Westernism spread in the clerical rank-and-file. In the 1980s the clergy started paving the way for the sainthood of two famous zealots, bishops Nikolaj Velimirović and Archimandrite Justin Popović, both outspoken anti-Westerners and opponents of inter-faith ecumenical dialogue. In the late 1980s and early 1990s both Church leaders were aggressively commemorated after the long silence during the communist era. Their banned writings were reissued and widely publicized. Velimirović's relics were transferred to Serbia in 1991. He was canonized in 2003. His canonization was partly a response to the Catholic Church's beatification of Croatian Cardinal Alojzije Stepinac who was always viewed by the SOC as an accomplice in the persecution of Serbs in World War Two (Perica in Kolstø, 2005: 143–57).

In the 1980s, a militant anti-Catholicism erupted in Serbia. The Vatican was a favorite topic for the new Serbian historiography and radical political journalism. The popes were portrayed as fanatically anti-Serbian, instrumental in the destruction of the interwar Yugoslav kingdom, and involved in the genocide against Serbs in the pro-Axis Independent State of Croatia. Another serious accusation blamed the papacy for the penetration and advancement of Islam into Europe from the fall of Constantinople to the Kosovo crisis of the 1980s (Perica, 2002: 145–46). The priest-historian Bogdanović wrote that the Roman Catholic Church was not only a passive witness but also an active participant in the Turkish-Albanian conquest of the Balkans (Bogdanović, 1985: 81). According to Bogdanović, the Vatican has always been primarily interested in the conversion of the Eastern Church. The popes of the Counter-Reformation era would take advantage of Eastern Churches' exhaustion and weakness caused by the struggle against the Muslim invader to force them into ecclesiastical union with the papacy (Bogdanović, 1985: 244–57). Drawing analogies from this historic role of the Vatican in the Balkans, Bogdanović and other Serbian historians pointed out that the Vatican did not properly understand the implications of the most recent Muslim-Albanian awakening in Kosovo, Bosnia, Sandjak, and Macedonia (Perica, 2002: 146).

Anti-Westernism and revivalist "new Orthodoxy" penetrated Serbian media, art, science, and popular culture. A document entitled

"A Proposal for a Serb Church–National Program" published in 1989 stated that Serbia would not be a "servile junior partner of western Europe and blind emulator of alien models ... we want a truly Christian Europe, with a genuine and creative 'theodemocracy' instead of a formal, arid, Western democracy" (Perica, 2002: 131). Upon his ascent to power in 1987, Slobodan Milošević was reserved toward the Church even though he did not remain indifferent to the appeal of the captivating myth and awakened tradition (Perica, 2002: 129–30). Milošević's foreign policy at first adopted the resurgent anti-Westernism somewhat softened during the war. Milošević sought allies in the East (e.g. Russia and China with a special role for Greece as a benevolent liaison with the EU). Some SOC bishops strongly backed Milošević but a majority remained cautious and Milošević's candidate for Patriarch did not win. The issue of restitution of Church property remained unsolved, Serbian historic and holy lands remained "unredeemed," and Church–state relations continued to be tense and even worsened after the war (Perica, 2002: 143–44, 202–05).

As early as the mid-1980s the SOC considered a partition of former Yugoslavia and, after its break-up, of Bosnia and Herzegovina. In the October 1987 issue of the SOC Patriarchate's semi-official journal *Pravoslavlje*, a senior cleric proposed partition of the then still united Yugoslav federation into two "civilizational blocks." As the article argued, "the two incompatible worlds sharply differ from one another in religion, culture, historical development, ethics, psychology and mentality, and therefore previous conflicts that culminated with massacres of the Second World War could repeat." The text concluded prophetically, calling for partition that must be accomplished as soon as possible or else "suicidal and self-destructive wars over borders will break out in the disintegrating Yugoslavia ... Western Europe will be watching it indifferently" (Perica, 2002; Radić in Popov, 2000). The cited article was not the work of a single zealot but represented the prevailing perspective of the Church. Several Serb Church leaders, including the cautious and pragmatic Patriarch Germanus Djorić, spoke in public about the partition of Yugoslavia into the Eastern-Orthodox and Western-Catholic spheres as the only way to avert a civil war (Perica, 2002: 158–61). It is interesting that these proposals implicitly or even openly invited the Catholic Church to take part in partition negotiations. It was quite clear that according to the Serbian proposal, Yugoslav Catholics and Orthodox would strike a deal at the expense of Muslims in Bosnia and Herzegovina and other parts of the country. In 1991, the nationalist leaders Milošević and Tudjman would indeed secretly discuss this kind of partition. On this occasion Serbian Church leaders invited their Croat Catholic counterparts to the negotiation table but the Vatican vetoed the participation of the Catholics. Even though many Croat Catholics, including Church leaders, tacitly endorsed the partition idea, the Vatican urged the Church in Croatia to oppose partition plans. Cardinal Archbishop of Zagreb Franjo Kuharić and the young Archbishop of Sarajevo Vinko Puljić defended in public the unity of Bosnia and Herzegovina, although the latter eventually lost his faith in Bosnia as a viable nation.

The partition idea emerged in the SOC at the time of the collapse of communism in Europe when many Eastern Christian Churches hoped that a new Eastern-Orthodox cultural bloc would replace the former Soviet bloc. In response to this, Orthodox zealotry and nationalism grew in many Orthodox Churches, notably in Russia, Bulgaria, Serbia, and Montenegro, and even in Greece despite this country's EU membership. The Belgrade Patriarchate intensified foreign policy efforts aimed at winning support for the "restructuring" of Yugoslavia by splitting it into the Eastern and Western "cultural blocs." The Church and nationalistic forces in Serbia hoped for the recovery of Russia as a world power and potential sponsor of a new "Orthodox Commonwealth." Contacts between patriarchies of Belgrade and Moscow were frequent and involved both public symbolic display of partnership and dynamic diplomatic activity – mostly through private channels. After four summit meetings in the 1970s, Russian Patriarch Pimen again came to Yugoslavia in November 1984, when he visited Kosovo and received a spectacular welcome by a crowd of local Serbs at the historic Gračanica church. As the old Uniate issue reappeared with the collapse of communism, Orthodox Churches gathered at several international conferences seeking pan-Orthodox solidarity and publicly protesting the apparent offensive from the Vatican to the East (Perica, 2002: 159–61). For example, in March 1991, Serbian Church representatives voiced radical views at the pan-Orthodox symposium "Roman Catholicism and the Orthodox World" in Ukraine. This conference sent a message to the Pope warning the Vatican not to send missionaries to the East. The conference also sent a message to Mikhail Gorbachev reminding him of the tradition of Russian Orthodox tsars, and invoking his sacred duty to defend religious rights and the cultural identity of Orthodox countries and Orthodox peoples. Such pressures on Gorbachev from the Orthodox Church in Russia and anti-Western nationalistic parties mounted in the wake of Gorbachev's historic 1989 speech in which he spoke about a "common European home," implying Russia's future joining of the EU. Continuing the dynamic pan-Orthodox campaign, a high delegation of the Serbian Church visited Moscow in May 1991. The Patriarchate's journal reported about the meeting on the front page under the title

"Now it is Time for all Orthodox Peoples to Join Forces."[5] As the Serbo-Croatian war escalated, the SOC sought support from an Orthodox ecclesiastical summit conference convened in Istanbul on March 12–15, 1992. This ecumenical conference issued appeals for peace in the Balkans and called the European Community to show respect to and cooperate with Orthodox countries in the process of European unification.

In the recent Balkan war the Serbian nationalist movement revived the "warrior-nation" myth. War is said to be the "Serbian way" and, as the writer and former federal president Dobrica Ćosić implied, only through war would Serbia recover the losses incurred during peacetime. State institutions and political parties, intellectual circles, the media, the Church, and the military supported the myth and conveyed it to the people (Popov, 2000). During the war, the Church assisted military efforts and diplomacy aimed to win Western support for Serbian causes. Seeking advantage from the growing West–Islam conflict, Serbia justified her militant course as an appropriate response to an alleged penetration of Islamist politics in the Balkans via Albanian and Bosnian Muslim communities. In 1990, Bishop Pavle, then the local bishop from Kosovo and future Patriarch, visited Washington and appealed for protection of Serbian medieval shrines in Kosovo, as "the most valuable pieces of evidence to prove the Serbian, Christian, European and civilizational character of the culture they represent" (Perica, 2002: 203). As the truth about Serbian "ethnic cleansing" reached the West, Serbia and Western democracies drifted apart moving toward the point of an overt conflict. The Dayton Accords temporarily eased tensions, but in 1998 a Serbo-Albanian war broke out in Kosovo – this time provoked by Albanian militant groups. Slobodan Milošević's attempt to use it as a pretext to cleanse Kosovo of Albanians was halted by the NATO attack on Serbia in 1999.

On March 24, 1999, NATO resumed massive air raids on Serbian towns and military targets. Western democracies supported the bombing. Russia could not stop it but nonetheless provided political and economic support for Serbia. The Russian Orthodox Church lobbied politically and symbolically for its Balkan brethren. On March 31, 1999, the holy icon of the miraculous Madonna (*Bogoroditsa*) of Kazan arrived in Belgrade and was presented before the faithful in several of Belgrade's churches. On April 20, 1999, the Patriarch of Moscow and All Russia, Alexy II, who earlier visited Serbia, Bosnia, and Kosovo during the Bosnian war, again came to the Yugoslav capital. After holy liturgy at the memorial temple of Saint Sava the Patriarch of All Russia addressed the crowd of 15,000 in the church and nearly 100,000 around it. He used strong words to condemn NATO's "arrogance and injustice" and spoke friendly words of support for "Serbian brothers."[6]

An Italian observer of global affairs noted that the NATO intervention triggered a vehement anti-Westernism in which Orthodox Churches of Serbia and Russia appeared as the founders of a new "anti-western Axis."[7] The Serbian Church press reported that NATO bombs intentionally targeted sacred monuments "like the Romans despoiled the Jerusalem Temple" and talked of "Antichrist's army."[8] Belgrade right-wing monthly *Duga* wooed Germany arguing that the USA set out to turn the world into its own mirror image by undermining homogeneous nations and forcibly intermixing the world population. According to the *Duga*, the principal hindrances to this US plan have been Serbia and Germany – the two European nations "with the most vibrant and enduring national identities and nationalist sentiments."[9] America's plan, the article also argues, aims at supporting Muslim states along the borders of Russia in order to surround the largest Orthodox country with Muslim states allied with the USA. In May 1999, the Yugoslav federal Parliament even voted in favor of Yugoslavia's adherence to the Union of Russia–Belarus but Moscow remained reserved.

A few weeks before Saint Vitus Day 1999, Serbian military and police withdrew from Kosovo. Columns of Serb refugees followed the troops and a new "great migration" of Serbs invoking the mythical exodus of 1690 was recorded in Church chronicles. By the summer of 2000, less than 100,000 Serbs were left in the province. Yet, the Church and the shrines remained and pilgrimages continued. Serb Church leaders sought revenge, blaming Milošević. Bishops' sermons and Church press portrayed him as an unrepentant communist and atheistic Marxist at heart. Milošević alienated the Church during his ten-year rule symbolically, economically, and politically. He did not attend liturgies or show public respect for the Church; he did not restore Church property lost under communism; and perhaps worst of all, he lost the war for Greater Serbia and left Kosovo, Macedonia, parts of Croatia, and Bosnia and Herzegovina in the hands of Muslims and Catholics.

The Church therefore backed an increasingly strong anti-Milošević domestic opposition. Concurrently, it stepped up collaboration with the West, knowing that both Washington and Brussels wanted the Balkan dictator out of power. In June 1999, on the occasion of the 610th anniversary of the Kosovo battle, Patriarch Pavle described Slobodan Milošević before Western TV cameras as the "main source of evil." Bishop Artemije, from Kosovo, representing Patriarch Pavle, spoke against Milošević in the United States, Canada, Western Europe, and Australia.[10] The Church's campaign was something quite unusual and infrequent in the long history of Church–state relations not only in Serbia but also in the Orthodox world. Orthodox Churches only reluctantly challenge secular authority. Milošević, however, angered the Church above all for the loss of the "holy land" of Kosovo and neglecting material support for the Church.

After the NATO bombing: neo-conservative revival in Serbia, 2000–2004

After the ending of the war in Croatia and Bosnia-Herzegovina in November 1995, Serbia saw a period that could be described in terms of "trauma" and "catharsis," as did a volume edited by Nebojša Popov and published at the time. The Milošević regime was losing legitimacy, urban protests organized by liberals and progressives mounted, and conservative nationalistic forces lamented over the complete loss of the Krajina region in Croatia and an ambiguous situation in Bosnia and Herzegovina, not to mention the Macedonian question, separatist tendencies in Montenegro, and volatile Kosovo. In short, Serbia was by and large defeated; only the Bosnian "Serb Republic" could be seen as a success of sorts, more thanks to mistakes of the West than the heroism of the Serbs.

Serbia was exhausted, disillusioned, and vulnerable. The nationalist mobilization triggered in the 1980s had lost momentum. The Albanian Kosovar separatist movement that patiently waited and maneuvered for almost two decades under the leadership of Ibrahim Rugova, now came under the influence of radicals that started an armed struggle. With the help of NATO they won. Although this led to the fall of Milošević, the foreign invasion of Serbia and the Albanian takeover in "Serbian Jerusalem" awoke the historical memory and mythical consciousness of the Serbs, giving a new impetus to radical ethnic nationalism.

In 2000 Milošević lost the elections. Under Western pressure, he was soon extradited to the International War Crimes Tribunal for Former Yugoslavia at The Hague. There, the number of Serbs indicted for war crimes surpassed all other nationalities combined, and the first head of state to be tried by an international criminal court was Milošević. Many Serbs view the International Court as biased, anti-Serbian, and a mere instrument of the great powers. The NATO bombing reminded Serbia of 1914 and 1941 Western attacks and the loss of Kosovo and parts of Bosnia to the Muslims as a repetition of the medieval catastrophe. Only the SOC with a few parishes and highly dedicated monks and nuns remained as a guardian of memory in the historic sacred center of "Old Serbia." Consequently, although the pro-Western liberals dominated the government, the people felt humiliated and victimized. The new government's legitimacy was weak. Serbian conservatives and ethnic nationalists fostered a "besieged-fortress" mentality combined with a sense of collective self-pity and "martyr-nation" image. Both Church and national intelligentsia (earlier mostly secular) emphasized a new form of the old ideal of Serbian unity, this time called "spiritual unity."

The Church publicly condemned the former regime's policies but sent spiritual advisers to attend to the Hague prisoner. Meanwhile Church leaders repeatedly called for national unity. Some zealot bishops hoped for Milošević's spiritual awakening, repentance, and public conversion and viewed him as a Serb patriot and basically another victim of Western games with small nations. In November 2000 the new Djindjić–Koštunica government applied for membership in the Council of Europe. President Vojislav Koštunica assumed an ambivalent outwardly West-friendly, but domestically and during his visits to Orthodox countries, "Slavophile-traditionalist" image. He frequented Church liturgies, appeared in public with Church leaders and revived Orthodox symbolism and conservative religious discourse in public. By contrast, the youthful looking, well-mannered Western-educated Premier Zoran Djindjić became a darling of the West. In Serbian society, the "neo-Slavophile anti-western" and extreme ethno-nationalistic forces remained strong. In his 2000 speech "Europe and the Serbian Question" at the Belgrade symposium "Serbia and the West: Roots of Misunderstanding," Slobodan Rakitić, chairman of the National Writers' Association, saw little responsibility for Serbia. According to Rakitić there exist two currently dominant perceptions of the "new" Europe, i.e. the European Union as "Christian Europe" and "secular Europe shaped by the Enlightenment." Rakitić argues that Serbia belongs to both. Yet in his opinion, "at the beginning of the 21st century Serbs again suffer due to misunderstanding with the West."[11]

After the 1999 NATO bombing, the conservative-nationalistic revival gained ground in some places where the liberals earlier dominated, such as major urban and university centers. A cultural movement for "Defense of the Cyrillic alphabet" spread across Serbia and diaspora communities in the West. At the Belgrade University students founded clubs and held seminars that celebrated the Russian writer and conservative-Slavophile philosopher Fyodor M. Dostoevsky. Dostoevsky is called the "Great Apostle of the Slavs" and his anti-Western rhetoric echoes in academic circles and in the conservative media. Although Dostoevsky's brand of Slavophilism was ambivalent and several of his famous speeches called for Russo-European mutual understanding and interaction between the two civilizations, the "Dostoevsky revival" in today's Serbia emphasizes only his attacks on the immoral, materialistic-individualistic and "soulless" West. The Serbian student youth also joined ultra-conservative clubs such as "Students' Association of Saint Justin the Philosopher." The conservative-nationalistic umbrella organization called *Srpski Sabor Dveri* – a national assembly of sorts named after the most sacred section in Orthodox Churches – penetrated student circles and organized frequent conferences, lectures, and mass rallies. The *Srpski Sabor Dveri* publicly launched its political slogans such as "For Orthodoxy; For Patriotism; For Monarchy – Against Communism and Globalization" (instead of globalization they interchangeably used terms such as "cosmopolitanism" and "mondialism"). Together with the Church, this organization and the entire Serbian neo-conservative movement labored to restore monarchy in Serbia and revive traditional values and forgotten festivals and folk customs. Principal enemies of this movement have been the liberal capitalist-imperialist West, Islam, and communism which is said to be recovering after its 1989–91 crisis.

Another momentum for the conservative-nationalist movement came in 2004 as Serbia commemorated the bicentennial of the First Serbian Uprising. The war under "Karadjordje" Petrović is also known as the Serbian Revolution that created the modern Serbian nation. On February 16 in Belgrade, at the event called "Spiritual Academy: The Serbian National Question Two Hundred Years Later," prominent Church leaders bishops Amfilohije and Atanasije spoke about Serbia's relations with the West. Metropolitan of Montenegro Bishop Amfilohije said that the most valuable Serbian tradition coming from the past 200 years is the idea of unity between Church and state as the basis for the rebuilding of unity of the whole nation. So united, he says, Serbia must fight for liberation from colonialism, and according to Amfilohije, Serbia is still under colonial rule. Thus, Amfilohije continued his anti-Western barrage which he most openly spelled out at a massive public event – the funeral of the assassinated pro-Western Prime Minister Zoran Djindjić. Bishop Amfilohije exploited this political murder in which Serbian mafia circles and corrupt politics worked together to stall democratization of Serbia, to attack the West which he blamed for Djindjić's death. To all intents and purposes, the Metropolitan Amfilohije has launched his candidacy as heir-apparent of the ageing moderate Patriarch Pavle. The vehement anti-Westernism will be his campaign's emphasis. Amfilohije is a serious candidate even though the predominantly moderate *Holy sabor* (council) of Serbian bishops otherwise does not appreciate his extremism. Nevertheless, Serbian ethnic nationalism including anti-Westernism is the ideology of the day with a considerable popular following and the *Holy sabor* will have to take it into account. Besides, Amfilohije also heads the diocese in the separatist-minded Montenegrin republic and as a patriarch would symbolically maintain unity between the two peoples and states. Amfilohije's close ally, the retired Bishop of Herzegovina Atanasije Jevtić delivered a fiery speech at the above-mentioned jubilee. He said, among other things, the following:

We Serbs have never been foreign puppets and we want to know what the new Europe and the West have to offer to us. In 1914 and 1999, wars of aggression came from the West to Serbia. (The West abhors our bellicose Balkan mentality but) it was (Western) Europe, not the Balkans, which invented the gas chambers of Auschwitz (and burned the six million in them). What did Churchill's (Western) Europe offer to us at the Yalta conference? We were sold to the communists. Likewise, the Dayton Accords and UN resolutions on Kosovo have been imposed upon and dictated upon our *narod* (people). We therefore must daily educate our *narod*. We need to unveil the hypocrisy and explain the forms of the contemporary Western neo-colonialism. Now that same Europe is staging a war crimes trial against our Balkan tyrant Slobodan Milošević. But, see, they find it hard to sentence this hardened criminal because their Western leaders are worse criminals than him. They could have just killed Milošević and Saddam any time. Yet, they keep them alive and put them on televised trials. So that they can continue the humiliation, the bombardment and obliteration of the entire peoples that the two tyrants earlier led. That is what the West is like and that is the real character of Europe. They do not allow us to put our Balkan home in order. They call the Balkans a madhouse. Because they want to maintain the disorder. And so long as the disorder reigns here they will be masters and we slaves. But we will keep on fighting if necessary two hundred more years and we shall prevail in the long run and kick them out of here. That is the message of the two hundredth anniversary of the Serbian revolution and the memory of its leader Prince Karadjordje Petrović.[12]

The post-1999 neo-conservative revival in Serbia deepened the conflict between the pro-Western Serbian liberals and the clericalist-nationalists. An emphatic anti-clericalism became a hallmark of Serbia's liberalism and Westernism. In Belgrade and other urban and university centers Serbia's "Westernizers" have been at war with the conservative-nationalists at least since Milošević's coming to power and through the wars of the 1990s. They formed the "European Movement in Serbia" and other similar organizations. The pro-EU activists consider the Church to be a pillar of reactionary conservatism, nationalism, and anti-Westernism that cost Serbia dearly. Sonja Biserko and Latinka Perović, Belgrade-based Serbian human rights activists, argue that the Church, the military, and the nationalist intellectual elite critically influence and shape the majority public opinion in contemporary Serbia. This majority, the two activists argue, "is trying to turn the clock back ... by their attitude towards two key issues – modernization of the state and society, which always implied

Europeanization of the two, and war crimes as the ultimate consequence of a policy, the political forces in the majority showed that they still held Serbia in the criminal symbiosis of state socialism and nationalism."[13] Another liberal Belgrade intellectual, historian Olivera Milosavljević, emphasizes the unwavering nationalists' and clericalists' denial of any responsibility on the part of Serbia for the evidently disastrous consequences of recent Balkan affairs. To illustrate this uncritical attitude Milosavljević quotes the writer Dobrica Ćosić who admits "a portion, perhaps" of the Serbian intelligentsia's responsibility but insists that "the others much more powerful than us Serbs must be much more responsible for our suffering." Milosavljević also points out that the Serbian cult of unity (implanted symbolically in the Serbian ecclesiastical and royal coat of arms), stalls democratization and liberalization of Serbia's society. In the most recent clerical-nationalistic discourse the old unity cult has been reinvented and more appropriately renamed into "spiritual" unity (Milosavljević, 2002).[14] Thus, Serbia itself remains ambivalent toward the EU and Europeanization as the two bitterly conflicting domestic camps either emphatically call for belonging to Europe without reservations or show anti-Western sentiments, distrust, and sometimes even hatred.

"Byzantine diplomacy"

The Serbian Church has a rich experience in relations with both states and other Churches. Orthodox Churches are heirs of the Byzantine tradition and this also includes the notion of "Byzantine diplomacy." The phrase sometimes has a pejorative meaning but in reality it captures a rational-pragmatic political style. In Serbian Church leaders' jargon, it is called "economics" as opposed to various forms of zealotry or "strictness" in application of sacred texts and theology. The SOC's highest hierarchy and married parish clergy have always been dedicated to this "Byzantine" or "economic" way of conducting relations with churches and states. Zealots are typically monk-priests and monk-theologians some of whom became influential bishops. Today in the SOC the zealots rally behind the cults of the saintly Bishop Nikolaj (Velimirović) and saintly candidate Archimandrite Justin (Popović). Leaders of the zealot faction are two former abbots and theologians, now bishops, Amfilohije (Radović) and Atanasije (Jevtić).

The Balkan peace process opened a window of opportunity for the SOC to get involved and it did, yet again, in the tradition of its "Byzantine diplomacy." The international conflict management in the Balkans hoped to get a wide range of independent factors involved and

Churches enjoyed a special role. The SOC took advantage of Western, particularly US, funding and American politics' ideological sympathies for this "religious statecraft" which partly saves the face of religion while otherwise fueling conflict and violence in numerous places in the contemporary world. The results of this "religious statecraft" in the Balkans have been ambiguous, to put it mildly (Perica, 2002: 179–85). Nevertheless, the SOC recognized the opportunity and took part in a number of peacemaking and humanitarian activities funded by the West. At an international conference in Washington DC discussing the peace process in the Balkans, SOC representative Irinej Dobrijević said the following: "In Orthodox nations, when government fails the Church assumes leadership until the crisis is over. Today, in Washington, the role of religion has been defined as track-two diplomacy: faith in action."[15] The problem is that the same faiths used to be the catalysts of the same deadly conflict (Radić, 2000; Perica, 2002; Ramet, 2002).

In the meantime, the Church did try to improve its image in the West. The Serbian historic site of Dečani monastery in the Kosovo province carried out effective "internet politics" and public relations with Western media under the management of Western-educated monk Father Sava. Concurrently, the Serbian Church's missions in Western Europe labored to improve relations with host governments and domestic churches. Serbian administrator for Central and Western Europe Bishop Konstantin stated in an interview as follows:

The West may be doing unnecessary injustice to us insofar as the western countries want to force upon us their model of democracy. It is based on economic rationale and economic interests alone; but the West does not understand or does not take seriously the peculiarities of our culture and the historical conditions under which our people and other people who share similar historic fate have grown. They often criticize us but I would rather not comment on that, except to note that they actually do not pay very much attention to us as many of us think.[16]

Relations with Russia, the EU and the United States have become the Serbian Church's foreign policy priorities. The friendship with Russia in which national Orthodox Churches played crucial roles has been successfully maintained ever since the early 1970s and upgraded after the fall of communism. The Church's diplomacy dealing with the EU and USA perceived the two foreign powers as partners for collaboration out of necessity but hoped to play them off against one another. Among recent examples of this diplomacy is the above-mentioned 1990 SOC delegation visit to Washington to appeal for containment of Islamic fundamentalism in the Balkans. The Church did not win what it sought but it did not give up and continued its diplomatic maneuvering during the war. In 1999 the Serbian Patriarchate established a de facto embassy or "Office for External

Church Affairs" in Washington DC. The Church's official representative was priest Irinej Dobrijević, a Western-educated experienced diplomat. In his public statements he often criticized the West for allegedly imposing upon Orthodox countries alien values and concepts such as notably the principle of separation between Church and state.

In order to successfully manage the Kosovo question and other regional issues, Church leaders occasionally had to make concessions and yield to Western pressures. Thus two factions in the clerical rank-and-file emerged. The vehemently anti-Western, not to mention anti-Muslim, "Serb" faction refused any compromise and called for struggle, including war, if necessary. The "Greek" faction called for a cautious collaboration and sought diplomatic solutions. The "Greek" label must not lead us to the conclusion that the Orthodox Church of Greece, due to its EU membership, stands for a moderate branch of Eastern Orthodoxy – rather, it means a "Byzantine diplomacy" and political pragmatism. Thus the Greeks' foreign policy in recent years built contacts with leaders of the Roman Catholic Church and conservative politics in Europe and the USA. Taking advantage of the Islamic militant upsurge and terrorism worldwide (including Albanian riots in Kosovo and Macedonia and the hopeless situation in Bosnia) they tried to win over the conservative Christian circles in the West for the Serb cause in the Balkans and pursued the idea of a grand anti-Muslim coalition.

In contrast to the "Greeks," the "Serbs" seek conflict and even renewal of the Balkan wars. During the 1999 NATO bombing the "Serb" faction held a rebellious clerical synod at the historic Sopoćani monastery. The dissenting clerics threatened schism and called for continuation of war. They opposed the papal visit to Serbia otherwise favored by Western diplomacies as a mission of peace and urged the Patriarch not to negotiate with the Pope and Western leaders. They even rejected minor symbolic gestures of good will such as changing obsolete customs in the Church. The "Serbs" rebuffed the Church of Greece's recommendation to introduce calendar reform or service worship in English for businesspeople and tourists so as to please the EU's loan-givers and persuade them to help their country in its dire economic situation, but they did applaud some Greek churchmen's sporadic outcries about "dark forces" of secularization and separation between Church and state threatening Europe's Orthodox countries from the West.[17] Historian Radmila Radić, who is a Belgrade-based analyst of the Serbian national Church, has stated recently for the Western media that inside the Church two clerical factions that are known in circles close to the Church as "Serbs" and "Greeks," argue over critical issues in domestic and world affairs trying to influence the Church and government. Again, these "Serbs" and

"Greeks" are yet another variant of the standard zealots–moderates dichotomy with the Serb label now standing for zealotry. According to Radić, most bishops are pragmatic diplomats ("Greeks") except the zealots Bishop Atanasije (Jevtić) and Bishop-Metropolitan Amfilohije (Radović). The zealots ("Serbs") hate compromise and fuse religion with extreme nationalist ideology. Their champions are Amfilohije and Atanasije and a group of monks and priests who are admirers of the cults of the saintly Bishop Nikolaj Velimirović and saintly candidate Archimandrite Justin. Radić plays down the "menace" of clerical zealotry, however. She insists that the Church of Serbia is a state religion and institution dependent on government financial support; that most clergy are state-salaried moderates and family men, and zealots are always minority groups of monks and monk-bishops. Hence the Church hardly ever contradicts the political authority of its "own state" and although its public statements are worded strongly it rarely makes a real difference in politics.[18] Radić also noted that the attribute "Greek" does not necessarily mean moderation, much less "pro-Western" in spite of Greece's prominent EU membership – monasteries and seminaries in Greece are traditional fountains of zealotry and a number of young monks and theologians returning to Serbia from seminaries in Greece tend to be anti-Western zealots. In Radić's view, the anti-Western zealots in Orthodox churches of Serbia and Greece actually differ only in the "Serbian way," which is less cautious and more boastful and straightforward in its public political pronouncements.[19]

International ecumenical organizations such as the World Council of Churches (WCC) and the Conference of European Churches (CEC) have been important channels for the SOC's foreign policy. Through the 1990s, the SOC sought support from these organizations for the Great Serbian agenda and passed propaganda messages through to the world public opinion. In May 2003 when Orthodox Churches of Europe commemorated the 550th anniversary of the fall of Constantinople, Patriarch Pavle used this opportunity to undo the recent Western media portrayal of the Balkan peoples as bellicose and mutually hateful. In his message to the ecumenical Patriarchate in Istanbul, Pavle called for understanding of the principle of separation between Church and state and invited further interfaith cooperation.[20] The SOC also participated in the conference entitled "Globalization in Central and Eastern Europe – Responses to the Ecological, Economic and Social Consequences" held in Budapest, June 23–29, 2001. The meeting used strong words to criticize practices of neo-liberal capitalism and privatization in ex-communist countries.

SOC diplomacy also included contacts with the Holy See. Since the Second Vatican Council, the two Churches' relations saw ups and downs but somewhat improved in the late 1990s. Patriarch Pavle's meeting with Pope John Paul II and contacts among bishops and special priestly envoys included talks on the issues of Kosovo, Macedonia and Bosnia-Herzegovina; Catholic–Orthodox and Christian–Muslim relations; the international peace process in the region; and EU enlargement. Relations between the SOC and the Vatican remained perplexing but not hostile. Although the SOC and the Vatican disagree over issues of Bosnia, Kosovo and Macedonia, tensions in Christian–Muslim relations in the region have brought the two Christian Churches together as evident from public statements of Catholic and Orthodox prelates in Bosnia. Concurrently, the SOC and other Orthodox Churches and the Vatican also worked together lobbying the EU to provide appropriate constitutional reference to Europe's Christian heritage and define the new association's identity in religious terms. Orthodox Churches demanded explicit references to Christianity as the pillar of continental and civilizational identity with the West. Orthodox Churches used strong rhetoric to condemn the emphasis on ideas of the Enlightenment in the draft EU constitution. In May 2001 the CEC released in Brussels a lengthy document entitled "Churches in the Process of European Integration" which states that "the EU is conceived mostly in terms of prosperous materialism" but success will not be possible without spiritual unity and shared values.[21]

Similar overtones with some more specific Balkan concerns could be heard at the conference "Christianity and European Integration" held in Belgrade on February 8–9, 2003. The conference's declarations stated that Europe is in "spiritual and ecological crisis" and that the ongoing integration of Europe can succeed only if it integrates divided Christianity rather than creating a new "multiculturalism." In other words, the declaration said that only unification of all Christians would help to articulate Europe's identity and avert the Yugoslav tragedy that may even yet befall the EU. The conference also asserted that the new unifying Europe needs a new accurate history of Europe and her peoples and again, that Christian Churches' role in forging Europe's image and identity is essential.[22]

The "war on terrorism" and George Bush's religious-conservative administration seem to have created better conditions for SOC efforts in the United States. In February 2004, Bishop Artemije returned pleased from one of his frequent visits to Washington. Artemije's chief adviser, the Belgrade university professor and top Serbian expert on Islam, Miroljub Jevtić (a vocal supporter of wars in Bosnia and Kosovo), stated for the press that "today in the United States religion has an incredibly strong influence on government and politics ... the highest representatives of the American administration share our conviction that the situation concerning Kosovo Serbs' continuous suffering is intolerable ... our hosts showed a particular interest in the aggressive attacks against Christian symbols and Christian culture in Kosovo."[23]

At the end of 2004, the Church turned its attention to Russia. A delegation from Serbia, led by president-elect Borislav Tadić and Patriarch Pavle, traveled to Moscow for a very successful visit. The Patriarch met with Russian Patriarch Alexy II on several spectacular occasions and received the highest "Prince Vladimir" decoration. The Russian Church also raised money for the finalizing of the construction of the grandiose Saint Sava's memorial cathedral in Belgrade. The two nations and their national Churches affirmed special friendly relations and as churches love to say "fraternal" ties.

Accordingly, as Belgrade human rights activist Sonja Biserko pointed out, "the Serbian elite constantly endeavors to make its way up on a potential conflict between Europe and the United States, and on Serbia's 'unquestionable' geostrategic significance."[24] Recent escalation of Islamist militancy in the Middle East played into the hands of Serb nationalists. Incidentally, in March 2004, a new wave of Serbo-Albanian clashes broke out in Kosovo. The riots left nineteen dead, nearly 900 injured, over 700 Serb, Ashkali and Roma houses, up to ten public buildings and thirty Serbian churches and two monasteries damaged or destroyed, and roughly 4,500 people (mostly Serbs) displaced. A Serb church leader told the media that the Albanian assault on Serbs and their cultural heritage in Kosovo "was a real *Kristallnacht*," referring to the Nazis' attack on Jews, synagogues and Jewish-owned businesses in Germany in 1938.[25] Another Serb nationalist leader described the event as a *pogrom*, again borrowing from Jewish history. He invoked the rhetoric of the wars of the 1990s in which Serbia portrayed herself as an "Israel of the Balkans." This idea is not senseless, but Serbia's problem is that the USA is not interested geopolitically in the Balkans and the EU will never treat Serbia as the USA treats Israel.

As the crisis in Serbia continued, the European Union moved on with the project of Eastern expansion. On May 1, 2004 eight East European countries were admitted to full membership in the European Union. Most of these countries had earlier reinvented themselves to become "Central" or "East-Central" European. Incidentally, this new Central Europe is Catholic Europe. The predominantly Orthodox Balkan region has been constructed as the new "other," i.e. some sort of a "new wild East." The new East-Central Europe has been relieved from the negative image at the expense of the Balkans (and perhaps the farther East such as

Ukraine and of course Russia). The Balkan region has now been given the role of the negative other that the whole of Eastern Europe carried on its shoulders from the Enlightenment to the end of the Cold War (Todorova, 1997; Wolff, 1994, 2001).

The new EU East, more or less "wild" – and Serbia as an epitome of the latter – seems as ambivalent as ever. It is prideful, defiant and anti-Western, yet at the same time longs for unity with Western and Central Europe. The West has been ambivalent in its own right regarding its policies toward Serbia. The West seems anti-Serbian insofar as the Balkan peace process involved the NATO bombing of Serbia and the Hague tribunal is full of Serbs. Yet several international peacekeeping incidents and observations by competent analysts of the Balkan crisis testified to the persistence of strong pro-Serbian sentiments in some Western European nations such as notably France and Britain (Ramet, 2002).[26] Likewise, according to historian Gale Stokes, Serbia has received substantial Western aid over the last ten years although it does not even qualify among the several countries awaiting the next round of EU enlargement scheduled for 2012.[27] After Milošević's fall, Belgrade's governing elites declared Serbia's "European" course, but in reality tried to imitate the Church's neo-Byzantine diplomacy. Meanwhile, domestic public opinion was more often anti- than pro-EU. Although the voices of anti-Western zealots have become quite common in Serbian daily life, culture, and politics, this still does not mean that Serbia is hopelessly anti-Western. Again, the keyword is "ambivalence" and the Serbia–West relationship involves mixed feelings on both sides. The anti-Western zealots never spoke for Serbia as a whole and not even for the SOC as a whole. There has always been a pro-Western and European Serbia culturally, not to mention that, historically, Belgrade governments sided as many times with the West as they did with Russia. Likewise, the Serbian Church has conducted diplomacy with all European powers and empires of the West and East and has recently focused on the European Union and the United States. After the May 2004 EU enlargement, Belgrade media called special attention to the newly admitted Cyprus. The future of the Cyprus question is seen in Belgrade as a test of whether the EU is capable of managing Kosovo, Macedonia, Bosnia, and other Balkan flashpoints. As if the EU headquarters sensed this mood, EU foreign ministers called for more effective management of the Kosovo question and put it among Brussels's priorities.[28] In the meantime, the conservative anti-Westerners and pro-Western liberals vied with each other in Serbian politics. The former won parliamentary elections in December 2003 and the latter presidential elections in June 2004. The Church did not interfere directly. It focused on the renewed Kosovo crisis.

Patriarch Pavle led Vidovdan celebrations in Kosovo in 2004 under protection of KFOR tanks and patrols. On this occasion Church leaders called for the return of Serb refugees and handed out medals to Kosovo Serb families with more than four children which continued the bitter demographic competition with local Muslims and provided young priestly troops for the Church. Yet if the Cyprus question is the good news, there is always the bad one, too. Thus, the recent beginning of Turkey's formal admission process to the EU has caused concern in Serbia's conservative circles while Serbia's liberals and Westerners tried to play it down.

All things considered, the Balkan crisis ended in defeat for the Serbian national project, but the region remains unstable. Ethnic nationalist extremists remain influential. Chauvinist and anti-Western rhetoric can still be heard in public. However, the cooperative and even pro-EU course inaugurated by the post-Milošević Belgrade regimes has remained unchanged. For example, the hard-line nationalist writer Vuk Drašković as the new Belgrade foreign minister has for several years now spoken the language the EU likes to hear. Concurrently, the pro-Western urban liberal-secular forces continue campaigning for a "modern European Serbia and Montenegro." These liberals are presumably more intolerant of the Church and conservative-nationalist circles around it than the Church is toward the liberals (in the Church's view "we are all Serbs after all" and unity is Serbia's sacred ideal). And the Church has its moderates who voice EU-friendly rhetoric. In his New Year's interview to a Belgrade daily newspaper, Serbian Patriarch Pavle pointed out the following:

Many Serbs today want to join the European Union: "Serbia wants to be in Europe," they say. Fine, I think that is good what they say. We, as the people of Saint Sava, have lived in Europe for centuries now and we lived in a Europe that cherishes the higher spirituality that spread from the East to the West; let us just be ourselves – we Serbs did fight many wars but we are not a nation of warriors and bandits; we know how to be humane, generous, and friendly.[29]

The Church, of course, insists on preservation of the nation's identity and traditions and fears the secular, materialistic and liberal West. To this end, the Church campaigned for transformation of Serbia and Montenegro into a constitutional monarchy under Crown Prince Aleksandar Karadjordjević, a British businessman who has divided his time between the West and Serbia to prepare for the potential role of the monarch. On the occasion of the bicentennial of modern Serbia, Patriarch Pavle once again released a statement in support of constitutional monarchy under Karadjordjević. For his part, the would-be Serbian monarch made a number of public statements on the Serbia–EU relationship according to which he seems to be an unambiguous Euro-enthusiast. Consequently, both secular urban pro-Western liberals and moderate conservatives, secular and clerical alike, back Serbia's EU course. Each of these forces, of course, does this for different reasons. The former idealize the West for its liberalism, economic, technological and scientific progress, and promise of prosperity. The latter also pragmatically realize that presumably the only way out of the dire poverty leads through the EU. Yet the conservatives seem also to have realized, and through their earlier-described international agenda demonstrated, the necessity of collaboration. They are aware that Eastern Orthodox Christianity is a faith on the defensive in contrast to resurgent Islam, rejuvenated Catholicism, and the ever-active and eastward-oriented missionary Protestantism. Besides, like earlier in history, European Orthodox Christianity cries out louder than other Christian faiths about the Islamic challenge. In consequence, the SOC has lately improved its relations with Roman Catholicism. The SOC is islamophobic as opposed to Roman Catholicism that could be better described as concerned about certain tendencies in contemporary Islam. As the SOC used to argue in the 1980s and does so again today, Muslim communities in Europe grow, taking advantage of Christian communities' low birth rate. Indeed, the SOC has "lost" several historic territories to the growing Muslim local communities (e.g. Kosovo, Sandjak, Macedonia, some parts of Bosnia and Montenegro). Meanwhile, the SOC has become increasingly politically dependent on the EU and international peacekeepers in order to maintain cultural life among local Serb minority communities and "spiritual unity" of all Serbs. Serbia's links with the Serb diaspora in the region lead through the EU and require its cooperation. The pragmatic "Greek" faction in the SOC therefore calls for cooperation combined with its neo-Byzantine diplomacy. They are prepared to legitimize the EU with reservations while still trying to play off the EU against the USA and keep special ties with Russia, and together with Greece to build some kind of an "Orthodox cultural lobby" within the EU. Turkey's admission to the EU will likely make this Orthodox lobby even more cohesive so that Turkey could be kept in check and its influence on Balkan Muslim communities curtailed. Yet it could also open a window of opportunity for both Turkey and the Orthodox of the Balkans to join forces and occasionally find common interests against the EU center or other regions insofar as the pragmatic conservative politics combined with the Euro-enthusiastic pro-Western liberals prevail in both Eastern Orthodox and Muslim societies.

Conclusion: the Orthodox will be Orthodox but they are Europeans

Oh, do you know, gentlemen, how dear this very Europe, this "land of sacred miracles," how dear it is to us, Slavophile dreamers – according to you – haters of Europe! ... This is our need to serve humanity, although it might be to the detriment of our dearest and most essential interests, our reconciliation with the civilization of Europe, the understanding and justification of their ideals, even though they did not even harmonize with ours. (F. M. Dostoevsky, *The Diary of a Writer*, 1877)

To conclude, in this chapter I have insisted on the idea of ambivalence, specifically analyzing a religion that carries out an ambivalent politics in the "public square." Countries of Byzantine Eastern-Orthodox Christian tradition on the EU's eastern periphery receive Europeanization with mixed sentiments. Acceptance and resistance combine and interact. In the Serbian case the latter has prevailed in recent decades. Serbia proudly emphasizes that Serbs are Europeans. It "imagines" the traditional Christian Europe with its two centers in the West (Rome) and East (Constantinople). Drawing from the historic interaction between the two branches of Christianity, in the East there exists a "culture" or "tradition" of anti-Westernism. It idealizes Europe or perhaps the whole world as a Christian commonwealth or godly kingdom on earth but ascribes a moral superiority to Eastern Christianity and views the West as corrupt. Eastern Orthodox Churches are repositories of such visions and sentiments. Yet this culture, or any other non-Western or even anti-Western cultural current, should by no means prompt the EU to launch some kind of a *Kulturkampf*. There are numerous cultural rivalries worldwide but few wars come out of it. Orthodox societies are hard to Europeanize, but not so much because of their character and culture and not even because of sporadic outbursts of Orthodox religious zealotry, ethnic nationalist excesses, and conservative leaders' anti-liberal rhetoric. As I argued elsewhere, one of the real difficulties for the liberal project is Eastern Churches' symbiosis with the state and weak contribution to the strengthening of civil society (Perica, 2002: 216). Eastern Churches have always been *de facto* organs of the government. Consecrating the ideal of national–ecclesiastical unity, they view civil society as an "intruder" between the people and the state–Church. They also see it as a domain of "sects" and various other challenges to tradition and identity of the nation such as progressive voluntary associations. They call for administrative surveillance over civil society and suppression of what the Church identifies as perilous tendencies. Thus Eastern Churches hamper liberalization. This is hard to change.

Europeanization must tolerate it. To be sure, democratization without a strong civil society is almost unimaginable. But the EU cannot force Orthodox churches "into civil society" like Stalin merged "by a decree" the Uniate churches with the Russian Orthodox Church.

Regarding the phenomenon of Orthodox zealotry and extremism exemplified here in the "warrior church" of Serbia, again, it is a part of this "culture of anti-Westernism" in the East. However, excesses are sporadic and temporary. Specifically, the SOC has been exceptionally militant during the final decades of the twentieth and early twenty-first centuries. This does not mean that the SOC has always been such. This only means that this is a time of landmark change and crisis on a global scale. Let us recall the Balkan crises leading to the Congress of Berlin in 1878, and that which involved the Balkan wars of 1912–13 and precipitated World War One. Analogous was the crisis during the final years before and decades after the end of the Cold War. Contrary to myth, Serbia is not a "warrior nation." It is rather a remarkable barometer of landmark historic changes and for that matter the tiny Serbia and Montenegro could teach us history perhaps more effectively than the cases of gigantic China and India.

In the eyes of the Serbian Church and Serbian conservative-nationalist forces around it, the EU is not the epitome of an ideal order. The EU has still to prove that it is something essentially different from the empires of the East and West with which Serbia, for example (but also many other small nations), vied in the past. Yet, even the conservative Serbia has recognized the EU as a historical necessity and opportunity. After the Balkan wars, Serbia is becoming more and more dependent on EU political and economic assistance concerning both domestic development and communication with "Serbian historic lands" and ethnic communities now beyond Serbia's borders. The grand failure of the Great Serbian project has done much harm to the peoples of what used to be Yugoslavia including Serbs, and it exhausted Serbia's resources. New battles for Serbia now seem unlikely if not totally excluded.

In the light of transnationalism theory, the Eastern Churches are transnational in their own right. Transnationalism theory so far has discovered a considerable potential in Roman Catholicism above all thanks to the supranational institution of the papacy that coordinates interaction among national churches, other faiths, and states (Byrnes, 2001). In spite of the absence of an equivalent to the papacy in Eastern Orthodoxy, transnationalism can count on Eastern Churches thanks to the pragmatic-diplomatic tradition that will recognize the need for transnational cooperation as the European Union continues to fragment and weaken national states, creating economic opportunities and making visible the advantages of regional development. Specifically in the Serbian case, the EU and transnationalism are channels of communication with "unre-deemed holy lands" left behind the national borders. The EU center is also a generous provider of assistance to Orthodox Churches via the peace process, humanitarian efforts, and cultural and environmental programs. Both the EU and the Serbian state now aid the SOC in maintaining the "spiritual unity" of all Serbs. Regarding the incompat-ibility between liberalism championed by the EU and traditionalism of the Orthodox world – Orthodox will be Orthodox. Yet, they are also Europeans and apparently very proud of it. However, in times of crisis the warrior church is likely to turn militant and the volcanoes of ethnic nationalism and anti-Westernism will erupt. Hence, Europeanization of the East will take time. It will perhaps never be complete but a continuing process with its ups and downs.

Notes

1 I refer to a recent follow-up to my *Balkan Idols* (New York, 2002) and also draw from some recent sources cited below including my contribution to Kolstø, ed., *Myths and Boundaries in Southeastern Europe* (London, 2005).
2 In the final stage of writing I received many valuable comments and sugges-tions. I wish to acknowledge with special gratitude the benevolent critique, useful new information, and inspiring suggestions from Sabrina Petra Ramet, Radmila Radić, the editors Peter Katzenstein and Tim Byrnes, and the anony-mous reviewers who read this manuscript during its preparation for publica-tion. I also learned a great deal of new information and heard important discussions related to this topic at the scholarly conference "Churches in Former Yugoslavia" in Münster, Germany (October 2004) sponsored by the German Catholic Bishops' Conference and chaired by Thomas Bremer from Westfälische Wilhelms-Universität, Münster. I especially appreciate what I have learned at this meeting from Olivera Milosavljević, Radmila Radić, Dubravka Stojanović, and Bojan Aleksov.
3 See Andrzej Walicki, *A History of Russian Thought. From the Enlightenment to Marxism*. Translated from the Polish by Hilda Andrews-Rusiecka. Stanford, CA: Stanford University Press, 1979, especially pp. 92–114 and 309–48.
4 Read at http://bocs.hu/chp/osijek/marcodjuric_sr.htm.
5 *Pravoslavlje*, July 15, 1991.
6 Alexy II said among other things: "Several powerful and wealthy countries arrogantly appropriated the role of a supreme judge who determines what is good and what is evil … NATO military actions have another objective: to impose a new world order based on their dictate and their power. But injustice and hypocrisy will not prevail … God is on your side my dear Serbian brothers … But I beg you to make peace in the holy Serbian land of Kosovo and let all peaceful people return to their homes." *Pravoslavlje*, May 1–15, 1999.
7 Francesco Maria Cannata, "Mosca-Belgrado: L'Asse Ecclesiastico Antioccidentale," *LIMES*, No. 1/2000, Rome, June 2000.

8 *The Serbian Orthodox Church: The Bombardment of the Serb Holy Places*, at http://www.spc.org.yu/Svetinje, 11 October 1999; *Istocnik*, no. 43 (Toronto, Canada: Serbian Orthodox Diocese of Canada, 1998).

9 *Duga*, no. 1723, 9 October 1999.

10 Bishop Artemije spoke at two 1998 US Institute of Peace briefings on the prospects for democracy in Serbia and publicly blamed Milošević for Serbia's troubles. *Peace Watch* 5, no. 1 (Washington DC: US Institute of Peace, 1998).

11 "Evropa & srpsko pitanje", in *Sloboda – list srpske narodne obrane u Americi*, at http://www.snd-us.com/archive/1764/lat/sr_1764L.htm.

12 According to my translation from *Danas*, Belgrade, February 16, 2004, at http://www.danas.co.yu/20040216/hronika3.html#2.

13 Sonja Biserko "Editorial: Anti-European Vertical Scores Off," Helsinki Charter, November–December 2003 at http://www.helsinki.org.yu.

14 The quotes are from Milosavljević's interview to *Ekonomist Online* at http://www.ekonomist.co.yu/magazin/em152/med/med2.htm.

15 Quoted at SOC office in Washington's website http://www.oea.serbianchurch.net/.

16 Quoted from Bishop Konstantin's 2002 interview with Belgrade journal *Blic* according to Serbian church's website http://www.spc.yu/News/Intervju/konstantin_c.html.

17 *The Greek Star*, January 8, 2004.

18 Evropski pokret u Srbiji at http://www.emins.org/publik/dugo_putovanje/index.htm.

19 According to my conversation with Radmila Radić on several occasions during the writing of this article.

20 The Information Service of the Serbian Orthodox Church, Belgrade, May 29, 2003, at www.serbian-church.net.

21 Conference of European Churches – Church and Society Commission – Working Group on European Integration Process, "Churches in the Process of European Integration," Brussels, May 2001, at http://www.cec-kek.org/English/IntegrationprocE-print.htm.

22 *Informativna služba Srpske Pravoslavne Crkve*, February 11, 2003, at http://www.spc.org.yu/Vesti-2003/02/11-2-03_13.html.

23 Quoted from Belgrade daily *Danas*, February 17, 2004, online edition at http://www.danas.co.yu/20040217/hronika1.html#0.

24 Sonja Biserko, "Editorial: Anti-European Vertical Scores Off."

25 Forum 18 News Service, Oslo, Norway: http://www.forum18.org/.

26 See the section "Belgrade's Friends in the West," in Sabrina Petra Ramet, *Balkan Babel. The Disintegration of Yugoslavia from the Death of Tito to the Fall of Milošević*. Boulder, USA and Oxford, UK: Westview Press, 2002, pp. 219–22.

27 Gale Stokes, "Can Money Buy Stability in the Western Balkans? Lessons from the Recent Past," AAASS President's Address, Toronto, November 22, 2003, *NewsNet*, January 2004, vol. 44, no.1. p. 4.

28 At the EU foreign ministers' meeting in Brussels on February 23, 2004, EU diplomacy "expressed concern over the development of political situation in Serbia." The ministers expressed support for a "European perspective" in

the management of the Kosovo crisis including foundation of a special "European partnership for Kosovo." *Danas*, February 24, 2004, at http://www.danas.co.yu/.

29 My translation from *Danas*, New Year edition 2004, December 31 2003–January 2, 2004, http://www.danas.co.yu/20031231/vikend8.html.

8 Europeanizing Islam or the Islamization of Europe: political democracy vs. cultural difference

Bassam Tibi

This chapter argues that Europe and Islam are in conflict, because European secularism and traditional Islam are based on different world views and both need to adapt in their mutual encounter: Europe by reacquainting itself with its specifically Christian roots within the context of secularism, Islam by adapting itself to a new European context marked by different values. European enlargement and transnational Islam are heading toward a fateful choice, not an unavoidable clash. The Europeanization of Islam, properly understood, will benefit both, Europe and Islam. The Islamization of Europe will be of enormous cost to both Europe and progressive elements in Islam. Some parts of my argument contradict fashionable and comfortable notions that Europe's encounter with Islam, in the form of immigration and European enlargement, will bring into reach the multiculturalism that has eluded Europe for so long. This is the argument of Hakan Yavuz in chapter 9 of this book. Nothing could be further from the truth. The eventual outcome of the renewed encounter between Europe and Islam is far from clear. It depends on how European states and the European Union will react to the growing number of Muslims in their midst and which strand of Islam will eventually prevail politically in Europe's Islamic diaspora, in Turkey, and in the Islamic world at large. Rather than hoping for the best outcome and hiding unpleasant realities, this chapter provides the descriptive analysis that identifies the players, most of them not known to specialists in European affairs or international relations, and the enormous political stakes. This chapter is guided by the assumption that the Europeanization of Islam is both possible and desirable. This does not hold, however, for political Islam, in this chapter used as a synonym for Islamic fundamentalism. In the interest of candor I would like to note at the outset that I write this paper with a strong political engagement and with an unusual biography. As an ethnic Arab Muslim of an *ashraf* background (Islamic nobility) and a German citizen who has not been accepted by the society in which he lives, my values favor the principle of political inclusion and agree with those informing

Europe's "open society." I believe strongly that inclusion in Europe comes with the commitment to accepting the values that constitute what it means to be European. What do I mean by Europe, Islam, and Europeanization? In using these concepts I seek to avoid the traps posed by essentialism and reductionism. The late twentieth century is witnessing a "revolt against the West"[1] and also against the model of universal Europeanization that is directed not only against Western hegemony but also against "Western values as such" (Bull, 1984: 223). The contemporary continuing revolt is intensifying and reaches Europe in the form of migration. The emergence of political Islam as a transnational, universal religion marks the arrival of a political vision that seeks to displace the West rather than live amicably side by side with it. Political Islam poses a fundamental challenge to the cultural foundations of the present world order organized in a secular framework. Dan Philpott (2002) describes that framework as the "authority structure of the Westphalian synthesis." And political Islam challenges also the validity of the principle of *laïcité*, of secularity in Europe itself. The Arabic-Islamic term *hijra* (Tibi, 2002: 258–88) is not only restricted to describing the migration of people from one place to another; it does much more. The religious doctrine of *hijra* obliges migrants – as believers – to proselytize. From this perspective the Islamic migration to Europe cannot be accommodated easily, as supporters of a European multiculturalism like to believe, without affecting a fundamental change in Europe's secular collective identity (Tibi, 1998a, 2002; Spuler-Stegemann, 2002). Should Europeanization prove unworkable and Muslims fail to shed their belief in the doctrine of *hijra*, then Europe will fail to integrate Muslim migrants and massive social and political conflicts lie ahead. While a secular Turkey would be a boon for those seeking to create a new framework for Euro-Islam, an Islamist Turkey would be a disaster.

After providing a historical account that situates my analysis, this chapter discusses the experience of Muslim migrants in Europe as well as in individual countries and reviews Turkey's complicated accession bid with the EU.

History and the political possibility of hybridization

Historical and geographic differences are so noticeable as to invalidate all views of a uniform Europe and a monolithic Islam. In the medieval era, for example, Islamic civilization was much more advanced than Europe's. In the twentieth century, however, Shakib Arslan (1939), a prominent Muslim thinker, asked in the title of his influential and widely noted book: "Why are Muslims set back to backwardness, while others have advanced?" Spatial differences are equally striking. Islam is not the same in Indonesia as in Morocco (Geertz, 1971). And there exist, of course, religious varieties of Islam and varieties of secularism in Europe. This is not to deny significant commonalities. Shaped by Roman-inflected law, Western Europe is united by value-orientation and institutional form (Braudel, 1994: 307–426). The same is true of Islamic civilization (Hodgson, 1974).

A non-essentialist understanding of the concept of civilization informs the analysis of secularization as a social process of functional differentiation (Tibi, 1980). To varying degrees, all West European states and societies separate religion and politics, institutionalize civil society, and build secular democracies based on substantive citizenship and human rights. In view of this fact it is a mistake to view the EU as an exclusive "Christian club," for on all counts its identity is secular. Like Europe, Islam is also a civilizational entity characterized by the world view of *Dar al-Islam*. In Islam there is a civilizational unity of the *umma* existing along recognized lines of local cultural diversity. As a light-skinned Arab I was treated in Senegal as a brother, while Afro-Americans seeking a cultural home there were turned down as aliens. Similarly in Indonesia and elsewhere in non-Arab parts of *Dar al-Islam* I have never been treated as "alien." Doctrinally orthodox Islam (Salafism) is not only a spiritual faith, but a transnational religion with a legal system (*shari'a*) based on a universal world view that is, if it is not adjusted, arguably incompatible with Europe in terms of values, law, and related institutions. This is not to deny the possibility that a reformed Islam can be "rethought" (Arkoun, 1994). Islam could be Europeanized. But an Islam defined by *shari'a* and *jihad* is unacceptable to a Europe intent on maintaining its civilizational identity.

There existed periods both in Islamic and European history during which it was possible to cross imagined thresholds between these two civilizations. Cultural borrowing and inter-civilizational cross-fertilization came about through the Hellenization of Islam and later through the impact of Islamic rationalism on the European Renaissance. Historians agree that Charlemagne was the founder of Europe and the Belgian historian Henri Pirenne (1939) linked the emergence of Europe under Charlemagne to the Islamic challenge.[2] He argued that Europe took form as a civilizational entity in the Carolingian age under the impact of the Islamic challenge. Many historians have followed Pirenne in their interpretation of the framework of the encounter of Europe with Islamic expansion. From Carolingian times until the Renaissance one can speak of "Western Christendom" and of a Christian Europe (*Abendland*) constituting one entity (Brown, 1996). Since the Renaissance – and more generally with the rise of the West (Burckhardt, 1988; Parker, 1988) – Europe has transformed itself into a secular entity. As Leslie

Lipson (1993: 63) puts it: "The main source of Europe's inspiration shifted from Christianity back to Greece, from Jerusalem to Athens. Socrates not Jesus, has been the mentor of the civilization that in modern times has influenced or dominated most of the planet."

And paradoxical as it may sound to those who today are essentializing civilizational differences, Islamic influences helped Europe move in this direction:

Aristotle crept back into Europe by the side door. His return was due to the Arabs, who had become acquainted with Greek thinkers . . . Both Avicenna and Averroës were influenced by him. When the University of Paris was organized, Aristotle was introduced there from Cordoba. (Lipson, 1993: 62)

As the Hellenization of medieval Islam was possible then, so a Europeanization of segments of Islamic civilization ready to join Europe is possible now. The *shari'a* schools of *Fiqh* Islam (sacral jurisprudence) stood in conflict with the rationalist Islam of the Hellenized philosophies of Farabi, Ibn Rushd, and Ibn Sina (Davidson, 1992). Sufi Islam – a spiritual Islam adopted by local non-scriptural cultures (mostly in West Africa and Southeast Asia, but also in Turkey, and Morocco) – was also in conflict with rigid, totalizing and essentializing *shari'a* Islam. Islamic medieval rulers were secular in practice as they separated *siyasa* from *shari'a*. As Joseph Schacht (1964: 54–55) writes, in medieval Islam there was a real difference between state administration/*siyasa* and *shari'a*: "a double administration of justice, one religious exercised by the *Kadi*, on the basis of the *shari'a*, the other secular and exercised by the political authorities . . . prevailed in practically the whole of the Islamic world."

At issue is a basic distinction between *shari'a* Islam (Salafism) and political Islam (Islamism). The existence of doctrinal Islam need not prohibit the evolution of a reformed Islam more favorable to Europe. With roots in the Renaissance, Europe's identity is based on a minimum civic culture of secular democracy and a civil society. It is highly questionable whether European roots do make it inevitable that the concept of "civil society does not translate into Islamic terms" (Mardin, 1995: 279). On the contrary, I argue here that citizenship, pluralism, tolerance, and modern positive law can be established in Islam if the effort at accommodating them is legitimized in religio-cultural terms. Making distinctions is not the same as drawing cultural boundaries. An essentialized Christian, and at times secular, meaning of Europe as an *Abendland*, would "other" Islam and Muslims. Analogously Muslim migrants and Turkey can never become European if their beliefs are essentialized, presented in ahistorical definitions such as an exclusive *umma* or an equally exclusive *Dar al-Islam*. Both essentialisms are serious intellectual mistakes that lead into intellectual dead-ends.

European politicians react angrily to the accusation that the EU is a "Christian club" and maintain that the emerging European polity is an association of states bound together by a "community of values." In this understanding, the European Union is a civilizational entity oriented toward secular values. As some leaders of political Islam claim – and pursue – an Islamization of Europe (Spencer, 2003: 51–83), Islamism as a politicized religion increasingly touches on the identity and security of secular Europe. The emergence of political Islam as the ideology of a new internationalism of desecularization (Ayubi, 1991; Tibi, 1998c) is directly relevant to the processes of European enlargement. However, secularization understood as a decoupling of religion from politics, has precedents in Islamic history and philosophy. Political Islam as a trans-national religious world view is often mistaken as "Islam" in general. It is worth pointing out that political Islam and its neo-Islamic doctrine of "*din-wa-dawla*/unity of state and religion" are quite recent phenomena. Made by history they can also be unmade through politics.

The newly invented Islamic tradition of world peace as *Pax Islamica* (Nardin, 1993: 128–45) is based on a vision in which the *Islamicate* (*Dar al-Islam*) maps the entire globe. Dozens of contemporary Islamic books argue that the West prevented Islam from accomplishing its mission of peace and unification of humanity. This vision of an Islamic world peace, as constructed today by political Islam, is an expression of a transnational religion (Qutb, 1992). The ultimate goal is to be pursued through proselytization and Islamization, and this world view is incompatible with either the European understanding of religious pluralism or with the principle of *laïcité*. Islam can be related to Europe, but not through the incorporation of Europe into *Dar al-Islam*. It follows that this version of Islamization runs totally counter to Europeanization.

Islam is a universal religion, which implies a transnational political outlook. Behind the great diversity of local cultures there is a common world view binding Muslims to one another. The *umma* community exists as a majority population in fifty-seven states and as a minority in states such as India, where it counts about 130 million members. This *umma* community constitutes the Islamic civilization defined by world view and a transnational organization. In Islamic faith *umma* is a com-munity of solidarity, but following the politicization of Islam this *umma* can be the grounds for a concept of the international system that rivals secular notions. The question is: can both civilizations accommodate one another in a cross-cultural understanding that transcends the collective memories of mutual conquests through crusade and *jihad*? An analysis of the politics of European migration and European accession opens a window into the complex array of answers that contemporary Europe offers.

Islamic migration: *hijra* – proselytization or Muslim incorporation into a European *Wertegemeinschaft*?

Europeanization is a potential bridge between Europe, Muslim migrants, and Turkey, provided that both Europeans and Muslim migrants and their religious leaders make important changes in their religious and political beliefs and practices. Abandoning plans for a cultural assimilation of Muslims to Europe's secular standards is as important as is setting aside hopes for an Islamization of Europe. What matters most, for Muslim migrants and for Turkey, is a process of political incorporation premised on inclusive notions of legal citizenship as well as European political value orientations. *Euro-Islam* is a concept that offers a framework for such a process of political incorporation without cultural assimilation (Bistolfi and Zabal, 1995: 230–34). To be sure, Euro-Islam as a policy concept adopted by European governments, such as Sweden and France, is not the kind of "European Islam" spokesmen of the West European Islam diaspora like Tariq Ramadan use as a cover for their favored political strategies that aim at something quite different. For France the issue is posed most acutely in the incorporation of Muslim migrants from the Maghreb (Islamic North Africa) countries, associate members of the EU within the framework of the Euro-Mediterranean partnership (Hopwood, 1985; Brauch et al., 2000). French thinking has evolved remarkably toward replacing the idea of assimilation to French culture (Hargreaves, 1995) with the concept of integration restricted to an incorporation into the political practices and value orientations of France's civic culture of *citoyennité* and *laïcité*. The stark choice for Europe is aptly summarized by the title of Nezar AlSayyad's and Manuel Castells's (2002) book *Muslim Europe or Euro-Islam?*

Global migration (Weiner, 1995) is the engine that brings Islam from the Mediterranean borders of Europe to the heart of the continent. European states have reacted diversely to this challenge. Despite the influx of about 10 million migrants between 1989 and 1999, Germany acknowledged only in 2003, in the context of a national debate over a new immigration law, that it had become a country of immigration. In July 2004 the German Parliaments (Bundestag and Bundesrat) legislated the new law. With Muslims accounting for about 40 percent of all European immigrants, Germany has a large community of Muslim migrants. Political incorporation has become a necessity; simply issuing a passport is totally insufficient. Compared to Germany's half-hearted and belated attempt to address the issue, France is a model. The French are not devoted to a "secular fundamentalism," as uninformed Americans occasionally polemicize. The widely noted headscarf controversy is a conflict over the meaning of a secular France. At issue is the disputed acceptance of the *shari'a*. Headscarves serve as a symbolic claim that the divine, Islamic *shari'a* law is valid in France and Europe. Should French *laïcité* or Islamic *shari'a* determine public life in France? And should *shari'a*-Islam or *Euro*-Islam prevail in Europe? *Laïcité* and *Euro*-Islam favor the political incorporation of Muslim migrants. In contrast *shari'a* divides Muslims from France and Europe. Spread in European mosques and religious schools, the world view of *hijra*-Islamization and *da'wa/* proselytization or *jihad* poses an insurmountable barrier to political incorporation.

Muslim migrants are pouring into the EU from all parts of the Islamic world. They have two major characteristics: they are embedded in the institutional structures of a transnational religion and simultaneously separated from one another by ethnicity and sectarian religion, as are, for example, Kurds from Turks and Sunnis from Alevites. This pattern of diversity in unity corresponds with the general Islamic rule. In addressing national governments, European authorities, or the general public through the media, religious leaders of the Muslim diaspora, such as Nadeem Elyas, a Saudi who heads an association of Sunni German mosques (ZMD), pretend to speak for all Muslims when they advocate the doctrine of a supposedly universally shared Islamic obligation to proselytize (*da'wa*). This doctrine was pursued in a historical process. After the Islamic revelation in 610, the Prophet Mohammed migrated in 622 from Mecca to Medina to establish the first *umma* polity in Islam. From the *hijra* stronghold of Medina the Prophet spread Islam through *jihad* and proselytization all over Arabia. After the death of the Prophet his successors, the caliphs, continued to wage *jihad* wars for the proselytization of Islam and started the process of Islamic expansion beyond Arabia (Tibi, 1999). Within the framework of this *historical Islam* religious leaders have constructed a universal *hijra* doctrine prescribing migration into the non-Islamic world in an effort to proselytize for Islam. This *hijra* doctrine still shapes the world view of most Imams who preach to the Islamic diaspora in Europe. Since a Muslim is not allowed to submit to non-Muslim authority, the doctrine is clearly opposed to the European project of politically incorporating its Muslim migrants as Harvard's Charles Maier once put it as "citizens of heart."

Doctrinal barriers notwithstanding, Muslims are moving to Europe in large numbers. Around 1950 only about 800,000 Muslims were living in

Western Europe, mostly in Britain and France. Their lineage dated back to the nineteenth century. Most were in one way or another politically incorporated and even culturally assimilated. The growth in numbers in subsequent decades made social and political problems more acute (Teitelbaum and Winter, 1998: 221–40) as an "Islamic presence in Europe" emerged (Gerholm and Lithman, 1988). New waves of migration began, in particular from Turkey to Germany in the 1960s and have skyrocketed in the 1990s under the impact of crises in the Balkans, North Africa, South Asia, and the Kurdish problem in Turkey as well as in Iraq. At the turn of the century about 40 percent of the total of European immigrants are Muslims. According to an EU estimate the number of Muslims in the EU stood in 2003 at about 17 million. In Germany there are several cities, especially in the Rhineland industrial area, where 15–20 percent of the total population is Turkish and does not speak German. In many classrooms children of migrants outnumber Germans. The same is true in France and Scandinavia. Such high figures have boosted the perception that Muslims pose a growing threat to Europe's identity, while Muslims remain afraid of losing their "Islamic identity" as a result of incorporation as European citizens.

The diversity of Islamic civilization is reflected in its European diasporic community, which is divided along ethnic and sectarian lines. In Germany Muslims are from Turkey, in France from the Maghreb (North Africa), and in Britain from South Asia (Pakistan, India, Bangladesh). Yet none of these communities remains ethnically exclusive. In Germany 2.5 million Turks constitute only about two-thirds of a total Muslim diaspora of about 3.7 million – in the 1960s the label "Turk" was synonymous with "Muslim." The Islamic ghetto of Berlin-Kreuzberg, is no longer exclusively Turkish as a significant number of Palestinians has moved in, with little interaction between the two groups. Furthermore, 1.5 million Turkish migrants have now moved to European countries other than Germany.[3]

The comparison between Islamic migration to Europe and the US is illuminating. American Turks are American citizens and perceive themselves as such, while Turks living in Europe perceive themselves as Turks rather than as Europeans, even when they legally are citizens, as are 400,000 of Germany's 2.5 million Turks. The difference between the US and Germany is rooted in their different capacities to politically incorporate immigrant populations. Germany tends to be ethnically exclusive, probably more so than France and certainly more than the US (Brubaker, 1992). As a result of a change in legislation passed in 2000, it is now possible for Muslim immigrants to Germany to be issued a European passport; but this falls far short of being politically fully

Islam

incorporated into the structure of European political values. Only in exceptional cases does one speak of Turkish-Germans. It is much more common to address Turkish citizens in Germany as "Turks holding a German passport."

The difference between the political incorporation of American Turks and the ghettoization of Turks in Germany also involves factors other than host government policy. American Turks come from the Istanbul–Ankara–Izmir triangle. They are mostly middle class and hold Western outlooks. In contrast, Turks living in Germany tend to come from eastern Anatolia. They tend to be poor and poorly educated, on religious as well as secular issues. This is reflected in their strong rural and traditional Islamic outlooks. By and large since the 1960s the political incorporation of Turks into German society has not succeeded (Tibi, 2002). In contrast to earlier migrants, they enter the institutions, such as the mosque, of a gated diaspora culture that fosters exclusion. To become European it is not sufficient to have a German or French passport. Beyond legal citizenship immigrants must acquire the broader identity of political citizenship, subscribing to core elements of a polity's value-system (*Wertegemeinschaft*) and outlook. This "citizenship of heart" can be found in America, but not in Germany and other parts of Europe. Instead one finds parallel societies of Muslims in Berlin, Hamburg, Frankfurt, and suburban Islam in Paris and other French cities.[4] It would be wrong to blame exclusively either Muslim migrants or European host societies for this state of affairs; both are implicated. The political culture of countries like Germany is ethnic and often exclusive, and Muslims from rural backgrounds and traditional Islamic beliefs are inclined to self-ethnicization. Exclusion and self-ethnicization are different sides of the same coin. Britain, Sweden, and Italy, and even states with small Islamic minorities, such as Switzerland and Austria, differ from Germany in degree not in kind. Europeans and migrants are both responsible for failed Europeanization.

A full depiction of the life of the Islamic diaspora in Europe would require data on both the institutional and organizational forms of diaspora life and of the transnational connectors that bolster political Islam in Europe. Due to the lack of systematic data it is practically impossible to track the sources of funding for the construction of mosques and the running of religious associations (*Moscheevereine*), schools, and bookstores. This shortage of data and empirical research has four causes that illustrate the obstacles facing the process of incorporation into Europe. First, "gated diaspora communities" (Papastergiadis, 2000: 198) create a sense among Muslims in Europe of living surrounded by a hostile environment of *Dar al-Kuffar* (the House of Unbelievers) or, worse, of *al-Salibiyun* (crusaders). Many Imams teach this attitude in the mosques and affiliated religious associations and schools, where they call for *jihad*, as is the case in the Saudi-funded Fahd Academy in Bonn, Germany as disclosed by German media (*Der Spiegel*, 2003: 54–55). Scholars and the police find it virtually impossible to enter this gated community. Second, in striking contrast to their self-descriptions as the proselytizing spearhead of Islam in a world of unbelievers, the leaders of the Islamic diaspora seek purely instrumental dialogue with church and peace movements in Europe, and in most instances such dialogue deliberately sidesteps all contentious issues (Spuler-Stegemann, 2004). What Marvine Howe (2000: 5) has argued for the case of Turkish Islamists applies more generally to the leadership of the Islamic diaspora in Europe: Islamists "speak with contradictory voices." Third, the few leaders of the Muslim diaspora who speak European languages often engage in double talk if not outright deception.[5] They rely on very different discourses when speaking to non-believers and believers. This makes it virtually impossible to rely on interviews as an instrument of empirical research. When interviewed, Imams never reveal their true beliefs and never disclose facts about the community they lead. Instead they seek to deceive those who are interviewing them. This is the practice of Shi'i *taqiyya*, which Sunni Muslims have adopted as *iham* or deception. Fourth and finally, whenever a journalist or scholar, against all odds, succeeds in getting some data and publishes the findings, the investigator is subject to damaging libel suits. The case of Udo Ulfkotte, a German journalist working for the *Frankfurter Allgemeine Zeitung*, serves as an example. After the results of his investigative reporting appeared under the title "Der Krieg in unseren Städten" (The War in our Cities), his career was ruined and he lost his job. His personal story is a warning to anyone who intends to publish similar investigations (Ulfkotte, 2003). A colleague working as a journalist for Germany's most important weekly, *Der Spiegel*, told me that after every major article it publishes on the Muslim diaspora even this journal is routinely exposed to political pressure and damaging lawsuits.

Islam's diaspora in Europe is transnational. No Islamic country, including the formally secular and democratic Turkey, would tolerate Western intervention in its domestic religious affairs – organizing, say, in favor of Middle Eastern Christians or protesting against the discrimination of Alevites. Yet Turkey and Saudi Arabia, among others, claim the right to participate in the decisions affecting Muslim affairs inside Europe. In Turkey, the state office of religious affairs, the *Diyanet* authority (*Diyanet Isleri Baskanligi*) sends Imams to mosques in Europe. In Germany, the DITIB mosques are run by the Turkish state and, currently, are under the influence of moderate religious leadership. With some exceptions, specifically the Fahd mosque and its academy in Bonn, Saudi Arabia does not itself run mosques. It does, however, provide funds for building mosques and teaching the most orthodox Wahhabi version of Islam in *madrassa* schools (Schwartz, 2002: 181–255). Even secular Kemalist politicians, like former Turkish Prime Minister Mesut Yilmaz, insist that Turks living in Europe have Turkey as their first home country, and that European countries rank only second even for Turks born in Europe. In contrast to Turkey and Saudi Arabia, Morocco, with a rapidly growing population of emigrants in Europe, barely intervenes into the lives of Muslim migrants, and Moroccan private religious foundations, which fill some of the void, are less active than comparable Saudi and Turkish foundations (Spuler-Stegemann, 2002: 46–91, 92–121). In short, in different ways the Islamic states of Turkey, Saudi Arabia, and Morocco are embedded in transnational religious networks of Islam in Europe.

In the analysis of non-state actors we must distinguish between four varieties of Islam: orthodox Salafist Islam, Sufi Islam, liberal Islam, and Islamism. All four are represented in the Islamic diaspora of Europe and are fully integrated into transnational Islamic networks. For instance, as is true of the United States, the mosques of the Salafist orthodox Islam in Europe are mostly Wahhabi in belief, and are Saudi-funded (Schwartz, 2002). Despite the fact that they receive Saudi money, they act as non-state actors. In sharp contrast, the only liberal version of Islam in Europe, with an expressly European value orientation, is found in France. The Imam of Paris, Dalil Boubakeur, and the supreme Mufti of Marseille, Soheib Bencheikh, are prominent figures of a Europeanized Islam. They receive the support of the French government and are therefore despised by Salafists and Islamists. Their political base in the Muslim community is weak. Dalil Boubakeur, for example, was opposed to the establishment of an official council representing Muslims in their dealings with the state. When the French state insisted on setting up an elected council and appointed him president, the elections led to an overwhelming victory for the Muslim Brotherhood. Because Boubakeur could not count on his own constituency within the council he resigned, allegedly for "health reasons." No liberal Imams can be found preaching in Germany, Sweden, or Britain.

Islamism is extremely powerful in the European diaspora and its spread reflects the lack of both integration and Europeanization. Here it is important to distinguish between institutional Islamists (such as the Muslim Brotherhood or *Milli Görüs*) and the jihadists (such as *Groupes Islamiques Armées*/GIA). Significantly, the most important fundamentalist movements in Islam, such as the Muslim Brotherhood/ *al-Ikhwan al-Muslimun* (Mitchell, 1969), have their bases in Europe, especially in the major mosques of Germany, France, and Switzerland. Dating back to 1928, when it was founded by Hasan al-Banna in Cairo, the Muslim Brotherhood was Islam's first fundamentalist political organization. Hasan al-Banna's grandson, Tariq Ramadan, acts as Imam and teaches in Switzerland (Spencer, 2003: 64–67, 68–69). Despite its jihadist background, the movement is now considered institutional-moderate. This *Ikhwan*/Muslim Brotherhood movement is well represented in Europe, even in secular France. The institution representing this group at the federal level in Germany, the *Islamische Gemeinschaft Deutschlands*/Islamic Community of Germany, is on the list of extremist organizations kept by Germany's Office for the Protection of the Constitution, a police agency charged with tracking political radicals inside the country. There is a jihadist branch of Islam in Europe that supports al-Qaida. Like moderate Islamists, the jihadists act openly and without restraint in a variety of mosque associations. Although both the Muslim Brotherhood and the al-Qaida-oriented groups are basically Arab-Sunni organizations, they are clearly unrelated. There are also non-Arab fundamentalists in the Islamic diaspora in Europe, most prominently the Turkish group *Milli Görüs*.

Islam in Europe: country experiences

The choice between Muslim incorporation into Europe and Muslim proselytization in Europe is a European-wide issue. But it plays itself out differently in each country.

Germany

Despite the obstacles to empirical research the character of the political and religious representation of the Islamic diaspora in Germany is clear. Two exclusively Sunni Muslim organizations compete with one another (Spuler-Stegemann, 2002) and exclude virtually all non-Sunni Muslims, while claiming to represent the entire diaspora. The predominantly or exclusively Turkish *Islam-Rat* is close to the fundamentalist organization *Milli Görüs*. The predominantly Arab *Zentralrat der Muslime Deutschlands* (ZMD) is headed by a Saudi, Nadeem Elyas, who publicly denies being a Wahhabi or member of the Muslim Brotherhood despite widespread suspicion that this is truly the case. Germany has about 2,400 mosques, and most of them have affiliated religious associations. Although most of these mosques have foreign funding, the exact sources and amounts are unknown and never disclosed. Christian churches are also known to have received external financial support to sustain them in hostile environments. It is beyond doubt, however, that beside Turkish millionaires, the so-called Saudi and Gulf "welfare foundations" are among the major donors of the mosques association. And the ideology espoused by these donors is highly traditional and inimical in many ways to European interests. Mosques are divided along ethnic (Turkish, Iranian, Bosnian, Pakistani, etc.) and sectarian lines (Sunni, Shi'i, Ahmadi, Alevite, etc.). However, with the exception of those operating under the Turkish state authority that runs the Religious Affairs Turkish-Islamic Union (DITIB), most Sunni mosques are controlled by the *Islam-Rat* and the *Zentralrat* (Spuler-Stegemann, 2002). Although hard statistics are not available, most Muslims belong to no religious associations, and most experts think that, taken together, both organizations represent no more than 10 percent of the Islamic diaspora. For this reason, German courts have repeatedly denied these organizations to legally represent "Islam."

Although it is a secular democracy, Germany does not fully separate Church and state. The German state collects a religion-based tax for churches and synagogues, provides funds for church activities at schools, and above all guarantees the representation of churches in public institutions, such as the boards of public broadcasting stations. As long as they represent *one* religion, Article 7 of Germany's Basic Law guarantees any religious community state recognition as a Church. Thus the German government tolerates Church intervention in politics. The leaders of the German Muslim community would like to see this model applied to themselves, foremost in the areas of taxation and media. The Protestant and Catholic Churches do not like this Islamic bid for recognition, but yet do not oppose it, because they prefer the political recognition of Islam to the alternative: if the principle of strict secularity were applied they themselves would lose a great deal of power. The Islamic leaders of the *Zentralrat* sued the German state for lack of equal treatment with the recognized Christian Churches and asked for recognition as the sole representation of a unified Islam. German law and German religious politics would thus have enhanced the disproportionate political influence of Sunni-Salafist Islam and the political suppression of the religious Islamic diversity that actually exists. In this case, however, matters turned out differently. Even though Islamists typically receive favorable rulings from German judges, a Düsseldorf court found in 2001 that the *Zentralrat* represents only a small portion of the German Islamic diaspora; it denied the *Zentralrat*'s claim for sole representation.

France, Great Britain, and the Netherlands

In all of Europe France has developed the most advanced policies for dealing with its Muslim diaspora. In Britain, by way of contrast, virtually no such policies exist, since the state is denied any intervention in religious affairs. After September 11, 2001, Britain's then Secretary for Home Affairs, David Blunkett, worked hard to change this situation, without much success. His concerns centered on Imams trained in Afghanistan under the Taliban and with proven connections to al-Qaida. In their mosques they have called for *jihad* against the West and in their sermons they are spreading hatred against "Jews and crusaders," both of whom are labeled as "enemies of Islam." Led by a Syrian, Mohammad al-Bakri, jihadists of the Islamist group of *al-Muhajirun* celebrated in the streets of London what they considered to be the "heroic" September 11 attacks and the martyrs of the *jihad* waged against the West (Tibi, 2002: 260–72). The suicide bombings in London in July 2005 are likely to make for a radical change in British policy.

Is it a sign of a lack of democracy that nothing like this did or could happen in Paris? Before the early 1990s the policies of the French state aimed at the political incorporation and cultural assimilation of Muslims. As I argued above, in the early 1990s, however, French policy downgraded its expectation to a political incorporation that included Muslim acceptance of the values of France's civic culture but fell short of cultural assimilation. Immigrant populations were now required to cross a threshold that was lower than full cultural assimilation but included compliance with the principle of *laïcité* and the political identity of a *citoyen*. Such political rights and values are expected to trump membership in the Islamic *umma* and consequentially require abandoning adherence to *shari'a* law. Although demanding substantial religious reforms, it is simply wrong to regard this policy as a mere reflection of France's "secular fundamentalism." Instead, French policy expresses a strong commitment to civil society, secular democracy, and individual human rights as the core of Europe's civilizational identity. French policy is strongly opposed to introducing *shari'a* law through the back door. On this crucial point political concessions in the name of cultural relativism would amount to a cultural surrender of the French state to a new Islamic absolutism that does not countenance any compromise. In France as in Europe at large, most of Islam's religious leaders have little interest in fostering a process of incorporating Muslim migrants into Europe. They prefer instead to press for the adoption of an Indian model of coping with religious diversity. In India a Muslim minority of 130 million has the legal right to practice *shari'a* law (Muslim personal law). Under such a model

218   Islam

European states would sanction legal segregation, the creation of a dual legal system, and an end to a core defining criterion of Europe's civilizational identity as reflected in the cultural underpinning of Roman-inflected public law, an important source of European values.

Finally, brief mention should be made of a novel approach taken by the Netherlands. The Dutch government appears to have found its own distinctive solution for the predicament of the Europeanization of Islam. As far as possible, it insists on training European Imams according to European standards rather than importing them from abroad. This policy is not yet fully implemented. After the assassination of the Dutch film maker Theo Van Gogh in the fall of 2004 and numerous reprisal torchings of mosques it is too early to come to a final assessment of the policy's staying power and merits. However, the issues discussed in this chapter, hitherto mostly taboos, are now in the center of public debate that amounts to nothing less than a response to Islam that is both assertive and inclusive.

Europeanizing Turkey between secularization and political Islam

Turkey's potential accession to the EU is a politically charged aspect of the enlargement process. In the words of Prime Minister Erdoğan cited by the *Frankfurter Allgemeine Zeitung* after a meeting with Angela Merkel, the leader of the German opposition party: "On our agenda is only a full membership, not a privileged partnership; the Turkish people want to join Europe and we do not accept any other solution." Accession would help Turkey to become a modern Islamic state and allow Europe to demonstrate that it is not a Christian political community intent on excluding members holding different religious beliefs.

It is tempting to accept uncritically Hakan Yavuz's convenient argument that Turkey's EU membership would foster the Europeanization of that country and at the same time promote a Europeanized Islam. Political analysis should resist that temptation and come to grips with the existence of a great variety of Islamist political movements in Turkey and its European diaspora. Aside from the secular Kemalists and ordinary, apolitical Sufi Muslims, there exist two different generations of political Islamists in Turkey. First, there is the anti-Western Necmettin Erbakan generation, holding to an Islamist neo-Ottoman and pan-Turkish outlook. Secondly, there exists the Tayyip Erdoğan generation, with an instrumental Europeanism. The patron of political Islam in Turkey, Erbakan, succeeded, with the assistance of the Kemalist Tansu Çiller, in seizing power democratically. He was Turkey's prime minister in 1996–97. After he challenged Kemalism with his Islamist policies, the

Turkish Security Council forced Erbakan to leave office. His *Refah Partisi* was subsequently banned as was its successor, the *Fazilet Partisi*. Political crisis conditions, however, gave a boost to the Islamists. Under the new leadership of Tayyip Erdoğan, on November 3, 2003 a new party, the AKP, won a landslide victory in a democratic election, giving it a two-thirds majority in Parliament. As the successor of the preceding Islamist parties the AKP is clearly Islamist, despite the fact that AKP politicians present themselves as "conservative Muslims," similar in ideological orientation to those of the secular "Christian-Democrats" in Western Europe, rather than as political Islamists. The AKP has not offered a single conceptual elaboration of the presumed distinction between Islamism and Islamic conservatism, and it does not count a single well-known reform theologian among its ranks. The only prominent liberal Muslim theologian in Turkey, Yasar Nuri Öztürk, is a member of the Turkish Parliament and belongs to the Social Democratic Party (CHP), not to the AKP (Öztürk, 2003). The behavioral implications of this change are not yet clear. It is widely understood, for example, that in the Turkish diaspora in Germany the AKP has good relations with the Islamist group *Milli Görüs* while shunning liberal Sunni and Alevite Muslim communities. The Foreign Minister of Turkey, the Islamist Abdullah Gül, has publicly requested the German government to recognize *Milli Görüs* and to remove its name from the German list of extremist groups. And Prime Minister Erdoğan reportedly has refused to meet with Alevites during his visits to Berlin. The *New York Times* correspondent for Turkey, Marvine Howe, quotes the prominent Islamist Mustafa Karahasanoğlu as pointing to a fundamental similarity in the political strategies of former Prime Minister Erbakan and current Prime Minister Erdoğan whose views did not change at all as he moved from the role of a leading opposition leader to prime minister. They "share the same philosophy and ideology, although their strategy may differ" (Howe, 2000: 182). The AKP's reformist claim could only be taken seriously if its leaders had made any effort to present an Islamic underpinning for the suggested combination of secular-democratic concepts with Islamic thoughts as other Islamic reformers have. They have not. Instead the AKP is using the power of government to push Islamist legislation. For example, dominated by the AKP's two-thirds majority, on May 14, 2004 the Turkish Parliament passed a new law that upgrades the status of graduates of the well-known Islamist high schools of Imam Hatip. Since these schools were opposed to the principle of secular education from their very beginning, all previous governments have been at pains to curb their influence (Tibi, 1998b: ch. 9, in particular 308–19). Because their religious schooling does not prepare them for studying in the arts and science, prior to the 2004 legislation Imam Hatip graduates were only eligible to enroll in divinity schools. The new law opens all faculties to high-school graduates from Imam Hatip schools. This law occasioned massive protest from the academic establishment and secular Turkish students. The Kemalist president of Turkey Ahmet Sezer refused to sign the law. It is certain that Sezer will be replaced soon by the present AKP speaker of the Parliament. Then, there will be no more Kemalist obstacles to the AKP's political goals.

The rise of political Islam in Turkey creates new complexities. The AKP claims to be more democratic than its predecessor, the secularist Kemalists; yet the AKP is linked to the radical diaspora organization of *Milli Görüs*, which had objected to the secular *Diyanet* sending Imams to Germany. *Milli Görüs* and the *Diyanet* continue to be at odds; they maintain independent mosques in the diaspora, although now, under AKP rule, cooperation is evolving. A liberal Islam interpreted along the separation of religion and politics would make it easy for Turkey to join the EU. Such a Turkey would share common values with Europe. An Islamist Turkey would not. Public opinion in Germany understands this. It opposes full membership by a majority of more than five to one (*Frankfurter Allgemeine Zeitung*, April 21, 2004: 1, 5). Prime Minister Erdoğan and Foreign Minister Gül angered French President Jacques Chirac in December 2003 when they pushed him to take a positive stance toward Turkey's accession bid. Chirac reportedly answered "it is not enough to respect European law in order to be European; one needs also to be polite and civilized" (*Tagesspiegel*, December 14, 2003: 2). At the EU Summit of December 2004, despite long odds, the French and German governments agreed that, starting in October of 2005, negotiations over Turkey's EU accession (within a period of ten to fifteen years) could begin.

European–Ottoman history has been a story of war and conquest.[6] When, thanks to its "military revolution" (Parker, 1988), Europe managed to halt Ottoman incursions into Europe at the end of the seventeenth century, Muslim caliphs were advised to copy European military might. This process of "Importing the European Army" (Ralston, 1996: 43–78) was the beginning of a partial and instrumentally motivated adoption of European practices in the Ottoman Empire (Göcek, 1996). The Ottoman caliphs wanted to import European technology and modes of organization, but were not inclined to adopt European values and institutions. I have described this elsewhere as "the Islamic dream of semi-modernity" (Tibi, 1995). The modernization of the late Ottoman Empire[7] did not aim at the Europeanization of its values, and the strategy did not stabilize the Islamic Ottoman rule so much as accelerate its downfall. The Kemalist revolution grew from these historical roots. Unlike the Ottoman rulers Kemal Pasha wholeheartedly pushed the project of all-out Europeanization. By accepting European cultural modernity this founder of modern Turkey (Macfie, 1994), named Atatürk (father of the Turks), wanted to make his country a fully-fledged European country. He abolished the caliphate, closed Islamic *shari'a* courts and religious schools, forbade headscarves, and introduced European laws. In a sweeping reform altering both script and vocabulary, the Turkish-Osmanli language was Latinized in 1928.

The problem with Turkey's Europeanization through Kemalism was fundamental. Kemalism was a "revolution from above," imposing innovations on society without democratic participation and the necessary cultural underpinnings. It focused mostly on urban centers and barely reached the countryside. The result was the emergence of two different societies within one Islamic country: a more or less superficially Europeanized urban Turkey (Istanbul, Ankara, Izmir) and a rural Turkey deeply rooted in Islamic tradition (*Anatolia* in the limited meaning of the Eastern countryside). Ellen Trimberger (1978: 112) has described this process and its outcome in an analysis that deserves full quotation:

Turkish nationalism with its emphasis ... on secularism ... did try to create a common national consciousness that broke with traditional values – especially Islam as a basis of political identity and legitimacy. But the universal values of Turkish nationalism did not really appeal to the peasants ... The Turkish revolution did not try to change the peasants or integrate them into the new polity ... Rather, the Republican program implied that peasants were "backward" and would only be changed by transforming the laws of the land. Integration from the top down by imposing regulations had been the general approach also behind Ottoman social engineering ... In continuing this bureaucratic style, Kemalism was profoundly unrevolutionary despite the populist themes which the Republic developed. Kemalism did not even try to break down the centuries-old antipathy that villagers felt for the central state and its representatives ... *In fact, a major effect of the Kemalist program was to create two nations: one rural, traditionalist and underdeveloped; the other urban, modernist and developing.* [Author's italics] By not mobilizing peasants, Kemalism strengthened the traditional bond.

As contemporary Turkish politics illustrates, Kemalist political change has backfired. Different strands of political Islam are emerging in Turkey, united in the objective of reversing processes of cultural modernization, acculturation, and secularization into cultural retraditionalization, deacculturation, and desecularization. The overall goal is to reverse what Europeanization has taken place to date (Howe, 2000: 179–94; Kramer, 2000: ch. 5).

As a condition for accession, the EU is insisting on increasing Parliament's power while limiting the power of the purely secular Security Council, which is dominated by the Kemalist military. This is exactly what the Islamists want. In response to European criticism made in 2000 at the World Economic Forum in Davos of the power imbalance between the Council and Parliament, then Prime Minister Bülent Ecevet replied: "In your countries, secularity is well established and therefore, there is no need for a guardian, unlike Turkey in which secularity lacks firm foundations and always can be threatened, therefore the need to be protected."

In accordance with EU demands the Security Council of Turkey is slowly being robbed of its powers. The current Parliament has begun to move down the road of incremental desecularization through the formal rules of democracy. The Turkish writer Murat Cakir (2000) has characterized Islamists as "pseudodemocrats" who, under the cover of democracy, promote their religious goals, both among members of the diaspora and in Turkey. The difference between radical and moderate Islamism is related to means, not ends. The overall objective is the same for both: an Islamic *shari'a* state. Diversity among Islamists is not only ethnic, such as Turkish vs. Algerian Islamists. It also refers to the preferred means of the political struggle, such as *jihad* or participating in legitimate democratic institutions for reasons of convenience rather than because of an abiding commitment to democratic-secular values. Inconvenient as it may be to hear this message, and in undeniable contra-diction of the arguments that Hakan Yavuz advances in chapter 9, the Turkish model of an Islamic state (*din-ü-devlet*) is the goal of all Islamists, both moderate and radical. The choice between Islamic moderation or militancy of Islam is less important than replacing the goal of an Islamic order with the vision of a politics infused by an Islamic ethics. In Islam, religion and secularity can coexist. Therefore, a reformist version of Islam is needed which abandons the obligation to proselytize and ceases to put religious law above secular law. In sharp contrast, combining Islam with a concept of order is not compatible with the Europeanization of either Muslim migrants or Turkey (Tibi, 2004).

Conclusion

Islam is of increasing salience for Europe. European politicians speak much about the need for integrating Muslim migrants. And they argue that the accession of Muslim countries like Turkey will further that end. These speeches do not add up to a programmatic stance. Euro-Islam could present a solution as long as Europe's political leaders insist that the values related to standards of Europeanization are adhered to by all: Europeans, migrants, and candidate countries. At present the question remains, does Europe have an identity (Tibi, 1998a)? Europe needs to answer this question before it requires Europeanization from its migrants and accession countries. The Islamic challenge and the potential of Islamization are not well understood in Europe. The call for toleration of religious difference, without careful attention paid to different strands of Islam, is intellectually facile and politically risky. Instead, as one critic notes, the issue of immigration and integration has been "skewed in the direction of control and security . . . This securitization is reflective . . . of difficulties melding diverse immigration and immigrant policy paradigms at EU level" (Geddes, 2000: 171–72). Especially since September 11, 2001, securitization trumps issues related to culture and identity. Migration from Islamic countries blurs existing boundaries and changes Europe. Muslim migrants are embedded at various levels in the structures of transnational religious communities, many of which are fundamentally opposed to the European values that come with political incorporation. It would, however, be a great mistake to blame only Islamic migrants. European societies are not what they claim to be: models of secularism and non-ethnic societies. European churches enjoy privileged access to secular states, and thinking along ethnic lines is pervasive. To Germans of all different political persuasions, a boy whose name is Mohammed or a girl named Aysha cannot be German – even if they are German-born, are native speakers of German, and are German citizens. This pushes Muslims into the gated Islamic diaspora culture and indirectly contributes to supporting the efforts of those Imams undermining the incorporation of Muslims as "citizens of heart." In outlook, Germans tend to be either pre-modern (on issues of German ethnicity) or postmodern (cultural relativists whose lack of belief in any overarching values ends up in a stance of political indifference). With or without Turkish accession, Europe cannot escape the simple fact that Islam has become a part of Western Europe.

If we want to prevent the clash of civilizations (Herzog, 1999) in Europe, we will need, more than ever, to have a free debate, uncensored by political correctness, and combined with a dialogue that goes beyond the rhetoric of "Christian-Islamic understanding" in addressing the rock-bottom issues and engaging in conflict resolution (Foroutan, 2004: ch. 2). The Europeanization of the Islamic diaspora and of Turkey can be achieved only as the result of political choices by all the concerned parties: Europeans and those Muslims who honestly want to be part of Europe without seeking to Islamize it. It remains to be seen how Europe and Islam will accommodate each other in what looks like a difficult path ahead. As a Muslim migrant who found refuge in Europe I wish Islam to be included in Europe, not the reverse – Europe becoming a part of *Dar al-Islam*. Europe's identity is neither Christian nor Islamic – it is secular based on a civic culture.

Notes

1 I agree with Hedley Bull that the revolt against the Western values is best "exemplified in Islamic fundamentalism" (Bull, 1984: 223). For more details on political Islam see the books by Nazih Ayubi (1991), Oliver Roy (1994), and Tibi (1998c); on the desecularizing impact of Islamism see Tibi (2000). On political Islam three authoritative books in Arabic: al-Ashmawi (1987), Mustafa (1992), and Dharif (1992) are worth mentioning.

2 The Pirenne debate revolves around Islam and the origins of Europe. There is a great literature on this debate, including a Cornell University Press book by Richard Hodges and David Whitehouse (1983). I made an effort at reviving this debate in a book completed at Harvard and published under the title: *Kreuzzug und Djihad. Der Islam und die christliche Welt* (Tibi, 1999), herein in particular chapter 2.

3 These figures are compiled on the basis of collected data from a variety of sources, among others from German newspaper coverage, but also from interviews run by the author with authorities.

4 For more details on this see chapters 3 and 4 on *Parallelgesellschaft* and chapters 7 and 8 on how to change this in my book (Tibi, 2002). On the French case see Gilles Kepel, *Les Banlieus de l'Islam* (Kepel, 1987), and more recently Silverstein (2004).

5 In the German weekly *Die Zeit* (May 29, 2002: 9) and *Der Spiegel* (issue 51, 2001) the dishonest dialogue was addressed under the title "Selig sind die Belogenen," which generated a big debate. The contributions in the volume edited by Ursula Spuler-Stegemann (2004) continue this debate.

6 Kaegi (1992) focuses on the Arab conquests in greater Syria and Mesopotamia by Muslim-Arab tribes. This was continued by the Turks resulting in a combined Arabization and Turkification of Byzantium failing to "contain emergent Islam," as Kaegi suggests. These historical lessons are today pertinent to Europe: the issue is Europeanization versus Islamization via settlements of migrants. On early *jihad* conquests see also Fred Donner (1981).

7 The major research on Ottoman-Islamic history is reflected in a seminal study on the Ottoman Empire by the Harvard historian Cemal Kafadar (1995).

9 Islam and Europeanization in Turkish-Muslim socio-political movements

M. Hakan Yavuz

My essay examines how Turkey's diverse Islamic groups' attitudes toward Europe have changed from rejectionism to accommodation and embrace as a result of interactions with European institutions and changing conditions inside Turkey. In the process of interacting with Europe, a new accommodative cognitive map of Islamic identity has emerged. This new understanding treats Europe and Islam as potentially mutually reconcilable and not oppositional identities locked in constant struggle. Thus, not Islam or a *sui generis* Islamic civilization, but dialectical engagement shapes one's perception of the "other."

This essay differs from Bassam Tibi's essentialist image of a rigid and uniform manifestation(s) of socio-political Islam(s) and a frozen broader Islamic civilization. Tibi's analysis of Euro-Islam is marked by a triangular relationship between essentialism, chauvinism, and fear. He draws the boundaries of Islamic identity around the reified historical notions of *jihad*, *hijra*, and *da'wa*, and he does not want to entertain the possibility of symbolic meanings and multiple understandings of a text or tradition conditioned by and evolving due to internal and external factors in the manifestation of a given Muslim collective self. This essentialist and reductionist outlook amplifies the paradox identified by Edmund Burke for many secular nationalists in the Middle East, who have become inside-out orientalists in their quest for modernity. This is probably why Tibi opts for a "reformed" Islam, informed by and disciplined via the historically particular case of the Christian Reformation and European Enlightenment. Even if we set aside the moral ambiguities of politically imposing such a "reformation project," Tibi seems far from understanding the social, economic, and political conditions that can make such a "desired" liberal or reformed Islam possible. This ostensibly religiously expansionist, ethno-centered, and non-pluralist "Islamic world view" is presented in stark contrast to the ostensibly universal political values of "Western civilization."

Such a simplistically erroneous dichotomy fails to note how even in modern times both Muslim and Western societies have manifested examples of both bloody intolerance and flourishing pluralism. Disturbingly, Tibi seems to be willing to accede to a well-worn tradition of right-wing European bigotry and xenophobia in implicitly endorsing grossly exaggerated fears of "Muslim takeover" of Europe, as a result of migration and the possible membership of Turkey in the EU. Few things would be more likely to prevent a pluralistic and mutually enriching dialectic between nominally Christian and Muslim Europeans than a false dichotomy between a "clash of European secular humanism and Islamic fundamentalism." To view this as the normative basis of interaction between the two only serves to congeal the misplaced chauvinism and sense of cultural superiority of certain conservative Europeans who have witnessed on their soil the genocide of European religious minorities in World War Two and recently in Southeastern Europe, in contrast to the European Muslim record of rule in the Balkans and Iberia. It also allows certain Muslim conservatives to avoid confronting the need for pressing political and social reform in the broader Islamic world and the need for greater pluralism and gender equality in their own communities in Europe. It should be noted that in contrast to Bassam Tibi's fixed dichotomy of "European Islam or Islamic Europe," there is a very good and promising possibility for the emergence of "European Muslims" or "Muslim Europeans." If European elites could only avoid viewing their relationship vis-à-vis their Muslim minorities through the lenses of fear, supremacy, and antagonism, they could discover the historical opportunities for forging a democratic pluralistic Muslim world and a cosmopolitan and tolerant European identity, coexisting side by side.

The spheres of political Islam and the Turkish case

The history of Islam in Turkey is the story of changing and shifting Muslim attitudes toward Islam and Europe. In other words, the shared language of Islam does not prevent disagreements and discursive evolution but rather facilitates the emergence of competing versions of Islam. Turkish political Islamic movements used to identify themselves in opposition to closer integration with Europe and the Western world. Since the early 1990s, however, a dramatic cognitive shift has taken place in Turkey. Islamic political identity is shifting from an anti-Western to a pro-European position, while conversely, the Kemalist bureaucratic-military establishment, which has defined its historic mission as that of guardians leading the nation westward, has become increasingly recalcitrant in regard to integration with Europe. Today one of the few unifying platforms of Turkey's diverse ethnic and religious groups is one favoring membership in the EU. Significantly, this is not only due to promises of socio-economic advancement but also to the promise of greater political, social, and religious freedom. Since the elections of 2002, the more traditional and religiously inclined sections of Turkish society have been more adamant than many in the "secular Kemalist" political and bureaucratic establishment in defending the project of Europeanization. How can we explain this novel and perhaps counterintuitive development in Turkey? This chapter examines "why and how" Turkey's diverse religious socio-political actors reconstruct the meaning and role of European identity by addressing the following three questions: What does European identity entail for various socio-political forces in Turkey? How and why have Turkey's powerful Islamic movements rearticulated a positive view of integration with Europe? Finally, what does the Turkish example teach us about the possibilities of Islamic opposition movements in various authoritarian states adopting a more liberal-democratic ideology and praxis?

Unlike Samuel Huntington or Bernard Lewis, who see the term "Islamic" delimiting a homogeneous, unchanging, religious or civilizational entity, I understand Islam at present as comprising at least seven diverse competing and conflicting political zones (Yavuz, 2004b).[1] Conversion patterns, colonial legacies, types of nationalism, and political economies factor into these evolving separate zones. Yet, under certain political conditions, one sees the emergence of consensus and similarities of "public opinion" on various issues. For instance, the Arab–Israeli conflict and the war in Bosnia helped to forge a shared consensus under the rubric of the Organization of Islamic Conference (OIC), but no such unity has formed around conflicts involving indigenous Muslim populations in Nagorno-Karabakh, Kashmir, and Cyprus. Within each zone, the understanding of the political role of Islam varies among the numerous socio-political groups employing Islamic idioms and identity claims while at the regional level it is informed by national culture and diverse historical and economic factors. It must be stressed that in critically analyzing Islamic, or any other socio-political movements, one must always be cognizant of the specific historical and present-day socio-political contexts in which they operate and evolve. This caveat especially needs emphasizing in the case of scholarship on Islamic-oriented movements where, as noted above, there has been a tendency in certain cases for writers to present reductive and ideologically motivated caricatures that fail to take into account the dialogic contexts and permutations common to all socio-political movements (Qureshi and Sells, 2003).[2] Context and history matter as much as constructed ideological content, which is very rarely, if ever, fixed or eternal. Such a heuristic approach is essential to understanding the various contingent manifestations of political Islam, with the Turkish example underscoring how a context of growing tolerance and pluralism on the part of formerly authoritarian political establishments promotes similar traits on the part of oppositional Islamic movements. This positive and reciprocal interaction provides an invaluable insight that Muslims, Europeans, Americans, and many others would do well to heed.

Political Islam in Turkey clearly demonstrates the localization and accommodation of a universally oriented belief-system. As a result of this localization, one can identify several key characteristics of prevailing forms of Turkish Islamic expressions. Turkish Islam is heavily influenced by the Seljuk and Ottoman heritage of Sufism. Sufi Islam with its dense social networks transmitted the flow of ideas, and practices of various charismatic leaders, helping to link local to more universalistic visions of Islam. In Sufi Islam, there is a self within the self. Muslims are encouraged to encounter and discipline this "other" within the self through devotional thought and practice. The Kemalist campaign of persecution in the 1920s and 30s forced the Sufi orders to shift from a *tekke*-centric (Sufi lodges composed of teachers and disciples), to a text-centric understanding of Islam. In Turkey, print Islam, or textual Islam, has been the dominant discursive mode over the past twenty years. This has allowed a rather promiscuous diversity of political theories and interpretations, ranging from traditional Western liberal theories to that of prominent post-modernist thought, into the discourse of contemporary Turkish Islamic writings. Turkish Islam(s) has not produced prominent radical-Salafist writers, along the lines of Sayyid Qutb or Abu ala-Mawdudi. On the other hand, the Ottoman legacy of Sufi networks and the Kemalist Directorate of Religious Affairs (DRA) has prevented the penetration, from Egypt and Pakistan, of "foreign Islam": manifestations of political Islam that reflect the specific historic and socio-political contexts of those societies. Thus, the fragmentation of religious authority has not been as drastic as in other parts of the Muslim world.

Turkey was not colonized to the extent of other Muslim societies, and the struggle for independence (1919–23) was relatively short and swift, mainly carried out by a regular army, rather than by local insurgents. Thus, the violence of national independence did not set a pattern of opposition to the state, as was the case in Algeria, among the Turkish Sunni majority, and there was no deep sense of siege by the West among Turkish Muslims. The 1974 Cyprus "operation" further consolidated a Turkish self-confidence that stands in contrast to the traumatic and ongoing legacy of destructive Western military interventionism in respect to the Arab world and Iran. Turks have not to the same degree felt themselves to be victims of conspiracies and plots in their relations with the Western world.

Market conditions and the formation of the middle class have also played an important role in the evolution of a liberal and pluralist version of Islam. Turkey has no oil reserves that make an attractive focus for external conquest or internal societal strife and rent seeking. Instead, the country enjoys a tax-based economy with a large middle class and civil society, which allows many close connections between politics, society, and economy. The emergence of an Anatolian bourgeoisie has contributed to the rise and moderation of political Islam by supporting market-friendly and pluralist Islamic movements.

The historical evolution of Turkey's Islamic movements

Becoming European

Contemporary Islamic political thought evolved in relation to the question of modernity in general, and the nation-state in particular. These issues became the building blocks of Muslim thinking in the nineteenth century in the context of Islam's vexed encounter with Europe. European material and intellectual progress impressed the Muslim societies, which used a number of strategies of borrowing, adaptation, and imitation of European ideas and institutions. While imperial conquest and subjugation interrupted this process of reconciliation in many parts of the Muslim world, the governing elite and intellectuals in the Ottoman Empire engaged in a project of modernization of Islamic institutions and ideas in order to maintain and consolidate the power of the Ottoman state.

In the present day, Turkey's struggle to join the European Union (EU) is very much an extension of the historic contest within Turkish society over national orientation and identity. The European roots of this triple heritage (Ottoman/Islamic, European, and Turkic) have been the dominant factors in the Turkish Republic's domestic and foreign policy orientation. Today fully 77 percent of Turks consider themselves to belong to both the European and Muslim worlds, and often describe their position as a symbiotic "bridge between East and West" (Çarkoğlu, 2004). Turkey's Republican People's Party elite wished to construct a modern and successful nation-state out of the remains of the Ottoman Empire. Tragically, however, they equated "Westernization" with superficial, and draconianly imposed, modes of dress and decorum. They failed to appreciate the true basis of Western dynamism in the ideals of pluralism, democratic governance, and a form of secularism that allowed individuals to pursue their freedom of conscience. Thus, this authoritarian and flawed Kemalist conception of "Westernization" produced an axiomatic hostility on the part of many segments of

Turkish society, which were excluded from power. Only tentatively, from the reformist period of Adnan Menderes in the 1950s to the dramatic liberalization of the Özal era of the 1980s, did many Turks come to realize that their rights would be best respected in a system that identified Westernization and secularism with more universal conceptions of pluralism, human rights, and democracy.

The Ottoman Empire was predominantly a Southeastern European state in terms of geography, the origins of its governing elite, and state investment. Evidence that the Balkans were the heartland of the Empire while the Anatolian and Arab provinces were the hinterland deeply marks current socio-political debates in Turkey. Ottoman cultural and social networks were the densest between the Danube and the Drina rivers. Consequently, most of the governing elite came from the Balkan or Rumelian provinces. The forced mass exodus of Muslims from the Balkans provided the political elite of the modern republic.

One of the structuring principles of Turkey's domestic, and therefore foreign policy, has been its struggle to become a *European* nation-state, and thus validate the cultural and ideological revolution inaugurated by Mustafa Kemal (1881–1938), the founder of the Turkish Republic. The Cold War further facilitated Turkey's identification with the "West." However, while Turkey has been a part of the European "system" since the Crimean War of 1854, it was not accepted as a member of the European "community" (Yapp, 1992).

The government of the Republic of Turkey attested to its status as a new Turkish state based on an ethno-linguistic national identity by othering "Islamic" identity as a source of backwardness or a security threat. After 1924, Mustafa Kemal implemented a series of reforms to create a homogeneous secular nation-state by subordinating Kurdish and Islamic identities into a state determined and regimented ethno-linguistic Turkish nationalism. These reforms, known as Kemalism, sought to disestablish and control religion to create a newly disciplined and obedient nation. The state used the educational system, architecture, media, military service, and a dress code to impose this identity. Kemalism tried to coalesce diverse identities into a single hegemonic identity by aiming at a complete socio-political transformation from an Islamic community into an ethno-linguistic, secular national society. Therefore, the state played a key role in the construction and dissemination of a new national identity during, and after, 1925.

The policies of "catching up" with the West while legitimizing the unchallenged authority of the new Republican elite were the main concerns of the state. The Kemalist elite presented themselves as "secular" and "progressive," in opposition to Islamic forces.[3] The Westernization project was presented as "emancipatory" and "anti-religious" but did not include the critical post-Enlightenment values of tolerance, liberalism, and democracy. The Kemalists imagined themselves, in their encounters with "Islamic forces," as being "secular," "rational," and "Western," though they had a very incomplete knowledge of Western political thought and traditions or of the meaning of "secularism" in the Anglo-American sense of the term. A. Adnan-Adivar argues that the Kemalist conception of secularism, similar to logical positivism in Western thought, became the "official dogma of irreligion" and was "imposed on [Turkish society] just as Islamic dogma had been imposed in the past" (Adnan-Adivar, 1951: 128). In Turkey, Kemalism, as a form of radical, authoritarian societal transformation, became not only the ideology that created a new Turkish man but was also deeply involved in the establishment and regulation of a state-monitored public sphere. In the 1930s, responding to societal reaction to the imposed transformation, the state articulated a set of principles to define its ideology as Kemalism, which included six principles: republicanism, étatism, secularism, nationalism, populism, and revolutionism. These principles form the ideological basis of the state and determine the security concerns of the Turkish state by defining its enemies.

Although Turkey was never colonized, Kemalism's uncritical modernization project was effectively a voluntary internal colonization of Turkish society by the imposition of certain simple-minded premises of Orientalism on Islam and Ottoman society.[4] Burke aptly illuminates this paradox, in arguing that "nationalists are inside-out orientalists," who have adopted the orientalists' critique of religion and have "sought to portray themselves as secular, in opposition to the retrograde forces of religion" (Burke, 1998: 689). The rise of the bureaucratic elite in the name of reform and independence very much replicated the ideological superstructure of Europe (Gökay, 1995). The Kemalist elite, which considered itself to be European, indulged itself in a process of projecting Anatolian Muslims as "backward natives" to be emancipated from the "chains of Islam and tradition" only by accepting the Jacobin-positivist tradition of radical modernization *in toto*. The "native subjects" (read Muslims and Kurds), "the internal others" of Kemalist ideology, were delineated and marginalized from within Turkish society to justify the new authoritarian Republican elite's privileges and sense of manifest destiny.

By removing the centuries-old Islamic glue from everyday life and state–society relations, the state was confronted with the difficult task of crafting and disseminating a secularized national identity in its stead (Gellner, 1994). In contrast to the long evolution of European social and political values, with its tradition of a strong civil society outside the control of the state, in Turkey, secularization was imposed from above and independent societal institutions and popular allegiances were crushed. The result of this state-led engineering has been a "moral and intellectual crisis" where the tolerant pluralistic aspects of the Enlightenment, absent in the Kemalist understanding of "Westernization," could not function as a moral compass to temper the more deracinating aspects of modernization. Individualism in the context of Turkey was reduced to egoism, a self-centered hedonism that has made the construction of civic virtues difficult to attain. In short, the Kemalist project of identity in Turkey consisted of half-baked Westernization, radical secularization, and forced national homogenization. Islam, consequently, became an identity with which to oppose the centralizing policies of the state and its self-declared Westernization project.

In response to the heavy-handed policies of the Republic, counter-elites stressed their "authenticity" and right to contest the power of the governing elite within the multiparty system. Turkish society perpetuated and negotiated its own cultural identity as a result of the openings of new political and economic opportunity spaces. In the negotiation of the state-centric vision of national identity, cultural (Islamic) identity was incrementally politicized. Sufi networks, in particular Naksibendi orders and Nurcu groups, and neighborhood-based alliances played a formative role in the development of Islamic oppositional identity (Özdalga, 1999; Duran, 2004).

Foreign policy as a civilizing process

Since the state authorities' self-legitimization relied on creating a Westernized nation-state by adopting Western civilization in art, politics, social relations, and law, they used foreign policy as a tool for attaining ideological as well as "realist" material gains. Turkey's struggle to become European extended to foreign policy (Laciner, 1999). The state actors' attempt to join all European institutions "was seen as the culmination of Europeanization efforts at home. It was a cultural project" (Kubicek, 1999: 162). For instance, the Kemalist establishment's negative attitude toward the Arab world was an outcome of its domestic policies of de-Arabization and de-Islamization of society (Kürkçüoğlu, 1972). Mustafa Kemal and his successors in the Republican People's Party actively sought to isolate Turkey from its former Arab hinterland for ideological as well as self-aggrandizing reasons. Turkey's foreign policy identification with the West was a function of the political orientation and legitimization of the Kemalist elite. Mentioning any form of solidarity with the Islamic world or "outside Turks" was regarded as a "deviation from the West and reactionism" (Güzel, 1995: 121).

At the end of World War Two, Stalin's demands for bases and territory from Turkey were an additional imperative for Ankara to identify its foreign policy closely with the Western bloc, though the country did not really share the democratic attributes of many of the other members of the alliance. Since the Arab states did not have common frontiers with the Soviet Union, they were not concerned with the threat of Soviet expansionism and focused on independence from the European colonial powers. Thus, Turkey's relations with the Arab world were subordinated to its commitments to the West and especially to the US. Turkish Foreign Minister Fuat Köprülü articulated this policy very clearly in his speech to the Turkish Parliament in 1951: "Our national interests are identical from every standpoint with the joint interests of NATO and with its geographic and military requirements."[5] The state actors almost always supported Western initiatives in the Middle East. For instance, although Turkey voted against the partition of Palestine, it was the first and only Muslim state to recognize the state of Israel, in 1949, and established diplomatic relations in 1952. Turkey's policy toward Israel was an extension of its relations with the West, in general, and the US, in particular (Yavuz and Khan, 1992). During the Suez Canal crisis, Turkey also supported European initiatives. At UN meetings in 1957 and 1958, Turkey voted in favor of France and against Algerian independence.

The Turkish state's attempt to become a part of the European Community cannot be fully explained by material incentives alone, but rather, derives in large part from the Republican elite's ideological quest for legitimation. Thus, in their actions since 1923 they have sought to define the identity of the society as European, and, by internalizing the norms and roles of European society and state, obtain recognition as part of a broader "European community." This was reflected in Turkey's involvement in the Organization of European Economic Cooperation (1948), the European Council (1949), NATO (1952), completion of an association agreement with the European Community (1963), and the customs union with the European Union (1996). Such involvement has brought material benefits, but also, and more importantly, has engaged these institutions in justifying the privileged and unaccountable status of the Kemalist establishment. However, though the state elite was clear about what it wanted Turkey to become, Turkish society was unwilling to completely give up its Islamically informed cultural identity.

The Cold War further facilitated Turkey's institutional identification with Europe. Traditional "realist" security concerns and balance of power considerations helped Turkey to become a member of the

European state system, but not of the emerging European ecumene or community. Turkey has always been depicted as an ambiguous presence on the European borders. The Cold War stress on regional security alliances, however, pushed cultural identifications aside and reset the parameters of domestic politics. Within Turkey, this was a period of "diversification of Kemalism" that saw the emergence of a less authoritarian multiparty system and the gradual, though still limited, opening up of political spaces. It brought Muslim voices to the forefront and helped societal groups to realize the significance of democracy and the potential of a new understanding of modernization. With growing leftist challenges, the state increasingly co-opted Islamic and nationalist groups as an antidote to the "communist threat" in Turkey. At this time, Sufi orders and the Nur movement became staunch supporters of Turkey's entry into NATO.

Turkey first joined NATO in 1952 and signed the 1963 Association Agreement, which envisioned Turkey's gradual integration into, and eventual full membership in, the European Economic Community (EEC). When Turkey signed the 1970 Additional Protocol with the EC, the EEC's successor, it became the longest-standing associate member of that group. In 1987, Turkey applied for full membership to the EU on a direct track, different from the process outlined in the Association Agreement of 1963. The EU did not give a definitive response to this application, citing internal reforms in progress in Turkey, and instead eventually signed the 1995 Customs Union Agreement with Turkey.

The period of liberalization

Some aspects of the Republican era of modernization, in general, and the neo-liberal economic policies of Turgut Özal, who was a Naksibendi Sufi and publicly religious, in the 1980s, in particular, created conditions conducive to the emergence of more tolerant, pluralistically oriented Islamic socio-political movements. The revolutionary change in regard to the public sphere took place when the Özalian economic policies created a link between the public sphere, politics, and the market (Daği and Sezal, 2001). The emergence of a new bourgeoisie, along with new global consumption patterns, led to the proliferation of independent TV, radio, and newspaper outlets, which in turn blurred the boundary between the local and transnational. These new opportunity spaces forced Islamic groups to critically engage with other societal groups and diverse issues.[6] Political and economic liberalization allowed the formation of an Islamic public sphere as a counter or alternative public space that relied on global discourses of human rights and democracy (Casanova, 1994). In these new public spheres where a pro-European Islam is being formulated, Islam was reconstituted to meet the needs of a free market economy, democracy, globalization, and the discourse of universal human rights. These concerns show the key role played by the formation of a new economic class. In other words, with the new Özalian reforms, the public sphere was gradually freed from the ideological dominance of the state. The new Islamist intellectuals, communication networks, and pro-Islamic bourgeoisie very much played a role in the emancipation of the public sphere from the control of the state.

This growing salience of liberal forms of Islam in the public sphere in Turkey is an outcome of the formation of a newly Islam-conscious bourgeoisie and the new financial networks formed between Turkey and the diaspora communities – especially those in Germany and other EU countries. One of the major outcomes of new opportunity spaces has been a re-"zoning" of social life according to the needs of modernity. New opportunity spaces in politics, culture, and economy have empowered identity groups to bring their private identities to the public. In these new spaces, new lifestyles, identities, and codes of conduct were formed. Market conditions require competition and differentiation. This competition has been the engine of different imaginations and subsequent manifestations of "Islam" at the societal level, and new market forces are the basis on which new manners and consumption patterns have been formed.

The implementation of the neo-liberal economic policies created a set of new opportunity spaces, and these spaces plunged the Muslims into markets, politics, economics, the mass media, and education. Hitherto excluded Kurdish and Turkish Muslim groups gradually moved into the public sphere. Thus, going public became the major trend in Turkey. Many Turkish social actors have realized that EU membership is the best way to overcome the ideological faultlines in Turkey between democracy and authoritarianism, civilian and military, and secularism and Islam.

During these years, in order to secure these new opportunity spaces in the public sphere, Özal wanted a powerful legal and international protective framework and the EC was the only option to carry this out (Dağı, 2001). Moreover, by joining the EC, Özal wanted to effectively restructure the authoritarian Kemalist Leviathan. In April 1987, Özal applied for full membership in the EC "in an effort to bolster democracy in Turkey, as it had with Spain, Portugal, and Greece" (Kubicek, 1999: 163). Although the EC did not openly refuse, it did so effectively, citing four reasons: the poor conditions of the Turkish economy; a rapidly expanding Turkish population which could not be absorbed; democratic and civil rights which fell significantly short of EC standards; and finally, cultural differences between Turkey and the EC.[7] Although the first three factors were significant in the decision of the Commission, the last factor provided a cognitive basis for the other three. The EC's negative response to Turkey's membership application in 1989 constituted a turning point in the evolution of Turkish domestic identity and this, in turn, created a confused orientation in foreign policy, and "a generalized sense of isolationism, not present at any stage in Turkish history during the post-World War II period" (Öniş, 1999: 125). After eighty years of "domestication" within the European institutions, many Turks concluded that their "otherness" was irredeemable.

Instead of full membership, the EU offered a customs union as a means of anchoring Turkey to Europe. Many politicians and bureaucrats presented the customs union as a next step toward full membership, but the EU treated it, in effect, as the final stage Turkey could hope to achieve. After a long and tortuous process, the European Parliament endorsed the customs union accord and it came into effect in January 1996 (Kramer, 1996). The US lobbied vigorously for the union, arguing that having Turkey anchored in Europe was essential to preventing a "fundamentalist" takeover. The customs union offered an important vehicle for the pro-European elite to consolidate the country's European orientation and force European leaders' continued engagement with Ankara. The Turkish elite decided to accept the customs union arrangement, which reduced sovereignty without granting the full benefits of membership, in order not to break with the ideological raison d'être of the Republic. The customs union decision, which was essentially economic in nature, "was presented as a decision not only about the future of European–Turkish relations but about Turkey's future in general" (Kramer, 1996: 61).

A further blow to the march westward was when Turkey was left off the list of the December 1997 Luxembourg Summit for EU expansion. The report cited Turkey's "serious shortcomings" in democratization and human rights. Historic Christian European antagonism toward "the Turk" and the broader vexing issue of the growing presence of Muslim immigrants in European societies also played a significant role in resistance to Turkey's entry to the EU. To be fair, however, while such sentiments have been openly expressed by center-right parties in many West European countries, the fierce criticism of Turkey by center-left parties mainly stemmed from principled concerns over democratic norms and human rights.

The Bosnian Muslim genocide reminded European elites and public opinion about the deadly implications of religious exclusion and many intellectuals and public figures started to discuss a multicultural Europe that could include a reformed Muslim Turkey (Khan, 1995). Moreover, the generational change in the leadership of Europe (Tony Blair and Gerhard Schröder), along with the rise of Social Democratic parties to power coupled with the US campaign on behalf of Turkey led to an at least modified rethinking of Turkish membership among many in European elites and society.

This process reached a climax in December 1999 when the EU Council declared that Turkey is "destined to join the Union on the basis of the same criteria as applied to the other candidate States."[8] In many ways, this decision was as historic as the Tanzimat Reforms of 1839 in terms of Turkey's struggle to become a full member of the European society of states. The EU is expected to work with Ankara for Turkey's adherence to the Copenhagen criteria – the *sine qua non* of meeting socio-economic and political norms of liberal-democratic society.[9] The decision of the EU Council to grant "candidate" status to Ankara has already structured the debate over identity and foreign policy. In March 2000, the EU published a detailed plan in an Accession Partnership to identify the shortcomings of Turkey in order for its application to proceed. These included demands to legalize Kurdish broadcasting, ban capital punishment, remove all legal obstacles to freedom of speech and assembly, reduce the role of the military in governance, and make progress on the Cyprus question. In response to the EU demands, Ankara has reluctantly and gradually started to make all necessary constitutional changes (Kardaş, 2002).

The target of "becoming" European has radically, and in surprising ways, transformed domestic political debate in Turkey. While still officially committed to the Republican dream of becoming a part of Europe, the Kemalist elite and in particular the hard-line generals have, for the time being, drawn the line against adopting the substantive democratic and liberal norms of Western societies. Nevertheless, although membership would result in the erosion of military power in the political system, the military cannot openly say no to the EU because it would amount to a denial of the central Kemalist goal of becoming European (Kösebalaban, 2003). Ironically, it has not been the Kemalist establishment, but rather Islamic groups, along with the Kurds and Alevis, who have recently become the most enthusiastic supporters of Turkey's entry into the EU (Daği, 2003).

The February 28 coup was critical in the complete transformation of the Islamic social and political actors' attitude toward Turkey's integration into the EU.[10] They quickly understood that this process of "Europeanization" was central to finally securing democracy and human rights in Turkey. The "soft coup" was known as the "February

28 process" because once the Welfare Party-(WP) led government was removed, the coup leaders instituted an ongoing program of monitoring, controlling, and criminalizing most Islamic activism as a security threat and institutionalizing a permanent legal framework for ostracizing devout and/or active Turkish Muslims from the market, educational, and political spheres (Yavuz, 2003: 81–131). The resulting pro-Europe orientation among mainstream Islamic groups also came to be shared by many supporters of Kurdish rights and liberal-democratic Turks in general. It is perhaps the most important and promising indicator of an emerging consensus over Turkish identity and orientation. This cognitive shift among Turkey's embattled Islamic groups indicates that integration with Europe is the best way to guarantee human rights for all and consolidate democracy (Duran, 2004).

As these Islamic groups plugged into opportunity spaces and started to benefit from expanding markets and legal protection, their sense of self and their world views started to transform. The source of the cognitive shift in Turkey is, however, the expansion of socio-economic conditions and opportunity spaces. The bulk of excluded Turkish society, whether Anatolian Muslims, Kurds, Alevis, or leftists, now see the EU as an opportunity to overcome state authoritarianism and facilitate democratization. For the first time, Turkish Muslim groups formed their own human rights association, known as Mazlumder in Turkish, to defend the rights of other excluded groups as well as their own. In other words, "the right to be different" is utilized by the Islamists to promote their goals but the same rights are also used by other groups. So, one sees the gradual internalization of the human rights discourse and self-reflexivity in terms of recognizing that if the rights of one are threatened, the rights of all are as well. Although one may perceive this as tactical Europeanization, and understand the use of the rights discourse as an outcome of economic benefits and pressure from the state, one sees the gradual internalization and universalization of such a tactical position. Being "Western" and "modern" is redefined in terms of rights, democracy, and the market economy rather than as a dress code or a rigid interpretation of laicism.

Turkish Muslim response: entering into Europe without becoming European

In Turkey, there are two different discourses about Turkey's membership in the EU. The liberal Kemalist and secularist elite see EU membership as the realization of the Westernization project which aims to create a Europeanized society. It is about becoming European by giving up an Islamic identity and legacy. For this group, the EU project is about *assimilation* into European culture and freedom from a religious world view. Thus, for the first group, the EU is a melting-pot for becoming "European." Due to the hegemonic position this discourse held in the public sphere until the 1980s, Turkey's believing Muslims usually reacted negatively to the EU process (Alpay, 2002; Öniş, 2003).[11]

Today, Islamic groups in Turkey display, broadly, two mindsets as regards policies and reforms related to the Europeanization process: defensive and assertive. The defensive position argues that the reforms have made Turkey and Turkish culture vulnerable to European influence, if not manipulation. It is important, in this view, to have more political liberties but we should see what we are "compromising." Adherents argue that Europe is not honest and sincere in its human rights discourse; human rights are for Christians and Jews, not for Muslims. They frequently remind their audience about the genocides in Bosnia and Chechnya, the European Court of Justice's decision allowing the closure of Islamic parties (Welfare, Virtue), and endorsing forced dress codes against traditional Muslims. Thus, Europe has been portrayed as having a double standard when it comes to dealing with Muslim issues. In this view, reforms are not purely salutary: there is a hidden agenda.

The second approach is generally less skeptical about the policies directed at fulfilling the Copenhagen criteria. The criteria are seen as essentials of economic and democratic transformation. The cultural concerns articulated by the first group are construed as unsubstantiated: "We should not have anything to fear if we are confident about our values and culture. Why bother about European influences but not think about a possible positive Turkish Islamic influence in Europe; the free market of ideas and associational life will benefit Muslims."[12]

Recently, a fierce debate, expanding on prior contentions, broke out between the two camps over the new standards for missionary activities and the opening of places of worship. Articles circulated in the newspapers (*Milli Gazete, Vakit*), magazines (*Cuma*) and internet sites arguing that the reforms made it impossible to control missionary activities in Turkey and pointed to 20,000 new churches (or private places of worship) opened in the previous year, not to mention actual numbers of converts to Christianity. A conference was organized in Antalya on missionary activities in Turkey. Many articles went on to argue that interfaith dialogue is a Christian (Catholic) conspiracy. This made some liberal Muslim groups, like Fethullah Gülen and possibly some Nakşibendi groups, uncomfortable. They argued that the figures on conversions were exaggerated and interfaith dialogue and cultural encounters are necessities of the time, and they concluded that it is better to act assertively than to rely on defensive measures.

The issues all revolve around the posited gains and losses an empowered civil society will bring to Turkey. How will open borders, an open market for goods, services, and ideas affect Turkey's internal and external security? There is a mutual influence between the Islamic groups, and the state and government in these debates. The AKP government is mostly positive about reforms, but continues to have some security concerns about religious minorities.

The second pro-European-integrationist discourse does not see Muslim and European identities as mutually exclusive. Of the three different experiences of Europe common among Turks – (a) *a place to earn a living*; (b) *safe haven from persecution*; and (c) *a new homeland* – intellectuals and leaders of Islamic movements have frequently used Germany and Switzerland as an escape from state oppression especially after military coups (Erbakan, Sevket Eygi, Sevki Yilmaz, and Saadettin Kaplan among others). From those safe havens, they transmitted the contents of meetings, talks, and writings back to Turkey.

Turkey's socio-political Islamic landscape is shaped by four diverse groupings: cultural Islam, state Islam, political Islam, and diasporic Islam. Each grouping has pursued strategies of withdrawal, confrontation, and engagement vis-à-vis Europeanization along their own axes of concern. The tension between cultural Islam and political Islam has focused on the definition of the West. While Sufi and Nurcu groups were more open to a democratic, liberal, and capitalist West, the National Outlook Movement (NOM: Milli Görüş Hareketi) of Necmettin Erbakan defined itself more in opposition to the West, which it tended to equate with Kemalist authoritarianism and atheism.

Turkish state Islam: Directorate of Religious Affairs (DRA)

In order to subordinate religion to the political establishment, as in the communist bloc, the new Kemalist Republic created its own version of "state Islam" by establishing the Directorate of Religious Affairs (DRA). The goal was to control and domesticate Islam in accordance with the needs of the laicist state by crafting a national (Turkish) and secular (European) religion. Islam was reconfigured as a Turkish ideology, and a component of Turkish identity. For instance, article 136 of the constitution states that the "Directorate shall exercise its functions and duties in accordance with the principle of laicism." The state controls all 80,000 mosques in Turkey and employs their Imams as state functionaries. Sunni-Hanefi Islam constitutes the doctrine of the DRA, which does not recognize the autonomy of the Alevis or other sects. When the DRA opened a number of mosques to establish an ethno-religious understanding of Islam among the Turkish workers in Europe, it was transformed by the European realities. In 2000 and 2001, the DRA organized two conferences on the EU process and Islam. In these meetings, the DRA presented itself as the guardian of Turkish values, language, and institutions in Europe.[13] It has over 300 mosques in different European cities and directly hires the Imams of these mosques. Although it benefits from freedoms in Europe to disseminate Islam and establish its institutions, the DRA has been against Christian missionary activities in Turkey.[14] Moreover, it has been either against or very reluctant to allow Christians to open new churches in Turkey. During my interview with the head of the DRA, Ali Bardakoğlu, he presented the DRA as a "national and state" institution to organize the national-religious affairs of Turkish citizens. The main source of conservatism in the DRA is the widespread insecurity among its clergy about Islamic knowledge, faith, and supremacy. The DRA wants to remain visible in the public sphere and also be important within the laicist state system by catering to the modern needs of the population by approving the more secular interpretations of Islam while reinforcing its position within the state by stressing religion's role in national identity and deference to authority.

The DRA is not very sympathetic to the overall assimilation of Europe's large Turkish immigrant population. Its main objective is to keep Turkey's Muslim population in contact with the mainland culture, whose one fundamental aspect is Islam. It continues to see Europe as most Turks did in the 1960s: Europe is a place to earn a living, so it is crucial to keep in touch with the mainland. There are many Turkish TV channels in Europe that simply rebroadcast Turkish programs, and newspapers and magazines published for Turks in Europe appeal to the same tastes as those sold in Turkey so that Turks do not feel "alien" in Germany or other parts of Europe.

Social and cultural Islam: Nurcus and Fethullah Gülen

In the examination of Islamic movements in Turkey, one needs to examine the paradoxical connection between modern Turkish nationalism and Islam. Some of the dominant Islamic movements such as the movements of Fethullah Gülen and Süleyman Hilmi Tunahan are based on a specific synthesis between Islam and Turkish nationalism. Both movements offer a conservative blending of nationalism and Islam. In other words, the linkage between nationalism and Islam in Turkey creates a conservative and communitarian code of ethics. In this conservatism, nationalism and Islam are two mutually constitutive (communitarian) identities. Thus, the major modernizing transformations in the Turkish political landscape have occurred when conservative governments were in power (Adnan Menderes, Turgut Özal, and Recep T. Erdoğan). Conservative leaders calculated their interests, but they also used opportunities and constraints in order to transform the political and social landscape. They have justified new positions and institutions by using the shared ethno-religious language of the society.

These moderate neo-Sufi groups regard the EU as an instrument for democratizing (i.e. reducing the role of the military) and domesticating radical and marginalized Islamic groups and thus opening new spaces for the increased role of Islam in the society. According to the leader of the Nur movement, who lives in the United States, "democracy is necessary to control radicalism and integrate marginal groups and the EU is essential for the consolidation of democracy in Turkey."[15]

The major cultural Islamic group is the Nurcus, the followers of Said Nursi, an ethnic Kurd, who authored several volumes of exegesis of the Qur'an, known as *Risale-i Nur Kulliyati* (The Epistles of Light). The goals of this dynamic movement are: (1) synthesis of Islam and science; (2) raising Islamic consciousness by stressing the connection between reason and revelation; and (3) achieving this-worldly and other-worldly salvation within a free market and through a quality education. One of the most powerful Nur communities is led by the intellectually dynamic Fethullah Gülen. The Gülen-led Nur community seeks to redefine laicism and form a shared language by organizing conferences of intellectual leaders. For instance, the Gülen-initiated Abant Declaration of July 1998 not only sought to redefine the meaning of laicism as practiced in Europe but also reinterpreted Islamic theology to respond to contemporary challenges.

Gülen has defended Turkey's integration with European institutions, especially the EU (Kösebalaban, 2003). His pro-EU vision is based on the following social, economic, and political reasons. Gülen regards the EU as a democratizing and domesticating tool for integrating and containing radical and marginalized Islamic groups. I like to summarize my conversation with Gülen in the following way: democracy is necessary to control radicalism and integrate marginal groups into a political and economic system.[16] The EU is essential for the consolidation of democracy in Turkey. Thus, moderation requires Turkey's entry into the EU. Gülen has rejected the arguments of the anti-EU coalition that EU membership would lead to cultural and religious assimilation of Turkey without any way to overcome inherent "Christian animosity" against Islam. Gülen answered these two arguments, common among the more radical Islamic and nationalistic groups, by arguing that the interaction with diverse cultures can be a source of dynamism and a way of rejuvenating universal aspects of Islam to create genuine and universal human

understanding. Moreover, according to Kösebalaban, Gülen's "perception of the West as a partner rather than as a security threat is in line with
his advocacy of globalization and with his universalistic interpretation of
Islam" (Kösebalaban, 2003: 177–78). In short, the goal of the Gülen-led
Nur groups is to construct a new form of modernity that is consistent
with the fundamental precepts of Islam as well as the emerging global
paradigm of democracy and respect for individual human rights.

Lastly, some diaspora communities, especially Gülen's followers,
advocate integration with the host country rather than isolation and
ghetto formation. Gülen advises his followers to settle where they
"migrate," buy houses, establish permanent residences, and find decent
full-time jobs. The idea is to become a recognized part of the public
culture without, of course, losing one's Turkish-Islamic identity. The
Gülen movement uses print and the visual media abroad to address
both native (Turkish) cultural concerns and local issues by publishing
magazines and newspapers in the various European languages. In a
nutshell, the impact of transnational religious ties on Europeanization
depends on the attitude of the religious movements toward Europe and
their varying identifications of "opportunity."

Political Islam: Erbakan to Erdoğan

Political Islam constitutes one of the key faultlines vis-à-vis laicism in
Turkey. Although manifestations of political Islam are spread across the
center-right parties, the dominant force representing political Islam has
been the NOM, which after being closed down in succession formed the
National Order, National Salvation, the Welfare, and the Virtue parties.
The NOM in the 1990s was transforming itself from a strictly religious-
right to a center-right party but this process was halted by the intervention
of the military coup in 1997. It was the umbrella party of a new Anatolian
bourgeoisie, the urban poor, and the excluded Kurdish minority. With
the closure of the Welfare Party, the pro-Islamic parliamentarians formed
the Virtue Party. The NOM's strategy has been very much built and
carried out by Erbakan. He has been the integrative figure of the
movement.

By "othering the West" as the "enemy," Erbakan differentiated his
movement from the Kemalist establishment and from some other
Islamic groups. Erbakan defined his movement against the West, in
general, and the Kemalist vision of Europeanization, in particular. He
argued that "the children of this great nation cannot be assimilated in a
Christian pot [Common Market], its sovereign rights and liberties cannot
be abolished by a Christian community. Turkey's future and interests can

only be served and protected with the formation of Muslim Common Market in which cultural and historical ties are strong" (Cayhan, 1997: 89). Erbakan also wrote a book to explain the negative consequences of the Common Market in 1971 (Erbakan, 1971). In this book, Erbakan treated Turkey's attempt to join the Common Market as a process of becoming a colony of Europe. He proposed the formation of an alternative Islamic Common Market among the Muslim countries, under the leadership of Turkey. These views started to change in the mid-1990s as a result of economic development and the formation of new opportunity spaces and increasing knowledge about the EU and other Muslim countries. Until 1995, Erbakan remained very much anti-Europe and led the opposition against the customs union with the EU in the Turkish Parliament and portrayed the agreement with the EU as a disgraceful, colonial treaty. Although he was against the customs union, when Erbakan became prime minister in 1996, he adopted a much more pro-EU position. In the 1999 election, Erbakan adopted pro-EU positions and made Turkey's entry into the Union the primary foreign policy goal. In the 1990s, the attitude of political Islam toward the EU, in particular, changed. How should we explain this transformation of Erbakan? Is this transformation cognitive or merely tactical? I will first examine the fragmentation of the Erbakan-led world view within Turkish Islamic movements and the emergence of alternative readings of Turkey, Islam, and Europe.

Since the February 1997 coup, the NOM, along with many intellectuals, opted for a pro-European position. Almost all major Islamic groups and prominent scholars support Turkey's integration with the EU, stressing the significance of human rights and the rule of law. This discursive shift from the EU as the foe of political Islamic identity to a friend is an outcome of a number of factors. Many people construe this shift as a survivalist need under the military, legal, and economic pressure to form an alliance with liberal groups. This paper demonstrates that this shift is, instead, an outcome of the ongoing internal liberalization process of establishment political Islam, the growing power of the Anatolian Muslim bourgeoisie, and the expanding public sphere and inclusion of new intellectuals into the movement. The February 1997 coup triggered the fragmentation of Islam into two competing groups:[17] The Felicity Party (Saadet Partisi; SP) of Erbakan and the Justice and Development Party (Adalet ve Kalkinma Partisi; AKP) of Tayyip Erdoğan. The SP as the successor of the Welfare Party of Erbakan made a major change in its party program by arguing that the Turkish–EU relations are "important for the implementation and realization of human rights and democratic norms and the further development of Turkey with the close ties with Europe."[18]

The EU requirements for membership forced both the state and anti-establishment forces to change their perceptions and strategies in terms of adopting a new social contract for Turkey. After the February 28 coup process and the politicization of the judicial system, Islamic groups began to regard the EU institutions and norms as a source of protection against the authoritarian state and a natural ally for transforming its ideology. In order to receive necessary support from the EU, they in turn had to shed their old ideology and internalize the global discourses of human rights and pluralism. In short, the configuration of domestic and international factors impelled leading Islamic political groups to forge a more democratic and liberal reading of Islam.

The Justice and Development Party of Tayyip Erdoğan

The AKP, unlike many other Islamic political parties in the world, stresses human rights and social justice more than the politics of identity and authenticity. The party framed the question of identity, such as the headscarf issue, in terms of human rights and a personal choice to wear or not to wear a particular type of attire. Recep Tayyip Erdoğan, the ex-mayor of Istanbul, articulates a new politics of pragmatism and economic justice as a policy priority. The AKP is syncretic, rather than liberal, in economic terms. Its electoral base incorporates farmers, the new urban class, and the new Anatolian bourgeoisie (Vergin, 2004). These diverse sectors of the population came together around a "democratic Islamic identity" to bring the AKP to power. This represents a genuine effort at synthesizing Islamic norms of honesty, charity, equity, and familial integrity with liberal-democratic principles of representative government, pluralism, and civil liberties.

The AKP went further and connected its democratization agenda with EU policies. For instance, the program of the AKP claims that "Taking as a basis the principles pertaining to the democratization of the Copenhagen Criteria which constitute the minimum standards to which members of the European Union must conform, amendments which must be made in our national judicial system shall be carried out in the shortest possible time."[19]

The AKP pursued a very pro-EU policy: the leadership of the AKP aimed to reposition the party as a center-right party by accepting the secular nature of the political system and pursuing integration of the country with the EU. The party has made EU accession the main goal of its domestic and foreign policy and mentions the EU seventeen times in its party program. In other words, the AKP tried to expand its socio-political base by reframing all its policies in the language of the

European Union. In the November 2002 elections, it received 34.1 percent of the votes, and took over the Turkish Parliament with 363 of the 550 seats.

One of the four major reasons for the AKP's widespread support for EU accession is the search for political identity through the EU process. Due to its Islamic roots, the AKP wants to project a new form of conservative democratic identity by identifying itself with the European norms of the Christian Democratic parties. While all Milli Görüs-inspired political parties regarded the European Union (then the Common Market) as an attempt to undermine Turkey's Muslim identity and sovereignty, in the 1999 and 2002 elections, Islamic parties regarded the EU not as an enemy but rather as an ally of democratization and economic development. Consolidating democracy and raising human rights in Turkey were linked to the Copenhagen criteria for admission to the EU. These reforms, both constitutional and legislative, created new legal opportunity spaces for the redefinition of the state–society, Islam–secularism, and the public–private ties in Turkey.

Second, the AKP is more pro-EU than other political parties because it defines itself against the military and seeks to use the EU process to reduce the power of the military within the political system. In the transformation of political Islam, external factors such as the Kemalist ideology of the Turkish state and the EU's attitude played an important role. The policy of the state institutions rejecting any deviation from the secular nature of the state and its readiness to use the courts against Islamic parties forced these parties to act within the secular system. Moreover, military pressure and the limited zone of rights encouraged the AKP to closely identify with the EU in order to play a continued role in the Turkish political system. For instance, in its party program the AKP argues that "the National Security Council, which provides an exchange of views between the Armed Forces and the political powers in the areas of security and defense, shall be restructured in accordance with the standards of the European Union, taking into consideration examples in democratic countries."

Third, the AKP has no well-articulated projects to transform the political landscape but relies on the Copenhagen criteria as a compass for the change. In order to expand political space and implement demo-cratic control, the AKP needs the EU's support. However, this support has been conditional on the preservation of secularism and democratic rule in Turkey. After the closure of the WP of Erbakan, the leadership of the party took the case to the European Court of Human Rights and the court upheld the decision of the Turkish court to close the party.[20] The EU does not tolerate the use of Islam in politics or any discussion of the implementation of religious law. This EU position forced Turkey's Islamists to articulate their platform in secular terms. Thus, the AKP has been successful in reframing religious and local issues in terms of a broader European and universal language of human rights and political liberalism.

Transnational Turkish Islamic networks

Transnational European norms shape Muslim policy by helping Islamic groups articulate their interests. The EU has been an active teacher helping these groups to frame their religious rights in terms of international human rights norms (Kücükcan, 1999; Bilir, 2004). Islamic groups in Turkey adapted their policies and orientations so as to conform to these expected "universal" norms in order to gain EU support for their democratic rights. One thus sees the Europeanization of Islamic identity in Turkey as a result of Muslim actors' engagements and interactions with EU institutions and expectations. We see the close interactive relationship between Islamic identity and interest in joining the EU, which initially may have involved tactical considerations but inevitably developed a deeper structural and ideological basis.

EU-based, especially German-based, Muslim organizations played a key role in the positive image of the EU and the integration of Turkey into the Union became a main goal of these transnational religious networks. A gradual cognitive shift from an Arab-centric to Euro-centric understanding of Turkish Islam was also promoted by the contrasting labor migration experiences of Turks in some Arab countries and Europe. The stories of those laboring in Arab countries tended to be negative compared to the experiences of those in Europe. Coffee-house chitchat and conversation about experiences and political systems in Europe and many Arab countries facilitated Turkish identification with the EU. Many Turks argue that Europe is more Islamic than Arab countries in terms of respect for human dignity and think that "Islam is not what is preached and represented by the Arab world."

The dynamics of transnational religious networks and their influence are determined by the political and legal conditions in the host and home countries. For instance, some radical Islamic groups cannot organize in Turkey but freely form a web of networks in Germany by utilizing the German legal system. An ethnically derived Islam helped to structure both the mosque system and networks for Turkish-Muslim communities in Europe. Almost all Islamic groups have branches in Germany, and there is a circulation of ideas, skills, and money back and forth. However, in the transformation of Islamic movements in Turkey transnational

Islamic networks played a secondary role. The Arab-dominated version of Islam came either through the translation of Sayyid Qutb or Wahhabi-financed institutions competing with a vernacular Turkish Islam. However, the influence of these works of Arab writers and Saudi Arabia has been minimal due to their negative stand on Sufism, their rigidity, and the condescending attitude of some Arab groups toward Turkish Islam. Furthermore, the experiences of those Turkish workers in Europe and those in the Arab Gulf and Libya created a stark dichotomy. Many Turks felt alienated from the corruption and lack of social or legal justice experienced in many oil-rich Arab states. The stories of this alienated labor force played a more important role than the thought of political ideologues like Sayyid Qutb in determining the orientation of Turkish political Islam.

In a similar vein, we see the evolution and separation of German Islam from Turkish Islam in response to divergent local needs and experiences. According to a recent study by the Center for Studies on Turkey in Essen, a leading research center, there are about 13 million Muslims living within the European Union. Islam is overwhelmingly represented by South Asian Muslims in the UK, by Muslims from North African countries in France, and mainly by Turks in Germany. Of the 3 million Muslims in Germany, 2.4 million are Turks, followed by 384,000 Bosnian Muslims.

To analyze the relationship between the country of origin and the country of settlement, one has to focus on the role of different state strategies to diffuse their "official Islam" to prevent "unwanted Islamic activism." In order to prevent radicalization of the Turkish community in Germany and maintain their identity, the Turkish state has always insisted on maintaining religious education and services through the government-run Religious Affairs Turkish–Islamic Union (DITIB). In Germany, the DITIB is the biggest organization for immigrants.

In addition to the presence of a Turkish state–Islam infrastructure as well as affiliates of the mainstream Milli Görüs in Germany, there have also been some radical fringe groups among the Turkish population in Germany. Led by Metin Kaplan, now jailed in Germany, one of these groups once had as many as 4,000 members but is now believed to have only 1,000. The transplantation of Milli Görüs to Europe was an expansion of Turkey-based Islam. However, it has evolved within the German context and shaped the National Outlook Movement in Turkey through the circulation of political organizing skills, ideas, and financial resources. It is one of the major Muslim NGOs supporting educational and political projects and inviting many prominent Turkish Muslim students and scholars to visit Germany and give talks. These intellectual exchanges

by Turkey's Muslim writers and scholars have played a key role in opening up discursive spaces and an appreciation for freedom of thought
and speech in the political realm. In other words, it offers moral and
intellectual support to the Islamic political movement in Turkey while at
the same time drawing it closer to European norms than is characteristic
of the ostensibly European-oriented Kemalist establishment. Although
many in the Turkish military see the dynamism of these Western
European affiliates as a threat to their domination, many prominent
Turkish leaders such as Prime Minister Erdoğan and Foreign Minister
Abdullah Gül, have very close links with them.

　　Milli Görüs is the largest Muslim organization in Germany, with about
27,500 members. With regional associations in almost every state and
headquarters in Cologne, it claims to have 500 mosque affiliates in
Germany and 214 more across the Benelux countries, France, Austria,
Switzerland, and Scandinavia, though there is no independent confirmation of these figures. It is the European branch of the Erbakan-led
National Outlook Movement in Turkey. Because the Kemalist establishment has feared its financial and organizational means, it has been under
close surveillance by the Interior Ministry of Germany. Milli Görüs says it
represents the interests of immigrants and promotes the integration of
Muslims in Germany. It wants to exert its influence on as many Turkish
people living in Germany as possible and eventually promote Islamic
causes it favors in Turkey. In a globalized framework, its activities blur
the distinction between national and transnational, between country of
origin and new home country. Under the leadership of Mehmet Erbakan,
the organization focused on a strong electoral presence in European
countries and hence acquiring a degree of political power that cannot
be discounted. Thus, Milli Görüs organized campaigns to call on members to take their host countries' citizenship in order to obtain the right to
vote. The organization also wants to be recognized as an Islamic
"Church" in order to get legal protection and recognition, along with
financial support, in line with Christian and Jewish denominations.
However, the state-dominated DITIB opposes its recognition as the
main representative body of Turkish Muslims, and the Turkish state
claims that Milli Görüs supports sectarian and politicized religious
groups in Turkey. Milli Görüs wants to be involved in German politics
and Turkish politics at the same time.[21]

　　Generational change played the key role in the orientation of Islamic
movements in Germany. Although the older generation consistently
organized in relation to what was going on in their country of origin,
the new generation focuses on the local, and national, conditions of
their settled immigrant communities. In 2005, one sees the syncretic

emergence of a Turko-German form of Islam. Due to Turkey's attempt to join the EU, the Turkish state institutions still play an important role in the organization of religious life in Germany.

The European debate

The 2002 EU Copenhagen Summit became the "Turkish summit." Turkey's insistence on a date for accession talks defined this event (Zürcher and Linden, 2004).[22] Turkish commentators claimed that this was as important as the Tanzimat Reforms of 1839 and the Helsinki Summit of 1999, in which the EU accepted Turkey as a candidate country to join the EU. The new AKP government worked very hard to get a date for Turkey's accession talks on October 3, 2005 to consolidate democracy against the ongoing threat of another Turkish military-led coup and in order to build confidence in the Turkish economy. Turkey is radically reforming its political and judicial structure in a plan that will require Ankara to radically overhaul an eighty-year ideology of Kemalist modernization heavily dependent upon an authoritarian vision of politics and society. Moreover, as a further concession to Europe, the Erdoğan government has been keen to solve the Cyprus problem within the context of the Annan Plan.[23]

As Turkey tries to meet the Copenhagen criteria, there is a major debate going on over the meaning of European identity. What does European identity entail? Does the membership of Turkey and the presence of Muslim communities in Europe challenge European identity or empower it? How should we read widespread European negative reaction to Turkey's membership? Does it stem from the anxiety over the weakness of European identity or historical hostility against Islam? There is no clear definition of European identity. Yet many people argue that the Greek heritage, Roman law, and Christianity (for some) or Enlightenment values (for many cosmopolitans) define the content of European identity. So it is an identity in formation and the process of imagination is still under way. As far as Turkey's Muslims are concerned, Europe means "democracy and economic prosperity." Thus, they do not see these identities as mutually exclusive but rather look forward to being both European and Muslim within the framework of the EU.

What do grand reified constructs such as "the West" and "Islam" mean in terms of this ongoing dialectic? These are expressions for complex amorphous transnational formations, and sites of constant political, social, and cultural contestation. These collective identities, just like ethnic and national identities, are temporarily forged by erasing internal diversity and dissension. Yet, this erasure of internal diversity does not invalidate the use of European or Islamic terminology. In other words, there is an Islamic world that consists of diverse cultures, linguistic groups, networks, and histories that are connected under the generic rubric of "Islam." There is a constant struggle among these diverse groups and individuals to establish the "true" meaning of Islam or Western civilization in relation to a specific set of practices, norms, and institutions. Thus, there are invariably many different contested interpretations of Islam. These interpretive attachments vary from "Islam" as a national liberation movement, to an NGO, to an instrument for integrating into Europe, as in the case of some Turkish Muslims. For many Muslims, the meanings of Islam identity and praxis include "Protestant" notions of economic advancement, civic engagement, and political participation. The Turkish case, when contrasted with those of Algeria, Egypt, and Saudi Arabia, demonstrates that when opportunity spaces are severely limited for peaceful socio-political contestation and transformation, socio-political movements, Islamic or otherwise, are prone to radicalization and violence.

The former French President Giscard d'Estaing, the President of the European Convention, publicly stated what others in Europe have long maintained privately: Turkey is "a different culture, a different approach and a different way of life," and its admission would quite simply mean "the end of the EU." At present, there is also a major debate over the boundaries of European identity. The remarks by d'Estaing appeared to shift the debate from what Turkey does to the reductionist construct of what Turkey is. He told *Le Monde* that Turkey's "capital isn't in Europe, 95% of its population is outside Europe – this isn't a European country."[24] His remarks are not isolated and reflect what a sizeable part of the elite as well as the public think. As the US pushed to anchor Turkey firmly in the EU camp as part of its own "war on terrorism" some Europeans became even more suspicious of Turkey as a Trojan horse employed by Washington to forestall deeper integration within the EU. At the heart of the debate, although few of those opposed to Turkey's accession dare to say as much, is the sensitive issue of Europe's cultural – and religious – identity. The conservative leader Edmund Stoiber told the CSU party conference: "Europe is a community that is based on Western values. As a community of shared values, Europe has to deal with the question of its borders. These borders must be based on shared values, culture and history. Turkey's membership would breach these borders." The British, led by Tony Blair, have by contrast argued that an increasingly multicultural Europe and a post-September 11 world threatened by a "clash of civilizations" will both benefit from EU membership for a democratic Muslim country. Additionally, the EU spokesman Jean-Christophe Filori said Monsieur d'Estaing's views weren't shared by the leaders of the fifteen EU nations: "Turkey's candidacy is not being questioned by any EU head of state and government in Europe."

Conclusion

Leading Turkish Islamic movements' attitudes toward Europe have changed from rejectionism, to accommodation, to embrace. These ideational and policy reversals are an outcome of changing contexts and permutations within Turkish-Islamic socio-political movements themselves. Religious and social transformation at a broad societal level along with the ideological evolution of leading Islamic groups in Turkey is an outcome of economic development and expanding discursive and civic opportunity spaces. A pluralistic and liberal political system coupled with an unfettered market of ideas and goods is the one circumstance that is likely to promote liberal and pluralistically oriented Islamic socio-political movements sharing an idiom in keeping with increasingly universal discourses on human rights and representative government. When such opportunity spaces are absent or sharply curtailed, as in the tragic cases of Algeria or Uzbekistan, even pacifically inclined Islamic movements, not surprisingly, turn to an ideology of resistance, authenticity, and martyrdom. This siege mentality in turn helps consolidate a conservative and authoritarian understanding of religion. Due to the expanding opportunity spaces in Turkey, there is no single reading of Islam and it becomes one of many competing identities and forces of mobilization in the marketplace of ideas. Bassam Tibi's advocacy of a Euro-Islam is one of many options and it is more likely to be accepted via mutually respectful and tolerant communication in an expanding European public sphere, as opposed to the authoritarian fiat of state authorities and official campaigns of assimilation as was the case in the Turkish Republic. For this to happen, basic tolerance and respect for pluralism is required on the part of Muslim and non-Muslim Europeans alike.

The EU has played a positive role in the process of consolidating democracy and institutionalizing human rights in Turkey. Given the long and deeply ingrained tradition of "statism" in Turkey, it would have been very difficult to achieve the desired democratic transformation of the Turkish state and society relying on domestic factors alone. Domestic political issues involving religion, Kurdish identity, and human rights have been increasingly transnationalized as external non-state actors, such as the Kurdish and Islamic diaspora, NGOs, and the EU, became heavily involved in agenda-setting and policy-making in Turkey. These interventions and EU pressure to allocate sovereignty challenge the civilian-military bureaucracy which is fearful that its privileged position will be undermined by the EU process of integration. Turkish EU membership holds great importance for both Europe and the Islamic world. Turkish democracy is far from perfect and its market economy has major structural problems. Many Europeans are further concerned that with a population of 65 million, it is bigger than virtually all current EU members except Germany. Still, Turkey's Islamic heritage has been the major issue in the ongoing domestic and international debate over national orientation and identity. If Turkey is able to success-fully develop into a liberal, democratic, and economically vibrant Muslim country anchored in the EU, it will have played a world historic role as a true bridge between East and West dissolving constructed dichotomies between Orient and Occident and the Islamic and Western worlds.

Notes

I wish to thank Ihsan Daği for allowing me to read his unpublished essays on Turkey. I would also like to thank Bruce Rutherford and Etga Uğur for their extensive comments on the first draft of this paper, and Nihat Ali Özcan, Şaban Kardaş, Ersin Gürdoğan, and Talip Kücükcan.

1 These seven zones of Islam consist of Arab, Persian, Turkish, South Asian, Southeast Asian (Malaysia and Indonesia), African, and Diaspora.
2 Qureshi and Sells's important volume very effectively challenges the reductionist and anti-Muslim-tinged writings of Bernard Lewis, Fouad Ajami, Samuel Huntington, Daniel Pipes, and V. S. Naipaul.
3 Hilmi Yavuz, "Aydınlanma, Batı-dişi Kültür ve Özne," *Zaman*, 10 March 2000.
4 A group of prominent Turkish academics have offered an important critical reappraisal of the modernist project of Kemalism (Bozdağ and Kasaba, 1997).
5 *Ayın Tarihi*, No. 215 (October 1951), p. 18.
6 By opportunity spaces, I mean a forum of social interaction that creates new possibilities for augmenting networks of shared meaning and associational life. Such arenas include civic and political forums, electronic and print media and cyberspace, and the market. In these spaces, not only are individual and collective actions blurred but also the boundary between the public and private is constantly redrawn. Islamic social movements represent the "coming out" of private Muslim identity in the public spaces. It is not only a struggle for recognition of identity but also "going public" through private identities. In these public spaces, identities and lifestyles are performed, contested, and implemented.
7 *Commission Opinion on Turkey's Request for Accession to the Community, SEC (89) 2290 final/2*, Brussels (December 18, 1989). Turkey used the Gulf crisis in 1990 and fully allied itself with the West as a bargaining chip in seeking full membership in the EU, just as Adnan Menderes, prime minister from 1950 to 1960, secured NATO membership after sending troops to Korea. During the 1991 war, Turkish public opinion did not support sending troops to the Gulf. In the end, the Gulf War created more problems for Turkey by creating

a permanent power vacuum in northern Iraq and politicizing the Kurdish identity, while the expected political and economic dividends did not materialize.

8 See *Presidency Conclusions Helsinki European Council*, December 10–11, 1999.
9 As stated by the Copenhagen European Council in 1993, membership requires that the candidate country has achieved (1) stability of institutions guaranteeing democracy, the rule of law, human rights, and respect for and protection of minorities; (2) the existence of a functioning market economy as well as the capacity to cope with competitive pressure and market forces within the Union; and (3) the ability to take on the obligations of membership including adherence to the aims of political, economic, and monetary union.
10 The 1997 military coup is commonly known either as the "soft coup" or the "February 28 process." It is called a "soft coup" because the military mobilized the major business associations, media cartels, university rectors, and a judiciary long subservient to its commands to engineer an anti-RP drive to force the recently elected Erbakan government to resign. The coup posed Islamic identity as a national threat and proposed a number of directives to cleanse the Islamic presence in public spaces where it had been present even in the most zealous period of Kemalism.
11 For detailed statements of the anti-EU radical Islamist arguments, see (Alpay, 2002). In 2002, seventy-five pro-EU groups and associations, including liberal and Islamic foundations, formed the *Avrupa Hareketi 2002*.
12 Interview with Fethullah Gülen, May 10, 2004.
13 The proceedings of these conferences were published as *Uluslararası Avrupa Birliği Surası I-II* (Ankara: Diyanet Yayinlari, 2000). The two volumes include sixty-three research papers which examine the history of the EU and the interfaith dialog and the role of the DRA in the EU system; see also *Türkiye'nin Avrupa Birliği'ne Girişinin Din Boyutu Sempozyum 17–19 Eylül 2001*, Çanakkale (Ankara: Diyanet, 2003).
14 The DRA is organizing a series of activities against missionaries; see *Yeni Şafak*, February 13, 2005.
15 Interview with Gülen, May 10, 2004.
16 Ibid.
17 The Constitutional Court closed the WP on the basis of its anti-secular activities. Erbakan was banned from political activity for five years. The Fazilet Party was formed under the leadership of Recai Kutan, a close confidant of Erbakan, who tried to maintain Erbakan's legacy. Due to pressure from younger and reformist members of the party leadership, the 1999 election platform declared the entry into the EU to be the primary goal of Turkey's foreign policy. However, in June 2001, the court closed the Virtue Party due to its anti-secular activities and this led to division and transformation of political Islamic leadership.
18 See, for the party programme, www.saadet.org.tr.
19 http://www.akparti.org.tr/programeng3.asp.
20 European Court of Human Rights (ECHR), Refah Partisi and Others vs. Turkey (No. 41340/98).

21 William Boston, "Germany's Young Turks: Vulnerable to Extremism," *Christian Science Monitor*, September 13, 2002.
22 A major debate is going on in different EU countries; see E. J. Zürcher and H. van der Linden's "The Netherlands Scientific Council for Government Policy," in their *The European Union, Turkey and Islam* (Amsterdam: Amsterdam University Press, 2004).
23 The Turks voted for the plan and the Greek side voted against the unification on April 21, 2004. Only the Greek Cypriot part of the island joined the EU.
24 *Le Monde*, November 8, 2002. Many European leaders argue that "Turkey has no place in Europe" and that admitting Turkey to the EU would be the "end of Europe." These statements were made by former German Chancellor Helmut Kohl in *The Guardian*, March 7, 1997.

10 Religion, European identity, and political contention in historical perspective

Daniel Nexon

Religion is once again becoming a central source of contention in European politics. As the contributors to this volume note, European political and cultural integration is now expanding to include political communities that did not experience the same process of secularization that took hold in Western and Central Europe during the second half of the twentieth century. At the same time, growing transnational linkages between Europe and other regions, primarily the Islamic world, are profoundly influencing European politics. Both of these developments are making religious identity an increasingly powerful locus for political mobilization and claims-making in European politics.

My aim in this chapter is to place these trends in historical perspective. In some respects, they are not particularly surprising. Significant aspects of European identity are tied to a long history involving the consolidation of Latin Christendom as a political-religious community. We must always be careful about the dangers of naïve cultural essentialism, yet it is difficult to imagine that Europeanization and increasing transnationalism would not generate political tensions involving religion. Many of the moments and processes that constitute important markers of European identity invoke a history built on the exclusion of religious heterogeneity, or on the management of intra-Latin Christian religious disputes.

In fact, one of the most important moments in the creation of the contemporary European religious-political order was the Westphalian settlement of 1648. Westphalia was the first "pan-European" international treaty, and it largely ended the military dimensions of the schismatic conflict between Protestant and Catholic variants of Latin Christianity. The Protestant Reformations and Westphalia operate as important baselines for contemporary European developments in two distinct ways. On the one hand, they represent an actual historical moment in which the European political order nearly did not survive the impact of transnational, heterogeneous religious networks on political mobilization and claims-making. On the other hand, they are elements in a general narrative of the emergence of putatively core "Western" values of religious tolerance and state sovereignty.[1] Westphalia and the impact of the Protestant Reformations on the European political-religious order are important signifiers in ongoing debates about European integration and the nature of politics in the Islamic world.[2]

The first section of this chapter examines the construction of Latin Christendom and its continued relevance to Europeanization. The second, more substantial section deals with the Protestant Reformations and the Peace of Westphalia. International-relations treatments of religious dynamics in the sixteenth and seventeenth centuries focus almost exclusively on the question of whether the Protestant Reformations, through the Peace of Westphalia, created the sovereign-territorial state system. Far more important, for our purposes, is the more fundamental question of why the Protestant Reformations led to a profound crisis in European state formation.

The answer is of some significance for the issues raised in this volume. Early modern European states were composite political communities characterized by stark regional differences and indirect rule. In the early modern European period, aggressive rulers pushed for greater centralization and integration, setting off routine dynamics of consolidation and local resistance. The Protestant Reformations created transregional and transnational movements that both opposed and supported greater political centralization (Mackenney, 1993: 81). Because they crossed social, economic, and regional divisions, they undermined the ways in which European rulers had maintained their authority by dividing and ruling their subjects and holdings. Moreover, the injection of seemingly intractable doctrinal divisions into political bargaining reduced the room for compromise between different political factions; it complicated ordinary questions of taxation, rights, and privileges. The result was a series of devastating civil and interstate conflicts that altered the European political landscape (te Brake, 1998: 28; Nexon, 2004: 237–30).

I then turn to the broader issue of the status of the Protestant Reformations and the Peace of Westphalia as sources of the current political-religious order in Europe. The Protestant Reformations did create new categories and practices of rule that provided important resources for the secular, sovereign order that we now associate with the European state system. Yet a secular basis for civil society was not, as James Tracy notes, an outcome that religious reformers and their opponents either imagined or desired. Indeed, the immediate legacy of the political-religious struggles surrounding the Reformations was a closer identification between state, religion, and territory than had previously existed in many parts of Europe. Rulers established state religions, often sought to homogenize religious practices within their territory, and, in doing so, created a political-religious map divided along confessional lines (Tracy, 1999: 285).

In the third section, I reflect on the implications of these patterns for religious heterogeneity in contemporary Europe. The weight of history suggests that the contributors to this volume are correct: Europe faces a difficult road as traditional "others" to Latin Christendom increasingly find themselves within the European project. Moreover, the process of replacing the Westphalian system with a large composite polity in Europe – the European Union – may replicate some of the structural forces that render transnational religious movements particularly problematic. Nevertheless, Europe's future is unlikely to resemble its past. European states are not dynastic agglomerations; the European Union, however imperfectly, governs through principles of pluralism and representation.

Religion and Europeanization

The chapters in this volume focus on Europeanization as both the deepening and extension of the European community – in cultural, political, and economic terms. First, Europeanization involves the construction of a European "identity" of increasing importance vis-à-vis national identities, whether French, German, Italian, or British. Second, Europeanization is implicated in the process of extending political and cultural membership in the project of European integration further east, even potentially to Turkey. Europeanization, of course, is a much longer process of negotiating terms of membership in the European community of states and nations.[3] It is essential to recognize that this process predates the widespread adoption of "Europe" as a marker of a peninsula on the Asian continent.

Although one could trace the descent of Europe at least to late antiquity, there are many ways in which the cultural and political locus of Europe stems from the medieval formation of Latin Christendom. As Robert Bartlett argues, Latin Christendom emerged out of the cellular reproduction of Franco-Gallic liturgy and social organization. Aristocratic military entrepreneurs from a Frankish core conquered and colonized their neighbors, some of whom had adopted Christianity, others of whom were pagan. "As the men of Frankish Europe intruded upon societies around and unlike their own," he argues, "they found both non-Christians (in eastern and the Mediterranean lands) and local variants of Christianity (notably in the Celtic countries). Their response was to equate the two, if the Christian societies did not have the social and legal characteristics with which they were familiar" (Bartlett, 1993: 23).

With them, they brought merchants, more peacefully inclined church-men, and peasants who contributed to creation of broadly similar forms of social organization. Some communities adapted and reformed in the face of Franco-Gallic expansion, often adapting the trappings of Latin Christian society. Conquest and colonization, exemplified by the Norman conquest of England, the creation of Norman kingdoms in Italy, the Teutonic crusades in the Baltic, and the long *Reconquista* of Iberia created lateral networks of cultural and political commonality across much of contemporary Europe. It reached its limits in Eastern Europe and the Near East. In the latter case, the military and social technologies of the Crusaders proved inferior to those of their rivals (Bartlett, 1993; Moore, 1997).

Latin Christendom, therefore, emerged as a political-religious com-munity linked through common forms of social organization, common adherence to Catholic religious rite, and, at the elite level, bonds of kinship. It involved two crucial exclusions: Orthodoxy and Islam (Hay, 1968: 30–34; Herrin, 1987; Delanty, 1995: 34–35). Over the course of the Middle Ages the divisions between Orthodox and Catholic rite deepened and hardened, and conflict increasingly marked the frontiers of the two communities of Christians (Herrin, 1987; Bartlett, 1993: 255; Hamilton, 1997: 155–59; Moore, 1997: 595–96).[4]

During the early expansion of Latin Christendom, Islam was an utterly alien and not terribly significant influence on identity formation. With the start of the crusades, however, non-Iberian members of Latin Christendom recognized Islam as a major force, one in cosmological opposition to Christianity. Later, the rise of the Ottoman Empire brought this challenge into focus, ironically at a time when European powers such as France and England, driven by considerations of political expediency, began to form temporary alliances with the Ottomans against the Habsburgs (Neumann, 1999: 42–49).

Through its formation and consolidation, Latin Christendom largely pushed out or marginalized Islam and Orthodoxy alike. Minor Orthodox communities persisted in some areas of the Latin Christian core, but the general trend was assimilation, conversion, or at least subordination to Rome. The emergence of the Ottoman challenge threatened to reverse this process with respect to Islam.

For example, the Spanish, soon after the fall of Granada, dealt with their "Islamic" problem through forced conversion. The Morisco popu-lation remained a challenge for the Habsburgs. From 1559, Islamic Corsairs found allies among the Morisco population of Granada. The Ottomans plotted to rally the Moriscos against Philip II. In response, Granadan authorities began a campaign to forcibly assimilate the

Morisco population, which in turn led to a major Morisco rebellion from 1568–70. Philip responded by forcibly dispersing the Morisco population throughout Castile. Finally, the Habsburgs opted for expulsion, which they carried out from 1609–14 (Elliott, 1963: 110, 240, 305–08; Lynch, 1991: 313–18). Thus, very few of the major European powers within Latin Christendom had, within their core territories, a significant Islamic or Orthodox population until the second half of the twentieth century.

The re-emergence of significant religious heterogeneity, in the form of Protestantism, during this period played an important role in displacing "Christendom" (meaning, largely, Latin Christendom) in favor of "Europe" as a geographic and cultural marker. Until the seventeenth century "Europe" and "Christendom" were interchangeable terms. But during the religious struggles of the early modern period, Protestants increasingly came to associate "Christendom" and the *Respublica Christiana* with Catholic hegemony, specifically the prospect of a Habsburg or Bourbon *monarchia*. Since European particularism, in the form of independent states, protected the continued existence of Protestant and Reformed confessions, "Europe" became identified with a multistate system governed by balance-of-power principles. The Treaty of Utrecht (1713), which ended the war of Spanish succession and precluded the possibility of a union between the crowns of Spain and France, was the last international agreement to mention the *Respublica Christiana*. It was also the first to reference power asymmetries as a cause of war (Schmidt, 1966).

This shift did not, however, represent a radical rupture. Napoleon claimed that "for a few shadings, France, Spain, England, Italy and Germany have the same traditions, the same religion, the same costume . . . Except for Turkey, Europe is but one province of the world. When we make war, we make civil war."[5] Burke, no fan of French universalism, also identified a common history – that of Latin Christendom – as the basis of European community (Thompson, 1994: 39). Such views, however, fell into disfavor. An increasing number of thinkers looked back on the *ancien régime* with distaste, and most recognized that European unity could not be achieved in an era dominated by sovereign, national states (Thompson, 1994). My point here, however, is not to engage in a history of ideas. Rather, it is to stress that when we view Europeanization as a long historical process, we inevitably confront the creation of Europe as a community through, first, the extrusion of religious difference and, second, the management of religious schism within a broader Latin Christian community.[6]

I now turn to a longer discussion of the cause of that schism. The Protestant Reformations, as I have already noted, led to a redefinition of the Latin Christian community from one that focused on doctrinal and social unity to one that stressed elements of common culture and civilization within a framework of local, multistate, particularism. The Reformations also began the processes of privatizing religion and domesticating religion within the sphere of civil society. However, this was not, generally, through principles of domestic tolerance. If anything, the proximate outcome of the Reformations was a more thorough religious homogenization through a close association between state, confession, and territory. Toleration of religious dissent, almost always driven by necessity rather than preference, was an extremely rare outcome in the seventeenth and early eighteenth centuries.

The Catholic Church and the Reformations

The position of the Catholic Church in the later Middle Ages presents something of a contradiction. Its temporal authority was in serious decline. Rome negotiated with European princes on a more or less equal footing; the later Middle Ages are filled with concordats specifying terms of appointment and the scope of lay taxation, influence, and other prerogatives in the different polities of Europe. Local bishops, abbots, and clergy operated with ever greater autonomy. But the ideal of Christianity as homologous and interdependent, with the ordered structure of the spiritual world mirrored by a related ordering of the secular, was hollowed out by the decline of scholasticism and the rise of humanism. Yet the hierarchical structure of the Church remained, and most accepted the commonality of the Christian faith with the Pope as its ultimate arbiter. Monasteries, bishoprics, and other institutions of the Church took on more and more institutional functions in society, and their continued quasi-autonomy from secular rulers helped give the political landscape its patchwork quality (Leff, 1961; Barraclough, 1968; Bonney, 1991: 1–9; Thomson, 1998).

In 1517, the story goes, Luther nailed his ninety-five theses to a church door in Wittenberg. Most of them contained the usual complaints against Church practices – indulgences, abuse of power, worldly extravagances, and so forth. But buried within them was the germ of far more radical proposals for Church reform, particularly the notion that salvation is a matter of personal faith and that scripture is the sole source of religious knowledge.

The Protestant Reformations, however, involved a number of phases, movements, and theological orientations. Luther is obviously one of the most prominent figures of the Reformations. His major innovation was the systematic promulgation of two related doctrines: justification by faith, and the notion that scripture was the only source of knowledge about God. For Luther, it was only through personal faith that one's soul could be saved. This had enormous implications for the already eroded structure of the medieval Church. For one, it meant that individuals had a personal relationship with God; clergy could serve as facilitators or guides for Christians, but not as mediators between them and the Divine (Bonney, 1991: 18–19; Tracy, 1999: 47–55). Second, it meant that the Church had no business dictating political behavior. For example, Luther argued that heresy cannot be suppressed by force, since "worldly government extends to life and property, but over the soul it holds no sway" (Mitchell, 1993: 37–39). In short, Luther's doctrines involved a *privatization of religion*, and a strong *separation of the profane from the sacred*.

Luther's call for reform was, initially, more notable for the atmosphere it helped create than the success of Lutheranism as any sort of organized movement. Luther's cause, and his debates with other reform-minded theologians, sparked great expectations of spiritual and political renewal in Germany and Switzerland. These expectations created a potent atmosphere for a number of popular movements, some of which were quite radical. Luther also found support from a relatively small number of princes, who provided a crucial shield for his activities in the years ahead.

The most dynamic push for reformation in this period was in the towns. Wayne te Brake argues that the process of urban reformation in the period roughly from 1520–40 was dominated by pressure "from below" upon civic officials to appoint reformist preachers, resist attempts by higher authorities to discipline evangelicals, or otherwise to abet religious reformation. Sometimes they were radically successful, sometimes they were defeated, but more often popular pressure for religious reform led to political-religious bargaining resulting in incremental reform. Far rarer were those urban officials who themselves led the process of reformation, seeking to impose Protestant codes of behavior and preaching upon subjects and citizens (Moeller, 1982: 61–69; te Brake, 1998: 35–44). This process was not restricted to upper (southern) Germany, but, taking a variety of forms, occurred throughout lower (northern) Germany. Although the specifics varied, desire for religious reformation often came together with pressure for communal rule (Schilling, 1992: 190–92).

The relative success of pro-reform movements in collective mobilization did not only stem from the elective affinity between Protestant ideas and the aspirations of many social groups. Just as important was their comparative advantage in building and exploiting networks for popular mobilization. In many areas of Germany a kind of "vanguard," however unorganized, of Protestant preachers developed. Artisans, merchants, former soldiers, converts, and defrocked clerics fanned across Germany preaching various versions of reform, contrasting clerical abuses to the scriptural "word of God" (Ozment, 1975: 123–25; Bercé, 1987: 17). Until the forces of the Counter-Reformation finally organized, the Catholic Church lacked not only a set of coherent and vital anti-Protestant ideas, but also any means of forming comparable networks. With a few exceptions, the Church depended either upon more or less locally organized (and sometimes spontaneous) anti-Protestant mobilization or the coercive power of rulers to counter Protestant agitation.[7] Coercion often successfully contained reform movements, but depending upon secular power left the Church vulnerable to the shifting religious allegiances of rulers, whether magnates, urban councils, lay and ecclesiastical princes, or sovereigns (Brodek, 1971: 398–99).

Nevertheless, in the early 1520s most expected reform to go the way of earlier heretical movements: nowhere fast. The first military uprising tied to the Reformation occurred between 1522 and 1523, when a group of Imperial Knights rose against ecclesiastical authority. They failed to garner support from either princes or towns and were soundly defeated by the Swabian League. After 1523 the Imperial Knights ceased to be important key players in German politics. The revolt also accentuated the fears of both moderates and conservatives that reformation inevitably carried with it political instability. The German Peasants' War seemed, for a time, to confirm those fears (Holborn, 1959: 169–70).

The German Peasants' War (1524–25) illustrates how rebellions without a significant elite component or external support generally fared in early modern Europe. It represents a useful contrast for some of the cases of more general religious conflict discussed below. The German Peasants' movement originated with mass meetings of artisans, peasants, former soldiers, and others seeking to air their grievances against lords and nobles. It contained no organized religious doctrine, but clearly drew inspiration from reformist ideals and presented itself as trying to bring about a new social and religious order. It soon attracted participants who probably numbered in the low hundreds of thousands, and amounted to a combination of barely coordinated uprisings against local rulers After a period of fear and indecision, a coalition of authorities suppressed the rebellion (Stalnaker, 1979; Kittelson, 1986: S128; Stayer, 1991; Schilling, 1992: 191–201; Scribner, 1994; te Brake, 1998: 31–34).

The social radicalism of the movement inspired Luther and many of the more conservative reformers to expand upon those elements of their theology that were attractive to dynastic rulers and magistrates. In the period following the war, a rash of princes entered the Protestant camp. James Tracy argues that the Peasants' War convinced Catholic princes that "religious order imposed by heretical governments was better than the chaos that seemed to loom on the horizon" (Tracy, 1999: 73). Thus, in the first half of the 1520s there were few princely conversions to Lutheranism. Frederick of Saxony, Luther's first protector, supported the movement relatively early, if carefully. Philip of Hesse converted in 1524. Despite the delay before conversions among the princes began in earnest, Heinz Schilling reminds us that the distinction between communal and princely reformation is better viewed as analytically distinctive processes than chronologically separate stages (Schilling, 1992: 196–97). By the 1540s, the majority of German princes had embraced Luther's reformist position.

Luther's direct influence was not European in scope. For the most part, it was confined to Germany and the kingdoms of Scandinavia, whose rulers converted to Lutheran-style reform. His indirect influence was more widespread, and fears of "Lutheranism" and "Lutherans" (there was, at this point no such thing as a Lutheran sect) spread throughout Western Europe. When Henry VIII declared himself head of the English Church and began seizing ecclesiastical and monastic property, he had little interest in Luther's teachings, although some of his advisers certainly were influenced by Luther. At first, the most successful movement in expanding beyond Germany was Anabaptism; it lost much of its momentum after radical Anabaptists seized control of Münster in 1534, declared a new Kingdom of God on Earth, abolished property and instituted polygamy, and were subsequently massacred by forces who had widespread sympathy throughout Christendom (Bonney, 1991: 24–26; Stayer, 1991). Zwinglism also foundered after Zwingli himself was killed defending Geneva from an invasion by Catholic cantons (Elton, 1964: 73–74).

It was left to another Genevan reformer, Jean Calvin, to bring new vibrancy to the religious reformations and extend their effective reach beyond central Europe. Like Luther, Calvin rejected reliance on extra-scriptural authority; he shared Luther's focus on justification through faith. He departed from Luther in endorsing predestination – the notion that God has already decided who will and will not be saved – and in his virulent rejection of religious images.

Predestination, as Luther argued, had dangerous implications. In particular, it suggested that individuals need not engage in communion or otherwise carry out the scriptural requirements of faith. Calvin's solution was to stress discipline among members of the Church – through frequent communion, for example – such as to enable them to slowly overcome the corruptions of the profane world. Calvin's reading of the New Testament led him to advocate an independent structure for the Church. Each local Church should be governed by a minister and a board of elders, who together formed a consistory. Among the consistory's duties were the maintenance of cohesion and discipline among the flock. In practice, the consistory was supposed to function as a parallel governing institution, as it did in Geneva. Thus, Calvinism also involved a privatization of religion through faith and discipline, but it also put forth an institutional structure designed to give faith and discipline a very public face (Bonney, 1991: 44–52; Gorski, 1993; Tracy, 1999: 85–95).

From the 1550s onwards, Calvinism emerged as the most dynamic reform movement. It gained adherents in France, the Netherlands, Germany, Hungary, Bohemia, Poland-Lithuania, and elsewhere. The institutional structures of Calvinism, combined with the dispatch of missionaries from Geneva and the need to organize in an environment in which Calvinism faced persecution from authorities, created an ideal basis for coordination and mobilization. These features would prove incredibly important in the Dutch Revolt and the French Wars of Religion, as we shall discuss shortly (Koenigsberger, 1955).

Belatedly, the challenge of the Protestant Reformations prompted reforms within the Church. The Council of Trent (1545–47, 1551–52, and 1561–62), initially formed to reunify Latin Christendom, became the focal point of this reformist effort. It strengthened the power of bishops, moved to curb Church abuses, set up seminaries to better train Catholic clergy, and developed a coherent set of doctrines to rebut the Protestant challenge. In essence, it gave birth to the Counter-Reformation. The advanced guard of the Counter-Reformation was the Jesuit Order (founded in 1540). Jesuits were commissioned with coordinating, mobilizing, and otherwise effecting the Counter-Reformation. Some of their work was clandestine (Dunn, 1970: 9–11; Tracy, 1999: 97–102).

Both Protestantism and Counter-Reformed Catholicism produced religious impulses that personalized and, to varying degrees, privatized aspects of religious belief, obedience, and experience. These impulses, however indirectly, created important discursive resources for secularism, which José Casanova reminds us is a "knowledge regime" rather than an inevitable developmental condition, by implying that religious faith could be separated from political practice. Of course, the short- and medium-term effects were precisely the opposite: the Protestant Reformations created strong homogenizing impulses within European political communities.

Yet we need to be a bit careful about the relationship between theological doctrine and political mobilization around religious ideas and identities. As we shall see, theology could be a major barrier to alliance formation, and theological disputes often made political settlements difficult to achieve. In that sense, the content of religious ideas mattered a great deal.

Nevertheless, many of the elites and ordinary people who mobilized around religious identities had very little understanding of these theological debates.

In fact, the differences between the various movements of reform and counter-reform could be quite fluid – difficult to distinguish both for observers and participants. In that sense, religious practices proved far more important as a marker of exclusion and inclusion, in other words, as one basis for common identity and commensurate collective mobilization. A relatively clear demarcation of religious confessions was an outcome of the Reformations rather than a constitutive element of them.

I stress this for three reasons. First, it is easy to forget in the face of short-hand references to "Protestants," "Lutherans," "Calvinists," and so forth. Second, it helps make sense of some of the dynamics discussed below, in a way that focusing too much on the specific content of religious ideas can obscure. Third, because it suggests that even very diffuse notions of religious identity – of the type now found throughout much of Western Europe – can be rapidly triggered in the context of political contention. Of course, better organized and more cohesive religious groupings will have an advantage when it comes to political mobilization and claims-making. Indeed, we shall see that this asymmetry gave Calvinist rebels in the Low Countries a decisive advantage vis-à-vis Catholics and moderates in terms of shaping political developments. In France, however, the different sides were on a more equal footing, which helps explain the ultimate failure of the Huguenots.

The political consequence of the Protestant Reformations

The political impact of the Reformations is impossible to understand without reference to the structure of early modern European political communities. European polities were not sovereign-territorial states, nor were they national communities. In fact, Europe was composed of a patchwork of autonomous and quasi-autonomous clusters of political authority; Europe, in 1500, "included some five hundred more or less political units." These included cities, towns, duchies, counties, and ecclesiastical holdings (Tilly, 1975: 15).

Thus, historians now generally refer to early modern European polities as "composite states": composed of numerous subordinate political communities linked to central authorities through *distinctive contracts* specifying rights and obligations. Subordinate political communities thus often had their own social organizations, identities, languages, and institutions. Local actors jealously guarded whatever autonomy they had. Subjects expected rulers to uphold these contracts; to guarantee what they perceived as "customary" rights and immunities in matters of taxation and local control (Koenigsberger, 1986: 1–26; Elliott, 1992; Oresko, et al., 1997; te Brake, 1998: 14–17).

Dynasticism was the ascendant principle of rule in late medieval and early modern Europe. Indeed, it remained so until it came under severe challenge from notions of popular sovereignty in the nineteenth century, and was only fully supplanted in Europe after World War One (Bukovansky, 2002). Dynasticism comprised two basic elements: (1) rule by individuals who occupied titular positions usually based upon medieval ranks, and (2) the principle that an individual's claim to that position was based upon kinship ties. For "those who governed, the interests of the family were all important" and "the survival or extinction of the dynasty was the difference between peace and war, and the accidents of inheritance shaped the power blocs of Europe as a whole" (Mackenney, 1993: 219).

Dynasticism promoted the formation of dynastic agglomerations. As Wayne te Brake notes, "most Europeans lived within composite states that had been variously cobbled together from preexisting political units by a variety of aggressive 'princes' employing a standard repertoire of techniques including marriages, dynastic inheritance, and direct conquest" (te Brake, 1998: 14).

We can find a number of illustrative examples across Europe. The Valois dynasty controlled a French kingdom that was, in reality, a hotchpotch of different duchies, counties, and formerly independent kingdoms with different contractual relations to the monarchy. The kingdom of Aragon was an agglomeration of Catalonia, Aragon, and Valencia. Each maintained separate representative institutions, and was ruled as a separate entity. The dynastic rulers of Aragon had added Naples and Sicily to their domains, and these were also juridically independent states. Other large polities, such as the Holy Roman Empire and the Polish-Lithuanian commonwealth, were not precisely dynastic agglomerations, as the head of state was elective and territory was not generally added through marriage and inheritance. The rulers of such polities were dynasts in their own right, and thus we can place them broadly within the same institutional category (Koenigsberger and Mosse, 1968; Bonney, 1991; Greengrass, 1991; Collins, 1995; te Brake, 1998).

By the start of the sixteenth century, dynastic agglomerations were starting to show clear advantages over other forms of composite states, such as city-states and federations. These advantages stemmed, in part, from their economies of scale and the centrality of dynastic relations in alliance politics. In particular, changes in warfare undermined the ability of towns, federations, and local nobles to field effective military challenges to dynastic rulers (Koenigsberger, 1987: 42; see also Roberts, 1967; Bean, 1973; Hintze, 1975; Howard, 1976; Parker, 1976, 1988; Tilly, 1990; Downing, 1992; Eltis, 1995; Ertman, 1997).[8]

The most startling aspect of the ascendancy of dynasticism was the rise of the Habsburgs to European primacy. Between 1515 and 1519, through a series of contingencies related to dynastic marriages and premature deaths, Charles V became ruler of the rump Burgundian state (1515) – including Artois, Franche-Compté, and the Low Countries – Castile and its overseas possessions (1516), Aragon-Catalonia and the Aragonese Mediterranean holdings (1516), a claim to the Duchy of Milan, and the traditional Habsburg domains in Central Europe (1519). He was also the presumptive candidate for King of the Romans – the elected title of the Holy Roman Empire – which he achieved after much bribery and some proxy warfare in 1519 (Esteban, 2001; Blockmans, 2002). Concerns over the influence and resources of Charles V, and later of the combined house of Habsburg, provide one of the crucial political backdrops for the unfolding of the Reformations.

Everywhere across Europe – whether in Charles's vast composite monarchy or the micro-agglomerations in Italy – dynastic power overlaid upon the same topography that produced city-states, city-leagues, and effectively independent magnates. Thus, attempts to enhance dynastic authority triggered sources of friction among and between regions, lords, towns, and social classes who sought to preserve or expand their privileges and autonomy.

It is in this friction that we can understand both the strengths and weaknesses of authority in dynastic composite states. The institutional structure of dynastic agglomerations depended upon and facilitated the effective use of divide-and-rule strategies along two distinct axes: *across* constituent parts of composite states and *within* constituent parts of composite states.

First, the composite quality of all early modern states created strong firewalls against the spread of rebellions. Because subjects in different holdings had different identities and interests, and because they were ruled via different contractual terms, they had little motivation or capacity to coordinate their resistance to the centralizing demands of rulers. Thus, only when rulers severely overreached in their demands did they provoke simultaneous uprisings. Even then, generalized rebellions tended to founder on regional differences.

Second, since early modern European society was highly stratified on class and status lines, rulers frequently were able to play off different groups against one another within regions and localities. Rulers could extend guarantees or grant exemptions to, for example, nobles, to secure their loyalty during periods of urban revolt. The inevitable suspicions and cleavages between different classes and interests generally proved fairly easy to manipulate. These divisions, as we have seen, doomed the German Peasants' Movement.

An example not involving religion is illustrative here. In 1520–21 Castile experienced a serious uprising centered around chartered towns, known as the revolt of the *Comuneros*. There were a variety of long-term sources of the rebellion, but the immediate cause was the ascension of Charles – a foreigner who spoke little Castilian, appointed his cronies to important offices, and, most importantly, pushed an exceptional grant of revenue through the *Cortes* (estates) with little regard for the rights and privileges of Castilians. The revolt failed, in large part, because the *Comuneros* could not overcome their divisions with the great nobles, who in turn crushed the rebellion after Charles bought them off with grants and immunities. At exactly the same time, a major revolt was underway in nearby Valencia – over which Charles also ruled – but the two groups of rebels made no attempt to coordinate or collaborate. Both saw their concerns as local, and had no basis to join forces (Pérez, 1989; te Brake, 1998: 26–29).

Such dynamics were increasingly important as warfare became more resource-intensive and rulers' economy-of-scale advantages increased. The more wealth and manpower were required for effective resistance, the more challengers to rulers needed to overcome within-region and between-region divisions. At the same time, economic and military pressures, reinforced by growing "international" dynastic competition, gave rulers more incentives to centralize control and abrogate customary rights.

The composite nature of European states also helps explain the spread of the various religious reform movements. Local autonomy limited the ability of rulers to suppress religious dissent, while religious dissent found fertile ground in the social and political instability characteristic of early modern states.

The spread of various forms of religious heterodoxy – most notably the ideas of reformers such as Luther and Calvin – had the potential to undermine effective rule in composite states. It led to organized networks of co-confessionals across regional, status, and political boundaries, supplied them with common identities and interests, and provided a basis for legitimate resistance. Pre-existing conflicts over local autonomy and between court factions both fed and were fed by the introduction of religious cleavages into early modern polities. As political claims-making increasingly centered around religion, it became more difficult for rulers – and even actors trying to hold together resistance movements that involved multiple confessions – to negotiate compromises even when the roots of resistance involved fiscal demands or centralizing policies. We can see these dynamics in three of the major religious conflicts of the sixteenth century: the escalating religious tensions in Germany that ultimately produced both the 1555 Peace of Augsburg and Charles V's abdication, the French Wars of Religion, and the Dutch Revolt.

The Schmalkaldic War and the 1555 Peace of Augsburg

The events leading up to the 1555 Peace of Augsburg demonstrate how religious differentiation undermined effective rule in a composite state. As ruler of a vast monarchy that included the Empire – itself the most decentralized composite state in Europe – Charles had difficulty turning his attention and resources to the developing religious instability in the empire. This drove him to make concessions to the Protestants, in exchange for their support in his wars against the French and the Ottoman Turks. When he did take steps against heresy, he found his efforts undermined even by those who should have supported him – Catholic princes and towns, who feared any expansion of Charles's power and authority would undermine their own autonomy. These twin pressures led Charles to adopt oscillating policies of toleration and suppression toward Protestantism (Bonney, 1991: 3 and 15–16; Blockmans, 2002: 80–83).

Religious differences were a source of both unity and fragmentation within Protestantism. Philip of Hesse's early attempts to create a Protestant defensive alliance collapsed over intra-Protestant doctrinal disputes, particularly the status of the Lord's Supper. Lutherans and Zwinglians differed on the nature of Holy Communion. Luther himself instructed John of Saxony that he should not participate in an alliance, because it would lead to military conflict, force Lutherans to defend doctrinal errors, and contradicted biblical condemnation of human alliances. Subsequently, John wrote instructions to his representative at the intra-Protestant negotiations forbidding him "to enter into an alliance with those who accept Zwinglian views of the sacrament" (Christensen, 1984: 422–23).

Ultimately, it became clear to the major Protestant leaders that Charles aimed to impose Catholicism on Germany. In 1531, six princes and ten cities formed the League of Schmalkalden (Dueck, 1982: 55). In 1534, the League struck against Charles by invading the Duchy of Württemberg. Their success consolidated the position of the Schmalkaldic League. Common religious identity enabled military and diplomatic coordination of the kind most dangerous to composite polities. The League now acted as "a visible unit negotiating with Henry VIII of England and playing its part in the politics of Scandanavia" (Elton, 1964: 156).

It took over a decade before Charles responded with military force. By that time, he faced a clear problem: most of the German princes were now Protestant, yet Charles aimed to fight a war with the ultimate goal of restoring Catholic unity to the empire. He embarked on an attempt to divide and conquer his foes by deliberate subterfuge. Charles publicly claimed his goals as merely political: the suppression of disobedience to his and imperial authority. As he wrote to his sister Mary, "I decided to embark on war against Hesse and Saxony as transgressors of the peace against the Duke of Brunswick and his territory. And although this pretext will not long disguise the fact that this is a matter of religion, yet it serves for the present to divide the renegades" (Bonney, 1991: 188).

The problem with this strategy was that it could only work so long as Charles hid his true aims. Having defeated the Schmalkaldic League and set about consolidating his position, Charles could no longer pretend his goal was not the marginalization and elimination of Protestantism. Once he promulgated his "Interim" religious settlement, his Protestant allies deserted him and those who had remained neutral flocked to the side of their co-religionists. Throughout Germany, local rulers obstructed its implementation. "Protestant pamphlets decried the Interim as a diabolical trick and popery in disguise" (Bonney, 1991: 119). Renewed warfare, joined by the French in hopes of weakening their Habsburg rivals, led to Charles's defeat (Blockmans, 2002: 96–98).

When the imperial Diet next met, it was February of 1555. The Religious Peace of Augsburg recognized the Protestant Confession of Augsburg and ratified existing seizures of Church lands by Protestants, but also held that any future clerical converts to Protestantism would have to transfer their benefices to a Catholic cleric. Augsburg adopted what te Brake refers to as a "thoroughly authoritarian settlement" to the question of religion. Henceforth, each autonomous town's, region's, or princedom's religion would be determined by its representative in the Estates. This was the principle *cuius regio eius religio*: rulers would decide the religions of their subjects, and were prohibited from intervening in one another's territory in support of co-confessionals (te Brake, 1998: 48). Thus, the Reformation in Germany established, in principle, if not always in practice, a new, homologous relationship between ruler, territory, and religion. Religion, in this respect, was to be domesticated in the interests of general peace.

Between 1555 and 1556, Charles abdicated his titles, granting the Emperorship to the "Austrian" branch of the family and reserving his

Conclusion

Italian, Burgundian, and Spanish inheritances for his son, Philip II (1556–98). The move stunned his contemporaries, but bowed to the new realities of a Europe divided by religion, incapable, at least for the time being, of being unified under a great *monarchia* (Koenigsberger, 1971: 59).

The French Wars of Religion

The French Wars of Religion are conventionally divided into nine different conflicts, beginning in 1562 and ending in 1598 with the promulgation of the Edict of Nantes. Revisionist historians, such as Mack P. Holt, note that the Edict of Nantes did not end religious warfare within France, and extend the history of the French Wars of Religion until 1629 and the Peace of Alais. The political history of overt Protestantism in France extends beyond that, until Louis XIV revoked the Edict of Nantes in 1685 (Holt, 1995).

The immediate causes of the Wars of Religion were the spread of Calvinism in France and the death of the French king, Henry II, in a jousting accident in 1559. Henry's death led to a succession of young or feeble heirs, and ignited intense factional conflicts between the great houses of Guise, Montmorency, and Bourbon. In fact, the intensity and intractability of religious warfare in France stemmed from the intermingling of multiple factors. The first were the factional struggles of these powerful noble families. The second was the mobilization of extensive Huguenot and ultra-Catholic networks. The third was the support given to these networks by foreign sources, whether from Geneva, Germany, England, or Spain.

The Wars of Religion quickly took on a general pattern. Any attempt by authorities to steer a moderate course emboldened the Huguenots without assuaging their demands; at the same time, moderation antagonized the Catholic party. Complicating matters was the fact that by the Third War of Religion (1568–70), popular mobilization began to take on increasing significance. Of course, part of Huguenot strength derived from the way membership in the Reformed faith provided a way of overcoming divisions between nobles and townsfolk. But it was in this period that France also saw the rise of Catholic confraternities, which were, in many instances, "designed to provide arms and men for the church militant in a holy crusade against French Protestantism" (Holt, 1995: 67).

In fact, the later stages of the Wars of Religion saw the creation of Catholic Leagues, orchestrated by the Guise, that brought these processes of polarization and large-scale mobilization to fruition. The second Catholic League was formed after the death of Henry III's (1547–89) brother left Henry of Navarre, a Bourbon Huguenot, as the presumptive heir to the throne. This new "Holy League" was composed of prominent hard-line Catholic nobles who were, in turn, linked to a network of "urban notables and magistrates who would eventually organize League cells in city halls throughout the kingdom"(Holt, 1995: 122–23). This was an organizational structure on a par with that created by Calvinism, and its strength, if not its cohesion, was enhanced by the formation of independent cells. Catholic hard-liners in Paris created the "Sixteen" – an independent revolutionary organization in Paris devoted to the Catholic cause and widely embraced by Parisians of different social standings (Knecht, 1989: 60–61; Holt, 1995: 122–23).

Thus, when Henry III – who had turned against the League – was assassinated by a militant Catholic and Henry of Navarre (Henry IV, 1589–1610) claimed the throne, he faced strong opposition from ultra-Catholics but widespread support from moderates By mid-1593, fewer and fewer people had the stomach for continued fighting. Henry IV's conversion to Catholicism, when it finally came on 25 July 1593, completely isolated the most militant Catholics within France (Knecht, 1989: 60–61; Holt, 1995: 122–23; Tracy, 1999: 152).

Henry's conversion to Catholicism gave him control of Paris and most of France, but it alienated his base of support among the Huguenots. Huguenot communities stopped contributing royal taxes. Others threatened armed insurrection. In April 1598 the two sides reached an agreement: the famous "Edict of Nantes." As with previous compromises, the Edict satisfied neither Huguenots nor former members of the Catholic League. Nantes provided for limited toleration, complete freedom of conscience, equal political rights, and a number of other concessions including a temporary right to hold some 200 fortified towns and keep arms. The Edict also restored Catholic worship in Huguenot towns and regions, and mandated that the Huguenot population refrain from work on Catholic religious holidays (Knecht, 1989: 80–82; Holt, 1995: 164–65; Tracy, 1999: 152–53).

Although the Edict is often held up as an icon of religious toleration and reason of state, this was not the case. The intention behind the Edict was the eventual restoration, by peaceful conversion and political pressure, of a unified French religious community; "rather than religious toleration or modern reason of state, the underlying principles of the Edict of Nantes was the restoration of 'one king, one faith, one law' " – a formula of confessional homogeneity that had new significance after the Reformation (Holt, 1995: 163). The Edict of Nantes was a *domestic* solution to the problem of religious difference; to that extent, it represents the growing compartmentalization of religious policy as the province of particular states. Its revocation by Louis XIV signals how effective this policy was. The Huguenots, diminished in number and politically marginalized, could not resist the transformation of France into a thoroughly counter-reformed state.

The Dutch Revolt

The Dutch Revolt fits many of the patterns of the French Wars of Religion. Indeed, the two events were interconnected by interventions and co-religionist alliances. In the Dutch Revolt, Calvinist networks played an important role in building coalitions across regional and class differences; in the Netherlands, as well as in France, Calvinist organizational structure facilitated effective revolutionary mobilization against rulers. The rebellion was sustained by financial and military assistance from foreign co-religionists (Koenigsberger, 1955). Calvinism thus provided the backbone and resources for the Dutch Revolt. It made surrender a difficult proposition for those towns, mainly in Holland and Zeeland, where it had time to put down significant roots. The question of toleration – on both Catholic and Calvinist sides – prevented the kind of negotiated settlement to the revolt that might have left Habsburg sovereignty intact. The Catholics in the Low Countries, for their part, never formed, as they did in France, a militant and organized countermovement. Indeed, many Catholics supported the revolt at crucial stages. When they abandoned or eschewed it, they looked to their ruler, Philip II of Spain, for support (Nierop, 1995; Mout, 1999).

As Antonio Ortíz argues, "but for the indignation of Philip II at the excesses of the Calvinists the established order might have been maintained indefinitely in the Netherlands; it was the Calvinists, albeit a minority, who succeeded in giving coherence to the resistance of those who were initially lukewarm." The conflicts in the Low Countries "were not exclusively religious, but it is unlikely they would have broken out if there had not been religious disaffection. Catholics and Protestants were at one in their indignation at the new taxes and the presence of foreign troops, but it was the Protestants who first resorted to arms" (Ortíz, 1971: 73–74).

The Low Countries, unlike France, were part of a larger composite monarchy. They were ruled from Castile by a Castilian monarch, and thus their defense of customary rights against centralization had a distinctive flavor. Combined with the lack of a militant Catholic party, this meant that any attempt to suppress heresy was easily viewed by individuals of all religious faiths in the Low Countries as an infringement upon local rule and privileges. Thus, when Philip's plan for an ecclesiastical reorganization of the Netherlands became public, it prompted opposition from nearly every social group in the Netherlands and helped sow the seeds for the First Revolt (1556–57) (Israel, 1995: 133–34; Darby, 2001: 16).

The questions of heresy and centralization were so intertwined that negotiating acceptable compromises between central authorities and local actors – whether elites or ordinary people – became nearly impossible. In the early stages of the revolt, Philip's policies produced alliances against him that crossed religious divisions. In the end, however, divisions between Protestant extremists and Catholic moderates ultimately ended the possibility of a Netherlands-wide rebellion.

This process reached a climax in 1578, when militant Calvinists seized control of Catholic holdouts in Holland and Zeeland, including the towns of Haarlem and Amsterdam, as well as in towns in Brabant and Artois. In June, they mounted a successful coup d'état in Utrecht. Nearly everywhere that Calvinist-burgher coalitions took control, they followed the same pattern: iconoclasm and the suppression of Catholicism (Israel, 1995: 192–94; Koenigsberger and Mosse, 1968: 262; Parker, 1977: 188–90). Despite his best efforts, William of Orange, the leading luminary of the rebellion, could not persuade the Calvinists to relent; his efforts were ridiculed by militant Calvinists and Catholics alike. Many moderate Catholics defected to the Spanish, and revolt increasingly polarized along religious lines (Elliott, 2000: 177).

By 1590, when the States General declared the existence of a "sovereign republic," the revolt was centered in the northern provinces and had a heavily Calvinist flavor. It was not long before the revolt became, in essence, a conflict between two states. But even after Philip III (1598–1621) succeeded his father as king, and the war was clearly being fought for economic and strategic reasons, religion remained the crucial obstacle to some form of reconciliation, let alone peace. The Twelve Years' Truce of 1609 represented the *de facto* recognition by the Habsburgs that their former possessions were independent, but war began again in 1621. Eventually, at Westphalia, the Habsburgs were forced to recognize the independence of their former territories, but not before wars against the Dutch helped exhaust Habsburg power and destroy the Spanish bid for European hegemony (Allen, 2000).

The Dutch Revolt illustrates the dynamics by which religious movements and claims-making interacted with the structural proclivities of composite states. It has another element of significance: the fact that the Calvinists remained in the minority had significant implications for the religious institutions of the Dutch state. It embraced Calvinism as the state religion, but could not afford to adopt policies overly hostile towards other confessions. Over time, the Dutch Republic emerged as the first

Western European experiment in religious tolerance, an experiment that became particularly influential as a result of the rapid ascent of Dutch power in the seventeenth century (Tracy, 1999: 284–85).

The Westphalia moment and the post-Reformation European order

The 1648 Peace of Westphalia ended the Thirty Years War (1618–48). The details of that conflict do not concern us, but I should note that it followed a pattern that should now be familiar, in which religious and political grievances intersected in a variety of combinations and permutations to produce conflicts within and across political communities. The flashpoint was Germany, the proximate cause the ascension of a Habsburg head of state with a strong record of commitment to the Counter-Reformation. His ascension triggered a Protestant rebellion in the Habsburg domains of Bohemia and Hungary, and the conflict eventually expanded to include most of the major players in Europe. In the end, the Habsburgs were defeated by a coalition of Protestant princes, the Dutch, and the French (Wedgwood, 1961; Ingrao, 2000).

The Thirty Years War had a number of important consequences for the European political and religious order. It marked the end, of course, of the Habsburg bid for hegemony. But, over the course of the war, we can detect shifts in European statecraft that imply a changing relationship between religion and politics. It would, of course, be deeply anachronistic to argue that religion was not an important factor in the conflicts of the seventeenth century. The Thirty Years War originated from, and was often sustained by, conflicts over religion. Quite a few of the individual participants in the struggle, from kings to soldiers, understood the struggle in religious terms.

As the war in Germany expanded into a general European conflict, it took on the increasing character of a political power struggle rather than a religious war. The armies of both sides included Catholics and Protestants, and not a few commanders put fortune above faith. Richelieu's policy of opposing the Habsburgs even at the expense of the Catholic cause nearly led to his downfall, but in the end his policies triumphed over those favored by the French dévots. Similarly, the Spanish minister Olivares found himself, albeit reluctantly, financing Huguenot rebels against the French crown (Elliott, 1984; Tracy, 1999: 166; Bonney, 2002: 68–71).

To argue, however, that the Thirty Years War marked the complete triumph of raison d'état over reason of religion goes too far. It would be more accurate to say that many rulers and their deputies allowed political necessity to guide short-term decisions, and that they found ways to rationalize those decisions in terms of longer-term religious principles. Such modes of thinking imply the increasing momentum of a conceptual shift in understanding the relationship between politics and religion, one in which the "state" was viewed as being relatively autonomous from specific religious concerns. The experience of religious conflict, both within states and between them, was crucial to this constitutive change in European political relations (Elliott, 1984; Mackenney, 1993).

Was there, then, a "Westphalian moment" and a "Westphalian system" founded at the end of the Thirty Years War? The question of whether or not the Peace of Westphalia is the origin of the modern, sovereign-territorial state system is vociferously contested in both international relations and historical scholarship. I am skeptical of strong claims affirming the centrality of Westphalia in the development of the European state system.[9] Most of the texts of the treaties that comprise Westphalia deal with territorial adjustments or the reordering of the Imperial constitution. Yet it is undeniable that the treaties of Westphalia marked an important stage in the evolution of the religious-political order in Europe.

Westphalia gave final codification – both explicitly and implicitly – to the reality of the European religious landscape: confessional diversity was there to stay, and nothing would restore a religiously integrated Latin Christendom. It did so explicitly with respect to Germany, by affirming the Augsburg formulation of *cuius regio eius religio*. It did so implicitly, first because it strove for a general, lasting peace despite the fact that European Christendom remained divided, and second, because the Spanish monarchy explicitly recognized the sovereignty of the Dutch Republic, despite the fact that the Reformed Church was the official state religion of that polity.

One of the major effects of Westphalia was to accelerate the territorialization of religion. By reaffirming Augsburg 1555, Westphalia "established and delimited confessional spheres of influence; and, in the process, under the pressures of procedure and arbitration, it also brought the Churches together politically" (Gerhardt, 1998: 485). While this state of affairs did lead to greater religious toleration than one might at first assume, the general trend was toward the formation of polities in which territory, state, and confession were closely linked (Schindling, 1998).

Similar effects were felt outside of the empire. Since the experience of the Thirty Years War convinced rulers that endless warfare over religion was counterproductive, the Westphalian settlement also had the effect of leaving most states free to handle religion as they pleased (Dunn, 1970: 78; Bonney, 2002: 531). Results varied. Counter-Reformation was largely successful in the Austrian Habsburg composite state, as well as in France. After the English Civil War and the 1688 Dutch invasion generally called the "Glorious Revolution," Britain remained a multireligious composite state, although Catholics were unable to secure official toleration and remained the subject of social and political discrimination for some time. In this respect, the Netherlands was the exception of the seventeenth century, not the rule.

The "Westphalian moment," such as it was, leaves us something of a double movement. On the one hand, Westphalia represented a bargain by European rulers to accept diversity within Latin Christendom to the extent that they would no longer intervene in one another's affairs over religious matters. On the other hand, Westphalia produced a greater homogenization of religion *within* most of the polities of Europe. Hungary and Bohemia, for example, once respectively heavily Reformed and Protestant, are now predominately Catholic because of the success of Habsburg policies of counter-reformation. This makes it difficult to argue that Westphalia was a *defining* moment in the history of religious toleration, just as it is problematic to argue that Westphalia *established* Europe as a system of sovereign states.

Still, as we have seen in our discussion of the development and ideas of the Reformations, Protestantism also created the groundwork for a greater privatization of religion. When viewed in the context of the Enlightenment and later social and intellectual movements, this contribution turns out to be not at all insignificant for the formation of what José Casanova terms the "knowledge regime" of secularism that now predominates in Europe. Once religious experience is personalized and privatized, it becomes possible – however barely – for religious identities to take on a far more diffuse character, as they have for many Western and Central Europeans in the last half century.

Conclusions

I cannot help but point out a certain irony that runs throughout this volume. As a result of transnational linkages and political integration, Tim Byrnes argues in the next chapter, Europe is now the most "post-Westphalian" region of the world. At precisely the same time, Europe is once again confronting the tensions that arise from religious heterogeneity. Is there a relationship between these developments, or are we seeing a contingent confluence of events? Based upon both the scholarship in this volume and arguments presented in this chapter, I suspect that there are at least two reasons to believe this juxtaposition is not purely accidental.

At the most general level, we have seen that it is very difficult to separate religion from processes of Europeanization. A great many of the historical resources for articulating a common European identity are premised on a reduction of religious heterogeneity through the creation of Orthodoxy and Islam as important "others." While the triumph of secularism as a knowledge regime in Western and Central Europe provides opportunities for constructing more inclusive conceptions of Europeanness, it raises its own problems.

In brief, the *institutionalization* of Europe through processes of European integration has its immediate origins in the Marshall Plan, the Cold War division of Europe, the Christian Democratic political movement, and the economic circumstances of Western European Christian and social democracy. For over fifty years, European integration, as a political project, mapped more or less on to the secularizing democracies of Latin Christendom. Its current expansion, expressly understood as an integration of Europe, involves agglomerating polities with divergent historical narratives and experiences, particularly in terms of religion. This is not simply a matter of incorporating Orthodox or even Islamic states. As Ramet argues, the Catholic Church in Poland exercises a stronger, and more activist, role in Polish politics than in countries such as France, Belgium, Italy, or Spain.

Multiple modernities, therefore, are not simply a potential consequence of European expansion; they are already present, a consequence, in no small part, of divergences and convergences involving religion. This suggests that Europe will have to confront the underlying religious components of its political and cultural identity: a Latin Christian community, albeit one divided by the schisms of the Protestant Reformations. In some respects, secularization makes this a more difficult task. It constitutes the religious basis of European community, as well as the religious identities of its inhabitants, in diffuse terms. Religious markers of identity lurk below the surface, and are therefore more difficult to directly negotiate.

The process of political integration, a process that involves impulses for greater homogenization, necessarily highlights religious heterogeneity. Nearly every contribution to this volume makes clear the degree to which the Catholic Church, the Orthodox Church, members of the Islamic community, and important Protestant voices, are aware of this fact and alternatively recoil from, embrace, or seek to reconcile its implications.

The legacy of Westphalia, both historical and symbolic, looms large in this context. As Philpott and Shaw note, the Catholic Church has come to see European integration as a way of rolling back what it sees as the pernicious effects of the Peace of Westphalia – most notably, a secular, divided *Respublica Christiana*. Philpott and Shaw also identify a connection between Protestant ambivalence toward Europeanization and the historical importance of state sovereignty as a safeguard of Protestantism as a minority religion within Europe. Similarly, both chapters on Orthodox attitudes toward Europeanization point out that the historical model for Orthodoxy is neither Westphalia nor *Respublica Christiana*, but the Orthodox commonwealth that succeeded the Byzantine Empire.

To secular international relations scholars the attitudes of the Catholic and Orthodox Churches may seem somewhat quaint, as they invoke developments in the distant past, whether Westphalia or the sack of Constantinople. To dismiss them would be a mistake. There are, in fact, many respects in which European integration represents the reconsolidation and expansion of Latin Christendom in a new guise. By the same token, although the religious components of European identity are submerged beneath a broadly secular orientation among Western and Central Europeans, they may still be triggered by the right circumstances. One of the lessons of early modern European religious conflict is that even diffuse religious identities can emerge as a basis for intense collective mobilization.

In more concrete terms, European integration aims at the formation of a large, composite political community. Disagreements in Europe over the relative scope of central power and local control are not likely to be resolved in the immediate future, particularly as European expansion leads to greater heterogeneity within a united Europe. At the same time, pressures for devolution *within* European states show no signs of abating, in no small part because, in states such as Britain and Spain, national consolidation never overcame the essentially agglomerative basis of state formation. Combine these dynamics with the growing scope and salience of transnational religious communities in Europe, particularly in their Islamic manifestations, and we have a number of ingredients that suggest religion could easily emerge as a potent force for political mobilization and contestation.

Nevertheless, there are enormous differences between early modern and contemporary Europe. Contemporary Europe, simply put, lacks most of the circumstances that account for why the Protestant Reformations led to a crisis in state formation. Contemporary European polities are not overextending their resources through warfare. They are not governed by dynasts, but are (more or less) pluralist and representative regimes that work through interest aggregation and coalition building rather than divide-and-rule dynamics. However, the ways in which religious heterogeneity created the basis for political mobilization, shaped political brokerage, and led to crises of legitimacy have interesting parallels with the dynamics addressed in the other chapters of this volume. These are particularly striking in the context of Philpott's and Shaw's discussion of the role of the Church in democratization, but also more broadly in terms of the sections on Orthodoxy and Islam.

One could, of course, imagine a disagreement about common European policy that mapped on to religious divisions. In the immediate future, questions about the status and treatment of Muslim communities in Europe might have the strongest potential to activate religion as a basis of competitive mobilization and claims-making, as they are already doing in the Netherlands. Such disputes have the potential to be quite disruptive, as they immensely complicate bargaining over law, authority, and any more mundane policy issues that they implicate. Indeed, given the interaction of processes of Europeanization, the growth of transnationalism, and expanding religious heterogeneity, Europe's challenges may prove greater than many expect.

Notes
1 See, e.g., Wilson, 2002.
2 At the very least, this image of Westphalia has, as Tim Byrnes argues, contributed to the lack of interest among international relations scholars in religion before September 11, 2001.
3 "Europe" is an inherently difficult geographic unit, in that it lacks any clear basis of demarcation from "Asia." As Martin Lewis and Karen Wïgen (1997: 36) argue, there is no natural border that separates Europe from Eurasia. Finding that border is less an act of natural geography than a way of reinforcing "the notion of a cultural dichotomy between" Europe and Asia, "a dichotomy that was essential to Europe's identity as a civilization." See also Thompson (1994: 37).
4 The legacies of this conflict continue to be a problem for Catholic–Orthodox relations today. The Greek and Serbian Orthodox Churches still invoke their betrayal and humiliation at the hands of Catholic military entrepreneurs and Italian city-states, chiefly in the 1204 Sack of Constantinople but also in the Latin micro-empires formed in the Aegean and eastern Mediterranean even as Islamic forces threatened the survival of the eastern Roman Empire.
5 Quoted in Thompson (1994: 39).
6 We should be extremely careful, however, about overplaying the *practical* uniformity of local religious beliefs. On the one hand, many scholars argue for the existence of pagan rites and practices in local communities (see Munck, 1990: 277–79). On the other hand, various heresies and reform movements were potent forces in the centuries preceding Protestantism.
7 On the 1536 Pilgrimage of Grace, which provides a partial exception to this rule, see Zagorin (1982: 19–31). On the more successful – at least in the short term – Catholic popular mobilization in Scandinavia, see te Brake (1998: 54–55). Both cases involved attempts by sovereigns to impose versions of

Protestantism without substantial popular support. The Pilgrimage of Grace, in particular, demonstrates the limitations of depending upon such forms of counter-mobilization: one of the reasons the Pilgrimage failed was that it lacked any basis by which it could overcome regional division within England and Wales and thereby undermine the ability of Henry VIII to divide and conquer Catholic opposition.

8 In Eastern Europe, climate and geography led to different changes, but these too seemed to have favored dynastic agglomerations (Frost, 2000).

9 For differing viewpoints, see Gerhardt (1998); Gross (1948); Krasner (1993, 1999); Osiander (2001); Philpott (2000, 2001a, 2001b); Repgen (1998); Schmit (1998). My own view is developed in Nexon (2004).

11 Transnational religion and Europeanization

Timothy A. Byrnes

What began as a coal and steel compact among six Western European states has evolved over the last fifty years or so into an economic and political "union" spanning twenty-five states from each of the four corners of the European continent. Along with the fits and starts of this remarkable evolution have come recurring debates about the definition of Europe, and about the inclusiveness of the term "European." These debates are about matters of identity as much as they are about economics, or politics, or law, and these debates tend to be most acutely conducted around periods of expansion and growth. It is no surprise, therefore, that issues of identity and definition are being raised today with such clarity as the European Union expands from fifteen to twenty-five, and as it faces the apparently inevitable prospect of opening its doors to every polity and every society that can make a legitimate claim to being "European" in nature.

Current discussions center around two issues, both of which are closely related to religion and to the social and political role of religious communities. The first issue involves the question of how Europe and the European Union are defined at this moment of unprecedented expansion. Is "Europe" merely a geographic space? A polity? A legal compact? As Peter Katzenstein states in his introduction, the usual categories of integrative tissue may not be enough to hold the new, ever-expanding Europe together. In fact, the usual emphasis, at least in recent years, on legal and cultural Europeanization is being joined in the contemporary context by rhetoric and historical allusions with a decidedly religious flavor. Explicit references to a Christian heritage and implicit allusions to a shared religious tradition are quite common these days in discussions meant to hammer out a definition of a continent that was supposed to have been firmly secularized already by modernity.

Second, religion is also implicated in European discussions of the ultimate scope of the potential union, or put another way, of the appropriate border where Europe stops and something else begins. Places like Croatia or Romania are considered natural candidates for eventual membership in the European Union because they are unmistakably "European" countries. Turkey's accession, on the other hand, is constantly moved into the shifting future, while places like Morocco and Algeria are considered fundamentally ineligible. There are many reasons for these distinctions, not the least of which of course are the simple and obvious geographic ones. But we ought not to miss in this context what James Beckford has called the "paradox" that secular Europe's "boundaries are becoming more sharply defined in religious terms" (Beckford, 1994: 167)

The analyses that we have included in this book surely make the basic case that religion is profoundly implicated in the complex processes implied by the term "Europeanization." The Catholic Church, for example, is deeply involved in Polish politics, and therefore also deeply involved in Poland's "return to Europe." The universal Catholic Church, particularly in terms of the Pope and the Holy See, is also directly engaged in the wider debates over both the definition of Europe, and the scope of its legitimate membership. The Orthodox Church is even more profoundly connected to Serbian national identity than the Catholic Church is to Polish identity. The tradition of autocephaly within Orthodoxy links Church to nation in Serbia at the same time as the wider Orthodox tradition orients both that Church and that nation to an alternative vision of "Europe" that points as much to Russia as it does to Brussels. Islam, as it has so often been in the past, is being used once again by "Christian Europe" as a way of defining itself by placing the concept of Europe in contradistinction to the concept of the Islamic world. This dynamic immeasurably complicates the prospects for the "Europeanization" of Turkey. But perhaps even more profound challenges are posed for the concept of European identity by the millions of Muslims who are already resident inside the European Union. The Muslims who live and were perhaps born in Germany, or France, or the UK are surely living in Europe; about that there can be no controversy. But some within Europe view as very controversial the more significant question of whether these Muslims ought to be considered Europeans, without even a hyphen in their designation.

Katzenstein asks us in his introduction to consider the potentially significant implications of the recognition of "multiple modernities" in the European context. In short, some Europeans, particularly from the nations that have either just been admitted to the EU, or that hope to be admitted soon, are presenting notions of modernity, and even definitions of Europe, that have a much more religious foundation than secular moderns usually countenance. In fact, one of the central arguments of this volume is that the political contestation associated with these conflicting, or at least not readily congruent, understandings of "modern" and "Europe" is likely to significantly complicate the progression of what is usually called "Europeanization." Indeed, these conflicting understandings are likely to occasion disputes over what it would actually even mean, for example, to "Europeanize" Poles, or Serbs, or Anatolian Turks.

We decided to approach this question of religion's role in European expansion within the framework of the concept of transnational relations. In 1971, Keohane and Nye defined a "transnational interaction" as "the movement of tangible or intangible items across state boundaries when at least one actor is not an agent of a government or an international organization." As Bryan Hehir points out in chapter 4, the inclusion of Ivan Vallier's chapter on "The Roman Catholic Church: A Transnational Actor" in Keohane and Nye's original volume on the subject signaled that if a conception of International Relations (IR) took root where actors other than states were to be taken seriously, then some of those actors would probably turn out to be religious in nature. After all, the whole notion of transnationalism invites examination of institutions, religious and otherwise, that do not fit readily into the traditional paradigms of IR theory. To argue, as I have elsewhere for example, that the role of Pope John Paul II in the fall of communism in East Central Europe did not fit readily into analysis driven by state-based theory of any stripe is not to say that his role was merely epiphenomenal, or irrelevant (Byrnes, 2001). It is, rather, to suggest, as Katzenstein does in chapter 1, that we need to stretch our theoretical paradigms in order to take further into account the ways in which transnational actors, such as religious communities and religious leaders, participate in international political processes, and how those actors might actually independently influence international political outcomes.

This seems particularly germane at the moment given the dramatic shifts we are experiencing in the very structure and organizing principles of the international state system. Suzanne Rudolph has written in this connection of the declining sovereignty of individual states, and even of the very notion of the state as fading in the contemporary world of globalization, supranational organization, and ideological realignment (Rudolph, 2003: 141). One does not have to go quite that far, however, in order to reach the conclusion that something structural is going on in world politics today, and that shifts in the underlying foundations of international relations might well be responsible for a renewed interest in religion among IR scholars, and even a renewed salience for religion in actual world politics.

The so-called Westphalian system is not dead, of course; sovereign states still comprise the central building blocks of the international system. But the centrality of the state, or at least its overriding preeminence, is now being challenged by other actors. And in this new world of transnational relations, transnational space, and transnational society, religion is apparently much more welcome than it was before at the table of international relations as a field of inquiry (Rudolph and Piscatori, 1997; Dark, 2000; Carlson and Owens, 2003; Hatzopoulos and Petito, 2003).

In focusing in this way on the dynamic relationship between transnational religion and political structure, we are relying in part on the approach outlined a decade ago by Thomas Risse-Kappen and his collaborators when they came together for the purpose of "Bringing Transnational Relations Back In." The analytical focus of that volume was the degree to which the influence of transnational actors was mediated by the structures of the states and international contexts in which they acted (Risse-Kappen, 1995). The subtitle of the book, in fact, was "Non-State Actors, Domestic Structures, and International Institutions," and the stated purpose of the exercise was to "identify under which domestic and international circumstances ... transnational coalitions and actors who attempt to change policy outcomes in a specific issue area succeed or fail to achieve their goals" (Risse-Kappen, 1995: 5).

In part, the analyses offered by our contributors in the present volume can be understood in similar terms. It is evident, for example, that the role of the Catholic Church in Poland is shaped powerfully at the moment by the structure of the post-communist Polish state; the role of Islam in Western Europe is similarly shaped by the very specific way in which "Churches" and the state coexist in, for example, Germany; and the role of Orthodoxy in Serbia is being profoundly challenged at the moment by the developing nature of the Serbian state in the post-Yugoslav and post-Milošević era.

Our cases have also focused on the ways in which the role of transnational religious actors is affected and shaped by what Risse-Kappen called "international circumstances," but what we might also call the very structure of the international political system. When international governing structures change, as they arguably are now doing through processes like European integration, then transnational religious actors, and presumably other non-state actors as well, are challenged to organize themselves and articulate their interests in ways that are relevant to the changing context. It has always been thus, by the way, as Nexon has helpfully reminded us in chapter 10 through his recapitulation of the very complex relationship that pertained between religious and political authority during the so-called Westphalian moment when the modern state system was constructed in the first place. Indeed, this crucial relationship between structural political change and religious institutions and religious identities has been a central focus in virtually every chapter of this book. Yes, religious factors often play a role in shaping political institutions and political structures. But just as surely, those structures then powerfully define the roles that are relevantly available for religious leaders and religious institutions to play in any given context.

The political role of Catholicism under the Roman Empire, for example, was surely not the same as the role of Catholicism under the modern state system; Islam's position under the caliphate was not the same as Islam's position under Western colonialism; and Orthodoxy under the Ottoman *millet* played a very different role from that played by Orthodoxy within Yugoslavia or within the post-Yugoslav states of the Balkan peninsula. Given this evident relationship between religion and "international circumstances," transnational religion's role in European politics should be expected to evolve along with the evolution of European political structures through the large-scale expansion of the EU.

In terms of analyzing transnational religion's *effect* on that political evolution, however, the cases presented in this volume argue for the necessity of disaggregating the concept of religion. I will return at the very end to the matter of religion *per se*, and to the question of religion's likely role in the further integration of Europe. I will argue there, in fact, that the analyses offered by our contributors suggest that on the whole religion is far more likely to be a drag on European union rather than a catalyst for it. But for the bulk of this concluding chapter, I want to look individually, albeit in comparative terms, at Catholicism, Orthodoxy, and Islam and at the very different roles those very different entities are playing in the ongoing processes of Europeanization. In doing so, I will focus on two specific factors in particular: the relationship between a given religious community and traditional notions of European identity; and the degree to which that religious community's own institutional structure equips it for meaningful participation in the myriad transnational interactions that so profoundly define European politics in the contemporary age.

Transnational religion turns out to be a very complex category, and included within that category is a very diverse set of political actors. Some of those actors have close historic ties to conventional definitions of European identity; for others, such connections are far more problematic and contested, in both historic and contemporary terms. Moreover, the ways in which each of these religious communities structures itself are clearly distinct, one from the other, and I want to argue, politically significant. Roman Catholicism embodies one very particular form of transnational interaction, but Orthodoxy manifests a very different form of transnationalism, and Islam is defined by yet another. In chapter 2, Philpott and Shah argued that the postures of these various religious traditions toward European integration are functions of those religions' "characteristic ideas, institutional relationship with the state, and historical experiences of Europe." I want to supplement that claim here by pointing out another key factor in determining the variant nature of these religious communities' roles in contemporary European politics: the variant transnational structures of the communities themselves.

Roman Catholicism

Because of its institutional makeup, Roman Catholicism is generally considered the most straightforwardly transnational of the three religious communities we have considered in this project. Indeed, in some ways, the Catholic Church is almost paradigmatically transnational in structure. Most analysts of the Catholic Church in this regard focus on the papacy and its authority (Hanson, 1987; Willey, 1992; Kent and Pollard, 1994), and I will certainly do so here. But Catholic transnationalism, to coin a term, goes well beyond the authority and universal status of the Pope. Catholic bishops from around the globe are also transnational actors, both through their communal membership in a collegial *magisterium* (or teaching authority) of a global church, and also through the complex web of personal and institutional contacts that exist among and between individual prelates and national episcopal conferences across state borders. In addition, the Catholic population of the whole world, what Vatican II's *Lumen Gentium* called with characteristic grandiosity, the "people of God," is also fundamentally transnational in character (Abbott and Gallagher, 1966: 24). These three categories, or if you prefer, levels of transnationalism, are related, though not identical, to the institutional levels identified by Hehir in chapter 4. I do not want to duplicate his analysis, but I do want to address each of these levels in the explicit terms of transnational structure, and in terms of that structure's relationship to expansion of European unity, however it is defined.

To begin with the papacy, it is true, as most everyone already knows, that the Roman Catholic Pope is the central figure of a very centralized and straightforwardly hierarchical structure. The heart of modern papal authority, of course, is the First Vatican Council's declaration in 1870 that when the Pope "defines a doctrine concerning faith or morals to be held by the whole church," he does so infallibly, that is to say that "such definitions of the Roman Pontiff are of themselves, and not by the consent of the church, irreformable" (Tanner, 1990: 816). Infallibility, though very rarely exercised, grants an aura of finality to the Pope's every word,

and is a kind of logical end to an ecclesiology that views one man, the
Pope, as personally selected by God (the Holy Spirit) to lead the universal
Church.

The Pope's role in the Church goes well beyond this aura, however. In
practical terms, the Pope personally appoints each and every bishop across
the globe, and those bishops must meet with the Pope every five years
during what are called *ad limina* visits to Rome. Even more importantly, the
teachings of the Catholic Church are articulated most clearly and most
forcefully (even when not necessarily infallibly) in papal documents such as
Humanae Vitae, which was focused on the matter of birth control, *Pacem in
Terris*, a treatise on war and peace, and *Rerum Novarum*, an early defense of
the rights of labor. All of these levers of power and modes of authority were
highlighted by the centralizing instincts and peripatetic style of Pope
John Paul II. Whether he was denouncing communism, warning against
secularism, resisting legalized abortion, or punishing dissent within his own
Church, the late Pope sought to impose a coherent voice of papal authority
over a far-flung, very complex Catholic Church.

We can see how pervasive that authority is by looking just briefly at
Pope John Paul's attitude toward the European Union and its eastward
expansion. Lurking under the surface of Sabrina Ramet's analysis in
chapter 5 of the Catholic Church's role in Poland is the question of *why*
the Polish bishops, so otherwise distrustful of "the West," and so anxious
to establish an authentically Catholic Poland as a truly autonomous state,
have supported Poland's accession to the EU. As Ramet shows convincingly, this is a complex story. But surely one factor in that story is the
simple, but powerful fact, that EU accession was supported by the Polish
Pope. Given the decisive nature of papal authority, the Polish bishops are
simply not able to take a public stance that would contradict the Vatican's
position on an issue of such importance.

To be sure, the Polish Pope had a very particular vision of "Europe,"
and very particular reasons for wanting Poland to be a part of it (Sutton,
1997). For Pope John Paul II, Karol Wojtyła of Krakow, EU expansion is
an occasion for a "new evangelization" flowing from East to West. "The
Church in Poland," he argued, "can offer Europe as it grows in unity, her
attachment to the faith, her tradition inspired by religious devotion, the
pastoral efforts of her Bishops and priests, and certainly many other
values on the basis of which Europe can become a reality endowed not
only with higher economic standards but also with a profound spiritual
life" ("Ecclesia in Europa," 2003). This is what Casanova referred to in
chapter 3 as Poland's "apostolic assignment."

One could certainly question the extent to which this vision is likely to
be turned into a reality in modern-day Europe. But the important point

here is not the practicality of implementing a papal vision. Instead, the point is simply that the authoritative head of the Catholic Church supported Poland's entry into the EU. That alone is a significant political fact, both in terms of the internal politics of the Church and the actions of the Polish episcopate, just as it is also a significant fact in terms of the external politics of how East Central Europe's "return to Europe" is conceived of in the East and, to a lesser extent, in the West. Moreover, as Hehir clearly indicates in chapter 4, the role of the Catholic Church today is played out not only in relation to the *expansion* of the European Union. The Church, as it has always been, is also now interested in *defining* Europe, in saying what Europe is as an idea, and in saying what values European society should devote itself to.

As Philpott and Shah stress in chapter 2, it is not at all surprising that a Pope would articulate these values in decidedly Catholic terms. Pope John Paul II was fond of referring to Europe as a fundamentally Christian civilization, and he tirelessly called on Europe to renew its civilizational identity through a renewed commitment to its Christianity, as defined, of course, in Rome. "Ecclesia in Europa," issued in 2003, was in a way the culminating articulation of this world view, but this theme had been present throughout Wojtyła's pontificate. Duncan B. Forrester, in emphasizing John Paul II's vision of a modern-day neo-Christendom, quotes the Pope from as early as 1982 declaring that "European identity is not understandable without Christianity, and it is precisely in Christianity that are found those common roots by which the continent has seen its civilization mature" (Forrester, 1994: 41). When John Paul II implored Europe to "find yourself again, be yourself," he did so as a religious leader who believed that an authentic European identity and an authentic European unity are impossible without reference to the religious tradition for which he spoke authoritatively. This understanding of European history provided the late Pope with a powerful sense of legitimacy in terms of his and his religious community's participation in the processes of developing the political structures that will govern European society in the twenty-first century.

Besides the Pope, however, what I am calling Catholic transnationalism is also embodied in and articulated by the thousands of Catholic bishops who serve the Church in almost every corner of the globe. These men (they are all men, of course) exercise fundamentally local authority over a geographic area called a "diocese." But that authority is only exercised legitimately because these bishops are members of a collegial teaching authority that in communion with the Pope shares authority as a collective body over the entire global Church. This collegial body, along with each bishop's individual relationship with the Bishop of Rome (the Pope), renders Catholic bishops the central players in a kind of global/local dynamic that absolutely defines transnational Catholicism. At the same time, these bishops are also members of what are called national episcopal conferences, groups of bishops within each country that "form an association and meet together at fixed times" in order to "fulfill their office suitably and fruitfully" (Abbott and Gallagher, 1966: 424–25). What this means is that episcopal conferences are the specific vehicles for articulating and disseminating the social and theological teachings of today's Catholic Church (Legrand et al., 1988; Reese, 1989). These conferences have the effect of nationalizing the day-to-day activities of an otherwise transnational Church, but they also provide institutionalized avenues of communication and interaction for bishops from different, and especially neighboring, countries.

For our purposes, a particularly relevant element of this communication and interaction, alluded to briefly by Hehir in chapter 4, is the development in recent years of the Commission of the Bishops' Conferences of the European Community (COMECE). This body is made up of bishops who are delegated by their individual national episcopal conferences to a kind of Catholic episcopal supranational organization that is served by an administrative secretariat based in Brussels. Interestingly, the bishops' conferences of many of the countries who are candidates for admission to the EU are counted as "associate members" of COMECE. And not surprisingly, given the position articulated at the Vatican, the COMECE has come out explicitly in favor of EU expansion to the formerly communist countries of Europe. In fact, in a sentence that responds eloquently to the questions and concerns that guide this project, the bishops of the COMECE wrote that accession of these new members represents "not the 'enlargement,' but [rather] the 'Europeanization' of the EU" (website).

I am not making any extravagant claims, by the way, as to the influence that the Catholic hierarchy exercises in Brussels. What I am saying is that COMECE is emblematic of the extent to which the Catholic Church is prepared for transnational cooperation on the issue of Europeanization. Europe's bishops, like all Catholic bishops, are trained to view themselves as part of a broadly based college of Catholic leaders. And the structural levers of communication and influence that can bring that vision to life already exist as elements of the basic institutional structure of the Church itself. Put another way, discussions among Catholic bishops over the expansion of the EU, and over the role of the Church in that process, are regularized and institutionalized.

Less regular and less institutional, but perhaps in the end more important is the fact that the "people of God" also serve as a layer of Catholic transnationalism in Europe and in European politics. This has, of course, been true throughout European history to one extent or another. The original notion of Christendom, after all, was a Catholic notion. Indeed, medieval Christendom, though surely not a relevant model for modern political structures, is nevertheless often cited as an indicator that European politics has not *always* been structured around individual states, and therefore does not *necessarily* have to be structured around individual states in the future (Meyer, 1989: 399; Bull, 2002: 255). Nelsen et al. (2001) have argued, among others (Davie, 2001), in fact, that this historically based transnational world view renders the Catholic populations of Europe more amenable to notions of European identity and perhaps European government than their Protestant and Orthodox neighbors are. While research into that question continues, however, it is worth pointing out again that some of the most prominent founding architects of the modern European movement in the 1950s, men such as Adenauer and De Gasperi, were Christian Democrats, animated in part by echoes of Europe's Christian unity (Gehler and Kaiser, 2003). Indeed, Douglas Holmes has argued in his recent book on *Integral Europe* that the whole project of European integration was powerfully shaped from the very beginning by Catholic social teaching. (Holmes, 2000). He pays particular attention in this regard to the key concept of subsidiarity, the traditional Catholic notion, ostensibly transferred to the project of European integration, that governing authority should only be passed on to a "higher" authority when it is impractical to have it carried out at a lower level (2000: 52). In any event, the important point here is that like their bishops, though admittedly in very different ways, the Catholic *peoples* of Europe are also prepared by their shared religious identity to conceive of themselves as a European *people*.

Orthodoxy

If Roman Catholicism is the most transnational of the three religious traditions we have examined, then Orthodoxy would appear to be the least. The Orthodox Church, unified on doctrine and ritual, is institutionally structured around what are known as "autocephalous" national churches. John Meyendorff has defined autocephaly, "on the strictly canonical plain," as "the right granted to a diocese or group of dioceses to elect its own bishop or bishops" (Meyendorff, 1966: 42). But Meyendorff also recognized that over time the term came to refer to "the absolute independence of ... national churches" (1966: 42). Today this concept of autocephaly denotes the great depth of connection between Church and state, or perhaps better put between Church and nation, in the Orthodox tradition.

Unlike Roman Catholicism and its well-developed system of transnational authority, and its well-defined understanding of the global "people of God," the very close ties between individual churches and individual nations within Orthodoxy make any movement toward transnational or supranational authority structures (whether religious or political) an uphill struggle, to say the least. In part, these ties between Orthodox Churches and Orthodox nations are a function of specific historical developments that created a specific understanding of the relationship between Church and state.

Whereas in Western Europe, struggles between Pope and emperor led in time to notions of a clear distinction between temporal and divine power, in the East the relationship between Patriarch and emperor was conceptualized as one of "symphony," the idea that these two powers should work together in harmony (Meerson, 1988: 35). Of course, these distinctions were always more theoretical than real. The temporal power of the papacy died a long and difficult death, and "symphony," as Philpott and Shah also imply in chapter 2, was sometimes a cover for the cooptation of the religious by the political through a phenomenon known as Caesaropapism. But it is nevertheless the case that the ties between religion and nation are much more pronounced and organic in the Orthodox tradition than they are in the Catholic, or for that matter in the Islamic.

That said, however, the relationship within Orthodoxy between transnational unity and national autocephaly has always been a complex one. It is interesting to note, for example, that whereas Western imperialism dragged Islam reluctantly into the particularities of the state system, Islamic imperialism, in the form of the Ottoman Empire, actually had the opposite effect on the Orthodox Church. Under the *millet* system operated by the sultan, the patriarch of Constantinople was seen as the legitimate spiritual, and in some ways political, leader of all Orthodox believers living in the Ottoman Empire (Papadakis, 1988: 45–47). The patriarch was never a pope, that is true, but the patriarch was the dominant figure of an unmistakably transnational Church, even if that transnationalism was imposed from outside the tradition.

The pendulum swung back away from the transnationalism of the *millet*, of course, when the rise of nationalism and the break-up of the empire led to the creation of independent sovereign states in the Balkans, most of which were defined in part by their autocephalous Orthodox Churches. In fact, according to Ramet elsewhere, "the autocephalous church figures [in the Orthodox tradition] as an authentication of national identity" in the first place (Ramet, 1988: 7). "To be a nation," she has said, "meant to have a church of one's own, and to be entitled to one's own state" (1988: 4). The patriarch in Constantinople retained what is called "initiative," including the right to recognize autocephaly in specific national settings. But the center of gravity within the Orthodox world moved decisively toward the national.

Today, this relationship between national religious identity and transnational Orthodoxy is continuing to develop. It is not an either/or, settled for all time proposition. It is undeniably true that the autocephalous Churches in places like Romania, Bulgaria, and Serbia are very closely wedded to national identity and deeply implicated in shaping these societies in the post-communist era. Autocephalous national Churches define Orthodoxy today, so they also define Orthodoxy's relationship to politics, in Europe and elsewhere.

But as Ramet points out here in chapter 6, that does not mean that we can just completely ignore the degree to which doctrinal unity endures within Orthodoxy and coexists alongside of institutional differentiation. Just because Patriarch Bartholomew has less power than Pope Benedict XVI (and he certainly does), does not mean that the Orthodox Churches do not conceive of themselves as a unified religious tradition (they do). John Meyendorff, for example, warns "observers from outside" not to underestimate "the power – keenly felt by the Orthodox themselves – of a common perception of basic Christian truths, expressed particularly in the liturgy but also in frequent unofficial and brotherly contacts which hold *the Church* together" (Meyendorff, 1996: 235–36).

These brotherly contacts, by the way, have grown more formal and more regularized in recent years as clerical leaders across the Orthodox world have gathered together from time to time to recognize their powerful ties to each other, to salvage recognition of pan-Orthodox solidarity from the perils of caesaro-papism, and even to consider the convening of a "Council" that would re-emphasize their unity and reconfigure their relationships with each other and with the patriarchal office in Istanbul. In fact, Ramet has reminded us in chapter 6 that some of these contacts in recent years have been quite explicitly *about* relations between the Orthodox Church and the European Union. The proposed Council, however, has not yet been convened, and all of these brotherly contacts continue to be mediated through the straightforwardly nation-based institutional structures of contemporary Orthodoxy. I am not denying that Orthodoxy, at least in institutional terms, is the least transnational of our three religious traditions. All I am suggesting here is that that does not mean that the transnational ties that do exist are not real, or that they are not, at least potentially, politically significant.

What we learn quite clearly from reading the analyses offered by both Ramet in chapter 6 and Perica in chapter 7, however, is that any reaffirmation or public recognition of Orthodox unity would not necessarily mean that such unity would work in favor of ready integration of "Orthodox nations" such as Serbia into the European Union. Indeed, Orthodox unity, such as it is, might be just as likely, if not more likely, to hinder ready accession for Romania, Bulgaria, and perhaps especially, Serbia, rather than to facilitate it. For one thing, echoes of the historic rivalry between Constantinople and Rome seem to underpin the hesitation expressed by so many Orthodox leaders about accepting definitions of "Europe," and how it should be politically structured, from Western sources. Byzantium, one might want to conclude, is not anxious to take lessons from Rome on what it means to be European, or what it means to structure European unity.

Moreover, Orthodox leaders throughout Europe remain profoundly committed to what Ware has called the "bold claim" that their Church is the "one, true church" that has "received a precious and unique gift from God" (Ware, 1997: 246–47). This bedrock theological conviction is surely the fuel driving the desire that Ramet captures so vividly on the part of Orthodox leaders to protect their Church and their people from the moral degradation and secularism that have engulfed the West. Orthodox churchmen in places like Serbia apparently believe that this degradation has been accepted by the Catholic and Protestant Churches that define the West in religious terms. This is simply not a Europe, much less a European *Union*, that these churchmen are anxious to join.

For his part, Perica in chapter 7 sees Orthodox hesitation at the prospects of Europeanization *from the West* as a function of an alternative Orthodox vision for Europe, or at least for part of Europe, in the form of some kind of Orthodox Commonwealth. Looking to Russia and Istanbul, rather than to Brussels and Rome, the Serbian Orthodox Church is not against Europe or European unity *per se*. Far from it. Instead, Orthodox leaders tend to be wary of "Europe" and "European unity" only so long as those phenomena are defined by nations who are, after all, signatories to the Treaty of Rome.

This way of defining things suggests a number of potentially complicating factors that could get in the way of ready integration of Orthodox nations into the European Union. Russia's role in European politics is viewed quite differently, for example, from Belgrade or a purported Orthodox Commonwealth, than it is from Brussels or, for that matter, from Washington. Greece's very important traditional role in transnational Orthodoxy will also have to be taken into account as the EU decides in coming years which Orthodox nations merit being invited to join "Europe," and which do not. Whatever a very uncertain future holds in this regard, however, it is hard to see at this point how pan-Orthodoxy or transnational Orthodoxy could do anything but complicate the path of Orthodox nations to EU accession. This is a self-consciously European religious tradition not very interested in undergoing Europeanization, as that process is currently defined.

Islam

Though profoundly dissimilar in numerous ways, Islam resembles Roman Catholicism in one important respect: they are both religious traditions that are fundamentally transnational in nature, and that make universal claims for all persons, at all times, in all places. For Muslims, the Qur'an is the actual word of God, the record of the uniquely direct intervention of the divine into human history. That is not something which is true for some people at some times, or true in some countries but not in others. It is true all the time and everywhere, and Islam's overriding transnational character is derived from the fundamental universality of these basic theological claims.

Unlike the case of Roman Catholicism, however, we cannot move systematically through the institutional levels of Islam, assessing the degree to which the structures are transnational in nature. Indeed, as Carl L. Brown has put it, "Islam knows no 'church' in the sense of a corporate body whose leadership is clearly defined [and] hierarchical ... No distinctive corporate body equivalent to the church in Christianity exists," at least not in Sunni Islam (Brown, 2000: 31).

The Shia tradition is more corporate, more analogously similar to the clergy-led communities that make up Christianity, and that find their zenith in Catholicism. Nevertheless, throughout all of Islam, the *ulema*, the learned men who lead local communities, are not formal authority figures and members of an officially sanctioned clerical caste. As is said so often that it barely merits repeating: there is no such thing as an Islamic pope. In almost diametric distinction from Catholicism, in fact, Islam is a basically self-governing religious community that is not tied together by the formal structure of a papacy, or national and international conferences of ordained clerics, or really by any institutional ties at all, as that term is generally understood in Western Christianity. This lack of top-down clerical leadership accounts for much of the diversity that Yavuz has emphasized so clearly in chapter 9. At the same time, Islam's highly decentralized institutional structure can also limit the coherence and cohesiveness of the Islamic community, in both religious and political terms.

That said, the Prophet Mohammed's clear intention was to found a highly unified community that would be both religious and political in

nature, and that would brook no division within itself. Indeed, the original Islamic community under the Prophet, and under his immediate
successors, was the very model of a tightly knit religious community,
albeit one with imperial ambitions and universal claims. But within a
very short time following Mohammed's death, this community divided
itself in all sorts of ways. Shia split from Sunni; one Islamic empire
followed after another Islamic empire in Arabia, the Indian subcontinent,
and the Middle East; and the caliphate, the human symbol of Islamic
unity, became subject to claims, counter-claims, and subsequent dilu-
tions of authority until it was formally "abolished" by the post-Ottoman
Turks in 1924.

These divisions, however, were not, by and large, articulated in
national terms. In part, this was because the parameters of Islamic life
were set before the rise of nationalism as a force in international relations,
and before the division of the globe into individual legal entities called
states. But in time, the creation of the international state system, and
perhaps more significantly the development of Western imperialism in
subsequent centuries, combined to bring about what James Piscatori has
called "territorial pluralism" within Islam (Piscatori, 1986: 40–75). The
founding notion of *Dar al-Islam* (the Muslim world) and *Dar al-Harb* (the
non-Muslim world) had presupposed a certain degree of reflexive unity
among the world's Muslims. But, albeit reluctantly in some cases, hyphe-
nated Islam developed within *Dar al-Islam* as nationalism came to play
such a central role in world politics. In time, phrases such as Turkish
Islam came to denote more than geographical classifications. They also
came to mean that the Islamic religion, and highly dispersed communities
of Muslims, became closely associated with individual national identities
and with specific iterations of state integrity.

There always was, however, and still is, a significant and portentous
disjunction between the ideal of Islamic unity, and the reality of Islamic
"territorial pluralism." And that disjunction is rooted in the development
of relations between the Islamic religious community and state power.
From the days of the Prophet Mohammed, the notion of distance
between religion and politics – or to use the Christian terminology,
Church and state – had always been foreign to Islam. Distinctions such
as those between divine law and human law, temporal power and religious power, so central to the trajectory of Western political development, had been rejected in the Islamic community. Such distinctions, in
fact, had been seen as the central barriers to the realization of Islam's
central goal: a godly community that could live in harmony under Islamic
rule, governed by *shari'a*, God's law.

In times closer to our own, of course, when Muslim communities had to live under Western imperialism, Islamic notions of the appropriate relationship between Islamic religion and state power changed dramatically. Forms of Islamic nationalism developed all over the world; *shari'a* came in many places to be seen as an appropriate basis for *national* legal systems; and in Iran, the Ayatollah Khomeini established something called an Islamic Republic, satisfying himself and his people with something that in another context might have been called Islam in one state. Despite all these accommodations to an international state system designed and developed outside of Islamic precepts, however, the ideal, always to be sought in theory if not in everyday practice, was a unified Islamic community living under Islamic government, structured and articulated according to Islamic law.

The most relevant point for our purposes here is that the *umma*, the Islamic people of God, is not divided into a series of national communities across the dozens of states wherein Muslims predominate. On the contrary, there is in Islamic thought only one *umma*, one community of Muslims, bound together by its shared convictions that there is no God but God, and that Mohammed is His prophet. The *umma*'s devolution into "territorial pluralism" is, in other words, a shortcoming to be overcome, not a nationalist designation to be celebrated.

In fact, the *umma* has served as the foundation of recurrent transnational political movements that have been based on Islamic unity and that have sought to strengthen it. Usually referred to as "pan-Islam," these movements are based on a notion that grew up mostly in response to Western imperialism, and that envisioned a post-imperial political structure much more closely analogous to the original Arabian Muslim community than to the state-based system created by the West. According to Joseph Landau in *The Politics of Pan-Islam*, pan-Islamic movements (and there have been several) tend to favor the establishment of a kind of super Islamic state that would bring together all the world's Muslims under a unified governing entity that would be headed by a caliph, a revived office that would once again establish the traditional pattern of combining religious and political leadership in one person (Landau, 1990: 1–8).

The Organization of the Islamic Conference (OIC), on the other hand, is an international organization that presupposes a common identity for the world's Muslims, and a common set of interests for states wherein Muslims predominate. The OIC is a secular body, strictly speaking, but it grew out of the Islamic solidarity that at least spanned, if not superseded, state boundaries at the time of its founding in 1969. The goal of its founders, as defined by John Esposito, was to "create an Islamic organization to represent and seek a modern institutional expression of Islamic unity or panIslamic sentiment" (Esposito, 2001: xi). Indeed, the very first "objective" listed in the organization's charter is "to promote Islamic solidarity among member states" (Kahn, 2001: 316). Of course, that statement has right within it at least the potential for contradiction between "solidarity" and "territorial pluralism." The very fact, after all, that the OIC is by definition an *international* organization whose members are *states* sharply limits its ability to serve as a *transnational* Islamic actor that somehow represents the *umma*'s interests in world politics. Indeed, in practice, the coherence and cohesiveness of the OIC has been limited over time by the divergence of interests identified and articulated by its member *states*.

Nevertheless, despite the limited effectiveness of pan-Islamic movements and despite the state-based structure of prominent Islamic organizations, it is still clearly the case that the *umma* is a transnational religious community (Mandaville, 2003). Moreover, the European manifestation of this community is diasporic with close familial, cultural, and religious ties to other places and countries that are closely identified with Islam. The central question for us here, then, is what role this transnational or diasporic community is playing, or is likely to play, in either the expansion of the European Union, *per se*, or in the reconceptualization of the idea of "Europe" to include Muslims and/or states with majority Muslim populations. Can we envision the transnational *umma*, or the Muslim diaspora in Europe, in short, as either a catalyst for, or barrier to, EU accession for Turkey or a deeper, more integrated relationship between the EU and the Islamic states of the so-called Mediterranean Initiative?

The first thing to note in this regard is that if Roman Catholicism can be seen in some way as definitional in relationship to Europe, then Islam can be seen in a similar way as oppositional. European identity, and what we tend to call Western civilization, coalesced in considerable part around its relationship with, and distance from, Islam. Islam was "the other," if you will, that served as the foundation of Europe's self-definition. And Islam, or Islamic civilization, was also the benchmark against which Europe measured itself in political and cultural terms. As Sheikh has put it so straightforwardly, "the West is called the West because Europe and later its cultural offspring in the Americas were situated West of the Islamic caliphate. The very designation of 'the West' was derived from an Islamic preoccupation" (Sheikh, 2003: 7).

Clear echoes of this historical dynamic can be heard today in the renewed talk of a Christian Europe, of neo-Christendom, and of the potential conflict between the Islamic religion and European values, however the latter are defined. Catholicism and Orthodoxy, as we have seen, is each able to offer a definition of European identity that is derived in large part from its own religious tradition and institutional history. For Islam, the relationship between religion and identity in the European context, the relationship between Muslim tradition and European unity is much more problematic. Indeed, quite often in European history, Islam has been perceived by Christian Europeans as an external imperial power seeking to export its universal religious claims *to Europe*, to a Europe, of course, that was already in thrall to the similarly universal claims of Christianity. Some of the trepidation expressed today about the growing presence of Muslims in Europe, or about the accession of a Muslim country like Turkey to the European Union, is derived from historical memories of the great battles that took place over European religious and cultural identity in the distant but not forgotten past.

This observation is not meant in any way as an endorsement of simplistic notions of an unbridgeable distance or an implacable opposition between Islam and the West. The relationship between these broad, diverse entities has been varied and complex, and the question of where one ends and the other begins has not always been as clear cut as some might imagine, even in historical terms. Islam was a powerful presence on the Iberian peninsula, after all, for seven centuries, and the Muslim populations of places like Bosnia or Albania are not, to put it in absurdist terms, recent immigrants from "the East." This recognition of complexity is particularly germane to any informed discussion of Turkey's relationship to Europe. The Muslim country that is a candidate for EU membership, after all, is not Pakistan, or Malaysia, or even Morocco. It is Turkey, a country with deep European roots, and the successor state to what Yavuz reminds us in chapter 9 was to a significant degree a *European* Ottoman Empire.

Indeed, one of the central themes of Yavuz's contribution to this project is the complexity of the relationship between Islam and "the West" when viewed from a Turkish perspective. Atatürk's pursuit of "Westernization," of course, was not the same thing as Erdoğan's acceptance of "Europeanization." But the whole span of modern Turkish history does suggest that essentialist notions of a Christian West and an Islamic East are too simple. Such notions, in fact, are liable to hinder rather than advance our understanding of the very complex processes involved in Turkey's relationship with the European Union.

In this collaborative project, we have the benefit of three equally thoughtful but very different reflections on the degree to which transnational Islam is involved in the issues surrounding Turkey's prospective accession. Casanova introduces in chapter 3 the important matter of the millions of Muslims already living within the European Union, and the complex ways in which their treatment by European governments may be said to question the legitimacy of the basic norms of liberalism and tolerance ostensibly embodied by those governments.

Hakan Yavuz sees the ties between Turks living in the European Union and Turks living in Turkey as more of a national matter than a religious one. Nevertheless, he suggests that those ties are a potential push along the path of accession because of what he defines as the relatively positive economic and social experiences of the European Turkish diaspora. Acceptance of European norms in Turkey, he argues, is being eased and facilitated by Turkish immigrant experience with those norms in Germany and elsewhere. This may be an indirect form of transnational Islam, but it is a form of politically significant communication and influence between Muslims across international borders, practically the definition of transnational relations.

Bassam Tibi, of course, sees the role of the Turkish diaspora quite differently. For him, the failure of Muslims living within the European Union to adapt to the basic norms of European civic culture serves only to reinforce the unfortunate distance that already exists between Turkey and political leaders of the European Union. Tibi, both here and elsewhere, has called for the development of a distinctive "Euro-Islam" that he thinks could ameliorate inter-religious and inter-cultural conflict in Western Europe, and in time clear Turkey's path toward Europeanization, and ultimately, toward EU membership.

My role here is not to pick and choose between these very different analyses of the relationships between and among the Turkish state, the Turkish diaspora, and the future of the European Union. Suffice it for me to point out in this context that transnational Islam is deeply involved in all of these analyses, and deeply implicated in all of these possibilities. Catholic transnationalism and its effect on EU expansion and the processes of Europeanization can be defined in papal, clerical, and/or popular terms. Orthodoxy, as a religion and as a political force, is defined most clearly by the concept of autocephaly. But the Islamic case has to be defined in less institutional terms and according to the ways in which Muslim experience in one place is transformed into Muslim expectations in another. This may not be as clear cut as the Catholic or Orthodox cases. It may, indeed, be much more open to analytical disputation. But surely these transnational processes of communication and influence are the proper ones to emphasize when dealing with a religious tradition so clearly defined by the *umma*, the Islamic people. It is probably through complex transnational interactions between and among Muslims themselves that Islam will have its effect on European integration.

Conclusion

We have discovered through close examination of these three religious communities that each has its own very distinct relationship with the processes of European integration. To repeat a point I made earlier, the category of transnational religion includes a very complex and diverse set of political actors. This is a simple but important point to emphasize, I think. As the field of International Relations moves slowly and reluctantly to take seriously the religious entities within its field of study, it must do so with a very clear understanding of the diversity of religion itself, and with an equally clear recognition of the very diverse ways in which religion intersects with politics. It would be a real shame, after all, if the field's response to transnational religion and its role in world affairs simply shifted from one of disinterest to one of oversimplification.

That said, our aim in the present volume was to do justice to that complexity and to try to make sense of the effect that this diverse set of actors is having on a central aspect of contemporary international politics. In this concluding chapter, I have presented the three religious communities in comparative terms, one after the other. I have argued that Roman Catholicism is the best prepared institutionally for participation in these particular political processes in terms of both of the dimensions I have been emphasizing. Catholicism's traditional relationship to European identity and European unity is so clear and so long-standing that the Church's current leadership is emboldened to claim a central role in once again defining what Europe is, and laying out the values to which an authentic European union should be devoted.

At the same time, Roman Catholicism is also uniquely situated in an institutional sense to participate in European politics at all of its currently relevant levels of activity: the Holy See and its diplomatic corps; the COSCE and its secretariat in Brussels; the national episcopal conferences resident in every European state. These are institutional resources and institutional parallels to European political structures that would be the envy of any political group or force seeking to influence the future contours of European integration.

Orthodoxy, on the other hand, occupies a very different place from Catholicism on both of these dimensions. The Orthodox tradition certainly has its own definition of Europe to advance and defend. But that Europe of Constantinople, Byzantium, and Eastern Christendom seems, frankly, less directly relevant to European politics today even than did John Paul II's pipedreams of a "new evangelization." The facts of European political development are that modern notions and processes of continental unity have come overwhelmingly from the West. Talk of an

Orthodox Commonwealth, of a Europe that would once again balance Constantinople and Moscow against Rome (and now Brussels) is a provocative challenge to easy and simple definitions of Europe and European identity. But in practical terms, it seems fairly distant from the debates and processes that are shaping Europe and European unity today.

Moreover, the Orthodox devotion to autocephaly and to the close link between Orthodox Church and Orthodox nation has rendered it institutionally out of step with current European discussions of transnational civil society, the liminal space between the national and the international, and the stretching and sharing of sovereignty inherent in European integration. Orthodoxy is a tradition religiously devoted to the form of national sovereignty currently being challenged by Europeanization. Not only are its traditions at odds with these contemporary political dynamics, at least as importantly, its institutional structures are also poorly equipped for participation in these dialogues. Patriarch Bartholomew's visits to Brussels and the renewed brotherly contacts between and among leaders of the various autocephalous churches are a signal that even the leadership of today's Orthodox Church recognizes this disjuncture. It will be instructive to see in the coming years how far the national Orthodox churches are willing to go in accommodating the institutional imperatives of supranational European identity.

The case of Islam is the most difficult to peg with clarity and assurance. The Islamic presence in Europe today is at the very least a useful corrective to simplistic definitions of a Christian Europe. Such notions always insulted the contributions of the Jewish community as egregiously as they ignored the presence of Muslims on the European continent. Nevertheless, Islam is still today a minority faction in European society and politics. It is a religious community that challenges easy definitions of European identity, but because of its own minority status it cannot reasonably offer a religiously based alternative of its own. Instead, the Islamic presence in Europe implicitly calls for greater recognition of religious diversity within Europe, for the development of a continental identity that is based on political and legal principles rather than on shared religious experience. In this sense, of course, the relationship between the Muslim community in Europe and the development of a modern-day European identity may be closer than one would normally be tempted to think it would be. But even recognizing that rather ironic possibility, one cannot ignore the degree to which Turkey's potential accession to the European Union, and the full integration of Muslim populations into European society, are seen widely in European political circles as intractable problems to be delayed, rather than as provocative invitations to constructive redefinitions.

In structural terms, Islam falls into a very different category from either Catholicism or Orthodoxy. Its lack of a hierarchical structure and its diasporic character in the European context make analysis of its institutional role in European politics particularly problematic. To the degree to which European integration is a process through which European peoples come to think of themselves as Europeans as opposed to Germans, or Slovenes, or even Turks, then the Muslim *umma* and its fascinating history of religious unity within territorial pluralism might be seen as a relevant referent to the challenges of Europeanization. But when it comes to formal religious participation in the institutional politics of contemporary Europe, the Muslim community is at a kind of structural disadvantage that will not easily be overcome.

Having discussed these religious communities once again one by one, and having thus emphasized their very different structural and contextual approaches to European politics, the final task is to return to a brief assessment of the role that religion, *per se*, is playing in the processes of European integration. Is religion, one could ask, really fracturing an integrating Europe from the periphery? A definitive answer to that important question, of course, must await future events that we can only see the outlines of now. Nevertheless, it is surely not too early to conclude on the basis of the analyses included in this volume that religion, as a political force, will be more likely to hinder the further integration of the European continent than to advance it.

Roman Catholicism, after all, is the religious community most straightforwardly supportive of the prospect of European unity. But the leadership of Catholicism is supportive of greater European integration only because those leaders want to define that integrated Europe through their own teachings and values, and only because they want to challenge today's Europe to return to the ostensibly Christian unity of its past. It is important to keep in mind in this connection that the Polish Pope and the Polish bishops were only willing to have Poland "rejoin Europe" because they hoped that eventuality would lead in time to secular Europe coming to look more like Catholic Poland!

The Orthodox Church is at its very foundation wary of any effort to diminish the status and role of nations and states, particularly if that effort is perceived as coming from Western Christendom. Leaders of today's Orthodox Church see the European Union as a modern echo of a division of Europe that is over 1,000 years old, and they see supranationalism and European identity as potential threats to national religious and political identities that have been forged and defended at tremendous cost.

Finally, Islam, regardless of the intentions of individual Muslims or even of the Islamic community in Europe as a whole, still stands as a challenge to the ready integration of the European continent, not as a spur towards it. Admittedly, this is the case where the future role of a religious community is unclear and uncertain. It is possible, of course, to envision Islam being accommodated more readily within the European Union than it is now. But it is also possible to envision this religious factor as a long-term point of contention and faction within an integrating Europe.

If the economic and cultural cores of Europeanization do, indeed, prove to be insufficient bases on which to build a unified political and social life, then Europeans, at least many Europeans in places like Poland, Serbia, and Turkey will likely look to religion as an alternative source of meaning, and even of political structure. This dynamic is already underway, I would argue, and it is what is calling religion to the forefront, or at least away from the margins, of European life. But as religion becomes a more salient factor in European politics, religion also brings with it very particular notions of European identity and European union (small case "u"), indeed of modernity itself, that challenge the notions of European unity to which "secular Europe" has grown so accustomed over the last half century. What is even more striking, however, is that these challenges posed by religious conceptions of European union and European identity will be reinforced in the coming years by European religion's embodiment of a form of social and political diversity that may not succumb readily to the unifying effects of Europeanization. The fractious implications of that diversity are real, and they are likely to be recognized as an increasingly prominent element of European politics in the coming years.

Notes

The ideas expressed here were first developed over the course of a Mellon-Sawyer seminar at Cornell University, "Toward a Transnational and Transcultural Europe." I thank all of the participants in that seminar for their reactions and guidance. I am also grateful to the participants at a workshop held in April 2004 under the auspices of Colgate University's Center for Ethics and World Societies. Sidney Tarrow, Sabrina Ramet, and two anonymous reviewers from Cambridge University Press offered very helpful comments on an earlier draft of this chapter. Peter Katzenstein read every draft, and was, throughout, a tireless and provocative collaborator.

References

Abbott, Walter M. and Joseph Gallagher 1966. *The Documents of Vatican II.* New York: Guild Press.

Adnan-Adivar, Abdulhak 1951. "The Interaction of Islamic and Western Thought in Turkey," in T. C. Young (ed.), *Near Eastern Culture and Society*. Princeton: Princeton University Press.

Agence France Presse 2000. July 21, in *Lexis-Nexis*.

———— 2001. April 18, at www.q.co.za/2001/04/18-romania.html [accessed August 13, 2003].

———— 2002. August 30, in *Lexis-Nexis*.

———— 2003a. January 7, in *Lexis-Nexis*.

———— 2003b. February 6, in *Lexis-Nexis*.

———— 2003c. October 1, in *Lexis-Nexis*.

———— 2003d. October 21, in *Lexis-Nexis*.

al-Ashmawi, Said M. 1987. *al-Islam al-Siyasi* [Political Islam]. Cairo: Sina.

Alexy II, Patriarch n. d. "Message from His Holiness Patriarch Alexy II of Moscow and All Russia ... on the Bringing of the Holy Relics of St. Andrew the First-Called from Holy Mount Athos," *Russian Orthodox Church News*, at www.russian-orthodox-church.org.ru/ne30526b.htm [accessed August 13, 2003].

Alfeyev, Bishop Hilarion 2003. "Christian Witness to Uniting Europe," *Ecumenical Review* 55, 1 (January).

Allen, Paul C. 2000. *Philip III and the Pax Hispanica*. New Haven, CT: Yale University Press.

Almond, Gabriel A., R. Scott Appleby, and Emmanuel Sivan (eds.) 2003. *Strong Religion: The Rise of Fundamentalism around the World*. Chicago: University of Chicago Press.

Alpay, Kenan (ed.) 2002. *Avrupa Birliği ve Müslümanlar*. Istanbul: Özgür-der.

AlSayyad, Nezar and Manuel Castells (eds.) 2002. *Muslim Europe or Euro-Islam? Politics, Culture and Citizenship in the Age of Globalization*. Lanham: Lexington Books.

Ambrosewicz-Jacobs, Jolanta 2000. "Attitudes of Young Poles Toward Jews in Post-1989 Poland," *East European Politics and Societies* 14, 3 (Fall).

American Psychological 1994. *The American Psychological Association's Statement on Homosexuality* (July), as quoted in "Roman Catholics & Homosexuality," posted at *Alternative Religions*, at www.religioustolerance.org/hom_rom.htm [accessed August 13, 2003].

Anderson, Benedict 1991. *Imagined Communities*. London: Verso.

Anderson, John 2003. *Religious Liberty in Transitional Societies: The Politics of Religion*. Cambridge: Cambridge University Press.

Ansell, Christopher K. and Giuseppe Di Palma 2004. *Restructuring Territoriality: Europe and the United States Compared*. Cambridge: Cambridge University Press.

Appleby, R. Scott 2000. *The Ambivalence of the Sacred: Religion, Violence, and Reconciliation*. Lanham, MD: Rowman and Littlefield Publishers, Inc.

Aquinas, St. Thomas 2002. *Summa Theologiae*, in T. Aquinas, *Political Writings*, ed. & trans. R. W. Dyson. Cambridge: Cambridge University Press.

Arkoun, Mohammed 1994. *Rethinking Islam*. Boulder, CO: Westview Press.

Arslan, Shakib 1939. *Limatha Ta'akhara al-Muslimun wa Taqadamma Ghairuhum* [Why are Muslims Set Back While Others have Advanced]. Beirut: al-Hayat, reprint 1965.

Ash, Timothy G. 1989. *The Uses of Adversity: Essays on the Fate of Central Europe*. New York: Random House.

Associated Press Worldstream (February 5, 2002), in *Lexis-Nexis* (www.nexis.com) [accessed November 20, 2002].

2003. October 21, in *Lexis-Nexis* (www.nexis.com).

Ayubi, Nazih 1991. *Political Islam. Religion and Politics in the Middle East*. London: Routledge.

Banac, Ivo 1988. *With Stalin against Tito: Cominformist splits in Yugoslav Communism*. Ithaca, NY: Cornell University Press.

Barraclough, Geoffrey 1968. *The Medieval Papacy*. New York: W. W. Norton.

Barscy, Monika 1999. "Homosexuals as the Others in Romania," *Soros Society*, at www.soros.org.mk/image/WEB1999/etexts/bmhatoir.htm [accessed August 13, 2003].

Bartlett, Robert 1993. *The Making of Modern Europe*. Princeton: Princeton University Press.

BBC News 1998. August 27, at news.bbc.co.uk.

2001. May 4, at news.bbc.co.uk [accessed August 13, 2003].

2002. October 1, at news.bbc.co.uk.

Bean, Richard 1973. "War and the Birth of the Nation State," *Journal of Economic History* 33: 203–21.

Beckford, James A. 1994. "Final Reflections," in John Fulton and Peter Gee (eds.), *Religion in Contemporary Europe*, 160–68. Lewiston: Edwin Mellen Press.

Bell, John D. 1999. "The Radical Right in Bulgaria," in Sabrina P. Ramet (ed.), *The Radical Right in Central and Eastern Europe since 1989*. University Park, PA: Pennsylvania State University Press.

Bercé, Yves-Marie 1987. *Revolt and Revolution in Early Modern Europe*. Manchester: Manchester University Press.

Berger, Peter L. 1997. "Epistemological Modesty: An Interview with Peter Berger," *Christian Century* 114: 972–75, 978.

1999. "The Desecularization of the World: A Global Overview," in Peter L. Berger (ed.), *The Desecularization of the World: Resurgent Religion and World Politics*, 1–18. Ethics and Public Policy Center Washington, DC: William B. Eerdmans Publishing Company Grand Rapids, Michigan.

Berger, Peter L. and Samuel P. Huntington (eds.) 2002. *Many Globalizations: Cultural Diversity in the Contemporary World*. Oxford: Oxford University Press.

Berger, Suzanne (ed.) 1982. *Religion in Western European Politics*. London: Frank Cass.

Bernstein, Richard 2003. "Continent Wringing its Hands over Proclaiming its Faith," *The New York Times* (November 12): A4.

Beyer, Peter 1994. *Religion and Globalization*. London: Sage Publications.

Biedroń, Robert 2004. President of the Campaign Against Homophobia, in interview with Sabrina P. Ramet, Warsaw, June 24.

Bień, Magda 2004. Member of the World Youth Alliance, and Ella Kryczka, member of the board of directors of KSM, in interview with Sabrina P. Ramet, Lublin, July 1.

Bilir, Ünal 2004. "Turkey-Islam: Recipe for Success or Hindrance to the Integration of the Turkish Diaspora Community in Germany?," *Journal of Muslim Minority Affairs* 24: 285–94.

Binder, Leonard 1964. *The Ideological Revolution in the Middle East*. New York: John Wiley.

1988. *Islamic Liberalism*. Chicago: University of Chicago Press.

Bistolfi, Robert and François Zabal 1995. *Islam d'Europe. Intégration ou Insertion Communautaire?* Paris: Édition de l'aube.

Blockmans, Wim 2002. *Emperor Charles V, 1500–1558*. London: Arnold.

Bogdanović, Dimitrije 1985. *Knjiga o Kosovu* (with summary in English "The Kosovo Question Past and Present"). Belgrade: Serbian Academy of Sciences and Arts.

Bonney, Richard 1991. *The European Dynastic States: 1494–1660*. Oxford: Oxford University Press.

2002. *The Thirty Years War, 1618–1648*. Oxford: Osprey.

Borneman, John and Nick Fowler 1997. "Europeanization," *Annual Review of Anthropology* 26: 487–514.

Bozdağ, Sibel and Resat Kasaba (eds.) 1997. *Rethinking Modernity and Identity in Turkey*. Seattle: Washington University Press.

Brauch, Hans-Günter, Antonio Marquina, and Abdelwahab Biad (eds.) 2000. *Euro-Mediterranean Partnership for the 21st Century*. London: Macmillan.

Braudel, Fernand 1994. *A History of Civilizations*. New York: Allen Lane/ Penguin.

Breakwell, Glynis M. 1996. "Identity Processes and Social Change," in G. M. Breakwell and E. Lyons (eds.), *Changing European Identities: Social Psychological Analyses of Social Change*, 13–27. Oxford: Butterworth-Heinemann.

Brodek, Theodor V. 1971. "Socio-Political Realities in the Holy Roman Empire," *Journal of Interdisciplinary History* 1, 3: 395–405.

Broun, Janice 1988. *Conscience and Captivity: Religion in Eastern Europe*. Washington, DC: Ethics and Public Policy Center.

Brown, Carl L. 2000. *Religion and State: The Muslim Approach to Politics*. New York: Columbia University Press.

Brown, Peter 1996. *The Rise of Western Christendom*. Oxford: Blackwell.

Brubaker, Rogers 1992. *Citizenship and Nationhood in France and Germany.* Cambridge, MA: Harvard University Press.

Bruce, Steve 1996. *Religion in the Modern World: From Cathedrals to Cults.* Oxford: Oxford University Press.

2000. "The Supply-side Model of Religion: The Nordic and Baltic States," *Journal for the Scientific Study of Religion* 39, 1: 32–46.

Bruce, Steve (ed.) 1992. *Religion and Modernization: Sociologists and Historians Debate the Secularization Thesis.* Oxford: Clarendon Press.

Buglewicz, Urszula 2004. Editor of the Lublin edition of *Niedziela*, in interview with Sabrina P. Ramet, Lublin, July 2; Katarzyna Surowiec, interpreter.

Bukovansky, Mlada 2002. *Legitimacy and Power Politics: The American and French Revolutions in International Political Culture.* Princeton: Princeton University Press.

Bull, Hedley 1977. *The Anarchical Society.* New York: Columbia University Press.

1984. "The Revolt against the West," in Hedley Bull and Adam Watson (eds.), *The Expansion of International Society,* 217–28. Oxford: Clarendon Press.

2002. *The Anarchical Society: A Study of Order in World Politics* (third edition). New York: Columbia University Press.

Bull, Hedley and Adam Watson (eds.) 1984. *The Expansion of International Society.* Oxford: Clarendon Press.

Burckhardt, Jacob 1988. *Die Kultur der Renaissance in Italien.* Stuttgart: Kroener.

Burke III, Edmund 1998. "Orientalism and World History: Representing Middle Eastern Nationalism and Islamism in the Twentieth Century," *Theory and Society* 27: 685–507.

Butler, Jon 1990. *Awash in a Sea of Faith: Christianizing the American People.* Cambridge, MA: Harvard University Press.

Byrnes, Timothy A. 2001. *Transnational Catholicism in Postcommunist Europe.* Lanham: Rowman & Littlefield.

Cakir, Murat 2000. *Die Pseudodemokraten. Türkische Lobbyisten, Islamisten, Rechtsradikale und ihr Wirken in der Bundesrepublik.* Düsseldorf: GDF-Publikationen.

Calleo, David 1978. *The German Problem Reconsidered: Germany and the World Order, 1870 to the Present.* Cambridge: Cambridge University Press.

Canefe, Nergis and Tanil Bora 2003. "The Intellectual Roots of Anti-European Sentiment in Turkish Politics: The Case of Radical Turkish Nationalism," in Ali Çarkoğlu and Barry Rubin (eds.), *Turkey and the European Union: Domestic Politics, Economic Integration, and International Dynamics.* London and Portland: Frank Cass.

Carey, George 1999. "The Millennium and the Soul of Europe." Address to the Academie für Zahnärztliche Fortbildung [Advanced Dental Institute], Baden-Württemberg, Karlsruhe, Germany (March 27). Available at http://www.archbishopofcanterbury.org/carey/speeches/990327.htm. [Accessed February 4, 2005].

Çarkoğlu, Ali 2003. "Who Wants Full Membership? Characteristics of Turkish Public Support for EU Membership," in Ali Çarkoğlu and Barry Rubin (eds.), *Turkey and the European Union: Domestic Politics, Economic Integration, and International Dynamics,* 171–94. London and Portland: Frank Cass.

2004. "Societal Perceptions of Turkey's EU membership," in M. Uğur and Nergis Canefe (eds.), *Turkey and European Integration*, 19–45. London: Routledge.

Çarkoğlu, Ali and Barry Rubin (eds.) 2003. *Turkey and the European Union: Domestic Politics, Economic Integration, and International Dynamics*. London and Portland: Frank Cass.

Carlson, John D. and Erik C. Owens (eds.) 2003. *The Sacred and the Sovereign: Religion and International Politics*. Washington, DC: Georgetown University Press.

Carr, William 1991. *A History of Germany, 1815–1990* (fourth edition). London: Edward Arnold.

Casanova, José 1994. *Public Religions in the Modern World*. Chicago: University of Chicago Press.

1997. "Globalizing Catholicism and the Return to a 'Universal' Church," in Susanne Hoeber Rudolph and James Piscatori (eds.), *Transnational Religion and Fading States*. Boulder, CO: Westview Press.

2001a. "Religion, the New Millennium, and Globalization," *Sociology of Religion* 62, 4: 415–41.

2001b. "Civil Society and Religion: Retrospective Reflections on Catholicism and Prospective Reflections on Islam," *Social Research* 68, 4 (Winter): 1041–80.

2003a. "Beyond European and American Exceptionalism: Towards a Global Perspective," in G. Davie, P. Heelas, and L. Woodhead (eds.), *Predicting Religion*. Aldershot: Ashgate.

2003b. "Das katholische Poland im säkularisierten Europa," *Transit* 25.

2004. "Der Ort der Religion im säkularen Europa," *Transit* 27: 86–106.

Cayhan, Esra 1997. *Dünden Bugüne Türkiye Avrupa Birliği İlişkileri ve Siyasal Partilerin Konuya Bakişi*. Istanbul: Boyut Kitaplari.

Chayes, Abram and Antonia Handler Chayes 1995. *The New Sovereignty: Compliance with International Regulatory Agreements*. Cambridge, MA: Harvard University Press.

Checkel, Jeffrey 2003. "International Institutions and Socialization in Europe: Introduction and Framework", lead essay for a collection of papers in *International Organization* (forthcoming Fall 2005).

Christensen, Carl C. 1984. "John of Saxony's Diplomacy, 1529–1530: Reformation or Realpolitik," *Sixteenth Century Journal* 15, 4: 419–30.

Christian Century 1998a. August 12, at www.findarticles.com [accessed September 1, 2003].

1998b. December 9, at www.findarticles.com [accessed September 1, 2003], p. 2.

2000a. September 13, at www.findarticles.com [accessed September 1, 2003].

2000b. December 13, at www.findarticles.com [accessed September 1, 2003].

2002. July 31, at www.findarticles.com [accessed September 1, 2003].

Christian Science Monitor 2003a. April 10, p. 7, in *Lexis-Nexis*.

2003b. "Orthodox Leader Blesses Green Agenda," July 24, posted in *Orthodox News* 5, 33 on August 4, 2003, at www.orthodoxnews.netfirms.com/29/Orthodox%20leader%20blesses.htm [accessed August 29, 2003].

Chrypinski, Vincent C. 1989. "Church and Nationality in Postwar Poland," in Pedro Ramet (ed.), *Religion and Nationalism in Soviet and East European Politics*, rev. & expanded edn. Durham, NC: Duke University Press.

"Church Against Homosexuality" 2000. "The Church is Against Homosexuality: Open letter of His Beatitude Patriarch Teoctist against the Intention of the Romanian Parliament to abrogate Article 200 in the Penal Code, concerning the Homosexual Relations" (September 13), at biserica.org/Publicatii/2001?NoX/XII_index.html [accessed August 13, 2003].

Cisło, Auxiliary Bishop Mieczysław of Lublin 2004. And Rev. Dr. Tadeusz Kadziołka, Rector of the Seminary, in interview with Sabrina P. Ramet, Lublin, July 1.

Claver, Francisco 1986. "The Church and the Revolution: The Philippine Solution," *America* (May 3) pp. 356–59; (May 10) pp. 376–78.

Collins, James B. 1995. *The State in Early Modern France*. Cambridge: Cambridge University Press.

Collins, Richard 1994. "Unity in Diversity? The European Single Market in Broadcasting and the Audiovisual, 1982–92," *Journal of Common Market Studies* 32, 1 (March): 89–102.

Čolović, Ivan 2002. *The Politics of Symbol in Serbia: Essays in Political Anthropology*, trans. from Serbian by Celia Hawkesworth. London: Hurst & Co.

Conant, Lisa 2002. *Justice Contained: Law and Politics in the European Union*. Ithaca, NY: Cornell University Press.

Conway, John 1994. "The 'Stasi' and the Churches: Between Coercion and Compromise in East German Protestantism," *Journal of Church and State* 36, 4.

Corley, Felix 2003. "Georgia: Racist Vigilantes again Blockade Pentecostal Church," *Forum 18 News Service* (July 14), carried by WorldWide Religious News at www.wwrn.org/parse.php?idd = 9093 [accessed August 16, 2003].

Cornwell, John 2000. *Hitler's Pope: The Secret History of Pius XII*. New York: Penguin Books.

Daği, İhsan 2001. "Human Rights, Democratization and the European Community in Turkish Politics: The Özal Years, 1983–1987," *Middle Eastern Studies* 37: 17–40.

2003. *Batililaşma Korkusu*. Ankara: Liberte Yayinlari.

Daği, İhsan and İhsan Sezal (eds.) 2001. *Kim Bu Özal? Siyaset, İktisat, Zihniyet*. Istanbul: Boyut Yayinlari.

Dalton, Russell J. and Richard C. Eichenberg 1998. "Citizen Support for Policy Integration," in W. Sandholtz and A. S. Stone (eds.), *European Integration and Supranational Governance*, 250–82. Oxford: Oxford University Press.

Darby, Graham 2001. "Introduction," in G. Darby (ed.), *The Origins and Development of the Dutch Revolt*. New York: Routledge.

Dark, K. R. (ed.) 2000. *Religion and International Relations*. London: Macmillan.

Davidson, Herbert 1992. *Alfarabe, Avicenna and Averroes on Intellect*. New York: Oxford University Press.

Davie, Grace 1994a. "The Religious Factor in the Emergence of Europe as a Global Region," *Social Compass* 41, 1: 95–112.

1994b. *Religion in Britain Since 1945: Believing Without Belonging*. Oxford: Blackwell.

2000. *Religion in Modern Europe: A Memory Mutates.* Oxford: Oxford University Press.

2001. "Global Civil Religion: A European Perspective," *Sociology of Religion* 62, 4 (Winter): 455–73.

Delanty, Gerard 1995. *Inventing Europe.* London: Macmillan.

Dharif, Mohammed 1992. *al-Islam al-Siyasi* [Political Islam]. Rabat: al-Umma.

Dixon, Tomas 2003. "Ignoring God in the Constitution," *Christianity Today* 47, 7 (June), at www.christianitytoday.com.

Donner, Fred 1981. *The Early Islamic Conquests.* Princeton: Princeton University Press.

Doogue, Edmund 2001. "Future Direction of WCC in Question as Orthodox and Protestants" [title as given], *Worldwide Faith News archives – PCUSA News to PresbyNews* (February 1), at www.wfn.org/2001/02/msg00010.html [accessed August 13, 2003], 2–3.

Downing, Brian M. 1992. *The Military Revolution and Political Change: Origins of Democracy and Autocracy in Early Modern Europe.* Princeton: Princeton University Press.

Dueck, Abe J. 1982. "Religion and Temporal Authority in the Reformation: The Controversy Among the Protestants Prior to the Peace of Nuremberg, 1532," *Sixteenth Century Journal* 12, 2: 55–74.

Duina, Francesco G. 1999. *Harmonizing Europe: Nation-States within the Common Market.* Albany: State University of New York.

Dunn, Richard S. 1970. *The Age of Religious Wars 1559–1689.* New York: W. W. Norton.

Duran, Burhanettin 2004. "Islamist Redefinition(s) of European and Islamic Identities in Turkey," in M. Uğur and N. Canefe (eds.), *Turkey and European Integration: Accession Prospects and Issues,* 125–46. New York: Routledge.

Eberts, Mirella W. 1998. "The Roman Catholic Church and Democracy in Poland," *Europe-Asia Studies* 50, 5 (July).

"Ecclesia in Europa," *Origins* (July 2003).

Economist, The 2003. "Charlemagne: God Meets the Lawyers" (December 6): 48.

Economist, The 2004. "Real Politics, At Last?" (October 30): 60.

Ecumenism in Georgia n. d. "The Struggle against the Ecumenism in Georgia," at www.geocities.com/Athens/Thebes/1865/private.htm [accessed August 16, 2003].

Eisenstadt, Shmuel N. (ed.) 1986. *The Origins and Diversity of Axial-Age Civilizations.* Albany, NY: SUNY Press.

1996. *Japanese Civilization: A Comparative View.* Chicago: University of Chicago Press

1998. "Axial and Non-Axial Civilizations – The Japanese Experience in Comparative Perspective – The Construction of Generalized Particularistic Trust," in Hidehiro Sonoda and S. N. Eisenstadt (eds.), *Japan in a Comparative Perspective,* 1–17. Kyoto: International Research Center for Japanese Studies.

1999a. *Fundamentalism, Sectarianism, and Revolution: The Jacobin Dimension of Modernity.* Cambridge: Cambridge University Press.

1999b. *Paradoxes of Democracy, Fragility, Continuity, and Change*. Baltimore, MD: Johns Hopkins University Press.

2000a. *Die Vielfalt der Moderne*. Weilerswist: Velbrück Wissenschaft.

2000b. "The Reconstruction of Religious Arenas in the Framework of 'Multiple Modernities'," *Millennium* 29, 3: 591–612.

2002. "Multiple Modernities," *Dædalus* 129, 1: 1–29.

EKD Bulletin 2002. "Will the WCC become superfluous?" (4 – 2002), at www.ekd.de/bulletin/bulletin_bulletin_4_2003_33.html [accessed August 13, 2003].

Eliade, Mircea 2005. *The Myth of the Eternal Return: Cosmos and History*. 2nd pbk. edn. Princeton: Princeton University Press.

Elliott, J. H. 1963. *Imperial Spain, 1469–1716*. London: Penguin.

1984. *Richelieu and Olivares*. Cambridge: Cambridge University Press.

1992. "A Europe of Composite Monarchies," *Past and Present* 137: 48–71.

2000. *Europe Divided, 1559–1598*. Oxford: Blackwell.

Eltis, David 1995. *The Military Revolution in Sixteenth Century Europe*. New York: St. Martin's Press.

Elton, G. R. 1964. *Reformation Europe: 1517–1559*. Cleveland, OH: World Publishing Company.

Emmert, Thomas A. 1990. *Serbian Golgotha: Kosovo, 1389*. Boulder, CO: East European Monographs; New York: Distributed by Columbia University Press.

Enyedi, Zsolt 2003. "Conclusion: Emerging Issues in the Study of Church–State Relations," in John T. S. Madeley and Zsolt Enyedi (eds.), *Church and State in Contemporary Europe: The Chimera of Neutrality*, 218–32. London: Frank Cass.

Erbakan, Necmettin 1971. *Türkiye ve Ortak Pazar*. İzmir: İstiklal Matbaasi.

Ertman, Thomas 1997. *The Birth of Leviathan: Building States and Regimes in Medieval and Early Modern Europe*. Cambridge: Cambridge University Press.

Esposito, John L. 2001. "Foreword," in Saad S. Kahn (ed.), *Reasserting International Islam: A Focus on the Origins of the Islamic Conference and Other Islamic Institutions*. Oxford: Oxford University Press.

Esposito, John L. and Michael Watson (eds.) 2000. *Religion and Global Order*. Cardiff: University of Wales Press.

Esteban, Emila Salvador 2001. *Carlos V. Emperador de Imperios*. Pamplona: EUNSA.

Eurasian News 2002. "Russian Orthodox Church Sets out its Vision of European Integration," October 8, at prcenter.newmail.ru/news2002/8_oct_2002_orthodox_church.htm [accessed August 13, 2003].

Eurobarometer 2003. *Eurobarometer 59: Public Opinion in the European Union* (Spring 2003). Fieldwork: March–April 2003. Release 2003: July.

European Report 2003. June 18, in *Lexis-Nexis*.

Evenimentul zilei 1998. April 16, as cited in Lavinia Stan and Lucian Turcescu, "The Romanian Orthodox Church and Post-Communist Democratization," *Europe-Asia Studies*, 52 (December 2000), at www.findarticles.com [accessed September 1, 2003].

2001. November 3, as cited in RFE/RL (November 5, 2001), p. 5.

314   References

Everts, Philip and Richard Sinnott 1995. "Conclusion: European Publics and the Legitimacy of Internationalized Governance," in O. Niedermayer and R. Sinnott (eds.), *Public Opinion and Internationalized Governance*, 431–57. Oxford: Oxford University Press.

Fetzer, Joel S. and J. Christopher Soper 2005. *Muslims and the State in Britain, France, and Germany*. New York: Cambridge University Press.

Filatov, Sergei B. 1995. "The Russian Orthodox Church and the Political Elite," in *East–West Church & Ministry Report* 3, 3 (Summer), at www.samford.edu [accessed August 16, 2003].

Finke, Roger 1997. "The Consequences of Religious Competition: Supply-Side Explanations for Religious Change," in Lawrence A. Young (ed.), *Rational Choice Theory and Religion*, 45–65. London: Routledge.

Finke, Roger and Rodney Stark 1992. *The Churching of America, 1776–1990: Winners and Losers in Our Religious Economy*. New Brunswick: Rutgers University Press.

Fokas, Effie 2000. "Greek Orthodoxy and European Identity." Paper Presented at the Socrates Kokkalis Graduate Student Workshop, Kennedy School of Government, Harvard University, Cambridge, Massachusetts, February 12.

Foroutan, Naika 2004. *Kulturdialoge zwischen dem Westen und der islamischen Welt*. Wiesbaden: Deutscher Universitätsverlag.

Frost, Robert I. 2000. *The Northern Wars, 1558–1721*. London: Longman.

Fuchs, Dale 2003. "New Law Requires Roman Catholicism Classes in Spain's Schools," *The New York Times* (December 29): 27.

Fukuyama, Francis 1989. "The End of History?", *The National Interest* 16 (Summer): 3–18.

1992. *The End of History and the Last Man*. New York: Free Press.

Gazeta Wyborcza 2003. June 3, trans. in BBC Monitoring International Reports (June 3, 2003), in *Lexis-Nexis*.

Geddes, Andrew 2000. *Immigration and European Integration. Towards Fortress Europe?* Manchester: Manchester University Press.

Geertz, Clifford 1971. *Islam Observed*. Chicago: University of Chicago Press.

Gehler, Michael and Wolfram Kaiser 2003. "Toward a 'Core Europe' in a Christian Western Bloc: Transnational Cooperation in European Christian Democracy, 1925–1965," in Thomas Kselman and Joseph A. Buttigieg (eds.), *European Christian Democracy: Historical Legacies and Cooperative Perspectives*. Notre Dame, IN: University of Notre Dame Press.

Gellner, Ernest 1994. "Kemalism," in Ernest Gellner (ed.), *Encounters with Nationalism*, 81–91. Oxford: Blackwell.

Georgian Mobs 2001. *Georgia: Mobs Terrorize Non-Orthodox Christians* (New York: Human Rights Watch, August 29), at www.hrw.org/press/2001/08/georgia-0829.htm [accessed August 16, 2003].

Geremek, Bronisław 2003. "Welche Werte für das neue Europa?," *Transit* 26: 7–15.

Gerhardt, Volker 1998. "On the Historical Significance of the Peace of Westphalia: Twelve Theses," in K. Bussman and H. Schilling (eds.), *1648: War and Peace in Europe*, 485–89. Münster: Westfälisches Landesmuseum.

Gerholm, Tomas and Yngve Lithman 1988. *The New Islamic Presence in Western Europe*. London: Mansell.

Gillingham, John 2003. *European Integration, 1950–2003: Superstate or New Market Economy?* Cambridge: Cambridge University Press.
Girnius, Kestutis 1989. "Nationalism and the Catholic Church in Lithuania," in Sabrina P. Ramet (ed.), *Religion and Nationalism in Soviet and East European Politics.* Durham, NC: Duke University Press.
Glas javnosti 2002. "Budimo čisti kao deca," Belgrade, January 6–7, at www.glasjavnosti.co.yu [accessed January 7, 2002].
Göcek, Fatma Müge 1996. *Rise of the Bourgeoisie, Demise of Empire. Ottoman Westernization and Social Change.* New York: Oxford University Press.
Gökay, Bülent 1995. "From Western Perceptions to Turkish Self-perceptions," *Journal of Mediterranean Studies* 5: 259–69.
Goldhagen, Daniel Jonah 2002. *A Moral Reckoning: The Role of the Catholic Church in the Holocaust and Its Unfulfilled Duty of Repair.* New York: Alfred A. Knopf.
Gorski, Philip S. 1993. "The Protestant Ethic Revisited: Disciplinary Revolution in Holland and Prussia," *American Journal of Sociology* 99, 2: 255–316.
Gowin, J. 1995. *Kościół po komunizmie.* Krakow: ZNAK.
Grabowska, Mirosława 2002. "Unia Europejska i studia europejskie – nowa rzeczywistość i jej badanie," in Krysztof Koseła, Tadeusz Szawiel, Mirosława Grabowska, and Małgorzata Sikorska (eds.), *Tożsamość Polaków a Unia Europejska.* Warsaw: Instytut Badań nad Podstawami Demokracji.
Greeley, Andrew M. 1989. *Religious Change in America.* Cambridge, MA: Harvard University Press.
1994. "A Religion Revival in Russia," *Journal for the Scientific Study of Religion* 33, 3: 253–72.
2003. *Religion in Europe at the End of the Second Millennium: A Sociological Profile.* New Brunswick: Transaction Publishers.
Greengrass, Mark 1991. "Conquest and Coalescence: The Shaping of the State in Early Modern Europe," in M. Greengrass (ed.), *Conflict and Coalescence.* London: Edward Arnold.
Gregory, Fr. n. d. "Orthodoxy and Ecumenism," at www.orthodox.clara.net/ecumenis.htm [accessed August 16, 2003].
Gross, Leo 1948. "The Peace of Westphalia, 1648–1948," *American Journal of International Law* 42, 1: 20–41.
Group of Lisbon, The 1995. *Limits to Competition: The Group of Lisbon.* Cambridge, MA: MIT Press.
The Guardian 2003a. January 30, p. 17, in *Lexis-Nexis.*
2003b. June 7, p. 17, in *Lexis-Nexis.*
2003c. June 9, at www.guardian.co.uk.
Güzel, Hasan Celal 1995. "21.Asir Türk Asri Olacaktir," *Yeni Türkiye* 3: 121–28.
Haas, Ernst 1997. *Nationalism, Liberalism, and Progress: The Rise and Decline of Nationalism.* Vol. 1. Ithaca, NY: Cornell University Press.
2000. *Nationalism, Liberalism, and Progress: The Dismal Fate of New Nations.* Vol. II. Ithaca, NY: Cornell University Press.
Habermas, Jürgen 2003. *The Future of Human Nature.* Cambridge, MA: MIT.
Hadaway, Kirk, Penny Long Marler, and Mark Chaves 1993. "What the Polls Don't Show: A Closer Look at U.S. Church Attendance," *American Sociological Review* 58: 741–52.

Hale, Julian 1971. *Ceausescu's Romania: A Political Commentary*. London: George G. Harrap.

Hamilton, Bernard 1997. *Religion in the Medieval West*. London: Arnold.

Hanson, Eric O. 1987. *The Catholic Church in World Politics*. Princeton: Princeton University Press.

Hargreaves, Alec G. 1995. *Immigration, Race and Ethnicity in Contemporary France*. New York: Routledge.

Harlow, Carol 1998. "European Administrative Law and the Global Challenge," *EUI Working Paper*, RSC No. 98/23. Florence: European University Institute.

Hastings, Adrian 1997. *Religion and the Construction of Nationhood*. Cambridge: Cambridge University Press.

Hatzopoulos, Pavlos and Fabio Petito 2003. "The Return from Exile: An Introduction," in Fabio Petito and Pavlos Hatzopoulos (eds.), *Religion in International Relations: The Return from Exile*, 1–20. New York: Palgrave.

Hay, Denys 1968. *Europe: The Emergence of an Idea*. Edinburgh: Edinburgh University Press.

Haynes, Jeff 1998. *Religion in Global Politics*. London: Longman.

Hehir, Bryan 1990. "Papal Foreign Policy," *Foreign Policy* 78 (Spring).

Hehir, J. Bryan and John Paul II 1983. "Continuity and Change in the Social Teaching of the Church," in John W. Houck and Oliver F. Williams (eds.), *Co-Creation and Capitalism: John Paul II's Laborem Exercens*, 124–40. Washington, DC: University Press of America.

Herberg, Will 1983. *Protestant–Catholic–Jew*. Chicago: University of Chicago Press.

Héritier, Adrienne 2001. "Differential Europe: National Administrative Responses to Community Policy," in Maria Green Cowles, James Caporaso, and Thomas Risse (eds.), *Transforming Europe: Europeanization and Domestic Change*, 44–59. Ithaca, NY: Cornell University Press.

Héritier, Adrienne, Christoph Knill and Susanne Mingers, in collaboration with Rhodes Barrett 1996. *Ringing the Changes in Europe: Regulatory Competition and the Transformation of the State. Britain, France, Germany*. Berlin: Walter de Gruyter.

Herrin, Judith 1987. *The Formation of Christendom*. Princeton: Princeton University Press.

Hervieu-Léger, Danièle 2000. *Religion as a Chain of Memory*. New Brunswick, NJ: Transaction Books.

2003. "Religion und sozialer Zusammenhalt in Europa," *Transit* 26: 101–19.

Herzog, Roman 1999. *Preventing the Clash of Civilizations*. New York: St. Martin's Press.

Hintze, Otto 1975. *The Historical Essays of Otto Hintze*. New York: Oxford University Press.

Hirschman, Charles, Philip Kasinitz, and Josh de Wind (eds.) 1999. *The Handbook of International Migration: The American Experience*. New York: Russell Sage.

Hirst, Paul and Grahame Thompson 1996. *Globalization in Question: The International Economy and the Possibilities of Governance*. Cambridge: Polity Press.

HLI-EUROPA News 2004a. "Polish Parliament to open debate on easing abortion law," *HLI-EUROPA News* (March 11), at www.hli.org.pl.

2004b. "Izabela Jaruga-Nowacka promotes postcoital contraception," *HLI-EUROPA News* (April 26), at www.hli.org.pl.

2004c. "The Episcopate alarmed with the bill of an equal status of women and men," *HLI-EUROPA News* (April 29), at www.hli.org.pl.

Hodges, Richard and David Whitehouse 1983. *Mohammed, Charlemagne and the Origins of Europe. The Pirenne Thesis.* Ithaca, NY: Cornell University Press.

Hodgson, Marshall G. S. 1974. *The Venture of Islam. Conscience and History in a World Civilization,* 3 vols. Chicago: University of Chicago Press.

Holborn, Hajo 1959. *A History of Modern Germany: The Reformation.* Princeton: Princeton University Press.

Holmes, Douglas R. 2000. *Integral Europe: Fast Capitalism, Multiculturalism, Neofascism.* Princeton: Princeton University Press.

Holt, Mack P. 1995. *The French Wars of Religion, 1562–1629.* Cambridge: Cambridge University Press.

Hopwood, Derek (ed.) 1985. *Euro-Arab Dialogue. The Relations between the Two Cultures.* London: Croom Helm.

Hosking, Geoffrey and George Schöpflin (eds.) 1997. *Myths and Nationhood.* London: Hurst.

Howard, Michael 1976. *War in European History.* Oxford: Oxford University Press.

Howe, Marvine 2000, *Turkey Today. A Nation Divided over Islam's Revival.* Boulder, CO: Westview Press.

Huntington, Samuel P. 1973. "Transnational Organizations in World Politics," *World Politics* 25: 333–68.

1991. "Religion and the Third Wave," *The National Interest* 24: 29–42.

1993. "The Clash of Civilizations?", *Foreign Affairs* 72, 3 (Summer): 22–49.

1996. *The Clash of Civilizations and the Remaking of World Order.* New York: Simon & Schuster.

2004. *Who Are We? The Challenges to America's National Identity.* New York: Simon & Schuster.

Hurd, Elizabeth Shakman 2004. "The Political Authority Structure of Secularism in International Relations," *European Journal of International Relations* 10, 2: 235–62.

Iankova, Elena and Peter J. Katzenstein 2003. "European Enlargement and Institutional Hypocrisy," in Tanja Börzel and Rachel A. Cichowski (eds.), *The State of the Union: Law, Politics and Society,* 269–90. Oxford: Oxford University Press.

The Independent 1998. November 21, in *Lexis-Nexis.*

Ingrao, Charles W. 2000. *The Habsburg Monarch, 1618–1815.* Cambridge: Cambridge University Press.

Insel, Ahmet 2003. "The AKP and Normalizing Democracy in Turkey," *South Atlantic Quarterly* 102, 2/3: 293–308.

Interfax 2003. "Russian Orthodox Church raps EU for 'anthropocentric' slant" (Moscow), June, carried at the Serbian Unity Congress website, at news. serbianunity.net/bydate/2003/June_09/5.html [accessed August 13, 2003].

Israel, Jonathan 1995. *The Dutch Republic: Its Rise, Greatness, and Fall 1477–1806.* Oxford: Oxford University Press.

Ivanovs, Rev. Ernest 2004. Pastor of the Reformed Free Church of Poland, in interview with Sabrina P. Ramet, Piaseczno, July 6.

Jackowska, Natalia 2003. *Kościół katolicki w Polsce wobec integracji europejskiej.* Poznań & Gniezno: Instytut Zachodniego.

Janis, Mark W. (ed.) 1991. *The Influence of Religion on the Development of International Law.* Dordrecht, Netherlands: Nijhoff.

Jansen, Thomas 2000. "Europe and Religions: The Dialogue between the European Commission and Churches or Religious Communities," *Social Compass* 47, 1: 103–12.

Jęczeń, Rev. Dr. Jarosław 2004. Director of Radio Plus, in interview with Sabrina P. Ramet, Lublin, July 3.

Jelavich, Charles 1954. "Some Aspects of Serbian Religious Development in the Eighteenth Century," *Church History* 23: 144–52.

Jerschina, Jan 1990. "The Catholic Church, the Communist State and the Polish People," in Stanislaw Gomulka and Antony Polonsky (eds.), *Polish Paradoxes.* London: Routledge.

Johansson, Karl Magnus 2002. "Party Elites in Multilevel Europe: The Christian Democrats and the Single European Act," *Party Politics* 8, 4: 423–39.

John Paul II. 1992a. *Sollicitudo Rei Socialis,* in David J. O'Brien and Thomas A. Shannon (eds.), *Catholic Social Thought: The Documentary Heritage,* 395–483. Maryknoll, NY: Orbis Books.

   1992b. *Centesimus Annus,* in David J. O'Brien and Thomas A. Shannon (eds.), *Catholic Social Thought: The Documentary Heritage,* 439–488. Maryknoll, NY: Orbis Books.

   1995. *Ut Unum Sint: On Commitment to Ecumenism.* Encyclical letter given in Rome, May 25, 1995. Available at http://www.vatican.va/holy_father/john_paul_ii/encyclicals/documents/hf_jp-ii_enc_25051995_ut-unum-sint_en.html [last accessed on July 5, 2005].

   2003. *Ecclesia in Europa,* Post-Synodal Apostolic Exhortation. Given in Rome, June 28, 2003. Available at http://www.vatican.va/holy_father/john_paul_ii/apost_exhortations/documents/hf_jp-ii_exh_20030628_ecclesia-in-europa_en.html [last accessed on June 15, 2004].

Johnston, Alastair Iain 1995. *Cultural Realism: Strategic Culture in Chinese History.* Princeton: Princeton University Press.

Johnston, Douglas (ed.) 2003. *Faith-Based Diplomacy: Trumping Realpolitik.* Oxford: Oxford University Press.

Johnston, Douglas and Cynthia Sampson (eds.) 1994. *Religion: The Missing Dimension of Statecraft.* New York: Oxford University Press.

Kadżiołka, Rev. Dr. Tadeusz 2004. Rector of the Seminary, in interview with Sabrina P. Ramet, Lublin, July 1.

Kaegi, Walter E. 1992. *Byzantium and the Early Islamic Conquests.* Cambridge: Cambridge University Press.

Kafadar, Cemal 1995. *Between Two Worlds. The Construction of the Ottoman State.* Berkeley: University of California Press.

Kahn, Saad S. 2001. *Reasserting International Islam: A Focus on the Origins of the Islamic Conference and Other Islamic Institutions.* Oxford: Oxford University Press.

Kalyvas, Stathis N. 1996. *The Rise of Christian Democracy in Europe*. Ithaca: Cornell University Press.

Kant, Immanuel 1991. *The Metaphysics of Morals*, trans. from German by Mary Gregor. Cambridge: Cambridge University Press.

Karamanlis, Constantine 1981. Speech on the Accession of Greece to the European Union (January 1, 1981). A partial text of the speech is available at http://www.ellopos.net/politics/eu_karamanlis.html [accessed April 1, 2004].

Kardaş, Şaban 2002. "Human Rights and Democracy Promotion: The Case of Turkey–EU Relations," *Alternatives: Turkish Journal of International Relations* 1: 136–50.

Karsai, László 2001. *Holokauszt*. Budapest: Pannonica kiadó.

Katzenstein, Peter J. (ed.) 1997a. *Tamed Power: Germany in Europe*. Ithaca: Cornell University Press.

1997b. "The Cultural Foundations of Murakami's Polymorphic Liberalism," in Kozo Yamamura (ed.), *A Vision of a New Liberalism? Critical Essays on Murakami's Anticlassical Analysis*, 23–40. Stanford: Stanford University Press.

2005. *A World of Regions: Asia and Europe in the American Imperium*. Ithaca, NY: Cornell University Press.

Kellogg, Michael 2001. "Putting Old Wine Into New Bottles: The East German Protestant Church's Desire to Reform State Socialism," *Journal of Church and State* 43, 4.

Kent, Peter C. and John F. Pollard (eds.) 1994. *Papal Diplomacy in the Modern Age*. Westport: Praeger.

Keohane, Robert O. and Joseph S. Nye (eds.) 1971. *Transnational Relations and World Politics*. Cambridge, MA: Harvard University Press.

Kepel, Gilles 1987. *Les Banlieus de l'Islam. Naissance d'une religion en France*. Paris: Édition du Seuil.

Khan, Mujeeb R. 1995. "Bosnia-Herzegovina and the Crisis of the Post-Cold War International System," *East European Politics and Societies* 9: 459–88.

Kirill, Metropolitan of Smolensk and Kaliningrad 2001. "The Orthodox Church in the face of world integration: the relation between traditional and liberal values", *Ecumenical Review* (October), at www.findarticles.com [accessed September 1, 2003].

Kittelson, James M. 1986. "Renaissance and Reformation in Germany: An Agenda for Research," *Journal of Modern History* 58 (Issue Supplement: Politics and Society in the Holy Roman Empire, 1500–1806): S124–S140.

Klimon, William M. 1994. "Chesterton, Kossovo of the Serbians, and the Vocation of the Christian Nation," *The Chesterton Review* (February): 41–53.

Kloczowski, Jerzy 2000. *A History of Polish Christianity*. Cambridge: Cambridge University Press.

Knecht, R. J. 1989. *The French Wars of Religion, 1559–1598*. New York: Longman.

Koenigsberger, H. G. 1955. "The Organization of Revolutionary Parties in France and the Netherlands During the Sixteenth Century," *Journal of Modern History* 27, 4: 335–51.

1971. *The Habsburgs and Europe, 1516–1660*. Ithaca, NY: Cornell University Press.

1986. *Politicians and Virtuosi: Essays in Early Modern History.* London: Hambledon Press.

1987. *Early Modern Europe: 1500–1789.* New York: Longman.

Koenigsberger, H. G. and George L. Mosse 1968. *Europe in the Sixteenth Century.* London: Longmans, Green and Co.

Kolstø, Pål (ed.) 2005. *Myths and Boundaries in Southeastern Europe.* London: C. Hurst & Co.

Korboński, Andrzej 1995. "A Concordat – But No Concord," *Transition* (Prague) 1, 9 (June 9).

Kościanska, Agnieszka 2001. "Polish Governmental Report – the Embodiment of the Anti-cult Propaganda," *CESNUR – Center for Studies on New Religions,* at www.cesnur.org/2001/london2001/koscianska.htm.

Kösebalaban, Hasan 2003. "Making the Enemy and Friend: Fethullah Gülen's National Security Identity," in M. H. Yavuz and John Esposito (eds.), *Turkish Islam and the Secular State: The Gülen Movement.* Syracuse: Syracuse University Press.

Koseła, Krzysztof 2003. *Polak i Katolik. Splątana tożsamość.* Warsaw: Wydawnictwo IfiS PAN.

2004a. "Religijność młodych Niemców i Polaków," *Socjologia Religii* (Poznań), 2.

2004b. Professor of Sociology, Institute of Sociology, University of Warsaw, in interview with Sabrina P. Ramet, Warsaw, June 22.

Kotliński, Roman 2004. Editor of *Fakty i mity*, in interview with Sabrina P. Ramet, Łodz, June 28; Adam Cioch, interpreter.

Kramer, Heinz 1996. "The EU–Turkey Customs Union: Economic Integration amidst Political Turmoil," *Mediterranean Politics* 1: 60–75.

2000. *A Changing Turkey.* Washington, DC: Brookings Institution.

Krasner, Stephen D. 1993. "Westphalia and All That," in J. Goldstein and R. O. Keohane (eds.), *Ideas and Foreign Policy: Beliefs, Institutions, and Political Change.* Ithaca, NY: Cornell University Press.

1999. *Sovereignty: Organized Hypocrisy.* Princeton: Princeton University Press.

Krasner, Stephen D. (ed.) 2001. *Problematic Sovereignty: Contested Rules and Political Possibilities.* New York: Columbia University Press.

Kubicek, Paul 1999. "Turkish–European Relations: At a New Crossroads?," *Middle East Policy Journal* 4: 157–73.

Kücükcan, Talip 1999. *Politics of Ethnicity, Identity and Religion: Turkish-Muslims in Britain.* Avebury: Ashgate.

Kürkçüoğlu, Ömer 1972. *Türkiye'nin Arab Orta Doğusu'na Karşi Politikasi (1945–1970).* Ankara: S. B. F. Yayinlari.

Kurth, James 1998. "Religion and Globalization," The 1998 Templeton Lecture on Religion and World Affairs, Foreign Policy Research Institute (May).

Kurzer, Paulette 2001. *Markets and Moral Regulation: Cultural Change in the European Union.* Cambridge: Cambridge University Press.

Laciner, Sedat 1999. "Türkiye-Avrupa İlişkilerinde Kültür ve Medeniyet Boyutu," *Liberal Düşünce Dergisi* 13: 39–57.

Laitin, David D. 2002. "Culture and National Identity: 'The East' and European Integration," in Peter Mair and Jan Zielonka (eds.), *The Enlarged European Union: Diversity and Adaptation*, 55–80. London: Frank Cass.

Landau, Joseph M. 1990. *The Politics of Pan-Islam: Ideology and Organization.* Oxford: Oxford University Press.

Law on Radio and Television Broadcasting, as published in *Dziennik Ustaw* (Warsaw), January 29, 1993, trans. in US Department of Commerce, *Central and Eastern European Legal Texts*, January 29, 1993.

Leff, Gordon 1961. "Heresy and the Decline of the Medieval Church," *Past and Present* 20: 36–51.

Legrand, Harve, Julio Manzaneres, and Antonio Garcia y Garcia (eds.) 1988. *The Nature and Future of Episcopal Conferences.* Washington, DC: Catholic University of America Press.

Leonard, Karen Isaksen 2003. *Muslims in the United States. The State of Research.* New York: Russell Sage.

Leszczyńska, Katarzyna, 2004. "The Standpoint of the Roman Catholic Church in Poland and the Czech Republic towards Europe, the European Union and the European Integration Process," in Dinka Marinović Jerolimov, Siniša Zrinščak, and Irena Borowik (eds.), *Religion and Patterns of Social Transformation.* Zagreb: Institute for Social Research.

Lewis, Martin and Karen Wigen 1997. *The Myth of Continents: A Critique of Metageography.* Berkeley, CA: University of California Press.

Lewy, Guenter 2000. *The Nazi Persecution of the Gypsies.* Oxford and New York: Oxford University Press.

Liebert, Ulrike 2002. "Causal Complexities: Explaining Europeanisation," Jean Monnet Centre for European Studies, University of Bremen, *CEuS Working Paper* No. 2002/1.

Lipson, Leslie 1993. *The Ethical Crises of Civilizations.* London: Sage.

Luckmann, Thomas 1967. *Invisible Religion.* New York: Macmillan.

Luxmoore, Jonathan 2000. "Poland's Catholic Bishops Reject Criticism of *Dominus Iesus*," *Christianity Today* (posted September 20), at www.christianitytoday.com.

2001a. "Poland Rethinks Supervision of 'Sects' after Minority Church Complains," in *Christianity Today* (March 6), at www.christianitytoday.com.

2001b. "Eastern Europe 1997–2000: A Review of Church Life," *Religion, State & Society* 29, 4 (December).

Lynch, John 1991. *Spain 1516–1598: From Nation-State to World Empire.* Oxford: Blackwell.

Macfie, Alexander L. 1994. *Atatürk.* London: Longman.

Mackenney, Richard 1993. *Sixteenth Century Europe: Expansion and Conflict.* Basingstoke: Macmillan.

Madeley, John T. S. 2003a. "European Liberal Democracy and the Principle of State Religious Neutrality," in John T. S. Madeley and Zsolt Enyedi (eds.), *Church and State in Contemporary Europe: The Chimera of Neutrality*, 1–22. London: Frank Cass.

2003b. "A Framework for the Comparative Analysis of Church–State Relations in Europe," in John T. S. Madeley and Zsolt Enyedi (eds.), *Church and State in Contemporary Europe: The Chimera of Neutrality*, 23–50. London: Frank Cass.

Madelin, Henri 2001. "Vatican City State," in Joel Krieger (ed.), *The Oxford Companion to Politics of the World*, 886. New York: Oxford University Press.

322   References

Magazyn Trybuny 2003. Warsaw, November 29–30.
Manchester Guardian Weekly 2003. April 30, p. 33, in *Lexis-Nexis*.
Mandaville, Peter 2003. *Transnational Muslim Politics: Reimagining the Umma*. London: Routledge.
March, James G. and Johan P. Olsen 1989. *Rediscovering Institutions. The Organizational Basis of Politics*. New York: Free Press.
Mardin, Serif 1995. "Civil Society and Islam," in John Hall (ed.), *Civil Society*. Cambridge: Polity Press.
Maritain, Jacques 1951. *Man and the State*. Chicago: University of Chicago Press.
Martin, David 1978. *A General Theory of Secularization*. New York: Harper & Row Publishers.
2003. "Integration und Fragmentierung. Religionsmuster in Europa," *Transit* 26: 120–43.
Marty, E. and R. Scott Appleby (eds.) 1997. *Religion, Ethnicity, and Self Identity: Nations in Turmoil*. Hanover, NH: University Press of New England.
Marx, Karl 1975. "On the Jewish Question," in *Early Writings*. New York: Vintage.
Mazurkiewicz, Fr. Piotr 2001. "Autonomy of the Church and Freedom of Religion in Poland," in Gerhard Robbers (ed.), *Church Autonomy: A Comparative Survey*, Frankfurt-am-Main and New York: Peter Lang.
2004. Professor of Political Science, Cardinal Stefan Wyszyński University, in interview with Sabrina P. Ramet, Warsaw, June 28.
McClaren, Lauren M. and Meltem Müftüler-Baç 2003. "Turkish Parliamentarians' Perspectives on Turkey's Relations with the European Union," in *Turkey and the European Union: Domestic Politics, Economic Integration, and International Dynamics*, 195–218. London and Portland: Frank Cass.
Meerson, Michael A. 1988. "The Doctrinal Foundations of Orthodoxy," in Pedro Ramet (ed.), *Eastern Christianity and Politics in the Twentieth Century*. Durham: Duke University Press.
Meyendorff, John 1966. *Orthodoxy and Catholicity*. New York: Sheed & Ward.
with selected revisions by Nichols Lossky 1996. *The Orthodox Church: Its Past and Its Role in the World Today*, fourth revised edition. Crestwood: St. Vladimir's Seminary Press.
Meyer, John W. 1989. "Conceptions of Christendom: Notes on the Distinctiveness of the West," in Melvin Kohn (ed.), *Cross-National Research in Sociology*. Thousand Oaks: Sage.
Millennium 2000. "Special Issue: Religion and International Relations," 29, 3.
Milosavljević, Marijana 2001. "Pravoslavni protiv Madone," *NIN* (Belgrade), No. 2659 (December 13, 2001), at www.nin.co.yu/2001–12/13/21071.html [accessed December 20, 2001].
Milosavljević, Olivera 2002. *In the Tradition of Nationalism. The Stereotypes about "Us" and "Others" in the Works of Serbian Intellectuals of the 20th Century*. Helsinki Committee for Human Rights in Serbia, Beograd.
Milward, Alan S. 2000. *The European Rescue of the Nation-State* (second edition). London: Routledge.
Mitchell, Joshua 1993. *Not By Reason Alone: Religion, History, and Identity in Early Modern Political Thought*. Chicago: University of Chicago Press.

Mitchell, Richard 1969. *The Society of the Muslim Brothers.* London: Oxford University Press.

Moeller, Bernd 1982. *Imperial Cities and the Reformation: Three Essays.* Durham, NC: Labyrinth Press.

Mojzes, Paul 1992. *Religious Liberty in Eastern Europe and the USSR: Before and After the Great Transformation.* Boulder, CO: East European Monographs.

Monitor 2002. "Russian Orthodox Church Accuses Vatican of Trying to Poach its Flock" (The Jamestown Foundation), 8, 35 (February 19), at www.james town.org/pubs/view/mon_008_035_000.htm [accessed August 13, 2003].

Monitorul 2001. January 13, as cited in RFE/RL-NL (January 15, 2001), p. 5; also RFE/RL, *(UN)Civil Societies*, Vol. 2, No. 3 (January 18, 2001).

Monshipouri, Mahmood 1996. "The Christians in Socialism – and After: The Church in East Germany," *Journal of Church and State* 38, 4.

Moore, R. I. 1997. "The Birth of Europe as a Eurasian Phenomenon," *Modern Asian Studies* 31, 3: 583–601.

Moravcsik, Andrew 1998. *The Choice for Europe: Social Purpose and State Power from Messina to Maastricht.* Ithaca: Cornell University Press.

Moscow Patriarchate 1998. "Meeting of Delegations of the Russian and Georgian Churches," statement issued by the Moscow Patriarchate (March 18), at www.incommunion.org/moscow.htm [accessed August 16, 2003].

Moses, Fr. John 1999. "What is Ecumenism?", *St. Nicholas Russian Orthodox Church, Dallas, Texas: Articles* (June 25), at www.orthodox.net/articles/what-is-ecumenism.html [accessed August 16, 2003].

Moss, Vladimir 1998. "Christ and the Nations," *Holy Martyrs Sophia, Faith, Hope and Charity* (September 17–30), at www.romanitas.ru/eng [accessed August 13, 2003].

Mout, Nicolette 1999. "Reformation, Revolt and Civil Wars: The Historiographic Traditions of France and the Netherlands," in P. Benedict, G. Marnef, H. v. Nierop, and M. Venard (eds.), *Reformation, Revolt and Civil War in France and the Netherlands*, 23–34. Amsterdam: Royal Netherlands Academy of Arts and Sciences.

Munck, Thomas 1990. *Seventeenth Century Europe 1598–1700.* London: Macmillan.

Murakami, Yasusuke 1996. *An Anti-Classical Political-Economic Analysis.* Stanford, CA: Stanford University Press.

Murray, John Courtney 1964. "The Problems of Religious Freedom," *Theological Studies* 25: 503–75.

1966. "Church and State at Vatican II," *Theological Studies* 27: 580–606.

Mustafa, Hala 1992. *al-Islam al-Siyasi fi Misr* [Political Islam in Egypt]. Cairo: Markaz al-Dirasat.

Naff, Thomas 1984. "The Ottoman Empire and the European States System," in Hedley Bull and Adam Watson (eds.), *The Expansion of International Society.* Oxford: Clarendon.

Nardin, Terry 1993. *The Ethics of War and Peace.* Princeton: Princeton University Press.

Nau, Henry R. 2002. *At Home Abroad: Identity and Power in American Foreign Policy.* Ithaca, NY: Cornell University Press.

Nelsen, Brent F. and James L. Guth 2003a. "Religion and Youth Support for the European Union," *Journal of Common Market Studies* 41, 1 (March): 89–112.

2003b. "Roman Catholicism and the Founding of Europe: How Catholics Shaped European Communities," paper presented at the Annual Meeting of the American Political Science Association, Philadelphia, Pennsylvania, August 28–31.

Nelson, Brent F., James L. Guth, and Cleveland R. Fraser 2001. "Does Religion Matter? Christianity and Public Support for the European Union," *European Union Politics* 2, 2: 267–91.

Neumann, Iver 1999. *Uses of the Other: "The East" in European Identity Formation.* Minneapolis, MN: University of Minnesota Press.

News from Poland 1998. "Honors for Bishop Pieronek" (June–August), at www.polishworld.com/polemb/news/698/bishop.htm.

Nexon, Daniel 2004. "Religion and the Fate of Empires in Early Modern Europe," Ph.D. dissertation, Columbia University.

Niebuhr, Reinhold 1940. *Christianity and Power Politics.* New York: Charles Scribner's Sons.

Nierop, Henk van 1995. "Similar Problems, Different Outcomes: The Revolt of the Netherlands and the Wars of Religion in France," in K. Davids and J. Lucassen (eds.), *A Miracle Mirrored: The Dutch Republic in European Perspective.* Cambridge: Cambridge University Press.

Norris, Pippa and Ronald Inglehart 2005. *Sacred and Secular: Religion and Politics Worldwide.* New York: Cambridge University Press.

Novosti 2003. "Inter-Orthodox Talks on Draft Constitutional Treaty of European Union," Information Service of the Serbian Orthodox Church (Belgrade), April 4, at www.spc.org.yu/Vesti-2003/04/4–4-03_el.html [accessed August 13, 2003].

Nowicka, Wanda 1997. "Poland: Case Study on Legal Instability concerning Abortion," *Preventing and Addressing Unsafe Abortion* (Geneva: World Health Organization), at www.waw.pdi.net/~polfedwo/english/public/whoabor.htm.

2004. President of the Federation for Women and Family Planning, in interview with Sabrina P. Ramet, Warsaw, June 22.

Nowicka, Wanda and Monika Tajak 2000. "The Effects of the Anti-Abortion Act," in Wanda Nowicka (ed.), *The Anti-Abortion Law in Poland: The Functioning, Social Effects, Attitudes and Behaviors* (Warsaw: Federation for Women and Family Planning, September), at www.waw.pdi.net/~polfedwo/english/reports/report00/rep00_3.htm.

O'Brien, David J. and Thomas A. Shannon 1992. *Catholic Social Thought: The Documentary Heritage.* Maryknoll, NY: Orbis Books.

OBOP Center for Public Opinion Research, reported in PAP (October 20, 1989), in Foreign Broadcast Information Service (FBIS), *Daily Report* (Eastern Europe), November 2, 1989, p. 74.

The Ogam 2003. January 29, at www.creationcenter.com/boards/TheOgamNews/messages/1917.html [accessed August 13, 2003].

Olsen, Johan P. 1997. "European Challenges to the Nation State," in B. Steunenberg and F. van Vught (eds.), *Political Institutions and Public Policy:*

Perspectives on European Decision Making, 157–88. Boston, MA: Kluwer Academic Publishers.

2002. "The Many Faces of Europeanization," *Journal of Common Market Studies* 40, 5 (December): 921–52.

Öniş, Ziya 1999. "Turkey, Europe, and Paradoxes of Identity: Perspectives on the International Context of Democratization," *Mediterranean Quarterly* 10: 107–36.

2003. "Domestic Politics, International Norms and Challenges to the State: Turkey–EU Relations in the post-Helsinki era," in Ali Çarkoğlu and Barry Rubin (eds.), *Turkey and the European Union: Domestic Politics, Economic Integration, and International Dynamics*. London and Portland: Frank Cass.

Öniş, Ziya and Emin Fuat Keyman 2003. "A New Path Emerges," *Journal of Democracy* 14, 2: 95–107.

Orbis 1998. "A Special Issue on Religion in World Affairs," 42, 2 (Spring).

Oresko, Robert, G. C. Gibbs, et al. 1997. "Introduction," in R. Oresko, G. C. Gibbs and H. M. Scott (eds.), *Royal and Republican Sovereignty in Early Modern Europe*. Cambridge: Cambridge University Press.

Ortiz, Antonio Domínguez 1971. *The Golden Age of Spain, 1516–1659*. New York: Basic Books.

Osiander, Andreas 2001. "Sovereignty, International Relations, and the Westphalian Myth," *International Organization* 55, 2: 251–88.

Özdalga, Elisabeth (ed.) 1999. *Naqshbandis in Western and Central Asia*. Istanbul: Numune Matbaasi.

Ozel, Soli 2003. "After the Tsunami," *Journal of Democracy* 14, 2: 80–94.

Ozment, Steven E. 1975. *The Reformation in the Cities: The Appeal of Protestantism to Sixteenth-Century Germany and Switzerland*. New Haven, CT: Yale University Press.

Öztürk, Yasar Nuri 2003. "Die Zeit nach den Propheten," in Michael Thumann (ed.), *Der Islam und der Westen*, 107–16. Berlin: Berliner Taschenbuch-Verlag.

Paarma, Jukka 2002. "A Soul for Europe: Christians Question Themselves," address to the conference, Faiths and Cultures within Conflict and Dialogue, Palermo, Italy (September 1–3, 2002). Available at http://www.evl.fi/arkkipiispa/Palermo2002.htm [accessed on February 4, 2005].

Pagoulatos, George 2002. "Greece, the European Union, and 2003 Presidency." Groupement d'Études et de Recherches, Notre Europe. *Research and European Issues* 21 (December).

Pantel, Melissa 1999. "Unity-in-Diversity: Cultural Policy and EU Legitimacy," in Thomas Banchoff and Mitchell P. Smith (eds.), *Legitimacy and the European Union: The Contested Polity*, 46–65. New York: Routledge.

PAP 1989. November 15, in FBIS, *Daily Report* (Eastern Europe), November 20, 1989, pp. 78–79.

1999. January 5, in *Lexis-Nexis*.

2003. May 5, in *Lexis-Nexis*.

Papadakis, Aristeides 1988. "The Historical Tradition of Church–State Relations Under Orthodoxy," in Pedro Ramet (ed.), *Eastern Christianity and Politics in the Twentieth Century*. Durham: Duke University Press.

Papastergiadis, Nikos 2000. *Turbulance of Migration. Globalization, Deterritorialization and Hybridity.* Cambridge: Polity Press.

Pareskevaides, Archbishop Christodoulos 2003. "Europa Nostra," address to the University of Craiova, Romania (June 2003). Available at http://www.ecclesia.gr/English/Archbishops/speeches/europa_nostra.html [accessed on April 1, 2004].

Parker, Geoffrey 1976. "The 'Military Revolution' 1560–1660 – A Myth?," *Journal of Modern History* 48, 2: 195–214.

1977. *The Dutch Revolt.* Ithaca, NY: Cornell University Press.

1988. *The Military Revolution. Military Innovation and the Rise of the West.* Cambridge: Cambridge University Press.

Parsons, Craig 2003. *A Certain Idea of Europe.* Ithaca: Cornell University Press.

Pawlina, Ks. Krzysztof 2003. "Powołania kapłańskie i zakonne w Polsce na początku XXI wieku," in Piotr Mazurkiewicz (ed.), *Kościół Katolicki w przededniu wejścia Polski do Unii Europejskiej.* Warsaw: Instytut Spraw Publicznych.

Penn, Shana 2001. "'Breaking the Silence': How Poland's Abortion Law Jeopardizes Women's Health and Rights," *Tribunal on Anti-abortion Law in Poland,* at www.waw.pdi.net/~polfedwo/english/news/tribunal/shana_penn.htm.

2003. "Women ENews Article on Poland's Abortion Law," *Women Enews* (February 7), at lists.partners/intl.net/pipermail/neww-rights/2003-February/000807.html.

Pérez, Joseph 1989. "Los Comuneros," *Historia 16.*

Perica, Vjekoslav 2002. *Balkan Idols: Religion and Nationalism in Yugoslav States.* New York: Oxford University Press.

2005. "The Sanctification of Enmity. The Construction of Founding National Myths in Postcommunist Serbia and Croatia," in Pål Kolstø, *Myths and Boundaries in Southeastern Europe.* London: C. Hurst & Co.

forthcoming, 2006. "A History of 'The Church of the Croats' or the Ethnicization of Croatian Catholicism in the Twentieth Century," in Francisco C. Gonzales (ed.), *A Nation of the Faithful. Catholic Nationalisms and the Politics of Sovereignty in Multiethnic States.* Madrid.

Petito, Fabio and Pavlos Hatzopoulos (eds.) 2003. *Religion in International Relations: The Return from Exile.* New York: Palgrave.

Petrovich, Michael B. 1976. *A History of Modern Serbia: 1804–1918.* New York: Harcourt Brace Jovanovich.

Philpott, Daniel 2000. "The Religious Roots of Modern International Relations," *World Politics* 52, 2: 206–45.

2001a. *Revolutions in Sovereignty: How Ideas Shaped Modern International Relations.* Princeton: Princeton University Press.

2001b. "Usurping the Sovereignty of Sovereignty?," *World Politics* 53: 297–324.

2001c. *Revolutions in Sovereignty: How Ideas Shaped Modern International Relations.* Princeton: Princeton University Press.

2002. "The Challenge of September 11 to Secularism in International Relations," *World Politics* 55: 66–96.

2004. "The Catholic Wave," *Journal of Democracy* 15, 2 (April): 32–46.

Pieronek, Bishop Tadeusz, 1998. "The Catholic Church and European Integration" (June 9), at www.poland-embassy.org.uk/events/pier.htm.

Pierson, Paul and Theda Skocpol 2002. "Historical Institutionalism in Contemporary Political Science," in Ira Katznelson and Helen V. Milner (eds.), *Political Science: The State of the Discipline*. New York: W. W. Norton & Co.

Pirenne, Henri 1939. *Mahomet et Charlemagne* [Mohammed and Charlemagne]. London: Allen & Unwin.

Piscatori, James P. 1986. *Islam in a World of Nation-States*. Cambridge: Cambridge University Press.

Poland Outlook n. d. Warsaw. "Scared No Longer," at www.masterpage.com.pl/outlook/scared.html.

Poland.pl 2002. "Abortion – Yes or No?", at www.poland.pl/articles/view.htm?id = 30005.

Polish Business News 1998. "The Catholic Voice in the Polish Home," at www.masterpage.com.pl/outlook/catholic.html.

Polish News Bulletin 2000. March 16, in *Lexis-Nexis*.

2001a. August 27, in *Lexis-Nexis*; and Agence France Presse (September 11, 2001), in Lexis-Nexis.

2001b. September 28, in *Lexis-Nexis*.

2002. June 25, reprinting an article from *Newsweek* (June 25, 2002), p. 16, in *Lexis-Nexis*.

Polskie Radio First Program 1995. Warsaw, September 15, trans. in FBIS, *Daily Report* (Eastern Europe), September 15, 1995.

"Pope argues" 2003. "Pope argues for Inclusion of Christian Roots in Constitution," September 8, at www.goacom.com.

Pridham, G. 1982. "Christian Democrats, Conservatives, and Transnational Party Cooperation in the European Community: Centre Forward or Centre Right?," in Z. Layton-Henry (ed.), *Conservative Politics in Western Europe*, 318–46. London: Macmillan.

Puzewicz, Fr. Mieczysław 2004. Episcopal vicar and head of KSM in Lublin, in interview with Sabrina P. Ramet, Lublin, June 30.

Quataert, Donald 2000. *The Ottoman Empire, 1700–1922*. Cambridge and New York: Cambridge University Press.

Qureshi, Emran and Michael Sells (eds.) 2003. *The New Crusades: Constructing the Muslim Enemy*. New York: Columbia University Press.

Qutb, Sayyid 1992. *al-Salam al-Alami wa al-Islam* [World Peace and Islam]. Cairo: al-Shuruq.

Race, Alan and Roger Williamson (eds.) 1995. *True to This Earth: Global Challenges and Transforming Faith*. Rockport, MA: Oneworld Press.

Radić, Radmila 2000. "Serbian Church and the Serbian Question," in Nebojša Popov (ed.), *The Road to War in Serbia*. Budapest: CEW Press.

Radio Free Europe/Radio Liberty (RFE/RL) 1997. "Georgian Orthodox Church Quits WCC" (May 21), at www.stetson.edu/~psteeves/relnews/georgia2605.html [accessed August 16, 2003], p. 1.

2002. *(Un)Civil Societies* (March 6), at www.rferl.org/ucs.

Rahner, Karl 1979. "A Basic Theological Interpretation of Vatican II," *Theological Studies* 40: 716–27.

Ralston, David 1996. *Importing the European Army. The Introduction of European Military Techniques and Institutions into the Extra-European World, 1600–1914*. Chicago: University of Chicago Press.

Ramet, Pedro 1988. "Autocephaly and National Identity in Church–State Relations in Eastern Christianity: An Introduction," in Pedro Ramet (ed.), *Eastern Christianity and Politics in the Twentieth Century*. Durham: Duke University Press.

Ramet, Pedro (ed.) 1989. *Religion and Nationalism in Soviet and Eastern European Politics*. Durham, NC: Duke University Press.

Ramet, Sabrina Petra 1998. *Nihil Obstat: Religion, Politics, and Social Change in East-Central Europe and Russia*. Durham, NC: Duke University Press.

2001a. "The Classical Liberal Tradition: Versions, Subversion, Aversions, Traversions, Reversions," in Oto Luthar, Keith A. McLeod, and Mitja Zagar (eds.), *Liberal Democracy, Citizenship and Education*, 46–67. Niagara Falls, NY: Mosaic Press.

2001b. "The Church and the Liberal Project: The Case of Poland," in Oto Luthar, Keith A. McLeod, and Mitja Zagar (eds.), *Liberal Democracy, Citizenship and Education*, 119–43. Niagara Falls, NY: Mosaic Press.

2002. *Balkan Babel. The Disintegration of Yugoslavia From the Death of Tito to the Fall of Milošević*. Boulder, USA and Oxford, UK: Westview Press.

2003. "Kirke og stat i Romania før og etter 1989," *Nordisk Østforum* 17, 3.

Reese, Thomas J., S. J. 1989. *Episcopal Conferences: Historical, Canonical and Theological Studies*. Washington, DC: Georgetown University Press.

ReligiousTolerance.org 2001. "Russian Orthodox Church and Homosexuality," at www.religioustolerance.org/hom_russi.htm [accessed August 13, 2003].

Repgen, Konrad 1998. "Negotiating the Peace of Westphalia: A Survey with an Examination of the Major Problems," in K. Bussman and H. Schilling (eds.), *1648: War and Peace in Europe*, 355–72. Münster: Westfälisches Landesmuseum.

Reus-Smit, Chris 1999. *The Moral Purpose of the State: Culture, Social Identity, and Institutional Rationality in International Relations*. Princeton: Princeton University Press.

Rhodes, Anthony 1983. *The Power of Rome in the Twentieth Century*. New York: Franklin Watts.

Riding, Alan 2004. "A Common Culture (from the U.S.A.) Binds Europeans Ever Closer," *The New York Times* (April 26): E1, E5.

Risse, Thomas, Maria Green Cowles, and James Caporaso 2001."Europeanization and Domestic Change: Introduction," in Maria Green Cowles, James Caporaso, and Thomas Risse (eds.), *Transforming Europe: Europeanization and Domestic Change*, 1–20. Ithaca: Cornell University Press.

Risse, Thomas, Stephen Ropp, and Kathryn Sikkink (eds.) 1999. *The Power of Human Rights: International Norms and Domestic Change*. Cambridge: Cambridge University Press.

Risse-Kappen, Thomas 1995. "Bringing Transnational Relations Back In: Introduction," in Thomas Risse-Kappen (ed.), *Bringing Transnational*

Relations Back In: Non-State Actors, Domestic Structures, and International Institutions. Cambridge: Cambridge University Press.

Roberts, Michael 1967. *Essays in Swedish History.* Minneapolis, MN: University of Minnesota Press.

Robertson, Roland and William R. Garrett (eds.) 1991. *Religion and Global Order.* New York: Paragon.

Roof, Wade Clark (ed.) 1991. *World Order and Religion.* Albany: SUNY Press.

Roy, Oliver 1994. *The Future of Political Islam.* Cambridge, MA: Harvard University Press.

Rudolph, Susanne Hoeber 1997a. "Introduction: Religion, States, and Transnational Civil Society," in Susanne Hoeber Rudolph and James Piscatori (eds.), *Transnational Religion and Fading States,* 1–24. Boulder, CO: Westview Press.

   1997b. "Dehomogenizing Religious Formations," in Susanne Hoeber Rudolph and James Piscatori (eds.), *Transnational Religion and Fading States,* 243–61. Boulder, CO: Westview Press.

   2003. "Religious Concomitants of Transnationalism: From a Universal Church to a Universal Religiosity?," in John D. Carlson and Erik C. Owens (eds.), *The Sacred and the Sovereign: Religion and International Politics,* 139–53. Washington, DC: Georgetown University Press.

Rudolph, Suzanne Hoeber and James Piscatori (eds.) 1997. *Transnational Religion and Fading States.* Boulder, CO: Westview Press.

Russian Orthodox Church News 2003. "Metropolitan Kirill sends an Open Letter to Valery Giscard d'Estaing, Chairman of the Convention on the Future of Europe Presidium" (February 14), at www.russian-orthodox-church.org.ru/ ne302143.htm [accessed August 13, 2003].

Rychlak, Ronald 2000. *Hitler, the War, and the Pope.* Huntington, IN: Our Sunday Visitor.

Rydel, Jan 2001. "Sacrum Poloniae Millennium," in Michal Buchowski, Edouard Conte, and Carole Nagengast (eds.), *Poland Beyond Communism: "Transition" in Critical Perspective.* Fribourg, Switzerland: University Press.

Sanford, George 1999. *Poland: The Conquest of History.* Amsterdam: Harwood Academic Publishers.

Saponja-Hadžić, Milanka 2003. "Serbia: Unease Over New Saint," *Institute for War & Peace Reporting* (IWPR), BCR No. 436 (10 June), at www.iwpr.net [accessed August 13, 2003].

Schacht, Joseph 1964. *An Introduction to Islamic Law.* Oxford: Clarendon Press.

Schilling, Heinz 1992. *Religion, Political Culture and the Emergence of Early Modern Society: Essays in German and Dutch History.* Leiden: E. J. Brill.

Schindling, Anton 1998. "Neighbors of a Different Faith: Confessional Coexistence and Parity in the Territorial States and Towns of the Empire," in K. Bussman and H. Schilling (eds.), *1648: War and Peace in Europe,* 465–73. Münster: Westfälisches Landesmuseum.

Schlesinger, Philip R. 1994. "Europe's Contradictory Communicative Space," *Dædalus* 123, 2: 25–52.

2001. "From Cultural Protection to Political Culture? Media Policy and the European Union," in Lars-Erik Cederman (ed.), *Constructing Europe's Identity: The External Dimension*, 91–114. Boulder, CO: Lynne Rienner.

Schmidt, H. D. 1966. "The Establishment of 'Europe' as a Political Expression," *Historical Journal* 9, 2: 172–78.

Schmit, Georg 1998. "The Peace of Westphalia as the Fundamental Law of the Complementary Empire-State," in K. Bussman and H. Schilling (eds.), *1648: War and Peace in Europe*, 447–54. Münster: Westfälisches Landesmuseum.

Scholte Jan Aart 2000. *Globalization: A Critical Introduction*. New York: St. Martin's Press.

Schwartz, Stephen 2002. *The Two Faces of Islam. The House of Sa'ud from Tradition to Terror*. New York: Doubleday.

Sciolino, Elaine 2004. "Debate Begins in France on Religion in the Schools," *The New York Times* (February 4).

Scotsman, The 2003. May 28, at www.news.scotsman.com.

Scribner, R. W. 1994. "Communalism: Universal Category or Ideological Construct? A Debate in the Historiography of Early Modern Germany and Switzerland," *Historical Journal* 37, 1: 199–207.

Second Council of the Vatican 1965. *Nostra Aetate*, October 28. In Austin Flannery, O. P. (ed.), *Vatican Council II: The Conciliar and Post-Conciliar Documents*. Northport, NY: Costello Publishing Company, 1992 (new revised edition).

Sheikh, Naveed S. 2003. *The New Politics of Islam: Pan-Islam Foreign Policy in a World of States*. London: Routledge.

Shore, Chris 1996. "Transcending the Nation-State?: The European Commission and the (Re)-Discovery of Europe," *Journal of Historical Sociology* 9, 4 (December): 473–96.

Silverstein, Paul A. 2004. *Algeria in France*. Bloomington: Indiana University Press.

Simo, Ana 2001. "Violence Stops Yugoslavia Gay Pride", *the Gully.com* (July 5), at www.thegully.com/essays/gaymundo/010705gay_yugoslavia.html [accessed August 13, 2003].

Słowo Powszechne (Warsaw) 1985. February 15–17, p. 7, trans. in *Joint Publications Research Service*, No. EPS-85-045 (April 15, 1985): 68–78.

Soper, J. Christoph and Joel Fetzer 2002. "Religion and Politics in a Secular Europe: Cutting Against the Grain," in Ted Gerard Jelen and Clyde Wilcox (eds.), *Religion and Politics in Comparative Perspective: The One, the Few, and the Many*, 169–91. New York: Cambridge University Press.

Southern, R. W. 1970. *Western Society and the Church in the Middle Ages*. Harmondsworth: Penguin Books.

Spencer, Robert 2003. *Onward Muslim Soldiers. How Jihad Threatens America and the West*. Washington, DC: Regnery Publishing.

Sperling, John, Suzanne Helburn, Samuel George, John Morris, and Carl Hunt 2004. *The Great Divide: Retro vs. Metro America*. Sausalito, CA: PoliPoint Press.

Spohn, Willfried 2001. "Eisenstadt on Civilizations and Multiple Modernity," *European Journal of Social Theory* 4, 4: 499–508.

Sprawodanie 2003. Sprawodanie Rady Ministrów z wykonywania w roku 2002 ustawy z dnia 7 stycznia 1993 roku o planowaniu rodziny, ochronie płodu ludzkiego i warunkach dopuszczalności przerywania ciąży. Warsaw: Prezes Rady Ministrów, October 27.

Spuler-Stegemann, Ursula 2002. *Muslime in Deutschland. Informationen und Klärungen.* Freiburg: Herder.

Spuler-Stegemann, Ursula (ed.) 2004. *Feindbild Christentum im Islam. Eine Bestandsaufnahme.* Freiburg: Herder.

Stadtmüller, Elzbieta 2000. "Polish Perceptions of the European Union in the 1990s," in Karl Cordell (ed.), *Poland and the European Union.* London: Routledge.

Stalnaker, John C. 1979. *Towards a Social Interpretation of the German Peasant War.* London: Allen & Unwin.

Stan, Lavinia and Lucian Turcescu 2000. "The Romanian Orthodox Church and Post-communist Democratisation," *Europe-Asia Studies* 52, 8 (December): 1467–88.

Stanley, Alessandra 2000. "An Inseparable Church and State: On Greeks Playing the Euro Card," *The New York Times* (June 25), Late Edition (final), section 4, p. 4, col. 1.

Stanosz, Barbara 2004. Founder of *Bez dogmatu*, and Andrzej Dominiczak, member of the editorial board of *Bez dogmatu*, in interview with Sabrina P. Ramet, Warsaw, June 24.

Stark, Rodney 1999. "Secularization, R.I.P.," *Sociology of Religion* 60, 3 (Fall): 249–73.

Stark, Rodney and William S. Bainbridge 1985. *The Future of Religion.* Berkeley: University of California Press.

Stark, Rodney and Laurence Iannaccone 1994. "A Supply-side Interpretation of the 'Secularization' of Europe," *Journal for the Scientific Study of Religion* 33: 230–52.

Staron, Stanisław 1969. "State–Church Relations in Poland: An Examination of Power Configuration in a Noncompetitive Political System," *World Politics* 21, 4 (July).

Statystyka – Dzieciobójstwo i porzucenie, at www.kgp.gov.pl.

Stayer, James M. 1991. *The German Peasants' War and Anabaptist Community of Goods.* Montreal and Kingston: McGill-Queen's University Press.

Stehle, Hansjacob 1981. *Eastern Politics of the Vatican 1917–1979.* Athens, OH: Ohio University Press.

Stepan, Alfred 2000. "Religion, Democracy, and the 'Twin Tolerations'," *Journal of Democracy* 11, 4: 37–57.

2001. *Arguing Comparative Politics.* Oxford: Oxford University Press.

Stone Sweet, Alec, Wayne Sandholtz, and Neil Fligstein (eds.) 2001. *The Institutionalization of Europe.* Oxford: Oxford University Press.

Sutton, Michael 1997. "John Paul II's Idea of Europe," *Religion, State, and Society* 25, 1: 17–29.

Szostek, Andrzej 2004. Rector of the Catholic University of Lublin, in interview with Sabrina P. Ramet, Lublin, 2 July.

Szostkiewicz, Adam 2004. Deputy foreign editor and staff writer for religious affairs for *Polityka*, in interview with Sabrina P. Ramet, Warsaw, June 27.

Szyszkowska, Senator Maria 2004. In interview with Sabrina P. Ramet, Warsaw, July 6; Ania Konieczna, interpreter.

Tallberg, Jonas 1999. *Making States Comply: The European Commission, the European Court of Justice and the Enforcement of the Internal Market.* Lund University, Department of Political Science, Lund Political Studies 109.

Tanner, Norman P. (ed.) 1990. *Decrees of the Ecumenical Councils.* Washington, DC: Georgetown University Press.

Tchkuaseli, Varlam 2001. "Facing up to Religious Intolerance in Georgia," *Minority Web* (July 14), at minority.iatp.org.ge/files/english/Facingup.php [accessed August 16, 2003].

te Brake, Wayne 1998. *Shaping History: Ordinary People in European Politics, 1500–1700.* Berkeley, CA: University of California Press.

Teitelbaum, Michael and Jay Winter 1998. *A Question of Numbers. High Migration, Low Fertility and the Politics of National Identity.* New York: Hill and Wang.

Theiler, Tobias 1999a. "The 'Identity Politics' of the European Union," D. Phil., Oxford University, Oxford.

1999b. "International Integration and National Beliefs: A Psychological Basis for Consociationalism as a Model of Political Unification," *Nationalism & Ethnic Politics* 5, 1 (Spring): 46–81.

1999c. "Viewers into Europeans?: How the European Union Tried to Europeanize the Audiovisual Sector, and Why It Failed," *Canadian Journal of Communication* 24: 557–87.

2001. "Why the European Union Failed to Europeanize its Audiovisual Policy," in Lars-Erik Cederman (ed.), *Constructing Europe's Identity: The External Dimension*, 115–37. Boulder, CO: Lynne Rienner.

Thomas, George M. 2001. "Religions in Global Civil Society," *Sociology of Religion* 62, 4 (Winter): 515–33.

Thomas, Scott 2000. "Religious Resurgence, Postmodernism and World Politics," in John L. Esposito and Michael Watson (eds.), *Religion and Global Order*, 38–65. Cardiff: University of Wales Press.

2005. *The Global Resurgence of Religion and the Transformation of International Relations: The Struggle for the Soul of the Twenty-First Century.* New York: Palgrave Macmillan.

Thompson, Martyn P. 1994. "Ideas of Europe During the French and Napoleonic Wars," *Journal of the History of Ideas* 55, 1: 37–58.

Thomson, John A. 1998. *The Western Church in the Middle Ages.* London: Arnold.

Tibi, Bassam 1980. "Islam and Secularization," *Archives for Philosophy of Law and Social Philosophy* 66, 2: 207–22.

1995. "Islamic Dream of Semi-Modernity," *India International Centre Quarterly* 22, 1: 79–87.

1998a. *Europa ohne Identität? Leitkultur oder Wertebeliebigkeit.* Munich: Goldmann (second edition 2001).

1998b. *Aufbruch am Bosporus. Die Türkei zwischen Europa und dem Islamismus.* Munich: Diana; translated into Turkish: *Bogaz'in iki Yakasi. Avrupa ile Islamcilik Arasinda Türkiye.* Istanbul: Dogan Kitapcilik, 2000.

1998c. *The Challenge of Fundamentalism. Political Islam and the New World Disorder.* Berkeley, CA: University of California Press.

1999. *Kreuzzug und Djihad. Der Islam und die christliche Welt.* Munich: Bertelsmann.

2000. "Secularization and De-secularization in Modern Islam," *Religion, Staat, Gesellschaft* 1, 1: 95–119.

2001. *Islam between Culture and Politics.* New York: Palgrave.

2002. *Islamische Zuwanderung. Die gescheiterte Integration.* Munich: DVA.

2004. "The Quest of Islamic Migrants and of Turkey to become European," *Turkish Policy Quarterly* 3, 1: 1013–28.

Tilly, Charles 1975. "Reflections on the History of European State-Making," in C. Tilly (ed.), *The Formation of National States in Western Europe*, 3–84. Princeton: Princeton University Press.

1984. *Big Structures, Large Processes, Huge Comparisons.* New York: Russell Sage Foundation.

1990. *Coercion, Capital, and European States AD 990–1992.* Cambridge: Blackwell.

Tocqueville, Alexis de 1990. *Democracy in America.* 2 vols. New York: Vintage.

Todorova, Maria 1997. *Imagining the Balkans.* New York: Oxford University Press.

Tracy, James D. 1999. *Europe's Reformations, 1450–1650.* Lanham, MD: Rowman & Littlefield.

Trautner, Bernhard J. 1999. "The Clash *within* Civilisations: Islam and the Accommodation of Plurality," *InIIS-Arbeitspapier* Nr. 13/99. University of Bremen.

Trimberger, Ellen Kay 1978. *Revolution from Above. Military Bureaucrats and Development in Japan, Turkey, Egypt and Peru.* New Brunswick, NJ: Transaction Books.

Trondal, Jarle 2001. "Is There Any Social Constructivist–Institutionalist Divide? Unpacking Social Mechanisms Affecting Representational Roles Among EU Decisionmakers," *Journal of European Public Policy* 8, 1 (March): 1–23.

Turek, Bogdan 1998. "Poland: Tension Rises Over Crosses in Auschwitz," *Radio Free Europe Research* (August 10, 1998), at www.rferl.org/nca.

Turowicz, Jerzy 1987. "Kilka uwag o dyskryminacji," *Tygodnik Powszechny* (16–19 April), trans. into German as "Diskriminierung der katholischen Presse in Polen," *Osteuropa* 37, 12 (December 1987): A682–83.

Turska, Urszula 1996. "Radio Maryja – Our Lady of Contention," *The Warsaw Voice* 46 (November 17), at www.warsawvoice.pl/v421/Media00.html.

Ulfkotte, Udo 2003. *Der Krieg in unseren Städten. Wie radikale Islamisten Deutschland unterwandern.* Frankfurt: Eichborn.

Urban, Jerzy 2004. Editor of *Nie*, in interview with Sabrina P. Ramet, Warsaw, June 25; Piotr Szymczak, interpreter.

Vallier, Ivan 1971. "The Roman Catholic Church: A Transnational Actor," in Robert O. Keohane and Joseph S. Nye (eds.), *Transnational Relations and World Politics*, 129–152. Cambridge, MA: Harvard University Press.

Vardys, V. Stanley 1978. *The Catholic Church, Dissent, and Nationality in Soviet Lithuania.* Boulder, CO: East European Quarterly.

1981. "Freedom of Religion, Lithuania and the Chronicle: An Introduction," in *The Chronicle of the Catholic Church in Lithuania*. Chicago: Loyala University Press.

Vergin, Nur 2004. "Siyaset Ile Sosyolojinin Bulustuğu Nokta," *Türkiye Günlüğü* 76: 5–9.

Vink, Maarten 2003. "What is Europeanisation? And Other Questions on a New Research Agenda," *European Political Science* 3, 1 (Fall): 63–74.

Vreme 2003. Belgrade, May 29, trans. in *Bosnia Report* (Bosnian Institute), New Series No. 32–34 (December 2002–July 2003).

Walaszek, Zdzisława 1986. "An Open Issue of Legitimacy: The State and the Church in Poland," *Annals of the American Academy of Political and Social Science* 483 (January).

Walicki, Andrzej 1979. *A History of Russian Thought. From the Enlightenment to Marxism*. Translated from the Polish by Hilda Andrews-Rusiecka. Stanford, CA: Stanford University Press.

Ware, Timothy 1963. *The Orthodox Church*. London: Penguin Books.

1997. *The Orthodox Church* (revised edition). London: Penguin Books.

Warner, R. Stephen 1993. "Work in Progress Toward a New Paradigm for the Sociological Study of Religion in the United States," *American Journal of Sociology* 98, 5: 1044–93.

Warsaw Voice 2002. March 31, in *Lexis-Nexis*.

Weber, Max 1946. "The Protestant Sects and the Spirit of Capitalism," in H. H. Gerth and C. W. Mills (eds.), *From Max Weber: Essays in Sociology*. Oxford: Oxford University Press.

Wedeen, Lisa 2003. "Beyond the Crusades," *Items & Issues* 4, 2–3 (Spring–Summer): 1–6.

Wedgwood, C. V. 1961. *The Thirty Years War*. Garden City, NY: Doubleday.

Weigel, George 1992. *The Final Revolution: The Resistance Church and the Collapse of Communism*. Oxford: Oxford University Press.

1999. *Witness to Hope: The Biography of Pope John Paul II*. New York: HarperCollins.

Weiner, Myron 1995. *The Global Migration Crisis. Challenge to States and to Human Rights*. New York: HarperCollins.

Willey, David 1992. *God's Politician: Pope John Paul II, the Catholic Church, and the New World Order*. New York: St. Martin's Press.

Williams, George H. 1984. *The Law of Nations and the Book of Nature*, 1–18. Collegeville, MN: St. John's Abbey.

Wilson, Bryan 1966. *Religion in Secular Society*. London: C. A. Watts.

1979. *Contemporary Transformations of Religion*. Oxford: Clarendon Press.

Wilson, James Q. 2002. "The Reform Islam Needs," *City Journal* 12, 4.

Wolff, Larry 1994. *Inventing Eastern Europe. The Map of Civilization on the Mind of the Enlightenment*. Stanford, CA: Stanford University Press.

2001. *The Enlightenment and the Orthodox World: Western Perspectives on the Orthodox Church in Eastern Europe*. Athens: Institute for Neohellenic Research – National Hellenic Research Foundation.

The Word 1984. "Orthodox Statement on Homosexuality," January, pp. 6–11, posted at www.holy-trinity.org/morality/homosexuality.html [accessed August 13, 2003].

World Council of Churches 1999. "Sex – Almost a Non-Issue," *Eighth Assembly – World Council of Churches* (1999), at www.wcc-coe.org/wcc/assembly/prsex.html [accessed August 13, 2003].

Wrost (Warsaw) 1993. April 18, pp. 75–76, trans. in JPRS, *East Europe Report* (May 17, 1993): 10–11.

Yapp, M. E. 1992. "Europe in the Turkish Mirror," *Past and Present* 137: 134–55.

Yavuz, M. Hakan 1999. "Search for a New Social Contract in Turkey: Fethullah Gulen, the Virtue Party and the Kurds," *SAIS Review of International Affairs* 19 (1): 114–43.

2000. "Cleansing Islam from the Public Sphere," *Journal of International Affairs* 54, 1: 21–44.

2003. *Islamic Political Identity in Turkey*. New York: Oxford University Press.

2004a. "Islam and Europeanization in Turkish-Muslim Socio-Political Movements." In this volume.

2004b. "Is there a Turkish Islam? The Emergence of Convergence and Consensus," *Journal of Muslim Minority Affairs* 24: 1–22.

Yavuz, M. Hakan and M. R. Khan 1992. "A Bridge Between East and West: Duality and the Development of Turkish Foreign Policy Toward the Arab-Israeli Conflict," *Arab Studies Quarterly* 14 (Fall): 69–95.

Yesilada, Birol A. 1999. "The Worsening EU–Turkey Relations," *SAIS Review* 19, 1.

Zagorin, Perez 1982. *Rulers and Rebels, 1500–1600. Volume II: Provincial Rebellion, Revolutionary Civil Wars, 1560–1660*. Cambridge: Cambridge University Press.

Zaręba, Sławomir H. 2004. "Postawy Polaków wobec zasad moralnych religii katolickiej," *Kościół Katolicki na początku trzeciego tysiąclecia w opinii Polaków* (Warsaw: Instytut Statystyki Kościoła Katolickiego).

Zdaniewicz, Witold and Sławomir H. Zaręba (eds.) 2004. *Kościół Katolicki na początku trzeciego tysiąclecia w opinii Polaków*. Warsaw: Instytut Statystyki Kościoła Katolickiego.

Zenit News Agency. 2004a. "Robert Schuman's Cause of Beatification Advances," March 3. Available at http://www.zenit.org/english/ [accessed July 5, 2005].

2004b. "Schröder Hails Pope's Role in Europe's Unification," March 23. Available at http://www.zenit.org/english/ [accessed July 5, 2005].

Zolotov, Jr., Andrei 2001. "Russian Prelate Urges World's Churches to Adopt Orthodox Dates for Easter," *Christianity Today* (April 4), at www.christianitytoday.com [accessed September 9, 2003].

2003. "Orthodox Church Takes on Rasputin," *Moscow Times* (February 5), at www.rickross.com/reference/rs/rs38.html [accessed August 13, 2003].

Zolotov, Andrei and Stephen Brown 1998. "WCC agrees to set up commission to try to resolve Orthodox grievances," *Ecumenical News International: Special Reports from the Eighth Assembly of the World Council of Churches* (December 3–14), at www.eni.ch/assembly/0584.html [accessed August 13, 2003].

Zubrzycki, Geneviève 2004. "The Catholic Church and the 'War of the Crosses' at Auschwitz (1998–99)," in Michael Geyer and Hartmut Lehmann (eds.), *Religion und Nation. Beiträge zu einer unbewältigten Geschichte*, 176–204. Göttingen: Wallstein-Verlag.

Zürcher, E. J. and H. van der Linden 2004. *The European Union, Turkey and Islam*. Amsterdam: Amsterdam University Press.

Życiński, Archbishop Józef of Lublin 2004. In interview with Sabrina P. Ramet, Lublin, July 2.

Index

337

democracy (cont.)
  Orthodox Church view of 38, 154
  in Poland 144
  in Turkey 72, 222, 235, 236, 237, 252
  see also liberalism
democratization
  Huntington's "Third Wave" 95
  and level of religiosity 51
  role of Catholic Church in 12
Denmark
  joins EEC 17, 71
  resistance to supranational EU
    integration 53
differentiation
  as independence from state governance
    39, 47
  and national identity 40
  Orthodox Church and 49
  Protestant churches 51
  religious communities' concept of 39
  and strength of opposition to
    communism 50
  and transnational ties 40
  Turkish Islamism 50
Djindjić, Zoran 187, 188
Djorić, Germanus, Patriarch of Serbia 182
Dobrijević, Irinej 191, 192
Dostoevsky, Fyodor M. 187, 199
"Draft European Act" (1981) (Genscher-
  Colombo Proposal) 27
"Draft Treaty of the European Union"
  (1984) 27
Drašković, Vuk 197
drugs, national policies on 29
Duga magazine (Belgrade) 185
Dutch Revolt 274–76
Dvorkin, Aleksandr 172
Dyduch, Marek 139
dynasticism 267

Eastern Europe 148
  applications to join EU 34
  democratization 34
  revival of religion in 83
  role of churches in democratic revolution
    (1989) 41–45
  and role of Orthodox Church 148, 176
  see also individual countries; Serbia
Ecevet, Bülent, Turkish prime minister 222
ecumenism, Orthodox opposition to
    155–59, 193
education
  attempts at Europeanization of 24, 26
  failure to influence national school
    curricula 24, 25, 26

international exchanges 25
  Orthodox influence on 153, 160, 161
  in Poland 122
  Spain 1
  university 25
England
  as multireligious state 278
  Norman conquest 259
  Reformation 264
  see also United Kingdom
Enlightenment, the 31, 82, 102, 140
  critique of religion 85, 88
  Orthodox Church and 148
  in Poland 68
  relationship to Christianity 82
  and secular modernity 66, 278
environmentalism 146, 174, 175n
Erasmus program for university
    education 25
Erbakan, Necmettin, Turkish prime
    minister 218, 243–44
  and AKP party 245–47
  and EU draft constitution 142
Erdoğan, Tayyip, Turkish prime minister
    45, 73, 218, 219, 249
Estonia 14, 19, 63
Euro-Islam, concept of 209, 222, 225, 301
Europe (continent of)
  Catholic missionaries from 102
  complexity of moral and spiritual heritage
    81–83, 207
  emigration from 74
  historical failure of unification projects 15
  and immigrant religions 75, 90
  and incompatibility of Islam with
    205–09
  institutionalization of 279
  modern immigration to 75
  perceived Christian boundaries of 3,
    251, 260
  power asymmetries 260
  rates of religiosity in 66, 83
  relations with Islam 80, 204, 226, 300
  relations with Ottoman Empire
    220–21, 229
  role of transnational religions in 34
  secularization of 83–90
  status in world affairs 113, 256
  see also Christendom; European
    enlargement; European identity;
    European Union
Europe, Council of 233
  Romania 167
  Serbia 187
"European city program" 27

Index

343